THE FRENCH BLOOD IN AMERICA

December 22, 1980

It is my pleasure
to present this
informative book
to The Huguenot
Society of Michigan

Zelma Johnson

LIBERTY ENLIGHTENING THE WORLD

The French Blood In America

By LUCIAN J. FOSDICK

ILLUSTRATED

GENEALOGICAL PUBLISHING CO., INC.
BALTIMORE   1973

Originally Published
1906

Reprinted
Genealogical Publishing Co., Inc.
Baltimore, 1973

Library of Congress Catalogue Card Number 73-279
International Standard Book Number 0-8063-0552-5

Made in the United States of America

THIS VOLUME IS DEDICATED
TO ALL PATRIOTIC AMERICANS,
AND ESPECIALLY TO THE DESCENDANTS
OF THE HEROIC FRENCH PROTESTANTS,
EXILES FROM THEIR NATIVE LAND
ON ACCOUNT OF THEIR RELIGIOUS FAITH—
THE STORY OF WHOSE HEROISM,
AND THE PART THEY PLAYED IN THE
BUILDING OF OUR AMERICAN COMMONWEALTH
ON THE SOLID FOUNDATIONS OF
CIVIL AND RELIGIOUS LIBERTY,
IS TOLD IN THESE PAGES

CONTENTS

FOREWORD 11
INTRODUCTION 15

BOOK ONE
THE RISE OF PROTESTANTISM IN FRANCE

I. THE FRENCH SPIRIT 25
II. THE HUGUENOTS IN FRANCE 38
III. THE FRENCH EXILES IN EUROPE 64
IV. SUFFERING FOR THE FAITH 74
V. LIFE IN THE GALLEYS 80

BOOK TWO
EARLY ATTEMPTS AT COLONIZATION

I. VILLEGAGNON'S FAILURE IN BRAZIL . . . 93
II. DISASTROUS ATTEMPTS IN FLORIDA . . . 98
III. THE HUGUENOT COLONY IN CANADA . . . 112

BOOK THREE
THE FRENCH PROTESTANTS IN AMERICA

PART ONE—NEW ENGLAND

I. THE FIRST COMERS 125
II. THE OXFORD SETTLEMENT 134
III. GABRIEL BERNON 143
IV. THE NARRAGANSETT SETTLEMENT 151
V. THE FRENCH CHURCH IN BOSTON 157
VI. PAUL REVERE 168
VII. THE FANEUIL FAMILY 173
VIII. THE BOWDOINS, DANAS, AND OTHER FAMILIES . 183
IX. A DESCRIPTION OF EARLY BOSTON 192
X. FRENCH SETTLEMENT IN MAINE 196
XI. HUGUENOT INFLUENCE UPON PURITAN CHARACTER . 202

7

8 **CONTENTS**

Part Two—The French in New York

I. The Founders of New Amsterdam . . . 212
II. The French Church in New York . . . 225
III. New Rochelle, the Huguenot Settlement . 231
IV. John Jay, Statesman and Jurist 244
V. Alexander Hamilton, Statesman and Financier . 252
VI. Some Prominent Names 258
VII. John and Stephen Gano 279
VIII. New Paltz 283

Part Three—Pennsylvania and the Southern States

I. Pennsylvania and Delaware 290
II. Elias Boudinot and Stephen Girard . . . 301
III. The Bayards and Other Families . . . 308
IV. South Carolina 322
V. Francis Marion, ... 338
VI. The Huguenots in Virginia . . . 345
VII. John Sevier and His Brave Wife . . . 358
VIII. The Thrilling Experiences of an Exiled Family . 363

Part Four—The French in Various Relations

I. America's Debt to France During the Revolution 377
II. The Louisiana Purchase 383
III. The French in Freemasonry 386
IV. The Order of the Cincinnati 397
V. French Leaders in Reform and Invention . . 400
VI. Huguenot Home Life in America . . . 407
VII. An Early French Estimate of American Character 416
VIII. The French as a Factor in American Civilization 420

Appendix 429
Index 445

LIST OF ILLUSTRATIONS

Facing page

Liberty Enlightening the World . . . . *Title*

Joan of Arc Seeing Visions 26

Joan at the Crowning of Charles at Rheims . . 32

Calvin, Coligny, Henry and Margaret of Navarre . 44

The Huguenots, by Carl Hoff 54

Mayor John Guiton's Oath at La Rochelle . . 58

La Rochelle : the Square 64

The Huguenot Lovers, by Millais 74

The Mayflower in Plymouth Harbour . . . 126

John Alden and Priscilla, by Boughton . . . 132

Old Huguenot Chair and Boston State House . . 148

Paul Revere, Portrait by Gilbert Stuart . . . 168

Peter Faneuil, from Portrait in Faneuil Hall . . 174

Faneuil Hall and the Old Feather Store . . . 176

The Faneuil Mansion on Tremont Street, Boston . 180

Officers of the Huguenot Society of America . . 220

The French Church in New York at the Present Time 224

Original Bayard House and Rappelyea Estate in New
    York, from Rare Old Prints 228

Old Huguenot Houses at New Rochelle . . . 234

John Jay, First Justice of the Supreme Court . . 244

Alexander Hamilton 252

9

General Richard Montgomery and Quebec .   .   .   268

Freneau, Thoreau, Whittier and Longfellow   .   .   272

Old Huguenot Houses at New Paltz   284

Admiral S. F. DuPont and the American Armada at
Port Royal   314

Gabriel Manigault and His Marot Psalm Book .   .   322

Henry Laurens and Francis Marion   326

Lafayette at Mount Vernon with Washington .   .   380

Elizabeth Hamilton, Sarah Jay, John Bayard, and Dr.
Provoost   410

Professor Henry M. Baird, Huguenot Historian, and
Reverend A. V. Wittmeyer, Founder of the Huguenot Society of America   418

President Garfield, Vice-President Hannibal Hamlin,
General John C. Fremont, General Robert Anderson, Admiral George Dewey, Senator Robert LaFollette   422

Johannis DePeyster and the Family Plate .   .   .   426

Lucian J. Fosdick

FOREWORD

THE purpose of this work is to trace the presence and influence of the French Protestant blood in America, and to show how important a part it has had in the making of our Republic. In recent times no little attention has been given to the subject of the Huguenots in America and their descendants. Credit for this is due chiefly to Dr. Henry M. Baird, whose history of the Huguenots is an authority on both sides of the Atlantic. His exhaustive work deals with France for the most part; and his brother, Dr. Charles W. Baird, has undertaken to write in detail that part of the history which belongs to America. His task has not been completed, and his work is too elaborate and involved to secure general reading. Various local monographs have been published, giving the history of some settlement or famous family, and a number of romances have dealt with the theme. But there is no single volume which presents readably a comprehensive view of the Huguenots in France and their descendants in this country; which reveals and estimates at its true value the Huguenot influence as a factor in American religious, social, and commercial life.

The story of the courageous men and women who, for the sake of conscience and religious liberty, endured persecution and exile, and found graves or made for themselves homes in the New World, forms one of the most pathetic and at the same time fascinating and inspiring chapters of human experience. Inspiring, because in these trying experiences there was exhibited a nobility of character, a strength of soul, a superb quality of manhood and womanhood, that lends new dignity to human nature. Of this record every descendant of the Huguenots may

11

well be proud. With this history every American should be familiar. It is time that America's indebtedness to the French Protestants should be recognized.

To understand the French Protestants in America it is necessary first to know them in France. The first part, therefore, is devoted to the rise of religious reform in France and the two centuries of war and persecution which killed off or drove out of France her best class of citizens, permanently weakened her as a nation, and paved the way for the French Revolution. The second part gives account of the various disastrous attempts to found Huguenot colonies in North America; and the third takes up the story with the beginnings at Plymouth, New Amsterdam, and Virginia, and traces it to the present time. The fourth part groups various matters of interest germane to the subject.

This story has in it the elements of human interest that appeal to all classes and ages. It is the author's conviction that the French who of late years have been pouring into New England and other sections of the United States may be greatly stimulated by the example of their fellow countrymen of an earlier day, and be led to prize more highly the opportunities opened to them and their children through American citizenship. It was the distinction and one source of the wide spread influence of the early French settlers that they assimilated thoroughly and rapidly, as a rule, becoming American instead of striving to perpetuate race prejudice and peculiarity. In this way they undoubtedly lost recognition, but gained power as makers of the State. This lesson should not be lost on the French Canadians of to-day, who are sometimes wrongly advised to hold themselves aloof as a distinctive class.

While this work is intended for popular reading, great care has been taken to make it accurate and fair. Its facts have been gathered from every available source, and it would be impossible to give credit in detail. To those who have extended courtesies in the obtaining of material, and aid in other ways, the author expresses his grateful appreciation. He acknowledges special obligations to Professor Howard B. Grose, for services both in research and in preparing the volume for the press.

The author's earnest desire is that this work may be a means to promote patriotism, quicken appreciation of civil and religious liberty, and heighten in the Americans of to-day a sense of their responsibility to preserve those rights and blessings which, as this record reveals, it cost the Huguenots so dearly to claim and defend in France, and which they helped the English Protestants to establish firmly on our shores. As it was in the seventeenth century the mission of Protestant Christianity to found, so is it its mission in this twentieth century still further to develop and perpetuate, a free Republic in America; and in this glorious mission the French Protestants have their full share.

L. J. F.

Boston, January, 1906.

INTRODUCTION

I

MANY surprises are in store for the reader who comes to these pages possessed merely of the ordinary knowledge as to who the Huguenots in America are and what they have done. More than one Puritan and Pilgrim tradition has had to be given up in the light of later historical research. But as the true character of the people is disclosed, there will be no begrudging of the full meed of praise belonging to those French Protestants who, when driven from France, found in our land a home and that religious liberty denied them in their own, and in return gave of their best to their adopted country. Surprises of Later History

The whole number of the Huguenot emigrants to America was relatively small. Numerically, they occupied a position of comparative insignificance among the founders of the Republic. But, as John Fiske says, "In determining the character of a community one hundred selected men and women are more potent than a thousand men and women taken at random." And the Huguenot refugees were "selected," if ever a body of men and women had the right to be so called. For two hundred years France had been like a vast furnace ; the fires of persecution had been refining and testing until only the pure gold was left. For two hundred years the persecution which had sought to destroy, had been cultivating, instead, those heroic virtues which enabled the small band of Huguenot refugees to America to write their names so large upon the honour roll of the Republic. Selected Men and Women

15

Truly, the Huguenot emigrants were a selected people—selected for their love of liberty, their love of human rights, their devotion to principle, their unswerving loyalty to conscience. Free America, Protestant America, owes a vast debt to these Protestants of France.

II

Liberty and Protestantism Before giving a brief résumé of the services which the Huguenots rendered directly, let us consider for a moment the services they rendered indirectly, to the American Republic, through England. Guided by Divine Providence, the persecuted Protestants of France proved themselves a power in shaping the larger destinies of the Republic. Reading history in the light of to-day we can see that they helped to lay those foundations upon which the people of the New World have reared their structure of Protestant republicanism. The American Republic had its beginnings under England ; the hardy adolescence of the colonies was passed under the shadow of English political and religious institutions. American liberties grew out of Protestantism, and America was Protestant because England was Protestant. Now the Huguenot refugees helped to make England Protestant, and thus indirectly they helped to make America free.

Huguenots in England In the struggle between William of Orange and James II, when the fate of English Protestantism hung trembling in the balance, it was the Huguenot refugees who turned the scales. They formed the backbone of the staunch little army that followed William into England. "Amid the chilling delays on the part of the English people," wrote Michelet, "the army of William remained firm, and it was the Calvinistic element in it, the Calvinistic Huguenots, that made it firm." They formed the unflinching nucleus around which the Protestant forces of England finally rallied to drive James out of the kingdom, thus removing the royal power from the grasp of Rome. "But the struggle was not over," says Gregg.

"Louis XIV of France was mortified to think that his own refugees were the soul of this defeat. He determined to retrieve it. He fitted up an army and put James at the head of it. This army invaded Britain. It landed in the north of Ireland. There another battle was fought, the battle of the Boyne, and James was again and finally defeated. Who won that battle, the famous battle of the Boyne, which carried in it so much of the future and gave to Protestantism the possession of the British throne? A Huguenot. It was the Huguenot Schomberg who commanded the Protestant forces that day, and although he fell in the battle, he left the kingdom in the hands of William III. Thus it pleased the God of battles to use the persecuted and dispersed and down-trodden French refugees to turn the helm of the mightiest matters of destiny and to share in the glory of His providence over nations and over the march of truth." Battle of the Boyne; Schomberg

III

England is now ready to bring its Protestantism with its republican principles over to the New World. This it does. And here it has another battle with Romanism. It has to meet the same foe that it met by the River Boyne, namely, the foe that persecuted the Huguenots. Rome determined to have this New World, and so through Spain took possession of South America, and through France took possession of North America. As far back as the landing of the Pilgrim fathers at Plymouth Rock, Cardinal Richelieu founded New France in North America. He made this law: "Everybody settling in New France must be a Catholic." None of the hated Huguenots was to be allowed to enter. This was done to checkmate Protestant England. The English and French met at Quebec and fought out the question, To whom shall America belong? In the great battle of Quebec Montcalm led the French, General Wolfe led the Protestantism versus Romanism

English. Montcalm fought for the old régime, Wolfe
for the House of Commons; Montcalm fought for allegiance to king and priest, Wolfe for the *habeas corpus*
and free inquiry ; Montcalm fought for the past, Wolfe
for the future ; Montcalm fought for Louis XV, Wolfe
for George Washington and Abraham Lincoln. Although both men were killed in that battle, Montcalm
lost and Wolfe won. With the triumph of Wolfe commenced the history of the United States.

The decisive
"If"

"France should have won that battle ; she should
have held America for Rome. She had the advantage.
She had Quebec as her Gibraltar and she had a chain of
forts from Quebec through the heart of the country down
through the Mississippi valley to the very city of New
Orleans. She had also allies in many tribes of Indians
whom she converted to Catholicism. She might have
won that battle, IF—and the Huguenots were in that if—
if she had only used the forces against England which
she used in persecuting and driving out the Huguenots
from the home land. One historian says that ' the persecution of the Huguenots in France called from America,
the important centre of conflict, the forces that would inevitably have torn from the American Protestants the
fair heritage they now have.' "

IV

Intermarriage
and Assimila-
tion

The exact value of the contribution of the French
Protestants to the building of the Republic no human
wisdom can estimate, so early, so continuous, so complete
was the assimilation of this people into the English
colonial life. Intermarriage began before the Pilgrim or
Puritan or Huguenot came to America, and it continued
all through colonial years. The French refugees entered
with earnestness and vigour into all the hopes and plans
of the new nation. They gave property and life in behalf of the principles they had so eagerly championed in
France. They faced danger and had their full share of

suffering in the struggle for independence. A considerable number of those of direct Huguenot descent were men of large influence whose ability was widely and cheerfully recognized, and whose names were enshrined in the grateful affections of the people. Of these refugees as a whole body Henry Cabot Lodge speaks as follows : "I believe that, in proportion to their numbers, the Huguenots produced and gave to the American Republic more men of ability than any other race."

This statement may, at first, be met with incredulity, but a little investigation of the facts will soon convince one of its correctness. Faneuil Hall, "cradle of liberty," is an index to the part which Huguenots have played in American life. Its four walls have heard the advocacy of every great cause pertaining to the upbuilding of America. Standing in Boston, the old city of the American Revolution, it is a constant rebuke to all that is low and degrading in national life, and a constant inspiration to every brilliant conception in the American mind that makes for patriotism. The name of Faneuil awakens many precious memories ; thoughts of Huguenot patriots crowd thick and fast. There was Paul Revere, a leader of the Boston Tea Party and the hero of the famous "midnight ride" ; Richard Dana, the people's champion in their fight against the Stamp Act ; James Bowdoin, who proved himself a thorn in the flesh of the royal governors ; General Francis Marion, "Swamp Fox" ; Gabriel Manigault, whose generosity saved the colonial government from bankruptcy ; and a host of others. A Huguenot was the first president of the Colonial Congress, and out of the seven presidents of that body no less than three were Huguenots—Henry Laurens, John Jay, and Elias Boudinot.

No name in American history has greater prominence and honour than the name of John Jay, the first chief justice of the nation, and president of the Continental Congress, president of the American Bible Society, presi-

Faneuil Hall an Index

Eminent French Americans

dent of the earliest society for the emancipation of the slaves, and signer of the treaty of peace which brought the Revolutionary War to a successful close. Close beside Jay stands Alexander Hamilton, a Huguenot on his mother's side. With his genius for organization, his ability as a financier, and his abundant patriotism, he carved a niche for himself on a level with the greatest statesmen of his day. In the history of the American navy appears no more heroic spirit than that of Stephen Decatur. In the Mexican and Civil Wars the Huguenot blood was represented by Admiral Dupont, General John C. Fremont, and General John F. Reynolds, and in the Spanish War by Admirals George Dewey and Winfield Scott Schley.

Three Presidents

Descendants of the Huguenots have been prominent in other walks of life. Among statesmen may be mentioned Presidents Tyler, Garfield and Roosevelt; John Sevier, "the commonwealth builder"; Thomas Francis Bayard, and a host of others. In law and medicine their names are of frequent occurrence. Stephen Girard, Christopher Roberts, Matthew Vassar, James Bowdoin and Thomas Hopkinson Gallaudet stand out as philanthropists and promoters of education. The names of Maury, Dana and Le Conte stand high in the list of American scientists. Such men as William Heathcote De Lancey, Hosea Ballou and William Hague were leaders in the church. While in literature are to be counted such names as Philip Freneau, Henry D. Thoreau, Henry W. Longfellow, and John G. Whittier.

A Fine Characterization

Of the Huguenots it has been well said: "There have been few people on earth so upright and single minded, so faithful in the discharge of their duties towards God and man, so elevated in aim, so dignified in character. The enlightened, independent, firm, God-fearing spirit of the French Protestants has blended its influence with that of the Puritan to form our national character and to establish those civil and religious institutions by which we are distinguished and blessed above all peoples.'' So skilled were they in the arts, such a spirit of economy and thrift characterized them, such loyalty had they to the principles of our national life, such sane and tolerant views in religious matters, such uprightness and excellence and nobility of character, such high and commanding genius in statesmanship, that their presence, even though they formed but a small body as to numbers and were so assimilated as to sink their identity in the common body, exerted a moulding and ennobling influence upon the entire fabric of our national life. Deserving of high honour are Puritan and Pilgrim. Let orator and historian continue to sound their praises. But side by side with them, sharers in their sufferings, partakers of their perils, distinguished helpers in their great labours, stimulating and inspiring, stood a smaller company whose life and deeds and spirit were also important factors in giving this land those institutions of civil and religious liberty by means of which she is steadily fulfilling her high mission and successfully working out her great destiny.

BOOK ONE

THE RISE OF PROTESTANTISM IN FRANCE

CHAPTER I

THE FRENCH SPIRIT

I

JOAN OF ARC stands foremost among the renowned and remarkable figures of history. Every Frenchman is proud of her name and fame. Wherever patriotism, valour, consecration and faith are honoured, the Maid of Orleans finds veneration. It is fitting that she should have first place in this work, which undertakes to trace the French blood in America and tell of its achievements as represented by the Protestant element that came from the Old World to the New. To understand the nature of this element it is necessary to go back to the mother country and learn what it was there; to trace the beginning and rise of the independent reform spirit in religion which led to the Huguenot faith, persecutions and exile. Joan of Arc

In this study one is led back further than Luther and Calvin, the great Protestant Reformers whose names overshadow all others. The forerunner of the Protestants is found in Joan of Arc. She was a martyr to her faith, as dauntless as any that ever died rather than deny and recant religious belief. She refused to consider herself unchurched, in spite of ecclesiastical oppression and cruelty, which relentlessly encompassed her death at the stake; so that she may fairly be called an unconscious Protestant—a true leader upholding the right of the individual conscience in matters of religion. The same spirit was in Joan of Arc that moved Calvin and Coligny and the tens of thousands of brave and noble French who were willing to suffer, to leave homes and possessions, to endure exile, but would not surrender their rights of conscience and their religious liberty. The Forerunner of the Reformers An Unconscious Protestant

25

II

Early in the fifteenth century clouds and darkness had settled over France. A critical point had been reached in the nation's life. War was in progress with England, and the fortunes of France were low. English conquest seemed certain. An incompetent king, Charles VII, was disliked by the nobility and distrusted by the people. Paris had fallen into the enemy's hands, and an English army was besieging Orleans. It was "one of the turning points in the history of nations."

At this junction there came to the French commander a volunteer, declaring that she had a commission from God to restore to the king of France his kingdom.
Never in the records of history was there a more singular volunteer or declaration. For this new ally, this "warrior" from Lorraine, intent on such mighty mission, was a country girl, modest and retiring by nature, simple-hearted and deeply religious, who had spun and knitted with her mother at home, and helped her brothers tend the peaceful herds among her native hills. Joan of Arc was born in 1412 in the village of Domremy, in the northeastern part of France, on the borders of Lorraine and Champagne. From her early years she had displayed an unusual Christian fervour, which led to her being regarded as peculiar, though she was most exemplary in conduct, pure and artless. She began to hear voices, as she called them, by the time she was thirteen. In the quiet home life, out in the fields or at her weaving, she
experienced moments of religious exaltation. At such times she saw visions and dreamed dreams, and heard the solemn voices bidding her "go forth to the help of the King of France." She became so filled with the idea that she was divinely called to deliver her country from the English foe that she could not resist the impulse to act. Simple girl that she was, in 1429, when she was but seventeen, Joan was inspired with the belief that if she could get command of the French army, God and suc-

JOAN OF ARC SEEING VISIONS

cess would go with her, and the English be driven from Orleans and France. Persevering and dauntless, urged on by the voices sounding in her ears, she overcame seemingly insurmountable obstacles, until at length she reached audience with the French officer in command. No wonder he thought her mad, the victim of religious delusion. The real wonder is that he, commander of men, soldier and not sentimentalist, was at last so stirred by her spirit and story, and by something in her personality which he could not fathom, that he decided to send her with armed escort to the King.

A Divine Inspiration

This was the direct result of Joan's visions. St. Michael appeared to her in a flood of light and told her to go to the help of the King, and restore to him his realm. This she must do, since it was God's will. She had not only to persuade the commander but to meet opposition on all sides. Her father, when he heard of her audacious purpose, threatened to drown her, but without effect. Her appeals for aid to reach the King were again and again refused with contempt. But she persisted. "I must go to the King, even if I wear my limbs to the very knees. I had far rather rest and spin by my mother's side, for this is no work of my choosing; but I must go and do it."

Overcoming Bitter Opposition

They asked, thinking to confuse her, "Who is your Lord?" "He is God," was her reply. The theologians proved to their own satisfaction from their books that they ought not to believe her, but they could not move her. "There is more in God's books than in yours," she said. And by and by the French officer was sufficiently impressed to give her at least her coveted chance to make her strange story known to the King.

So at last she was ushered into the presence of the as yet uncrowned monarch, and a strange scene it was. This country girl, never before away from her simple home surroundings, appeared not the least daunted by the ordeal of a court presentation. She had a mission,

Maid and Monarch

and was so intent upon that as to give little heed to aught else. With the simplicity of a true greatness, she knelt before her sovereign and said modestly, yet with utmost assurance, "Gentle Dauphin, my name is Joan the Maid. The heavenly King sends me to declare that you shall be anointed and crowned in the town of Rheims, and you shall be lieutenant of the heavenly King, who is the King of France."

A Bold
Declaration

Imagine the scene and the sensation this created. The impression was profound. The King did not readily come to this conclusion, however. Her proposition to have troops placed under her command, that she might lead them to Orleans and raise the siege, was plainly absurd. Her persistency in it, and her calm assurance in her success, convinced him that she was possessed by a devil. She admitted that she was only a poor shepherd girl, not a soldier. "I am a poor maid," she said frankly. "I know not how to ride to the wars, or to lead men to arms."

The King was moved. He was in too dire straits to turn aside lightly any offer of help. This one seemed childish, yet there was something in the character and confidence of the Maid that gained friends for her, and her case was turned over to the parliament and university authorities at Poitiers.

Having made this point, Joan said : "I know well that I shall have hard work to do at Poitiers, but my Master will aid me. Let me go, then, in God's name." The learned doctors were amazed at the simplicity and force of her answers. Asked what signs she had, she replied : "Give me some men at arms and lead me to Orleans, and I will then show you signs. The sign I am to give you is to raise the siege of Orleans." The doctors decided in her favour, and the King placed her in command of the army.

Placed
in
Command

Nothing was wanting to make the scene dramatic. Arrayed in white armour on a black horse, with a small axe in her hand, the maid of Orleans rode forth, attended by two pages, two heralds, a chaplain, valets, and special guards. An army of ten thousand followed her from Chinon. They were rough men, but her influence over them was remarkably restraining. Her common sense was as strong as her imagination. She seemed supernatural to the soldiers, as she led them forward against the English who held Orleans in siege. Her enthusiasm and fearlessness were electrifying. She displayed skill in the management of forces, including artillery, that astonished experienced generals. Under such leadership the French were irresistible, and the maid's prediction that she would deliver Orleans and restore to the King of France his kingdom was fulfilled.

III

The coronation of the Dauphin at Rheims soon took place. Then Joan considered her mission ended and asked leave to go home, saying, "O gentle King, the pleasure of God is done." But the archbishop urged her to remain. "Would it were the King's pleasure," she said, "that I might go and keep sheep once more with my sisters and brothers; they would be so glad to see me again." She was not permitted to leave, and engaged afterwards in several battles and sieges, but her conviction was that the chief mission was performed. At the coronation she had occupied the highest place. She was hailed as the saviour of her country. Briefly she enjoyed the high honour rightly hers, and then began the tragedy which was to be a lasting infamy to France. She was betrayed into the hands of the English, who looked upon her as a sorcerer. She was brought to Rouen in chains, cast into a cell, and fastened by a large iron chain to a beam. So afraid were her captors that she would elude them by miracle that they caused this helpless girl to sleep with double chains round her limbs so

Joan's Prediction Fulfilled

Shameful Betrayal

that she could not stir, while three armed men guarded her by day and night.

A Form
of Trial

At length she was brought to trial. The bishop of Beauvais presided, and all the judges were ecclesiastics. The trial lasted for about a year. Every effort was made to entangle the maid, but she met her judges successfully at every point. They asked : "Do you believe you are in a state of peace?" She replied : "If I am not God will put me in it." They argued that God had forsaken her as her capture proved. She replied, "Since it has pleased God that I should be taken, it is for the best." They demanded : "Will you submit to the Church Militant?" "I have come to the King of France," replied Joan, "by commission from the Church Triumphant above; to that church I submit." She closed with intense feeling ; "I had far rather die than renounce what I have done by my Lord's commands." They deprived her of mass. She said weeping : "The Lord can make me hear it without your aid." The judges asked her :

A Real
Protest

"Do your voices forbid you to submit to the church and the pope?" When she saw the judges all against her she said : "I hold to my Judge, the King of heaven and earth. God has always been my Lord in what I have done. The devil has never had any power over me."

Travesty
of
Justice

Nothing was too base to attempt in order to secure a conviction. A vile priest was engaged to secure Joan's confidence in the hope that she might make admissions that could be used against her as evidence. The King she had placed upon the throne left her unaided. What were the charges brought against her? Principally these : That she had in a wicked manner, and contrary to the divine law, dressed herself in men's clothes, and committed murders with weapons of war ; that she had represented herself to the simple people as a messenger of God, initiated in the secrets of Providence ; and that she was suspected of many other dangerous errors and culpable acts against the divine majesty. Was there ever a greater

travesty on justice !   Of course her conviction was a fore-
gone conclusion.   On such flimsy charges the doctors of
the University of Paris declared gravely :

She has offended beyond measure the honour of God, abjured the **Charges**
faith in a manner not to be expressed, and extraordinarily defiled the **that were**
Slander
church.   By her idolatry, false doctrine and other innumerable crimes
have invaded the soil of France ; never, in the memory of man, would
so great hurt have been given to our holy religion, and such damage
to the kingdom, as if they were to let her escape without satisfying
the ends of justice.   But were they to deliver up the maid, they would
obtain the grace and love of God, and at the same time augment
the glory of the faith and splendour of their noble and illustrious
names.

IV

The venerable doctors of the University, with the
Bishop Beauvais, visited her from time to time to examine her, and to torture her with their questions.   On
one occasion they exhorted her to make her submission ;
they quoted Scripture, but without success.

As they were leaving the prison one hissed to Joan : **Joan's**
"If you refuse to submit to the church, the church will **Firm**
Position
abandon you as if you were a Saracen."   To this she
replied : "I am a good Christian—a Christian born and
baptized—and a Christian I shall die."   Before the bishop
left his victim he made another attempt to make her submit, presenting a bait that he thought would be sure to
catch her, namely, permission to receive the eucharist.
Said he : "As you desire the eucharist, will you, if
you are allowed to do so, submit yourself to the
church ?"   To this Joan replied : "As to that submission I can give no other answer than I have already
given you.   I love God.   Him I serve as a good Christian should.   Were I able I would help the church with
all my strength."

Some of the judges requested that in a more public **Public**
place than in her prison, Joan should be again admonished **Warning**
relating to the crimes of which she was accused ; and the

bishop accordingly summoned a public meeting of the judges to be held in the chamber near the Great Hall. On that occasion sixty-two judges were present. A celebrated doctor of theology, a man of great eloquence, presented the case and sought to break down Joan's will. The bishop admonished her that if she did not obey the advice given she would jeopardize her body and soul. He said all faithful Christians must conform to the church, and after arguing at length closed by saying that by not conforming to the holy church she placed herself in the power of the church to condemn and burn her as a heretic. She boldly answered: "I will not say aught else than I have already spoken, and were I even to see the fire I should say the same."

Threat of Torture

Then threat of bodily torture was tried. Joan was taken into the inquisitorial chamber, where ranged round the circular walls were the instruments of torture. The bishop of Cauchon, after an exhortation, said: "Now, Joan, if you refuse to speak the truth, you will be put to the torture. You see before you the instruments prepared, and by them stand the executioners ready to do their office at our command. You will be tortured in order that you may be led into the way of truth, and for the salvation of body and soul, which you by your lies

The Heroic Spirit

have exposed to so great a peril." Here was the severest test she had been exposed to. But her course rose to the moral sublimity of the Christian martyr. She said: "Even if you tear me limb from limb, and even if you kill me, I will not tell you anything further. And even were I forced to do so, I should afterwards declare that it was only because of the torture that I had spoken differently."

An elaborate sentence by her judges was pronounced against her. This is part of it:

The Sentence

Apostate after having cut her hair short, which was given her by God to hide her head with, and also having abandoned the dress of a woman for that of man; vicious and a soothsayer, for saying without

JOAN AT THE CROWNING OF CHARLES AT RHEIMS

showing miracles, that she is sent by God, as was Moses and John the Baptist; rebel to the holy faith by remaining under the anathema framed by the canons of the church, and by not receiving the sacraments of the church at the season set apart by the church, in order not to have to cease wearing the dress of a man; blasphemous in saying that she knows she will be received into paradise. Therefore, if after having been charitably warned she refuses to re-enter the Catholic faith, and thereby give satisfaction, she shall be given over to the secular judges and meet with the punishment due to her crimes.

The sentence was pronounced that Joan of Arc be put to death by fire, as a heretic. Her judges declared:

Decree of Death

By our present sentence, which, seated in tribunal, we utter and pronounce in this writing, we denounce thee as a rotten member, and that thou mayest not vitiate others, as cast out from the unity of the church, separate from the body, abandoned to the secular power as, indeed, by these presents, we do cast thee off, separate and abandon thee;—praying this same secular power, so far as concerns death and the mutilation of the limbs, to moderate its judgment towards thee, and, if true signs of penitence should appear in thee, to permit that Sacrament of penance be administered to thee.

Appeal for a Soldier's Death

When the maid heard the sentence from the bishop, she exclaimed, "Alas, am I to be treated so horribly and cruelly? Must my body, pure as from birth, and never contaminated, be this day consumed and reduced to ashes? I would rather be beheaded seven times over than on this wise. Oh! I make my appeal to God, the great Judge of the wrongs and grievances done to me. Bishop, I die through you."

On the 24th of May, 1431, two lofty scaffolds were erected, on which were to be seated cardinals, doctors, inquisitors and bishops, to feast their eyes in seeing the burning of Joan of Arc. On the other scaffold was to be placed the victim, with the fuel somewhat below, so the flames would rise and envelop her.

The Execution

The execution was ordered to be carried into effect. She was covered with a long white garment such as criminals and victims of the Inquisition were generally arrayed in. On her head was placed a mitre-shaped paper cap, on which were inscribed "apostate, idolatress." She was placed in a cart on which two priests mounted with her, accompanied by eight hundred troops marching along the road. A discourse was delivered by a monk by the name of Midi. After the sermon the preacher added: "Joan, the church, wishing to prevent infliction, casts you out of her. She no longer protects you, depart in peace." The bishop of Beauvais, the vile wretch who presided at her trial, was present still to torment her, and said: "We reject you, we cast you off, we abandon you according to the usual formula of the Inquisition." She ascended the platform and a chain was placed around her to fasten her to the stake. She exclaimed: "Oh, Rouen, must I die here? I have great fear lest you will suffer for my death." The fire was kindled. She saw it and shrieked. While the flames began to roll around her she cried out for water, and cried on God, and then said:

Last Words of the Martyr

"My voices have not deceived me." Her last words were "Jesus—Jesus!" Then her head fell on her breast and her pure spirit went to paradise. Many were melted to tears, and even the rude soldiers cried: "We are lost; we have burned a saint. Would God, my soul were where hers is now."

V

Estimates of Historians

Green

The eminent English historian, Richard Henry Green, says: "The one pure figure which rises out of the greed and lust, the selfishness and unbelief of the time, is the figure of Joan of Arc."

DeQuincy

In one of his most powerful essays DeQuincy deals with this subject. This is his conclusion from the facts: "Never from the foundation of the earth was there such a trial as this, if it were laid open in all its beauty of defense, and all its hellishness of attack. Oh, child of France! shepherdess! peasant girl trodden under foot by all around thee; how I honour thy flashing intellect, as

God's lightning to its mark, that ran before France and
laggard Europe by many a century, confounding the malice of the ensnarer, and making dumb the oracles of false-
hood."

To these estimates we add that of Mark Twain, who has   Clemens
made one of the most discriminating studies of the Maid
of Orleans, and given his mature conclusions in a recent
article entitled "Saint Joan of Arc." After a masterly
review of her military career—"the briefest epoch-mak-
ing military career known to history," lasting only a year
and a month—he says:

"That this untrained young creature's genius for war   A Genius
was wonderful, and her generalship worthy to rank with
the ripe products of a tried and trained military experience, we have the sworn testimony of two of her veteran
subordinates—one, the Duc d' Alençon, the other the greatest of the French generals of the time, Dunois, Bastard
of Orleans; that her genius was as great—possibly even
greater—in the subtle warfare of the forum, we have for
witness the records of the Rouen Trials, that protracted
exhibition of intellectual fence maintained with credit
against the master-minds of France; that her moral greatness was peer to her intellect we call the Rouen Trials
again to witness, with their testimony to a fortitude which
patiently and steadfastly endured during twelve weeks
the wasting forces of captivity, chains, loneliness, sickness, darkness, hunger, thirst, cold, shame, insult, abuse,
broken sleep, treachery, ingratitude, exhausting sieges of
cross-examination, the threat of torture, with the rack
before her and the executioner standing ready: yet never
surrendering, never asking quarter, the frail wreck of her
as unconquerable the last day as was her invincible spirit
the first.

"From the verdict (of Rehabilitation, twenty-five years   The Wonder
after she had been condemned and burned by the Church   of the Ages
as a witch and familiar of evil spirits) she rises stainlessly
pure in mind and heart, in speech and deed and spirit,

and will so endure to the end of time. She is the Wonder of the Ages. All the rules fail in this girl's case. In the world's history she stands alone—quite alone. . . . There is no one to compare her with, none to measure her by. . . . There is no blemish in that rounded and beautiful character. . . . Taking into account all the circumstances—her origin, youth, sex, illiteracy, early environment, and the obstructing conditions under which she exploited her high gifts and made her conquests in the field and before the courts that tried her for her life, —she is easily and by far the most extraordinary person the human race has ever produced.''

Reversing the Verdict Twenty years after the martyrdom it was concluded to attempt to revise the process. The then reigning pope pronounced the charges against Joan to be utterly false. He appointed the Archbishop of Rheims and two prelates to inquire into the trial, aided by an inquisitor to attend to that work. The decision of the prelates was that her visions came from God. They pronounced her trial at Rouen to have been wicked, and that she was free from any blame. The church had decided against the maid, and now it concluded to turn around. Thus the investigation resulted in the declaration of her innocence, or rehabilitation. In 1431 she was pronounced to be in league with the devil, a heretic, an idolatress, and was burned at the stake. In 1456 the French clergy, with the sanction of the pope, declared the memory of Joan of Arc free from all taint of heresy and idolatry. And now, by that same church, which would claim so illustrious a personage as its own, Joan has been canonized as a saint.

It is in view of all the facts that Joan of Arc is called a genuine Protestant martyr, although the term Protestant had not then come into use. She embodied the Protestant principle, as did Huss and Savonarola and Wycliff. As an American writer says:

Joan and Luther '' Joan of Arc was thus in the same position before this tribunal that Luther was before the Diet of Worms. Her

language and his were identical, except that he spoke of
the Word of God in Scripture, where she spoke of the
Voice of God in her soul. Both wished to obey the
church. This was God, speaking to the soul or speaking
in the Scripture. The time came to Joan when the church
said : 'Deny the Voices of God in your heart.' The time
came to Luther when the church said : 'Deny the Word
of God in the Bible.' Then both became virtually Protestants, and obeyed the higher law as against the lower
one. The girl of Domremy was a Protestant before the
Reformation." And her spirit was to live again in the
Huguenots.

Siege of Orleans

CHAPTER II

THE HUGUENOTS IN FRANCE

I

Huguenot Defined

THE term " Huguenot," as it is applied in history, and as it is to be understood throughout this book, means a member of the Protestant evangelical party in France. It is therefore equivalent to the expression used in the Edict of Nantes and other royal edicts, "member of the Pretended Reformed Religion." The Huguenot Church was the Reformed Church of France.

Origin of the Name

The origin of the word has been lost in obscurity, but many theories have been advanced as to its derivation; among which are the following :

1.   Hugon's tower at Tours, a place where the early Protestants secretly assembled for religious worship.

2.   *Heghenen,* or *huguenen,* a Flemish word equivalent to Puritans.

3.   Says Verdier, in his Prosopographic, " *Les Huguenots ont été ainsi appelez de Jean Hus, duquel ils ont suivi la doctrine; comme qui dirait les Guenons de Hus.*" (The Huguenots were so called from John Huss, whose doctrine they followed ; as one would say, the disciples of Huss.)

4.   *Hues quenaus,* which signifies in the Swiss patois, a seditious people.

5.   Benoît observes that some supposed the term had originated from an incorrect pronunciation of the word gnostic.

The Confederates

6.   The most generally received etymology is traced to the word Eignot, derived from the German *Eid-genossen— federati,* confederates or allied. There was a party thus designated at Geneva.

38

7. The word Huguenot was not applied to the Reformed Church of France as a distinctive epithet until about 1560. Then the term was applied to the whole political party which supported the claims of Henry of Navarre to the crown. It was intended as a reproach, and soon became synonymous with Reformer. Cardinal Richelieu captured the city of Rochelle, the stronghold of the Protestants, and by 1628 had broken up the political organization of the Huguenots, leaving only the religious organization as the bond of union for the Reformed in religion. In 1660 the religious organization was also practically wiped out of existence by the Revocation of the Edict of Nantes. But the name and the Reformed religion have both survived in France, while the descendants of the Reformers have spread their influence around the globe.

II

Early in the sixteenth century the corruptions and abuses of the Roman Catholic Church in France became so wide spread that thinking men could no longer remain blind to them, but were forced to recognize that ignorance, superstition and immorality prevailed throughout the whole organization. Corruption in the Church

The immorality of the clergy was notorious. So bad were the lives of most of the ecclesiastics that the expressions "Idle as a priest" and "Lewd and greedy as a monk" became popular proverbs. From bishop to friar the spiritual leaders of the people were debauched and corrupt. The great dignitaries of the church gave themselves up to a life of pleasure on a magnificent scale; no courtier could outrival them in their luxurious dissipation, their banquets, drinking bouts, games and revels. The only care of the priests was to extort as much money out of the people as they could possibly squeeze, and they saw to it that none of their wealth was wasted in helping the poor and distressed. Like their Immorality and Ignorance of the Clergy superiors they were devoted body and soul to a ceaseless round of sensual pleasures. The monastic orders were no better, and filth and gluttony rioted among them. In speaking of them, a contemporary Romish writer says : "Generally the monks elected the most jovial companion, him who was the most fond of women, dogs, and birds, the deepest drinker—in short, the most dissipated ; and this in order that, when they had made him abbot or prior, they might be permitted to indulge in similar debauch and pleasure."

The ignorance of the clergy in spiritual matters was equalled only by their debauchery. A few scraps of Vulgate Latin with which to conduct the mass, a slender stock of "Aves" and "Paters," sufficed for the rank and file of the priesthood. Of the Bible they literally knew nothing at all. But this cannot be wondered at when even the professed teachers of theology showed a marvellous ignorance of the Holy Scriptures. Robert Etienne, a famous scholar and printer who was born in 1503, wrote as follows concerning the Biblical knowledge of the theologians of the Sorbonne : "In those times, as I can affirm with truth, when I asked them in what part of **The New Testament Unknown** the New Testament some matter was written, they used to answer that they had read it in Saint Jerome or in the Decretals, but that they did not know what the New Testament was, not being aware that it was customary to print it after the Old. What I am going to state will appear almost a prodigy, and yet there is nothing more true nor better proven : Not long since, a member of their college used daily to say, I am amazed that these young people keep bringing up the New Testament to us. I was more than fifty years old before I knew anything about the New Testament !"

If the theologians had such a slight acquaintance with the teachings of Christ the people could well be forgiven for not having any knowledge at all of Him. There was no translation of the Bible into French, and as the popular education of that day did not include Greek or Hebrew, the Gospels remained safely hidden from the French people.

Superstition flourished in the soil prepared by immorality and ignorance. The worship of a living God was swallowed up in reverence for the relics of saints and for pictures and statues of them. There seemed to be no limit to the popular credulity, and the grossest deceptions aroused no suspicions among the faithful. In one church the hair of the Virgin was to be seen, in another the people were accustomed to worship the sword of the archangel Michael, in still another the veritable stones with which St. Stephen was killed were carefully preserved. Indeed there were enough of these stones in the churches of France to furnish sufficient material for a respectable wall, just as there were so many crowns of thorns as to lead one to believe that a whole hedge must have been used in the making of them. St. Dionysius' body lay in state at Ratisbon as well as at Saint Denis, but he was no more fortunate in this respect than the other saints, most of whom could boast of having two or three bodies; and much less so than the apostles, who were all credited with having at least four bodies apiece, besides numerous and seemingly unnecessary duplicate finger and toe joints. The extreme to which this worship of relics was carried may be seen from the following partial list of the treasures of the Sainte Chapelle in Paris: the crown of thorns, Aaron's rod that budded, the great crown of St. Louis, the head of the holy lance, one of the nails used in our Lord's crucifixion, the tables of stone, some of the blood of Christ, the purple robe, and the milk of the Holy Virgin.

Superstition Without Limit

But the superstitions fostered by the church were not confined to a belief in marvellous relics. The people were stimulated to fresh zeal and increased contributions by means of miracles which caused great amazement everywhere except in the minds of the ingenious priests

Popular Credulity

who got them up.   A fair example of these "miracles"
is that of the well-known "ghost of Orleans."   A wealthy
lady, having died, was buried without the usual gifts for
the welfare of her soul being made to the church.   The
Franciscans of that city accordingly hit upon a scheme
to make use of her for purpose of warning to others who
might also be tempted to forget the church in their wills.
A series of distinct tappings was heard to issue from her
tomb, and these were explained to the awe-struck people
as signs of her approaching doom and of her desire to
have her heresy-polluted body removed from consecrated
ground.   Unfortunately for their plans, one of their
number was discovered hidden above the ceiling whence
the mysterious sounds had come.   But for every one of
these impostures which was exposed there were a hundred which were widely credited as veritable miracles.

III

The First
Reformers
Guillaume Briçonnet, Bishop of Meaux, was among
the number who realized how urgent was the need of re-
forming the church.   Resolving to commence the work
Briconnet
of reformation in his own diocese, he invited to Meaux a
small handful of able and earnest men whom he knew to
be advocates of a purer and more spiritual Christianity.
LeFevre
Among them was the famous scholar Jacques LeFevre,
of Staples, and his no less famous pupil, Guillaume
Farel
Farel, whose staunch heart put courage and good cheer
into his comrades.   The teacher had prophetic insight.
Before the close of the fifteenth century, the amiable
Professor LeFevre said one day to Farel, "My dear
William, God will renew the world ; and you will see
it."   Dissatisfied with his own attainments in religion,
and with the standard of knowledge and piety around
him, this great scholar had begun to drink from the
pure fountain of the Gospel of Christ in the original
language, and was giving out liberal draughts to those attending upon his lectures.

The Bible was the cause of the Reformation in France, as in all lands. In the fifteenth century an eager demand had sprung up in France for the Scriptures, editions of which had been printed in Antwerp, some versions in French for the Walloons. The translation that super- **Effect of the Bible** seded all others in French was made by LeFevre, who may on this account be ranked as the first of the Huguenots. The effects were the same wherever the Book appeared. It was the accidental sight of a copy of one of Gutenberg's Bibles in the library of the Erfurt convent that transformed local monk Luther into the Protestant World Reformer. So in France, the reading of the Bible by the people was followed by an immediate reaction against the superstition, indifferentism and impiety which generally prevailed. There was a sudden awakening to a new religious life. The sentiment of right was created, and a new sense of manhood was born.

Under the protection of Margaret of Angoulême, wife of the King of Navarre and only sister to Francis I, King of France, the reformation at Meaux proceeded with great rapidity. The gospel was preached from the pulpits, and copies of the Bible were spread broadcast among the people. In the pure light of God's Word the gross superstitions of the Romish church faded as mists before the sun, and the inhabitants of Meaux soon came to value spiritual truths above saintly relics and waxen images.

But all this did not escape the jealous eyes of the **Power of the Church** church which based its wealth and power on the ignorance of the people. Strong pressure from Rome was brought to bear on the King, and in spite of the efforts of Margaret, who was distinguished by her humanity towards the Protestants from first to last, the work of stamping out the heresy was begun. Briçonnet, in order to save his life, was forced to aid in the work of blotting out the reforms he had himself helped to institute. One by one the reformers were compelled to leave Meaux and take up their work more quietly in other places. But the poor people of the town remained behind, and the tenacity with which they clung to the "new doctrines" showed how crying had been their need of a message of salvation.

Leclerc the
First Martyr

Jean Leclerc, a wool-carder, was the first upon whom the church vented its fury. Accused of irreverence, he was taken to Paris for trial and was condemned to be whipped through the streets of that city for three successive days, then to go through a like punishment at Meaux, after which he was to be branded on the forehead with a hot iron and banished from the kingdom. As the iron was being applied to his brow his aged mother cried out in her anguish, "Vive Jésu Christ et ses enseignes!" (Live Jesus Christ and His witnesses!) Leclerc then made his way to Metz and there took up his trade again. Undaunted by his terrible experience he continued to communicate his knowledge of the Gospels to all with whom he came in contact. He was seized a second time and was condemned for heresy. His nose, arms and breast were torn by pincers, and his right hand cut off at the wrist. A hoop of red-hot iron was then pressed upon his head. So far, no words had escaped his lips, but as the metal slowly ate its way into his skull he began calmly to repeat the words of the Psalmist, "Their idols are silver and gold, the work of men's hands." At this, dreading the effect of his words upon the people, his persecutors quickly stifled his voice by throwing him into the fire.

Bitter
Persecution

Other martyrs followed Leclerc into the flames in rapid succession. The faithful citizens of Meaux who held the reformed doctrines were liable at any time to the most bitter persecutions. If one of their number gave the priests the slightest pretext to act upon, he was proclaimed a heretic and given to the proper authorities, from whose hands he received punishment of the most inhuman kind. To aid in the work of extermination, spies were employed who were allowed to confiscate the prop-

King Henry of Navarre

Queen Margaret of Navarre

John Calvin

Admiral De Coligny

erty of any one against whom they could bring evidence
of heresy. But these efforts of the church failed to achieve
any lasting results, and tended to spread the work of reformation by driving the reformers into various parts of
France. Before a great while the faith which these early
martyrs had sealed with their blood was deeply rooted in
many sections of the country, making headway even in
Paris.

As the Huguenots increased in numbers the severity   The Vaudois
of the authorities grew more merciless and frightful.   Horrors
The most stringent laws were enacted and the sweet air
of France reeked with the smoke from hundreds of holo-
causts. Not content with burning a heretic here and
there, those in power commenced the persecution of
entire communities. The expedition against the Vaudois
was one of the most dreadful of these wholesale butcheries.

The Vaudois lived in the valley of the Durance, a few
miles east of Avignon. They were known far and near
for peaceable folk who strove to be honest in their deal-   1540
ings with men and to lead just and upright lives. But in
the minds of their bigoted enemies these facts did not
outweigh their hatred, for the simple reason that the
Vaudois were accustomed to read their Bibles and to
worship God after the fashion of the earliest Christians.
For a long time they had been the butt of various persecutions and had still remained steadfast in their faith, so
it was finally decided to make them such a signal example
as would frighten the very stoutest Huguenot heart. In
1540 the Parliament of Provence decreed that fifteen men
from the village of Merindol who had failed to come to
court to answer to a charge of heresy were to be burned
alive. If not "apprehended in person, they will be
burned in effigy, their wives and children proscribed,
and their possessions confiscated." Further than this,
the decree ordered that all the houses in the village
should be burned and that every trace of human habitation should be removed.

Several months passed before the execution of the order, and the Vaudois came to believe that the storm had passed safely over their heads. But on the 16th of April an army was hastily gathered together and the carnage began. The villages of Cabrierett, Peypin, La Motte and Saint-Martin were the first to be burned. At the approach of the troops some of the inhabitants fled to Merindol, while others sought escape in the neighbouring woods. The women, children and old men were hidden away in a forest retreat in the hope that if discovered their evident weakness would prove their best means of safety. But this hope was futile. The hiding-place was discovered and a massacre ensued. Gray-haired men were put to death by the sword and the women were subjected to the brutal lust of the soldiery, or if with child their breasts were mutilated and they were left to die with their unborn offspring.

Two days later the army arrived at Merindol, but the villagers had received warning of its approach and had taken to flight. A young man was the only person found within the limits of the town and upon him was vented the rage of his captors. As he was dying he cried out, "Lord God, these men are snatching from me a life full of wretchedness and misery, but Thou wilt give me eternal life through Jesus Thy Son." The soldiers then took up the work of destroying the town. Two hundred houses were burned and levelled to the ground, and the dwelling place of thrift and simple happiness was turned into a scene of utter desolation. Many of the fleeing Vaudois were overtaken and put to death or sent in chains to the galleys to serve with thieves and murderers. A party of some twenty-five of the fugitives was found hiding in a cavern, and with laughter and brutal jests a fire was kindled at the mouth of the cave to stifle the helpless victims like rats in a hole.

A large number of the Vaudois had taken refuge in the town of Cabrières, resolved to defend their wives and

Brutality and Massacre

Barbarous Cruelties

Treachery and Murder

children to their last drop of blood.   The army halted
before their weak intrenchments, hesitating to attack the
desperate defenders.   Word was sent to the Vaudois that
by voluntarily surrendering themselves they would avoid
needless bloodshed and their lives and property be spared.
Beguiled by these promises they laid down their arms.
They had no sooner done so than their persecutors fell
upon the defenseless town like a pack of wolves.   The
greater part of the garrison was murdered in cold blood,
while upwards of eight hundred women and children who
had crowded into the sacred precincts of the church were
there put to the sword.   Among the defenders of the
town was a band of forty heroic women, for whom the
crowning act of cruelty was reserved.   They were locked
into a barn and a torch was then applied to the flimsy
structure.   One soldier, moved to pity by the shrieks of
the frenzied victims, opened a way of escape, but his
comrades who were enjoying the spectacle barred the
exit with the sharp points of their spikes.   Thus, in one
way or another, over a thousand innocent persons were
killed and three times that number driven forth as homeless and destitute wanderers.   For weeks afterwards it
was no strange thing to come across the body of some
Vaudois lying by the roadside, overcome by hunger and
thirst, or to hear the wailing of a child that mourned
beside its mother who had fallen dead of exposure and
fatigue.   No charity could be shown these helpless people, for whoever gave them food, drink or shelter did so
under penalty of hanging for it.

Such was the fate that befell a people whose only fault
was that they were Protestants ; a people concerning **A High**
whom Governor de Bellamy reported to the King, **Tribute**
"They differ from our communion in many respects, but
they are a simple, irreproachable people, benevolent,
temperate, humane, and of unshaken loyalty.   Agriculture is their sole occupation ; they have no legal contentions, no lawsuits, or party strife.   Hospitality is one

of their principal virtues, and they have no beggars amongst them. They have neither locks nor bolts upon their doors. No one is tempted to steal, for his wants are freely supplied by asking."

"They are heretics," said the King sternly.

"I acknowledge, sire," said de Bellamy, "that they rarely enter our churches; if they do, they pray with eyes fixed on the ground. They pay no homage to saints or images; they do not use holy water, nor do they acknowledge the benefit to be derived from pilgrimages, or say mass, either for the living or the dead."

"And it is for such men as these you ask clemency! For your sake, they shall receive a pardon, if they renounce their heresies within three months, and seek a reconciliation with the mother church. Think you that I burn heretics in France, in order that they may be nourished in the Alps?" That was the spirit bred in the monarch by the Roman ecclesiastics who surrounded him and flattered him as the defender of the most holy faith.

IV

For thirty years the Protestant party had been growing stronger in spite of the terrible persecutions it received, until in 1555 a Huguenot church was established in Paris, the very centre of French Roman Catholicism. The example of Paris was followed rapidly by other cities; so rapidly, indeed, that six years later there were two thousand one hundred and fifty churches in France from whose pulpits the Word of God was preached. The growth of the Huguenot movement was phenomenal during these same six years, and its doctrines were embraced by all classes of the population alike.

Growth Under Persecution

The lower nobility, the provincial gentry, were chiefly Protestant. Benoît says, "The country churches were almost entirely composed of noblesse," and that "in some, one could count from eighty to a hundred families

Lower Nobility Protestant

of gentlemen." On the dissolution of a church their houses often formed a centre for the scattered congregation. To "seize the nobility" was the King's first order to the dragoons, showing his estimate of their influence and power.

Powerful nobles, like the great Prince of Condé and the illustrious Admiral Coligny, espoused the cause of the Reformed Church and demanded liberty of worship for its adherents. Finally, in 1561, it became evident that the old state of affairs could not go on ; the Huguenot leaders brought great pressure to bear on the throne, and after many vexing delays the famous "Edict of January" was issued, giving to the Huguenots the right to worship unmolested by rabble or clergy. The schools and hospitals were thrown open to all, and the Huguenots were permitted to hold all offices of dignity and responsibility. It was a great victory for freedom of conscience, and had it been faithfully lived up to, France would have been spared a series of devastating civil wars and the loss of so many of her bravest and most industrious sons.

Conde and Coligny

But it was not the intention of the Catholic party to admit their fellow-countrymen to anything like an equality of worship with themselves, and so they proceeded at once to break faith with the Huguenots. In vain were all appeals to the law, so that out of self-defense the Huguenots were compelled to take up arms. They did so, however, only after the greatest provocations : as for example, when no punishment was meted out to the murderers of over a hundred Huguenots who were peacefully worshipping in their tabernacle at Vassy. This massacre of Vassy was a needless and cold-blooded atrocity, and its perpetrators were known ; but in spite of these facts and in defiance of the "Edict of January," the murderers were allowed to go unscathed. Such outrages and such breaches of faith made a resort to arms imperative and gave rise to a series of civil wars that turned France into a bloody battle-ground for over thirty years, and inau-

Massacre of Vassy

Source of Civil Wars

gurated a long train of persecutions, broken promises, and repressive acts of legislation, which culminated in the revocation of the "Edict of Nantes," in 1685. It would be out of place in this brief sketch to go into the history of these wars and the troubles which followed them. A short account of the massacre of St. Bartholomew's Day will be sufficient to show the treachery and ferocity with which the Huguenots were treated.

St. Bartholomew's Day
August 24, 1572

In the month of August, 1572, Henry of Navarre, the nominal head of the Huguenot party, together with Admiral Coligny and the Prince of Condé with eight hundred gentlemen, entered Paris to celebrate the nuptials of Henry and Margaret of Valois, sister of Charles IX. They came as the king's guests and were under the protection of the "Edict of Saint Germain," in which the throne reiterated the promises of religious toleration made in the previous "Edict of January." The wedding was celebrated on the seventeenth with great magnificence, and the remainder of the week was devoted to various holiday sports and games. These festivities were, however, but a mask to cover the real intentions of the Roman Catholics and to throw the Huguenot gentlemen off their guard. On the eve of St. Bartholomew's Day the plans for an appalling massacre had been perfected, and the unsuspecting victims were already marked out for slaughter. The gates of Paris were locked so that none might escape, every house in which a Protestant lodged was marked with a piece of chalk, and soldiers were in readiness to begin their bloody work as soon as the great bell in the tower of the "Palais de Justice" should ring forth the appointed signal.

V

Murder of Admiral Coligny

The massacre was begun by the murder of Coligny, who was confined to his house by a wound he had received a few days before. Early in the morning he was awakened by an uproar in the street, followed by a loud demand for admittance in the name of the king. His servant, La Bonne, opened the door and was immediately struck down with a dagger by Cosseins, a captain of the guard. A motley band of troopers then pressed into the house over the fallen body, and easily overcame the resistance which Coligny's five Swiss guards were able to offer, though they contested bravely every inch of the passage to the Admiral's room. Meanwhile, Coligny, understanding what the clashing of arms signified, rose from his bed despite his wound, and prepared to meet his assassins like the honourable soldier that he was. To the little group of faithful friends and followers who were gathered about him he said, in a voice unmoved by fear, "For a long time I have kept myself in readiness for death. As for you, save yourselves, if you can. It were in vain for you to attempt to save my life. I commend my soul to the mercy of God." Obedient to his request, all his followers excepting Nicholas Muss fled to the roof and made their escape in the darkness. When the soldiers broke into the room they found Coligny awaiting them with the greatest composure, quite undaunted in the face of certain death. "Aren't you the Admiral?" cried one of the troopers. "Yes," replied Coligny. "I am he. But you are too young a soldier to speak thus to so old a captain, if for no other reason than respect for my age." With a curse the soldier struck him with his sword, and the old warrior was quickly put to death. His body was then thrown out of the window into the court below, where the Duke of Guise was waiting the news of his death. Taking out his handkerchief the Duke wiped the blood from Coligny's face and cried, "I recognize him, 'tis the Admiral!" After grinding his heel into the face of the fallen leader he shouted, "Come, soldiers, we have begun well; let us go on to the others!"

The head was then cut off and carried to the Louvre for Charles and his mother to feast their eyes upon. After they had satisfied their hatred they ordered it embalmed

A Noble Victim Undaunted

Ruffian Indignity

A Martyr Statesman

and sent to Pope Gregory at Rome as a token of the zeal with which religious freedom was being thwarted in France. The headless corpse was shamefully mutilated and with every show of ribald scorn it was dragged through the streets of Paris for the space of three days by a crowd of gamins. And so, in the fifty-sixth year of his life, passed away one of the greatest characters which France has ever produced. None of the ignominy which was heaped upon him could serve to cast the slightest stain on his loyalty, purity, and uprightness of life. As a soldier he showed indomitable pluck in the face of defeats which would have disheartened many a courageous man ; he was a master of strategy without a superior in that age of generals, a leader who never failed to inspire the confidence of his troops ; with only the slenderest resources behind him his qualities of generalship enabled him to wage war for many years against a powerful enemy who vastly outnumbered him. As a statesman he sought to save France from the ruin into which her dissolute sovereign was leading her, and was justly regarded as wise and far-sighted. But it is as a Christian gentleman that Gaspard de Coligny deserves most to be remembered. In that dissolute age he set a shining example to the other great nobles of his rank. Every act of his life felt the influence of his manly and straightforward piety. Whether at home, in his castle of Châtillon-sur-Loing, or in the rude camps of the field, he sought to emulate the example of his Master. It was his constant glory and delight to be a Christian.

One of France's Greatest Names

VI

Following the death of Coligny came the wholesale massacre of the Protestants. For three days and nights the carnage went on. Nothing availed to save the wretched victims : neither youth, age, nor sex prevented the swords of the Roman Catholic bigots from striking home. Venerable men were struck down in their feeble-

Wholesale Massacre Without Mercy

ness, babes were torn from their mother's breasts and spitted on the ends of pikes, women were treated to every bestial indignity, so that the blow which ended their suffering seemed like an act of mercy. So sudden was the attack and so scattered were the Huguenots that resistance was out of the question except in a rare instance or two where some doughty gentleman found time to buckle on his breastplate and grasp his sword. The Lieutenant de la Mareschaussée was one of these. With the aid of a solitary companion he defended his house against the onslaughts of the butchers for the whole of that day. Spurred on by the thought of the fate awaiting his wife and invalid daughter he fought like a madman until sheer exhaustion enabled his enemies to despatch him. To vent their spite the soldiers dragged his sick daughter naked through the streets until she died of their maltreatment.

Altogether, probably between five and six thousand persons were slain within the walls of Paris, though some authorities place the number as high as eight or ten thousand. Most of these bodies were dumped into the Seine, so that the river fairly flowed with blood for days afterwards. So numerous were the corpses floating in the stream that the lagging current was unable to carry them all away, and for miles below the city the shores were covered with putrefying remains. It is only fair to France to say that the blame for these atrocities of St. Bartholomew's Day falls heaviest on the Church of Rome, which for years had taught the doctrine that it was no sin to kill those who held other forms of belief; which had gone even further and stated that to do so was an act of signal piety. Indeed, when the news of the massacre reached Rome it was received with the greatest rejoicing, a jubilee was celebrated, and for three nights the city was brilliantly illuminated. King Charles who, under his mother's instigation, ordered the massacre that

The Number of the Victims

Rome's Rejoicing

shocked the world, died at twenty-five, the prey of terror and mental agony.

VII

Henry of
Navarre

When Henry of Navarre was made king of France he found it politically necessary to abjure his Huguenot faith and turn Catholic. But he never forgot his old allegiance to the Reformed religion, and strove in every way to give his former comrades their just rights as citizens of France. On the thirteenth of April, 1598, he set his name to "a perpetual and irrevocable edict," known as the Edict of Nantes, which granted liberty of conscience

Edict of
Nantes

to all Frenchmen. It restored to the Huguenots their full civil rights and gave them the freedom to worship God unmolested by priests or bigots. It was one of the most glorious steps towards human liberty that has ever been taken, and had its solemn promises been adhered to by Henry's royal successors, France would have been spared some of the blackest and most unfortunate passages in her history.

Louis XIV

But after the death of Henry IV, the beneficent provisions of the edict were one by one rendered inoperative, and the old round of petty and cruel persecutions was resumed. We must pass over these unhappy years until we come to the crowning act of despotism which marked the career of Roman Catholic intolerance,

Revocation of
the Edict

the Revocation of the Edict of Nantes. In 1685 Louis XIV utterly destroyed the few remaining liberties of his Protestant subjects by breaking the solemn promises made to them by Henry IV. According to the terms of the Revocation all Huguenot churches were to be torn down, the gathering of Protestants for the purposes of worship was forbidden, even religious services in the home were made punishable offenses. Protestant schools were abolished, all children were to be brought up in the Roman Catholic faith and were to be baptized by the parish priest, etc. Most tyrannical of all the provisions, however, was that which forbade any Huguenot from

THE HUGUENOTS, *by Carl Hoff*

leaving the kingdom under penalty of serving a life sentence in the galleys. Thus by a single stroke of the pen, Louis made life for the Protestants unbearable in France, and at the same time made it a crime for them to seek an asylum in other lands.

The condition of the Huguenots now became truly pitiable, for not content with robbing them of all their liberties the king desired their wholesale conversion. In the endeavour to accomplish this the most heartless methods were resorted to, chief among them being the fiendish process called "dragooning." A day was appointed for the conversion of a certain district, and the dragoons, who were carefully selected from among the most ruffianly swash bucklers in the French army, made their appearance accordingly and took possession of the Protestants' houses. Their orders were to make as much trouble as possible, and they obeyed them with barbarous exactness; converting a quiet home into a bedlam and subjecting the family to the grossest insults and most outrageous tortures. Woe to the unhappy wretch upon whom the troopers were quartered. They stabled their horses in his parlour, smashed his furniture at will, destroyed whatever they could not eat or drink, kept his family awake at night by their drunken uproar or by prodding them with their swords, exposed his wife and daughters to foul language and abuse, and taught his sons the vices of the soldiery. *Dragooning*

Rather than subject his loved ones to such treatment many a brave man, who would cheerfully have suffered the rack or the wheel for the sake of his faith, forced himself to become an unwilling convert to the "true religion." Those who refused to submit after the dragoons had been in their homes a few days were beaten without mercy, or starved, or half-roasted over a fire; mothers were bound securely and forced to see their young babes perish at their feet; some were hung in the chimneys and piles of wet straw burned under them until *Recanting to Save One's Family* they were nearly suffocated ; others were held under water till life was almost extinct.   These, and other crimes too horrible for mention here, were all committed under the mask of a religion which, professing to teach the love of God, inspired the hearts of its followers with a hatred of their fellow man.

VIII

From this condition of affairs large numbers of the Huguenots sought relief by fleeing over the borders of France into Switzerland, Germany, Holland and England, where they were warmly welcomed, both on account of the pity felt for their sufferings, and because they represented the most sober, industrious and intelligent class of the French people.   It is probable that at least four hundred thousand persons emigrated within a short time after the Revocation, and some historians put the figures as high as eight hundred thousand.   Their going struck a sore blow to France, and was the most potent cause of her loss of commercial supremacy.   For the majority of those who escaped were noblemen and gentry, wealthy merchants and manufacturers, bankers, or skilled artisans ; and while most of them were forced to leave their wealth behind them they carried away what was of far more importance—the knowledge of trades such as weaving fine cloths, making silks and laces, hats, etc., which had up to that time been confined to France.   The growth of England as a great manufacturing nation was due in no mean degree to the efforts and the skill of the refugees whom she received so hospitably.   But this emigration was not accomplished without the greatest hardships.   The guards along the frontiers were increased and every effort made by the government to prevent the outflow.   Those who were apprehended were certain to be consigned to the galleys, but this did not prevent the bolder spirits from making an endeavour to reach freedom.   The greatest variety of strategies was resorted to :

Fleeing Into Exile

France Lost her Skilled Artisans and Best Blood

some shipped themselves to England inside empty wine casks; noble ladies disguised themselves as peasants and drove herds of cattle across the Dutch frontiers; others ventured out to sea in open boats to board some friendly ship.

One aristocratic lady secured a passport from a Swiss servant and for weeks rubbed her face with nettles to produce the blotched appearance called for in the description.

Roman Catholics in later times have tried in every way possible to minimize the Massacre of St. Bartholomew, to deny that it was a Church measure, and to charge it upon the Protestants themselves as breakers of the peace. Roman Catholic historians have played fast and loose with the facts of history regarding the entire period of persecution. But the facts remain and cannot be wiped out or evaded.

Efforts to Efface the Stain

There is no question that when the Massacre of St. Bartholomew's day was announced to the world, the Romish clergy of France rejoiced; the King was hailed as the destroyer of heresy; and the Pope at Rome, as head of the Roman Catholic Church throughout the world, approved the infamous deed; going so far as by a special medal, representing the slaughter of the Huguenots, to make it a notable event in the history of the church. The Parliament of Paris followed his example, and on their medal engraved the words, "Piety aroused Justice." But within a hundred and fifty years, the great Roman Catholic preacher, Massillon, when pronouncing the eulogy of Louis XIV, and praising him for the Revocation of the Edict of Nantes—an act not less infamous than the massacre, thus speaks of the latter event: "Even by the recollection and injustice of that bloody day, which ought to be effaced from our annals, which piety and humanity will always disown, which in the effort to crush heresy, under one of our late kings, gave to it new fire and fury, and fumed, if I may venture to say it, from its blood the seed of new disciples." Thus

Blood of Martyrs the Seed of the True Church

this French Roman Catholic turned away in horror from the inhumanity of that earlier day, which he would have the world forget if he could.

IX

One of the greatest craftsmen France ever produced was Bernard Palissy the potter. It was his, too, to suffer for his Protestant faith and at last to give his life for it. He was as noble in character as he was skilled in his art. There was much of pathos and disappointment in his life, yet he lived it grandly, and sets an inspiring example of persistence and piety. Think of pursuing an ideal of beauty for a quarter of a century—working under every conceivable hardship and difficulty, yet never losing faith in ultimate success. That was the man who discovered a secret of enamelling that is the admiration of the world.

Born in 1510, in the south of France, where the reformation most developed, he was brought up to his father's trade—a worker in glass. His parents were too poor to give him any schooling. "I had no other books," said he in after years, "than heaven and earth, which are open to all." He learned glass-painting, drawing, and to read and write, by his own exertions. He was over thirty, married and with a family to support, when the

sight of an elegant cup, of Italian manufacture, first set him to thinking about the new art of enamelling. The sight of a cup changed his whole existence. He resolved to discover the enamel of which it was glazed, and persisted for months and years, spoiling furnaces and pots and drugs and his wife's temper, as she could not be expected to sympathize with his enthusiasm and extravagance when the children had to go hungry. On he worked, often in direst poverty, only to meet disappoint-

ment. Once, in a critical experiment, he burned up all the furniture to feed his furnace—and still failed. His wife and neighbours said he was mad, but he kept on. "Hope continued to inspire me," he says, "and I held

MAYOR JOHN GUITON'S OATH AT LA ROCHELLE

on manfully.   Worst of all the sufferings I had to endure were the mockeries of my own household.   For years my furnaces were without covering, and I have been for nights at the mercy of the wind and rain.   My house proved no refuge for me, I found in my chamber a second persecution worse than the first.''   Still he went on, and it was **Success at Last** sixteen years before he reached success and would call himself potter.   Ever after till death he proceeded from one improvement to another, aiming at perfection.

Fame and means were now his, but another suffering he had to endure.   He was bitterly persecuted because he was a Protestant.   As he was fearless of speech, Palissy was pronounced a dangerous heretic by the priests ; his **Persecuted as Protestant** workshop was smashed by the rabble, and he was even condemned to be burned.   From this fate he was saved by a powerful noble—not because the nobleman cared for the potter or his religion, but because no other artist living was able to execute the enamelled pavement which the nobleman had ordered for his magnificent château then in course of erection near Paris.   Thus Palissy's art, which cost him so much, saved his life literally.   The **Saved by his Art** King also was greatly interested in his work.

The persecutors could not let him alone.   When an old man of seventy-eight, owing to his open warfare against astrology, witchcraft and other impostures, he was again arrested as a heretic, and imprisoned in the Bastille.   He was threatened with death unless he recanted, but proved as persistent in holding to his religion as he was in hunt- **The King's Visit** ing out the secret of the enamel.   King Henry IV went to see him in prison, to use his personal influence to induce the old artist to recant.

'' My good man,'' said the King, '' you have now served my mother and myself for forty-five years.   We have put up with your adhering to your religion amidst fires and massacres : now I am so pressed by the Guise party that I am constrained to leave you in the hands of your enemies, and to-morrow you will be burned unless you become converted.''

"Sire,'' answered the unconquerable old man, "I am ready to give my life for the glory of God. You have said many times that you have pity on me; and now I have pity on you, who have pronounced the words, 'I am constrained.' It is not spoken like the King; it is what you, and those who constrain you, can never effect upon me—for I know how to die.''

The King, who admired the brave man and the great artist, did not permit Palissy to be burned, but did leave

him in prison, where he died—a real martyr to his faith —less than a year later. This was the kind of character and of ability that France lost. There was nothing left to replace such genuine religion, nothing out of which to create such type of citizens, who are the bulwark of the state as they are its glory. Palissy the potter deserves high place on the roll of honour of the Huguenot martyrs.

X

Louis XIV himself bore testimony to the high character of his Protestant subjects, whom he declared, in 1666: "Being no less faithful than the rest of my people, it behooves me to treat with no less favour and consideration.'' But this was the very year in which the "relapsed heretics'' were placed entirely at the mercy of the Roman Catholics, and subjected to all kinds of annoyances and persecutions. As one wrote, "The members of the reformed religion are so cruelly persecuted through the whole kingdom that, if the work go on, it is to be feared that nothing less than a great massacre must be looked for.'' Public worship was proscribed and even the singing of psalms prohibited on the highways or in private houses. The Protestants were forbidden to bury their dead in open day.

Perhaps nothing could show the condition and spirit of

the Huguenots in France in 1668 better than this trans- *Invincible Spirit*
lation of a letter written by one of their number :

These things make us justly apprehensive that in the end they will
break out in acts of open violence ; there being nothing which they are
not in case to undertake for accomplishing of our ruine. And unless
we be willfully blind, we cannot but see that they design to drive us
into some insurrection. (But that we never shall do, preferring rather
to suffer the greatest extremity and our blood to be shed, than in the
least to violate the respect which we owe to our prince.) And if they
cannot overcome our patience (as assuredly they never shall), then
their resolution is, By continual importunity to prevail with his
Majesty to drive us out of the kingdom. But we hope that the King
is so good and just that he will never gratifie them in such a thing,
without a parallel. *And if we should be called to such a trial, we hope
God will give us such strength and courage that we may serve Him where-
ever His providence shall call us.* And this in effect is the general resolution of all the Protestants in the kingdom.

That is the kind of Christian spirit and character that,
banished from France, was to enrich every European
country, and our own America. "Patient as a Huguenot" became a proverb, because the ministers were resolved to suffer for righteousness' sake rather than again
make appeal to arms.

"One might be tempted to suppose," says Poole, "that
not the least reason for the energy of the clergy in opposition to the Huguenots was suggested by jealousy of the
contrast between their own scandalous neglect and the
careful order and nice discipline of the Protestants." As
Gustave Masson, the historian, says : "The Vitality of
Protestantism in France, despite the severest persecutions
that can be imagined, is a circumstance which, while it cannot be denied, fills us with hope for the future." The hope
of Protestant France lies in the noble words which Theodore
de Bèze spoke to the King of Navarre : "Sire, it is the
part of the Church of God to endure blows, and not to
deal them : but your Majesty will please to remember
that it is an anvil which has already worn out many a
hammer."

XI

One of the most powerful influences of the Reformation
in France, as in Switzerland, was Clement Marot's Psalms.
The young Clement, whose father was a poet, was attached to the family of the Duke D' Alençon about 1520.
He was led to translate some of the Psalms into French
verse. Having put them into lively ballad measure, he
printed about twenty translations, dedicating them to the
king. The sweetness of the poetry won a great success
at the court, the king was pleased with the dedication,
and the demand for copies was large. The ecclesiastical
authorities censured the book, but the king and court
carried the day, and Marot's hymns began to be sung
everywhere. At all times and in all places the Psalms
might be heard sung to lively ballad tunes. They took
for a time the place of national songs. Marot paraphrased
thirty more of the Psalms, and the fifty were printed in
Geneva in 1543 with a preface by Calvin, and had a wide
circulation. No one then realized what part these Psalms
were to play later, when the persecutions came. In the
Netherlands they were sung in the field meetings of the
Reformed, and the effect on the crowds was electric and
resistless. The different Psalms were fitted to tunes according to the popular taste, and were sometimes accompanied by musical instruments. Calvin got two excellent musicians to set the whole number of Psalms to music, and words and music were printed together. That
was the original church hymn book, and oddly enough
for a time Roman Catholics as well as Protestants carried
and used the book. The Psalms were sung in private and
in company, and the effect was marked. Fearing that
the court would become too religious, the evil-disposed
tried to counteract their influence by translations of Latin
odes; but the influence of the Marot Psalms long continued even in those fashionable circles.

As for the Protestants, they found their rallying cry in
these hymns. The adoption of them as a part of public

Marot's
Psalms

Widespread
Influence

A Rallying
Cry

worship caused their rejection by the Romanists.　On
the field of battle, at the funeral pyre of the martyr, in
the prisons, all through the terrible period of religious
persecution and bloodshed, the Psalms of Marot could be
heard, and were the source of inspiration and courage.
It is well said that the influence of Marot on the language
and poetry of France has been enduring, and the good
accomplished by introducing the singing of David's
Psalms into the Reformed congregations and families cannot be estimated.　As Luther's Hymn, which is a translation of a Psalm, was the Protestant battle hymn of
Germany, so the Marot Psalms led the French forward
in their long struggle for religious liberty and human
rights.

— Massacre of Vassi

CHAPTER III

THE FRENCH EXILES IN EUROPE

I

Europe's Gain Through France's Folly

WHAT France lost and what the other countries of Europe gained at her expense by giving refuge to the Huguenot exiles is shown in detail by Weiss in his *History of the French Protestant Refugees*, and by Poole, an English writer, in his *Huguenots of the Dispersion*, a valuable essay. England was doubtless the largest gainer in the arts and manufactures, yet nearly all the countries of Northern Europe received valuable accessions in artisans and agriculturists, some reaching even into Russia. Skilled trades were thus carried into sections where they had previously been unknown.

Protestant Superiority in Skilled Industry

In almost every branch of industry the French Protestants greatly surpassed the Roman Catholics. Why, is an interesting question for discussion. Poole attributes it to the free spirit, fostered in the consistories and synods of the Protestants and in their schools of learning, which found an apt expression in the zest and success with which they devoted themselves to the improvement of manufacture and the extension of commerce. They were mentally quickened by a religion which exercised thought and reason, and their training in the administration of the church fitted them for business transactions. Whatever the reason, the fact is indisputable as to the immense vigour with which the Huguenots applied themselves to trade, and the excellence which, thanks to their tone of mind and the superior length of their working year, they attained in it. For holidays, for example, the Huguenots allowed only the Sundays and the two re-

64

LA ROCHELLE: THE SQUARE

ligious festivals of Christmas and Easter, while the Roman
Catholics had double the number in order to celebrate the
saints' days. Thus the Huguenots worked on 310 days
in the year, the Roman Catholics only on 260, which
made a decided difference, aside from the superior quality and speed of the Protestant workmen.

Weaving was one of the principal industries of France, Arts and Crafts
with over 44,000 persons engaged in it in 1669; and the
Protestants had a practical monopoly. Cloth in Champagne and the southeast, serges and light stuffs in Languedoc, the linens of Normandy and Brittany, the silks and
velvets of Tours and Lyons, glass in Ormandy, paper in
Auvergne and Angoumois, the tan-yards of the Touraine,
the furnaces of iron, steel and tin in the Sedanais—these
were Protestant industries whose products made France
known in every market. And it was this splendid industrial population which the infatuated Louis, at the be-
hest of his Roman Catholic advisers, scourged from his
kingdom.

Colbert, the great French minister of finance, and the
only French statesman who knew the value of trades, A Valuable Factor
recognized the worth of the Huguenots. "This great
man," says Ançillon, "was too able an administrator
to fail of being tolerant. He had learned that civil and
religious liberty was the principle of work, of industry,
and of the wealth of the nations." Thus he employed
the German Protestant Herward, his comptroller-general
of finance, and kept the Huguenots in the financial department as long as his influence prevailed at court. It
was not until the profligate king had wearied of his faithfulness and wise counsels that the fierce persecutions began,
and not until after his death that the Edict was revoked
and commerce lost to the France he devotedly loved and
served.

II

Holland at first received the intellectual and com- Holland
mercial flower of the French Protestants. Haarlem is

an illustration. The exiles reached there, as the munici-
pal records state, "in a sorely destitute state, lacking
the means of life, and in no wise able to sustain their
families." But not long did they require town help or
support. Their woollen manufacture increased till the
town became too small for them, and they built the
Nieuwe Stad (new city). Besides cloth, druggets, and
such woollen stuffs, they introduced into Haarlem a
variety of silk product, velvet, plush, and the like,
which, though coarser than the original manufactures
at Lyons, Tours and Paris, were long in great demand
abroad because cheaper. Haarlem was soon outstripped
in the woollen trade by Leyden, where the French made
the finest cloth, the best serges to be found in the country.
The comfort of these thrifty and expert immigrants was
such that even Roman Catholic soldiers would desert to
settle there.

But Amsterdam was the centre, and a whole quarter
of the city was settled by the Protestant workmen of
Pierre Baillé, the richest manufacturer of his district in
France. Before this, Amsterdam had been busied almost exclusively with maritime commerce. Now, industries were rising everywhere in silk and wool and
linen ; a new part of the city, as at Haarlem, was built
for the workers, and almost entirely occupied by hat
manufactories. Paper mills were in plenty also, and the
book trade was largely stimulated.

These cases are typical of the impulse given by the
French refugees to trade. What was true of Holland
and its cities was true also of England and Ireland, of
Germany and Switzerland, of Sweden and Austria, and
not least of America, where the French transplanted
their commercial, industrial, agricultural and religious
characteristics in full measure.

Here is what a writer in the *Nederlandsche Spectator*
of 1750, who does not quite like the dash and swing and
success of the newcomers, in contrast to the Dutch

*Woollen
Manufactures*

*A French
Section*

*A Dutch
Estimate 1750*

stolidity, says of the Huguenot immigration : "This people, oppressed and hardly handled, came over to us in so great swarms, that it seemed about to equal the number of the inhabitants, and scarcely to be provided with places to live in. Not alone were they received cheerfully as brothers and fellows in faith ; but people of every diverse sect lavished abounding gifts upon them : and everywhere, as guests, free from the charge of scot or lot, they were furnished and favoured with rare immunities. The engaging joyousness, which no tyranny could quench, the courteous grace which could gain an entrance by its modest tact everywhere, soon made so much impression here on the more and better part of the people, and so used its mind to their manners, that it came to be reckoned an honour the most to resemble the foreigners."

This is a high tribute indeed, and something of the same result was produced in America by those gracious qualities and graceful manners which found as much contrast in the New Englanders as in the Hollanders, who come of the same sturdy and conquering though less polished stock.

III

In Great Britain the French immigrants made lasting impress, and gave trade and manufacture an impulse and breadth never afterwards lost. The lace makers spread their manufactures over several countries, and made this industry famous and remunerative. Furriers and beaver hat makers in large numbers settled in Wandsworth ; and for forty years, until a theft restored the art, France was compelled to import all the best goods of this kind, made by Frenchmen, from England. It is said that even the cardinals of the Holy College had to buy their hats in English Wandsworth ; which ought to have been sufficiently humiliating to the high officials of the Church which drove the industry forth from France.

In Great Britain

London

To London the refugees came by thousands, "far the greater numbers in a state of persecution, empty and naked, to depend on the hospitality and charity of this good-natured kingdom." But never for long were they

1687

dependent. Workshops and churches sprang up together. In a single year the official account of the relief committee reported that 13,500 refugees had been helped in London; while two French churches were organized in Spitalfields and one by the Strand. Commerce and church went together where the Huguenots were. Among those thousands aided there were 143 ministers and 283 families of quality. Their children were sent to the best trades or into his Majesty's troops—the latter to

1688

the number of 150. In the next year the French ministers in and about London were incorporated, with power to purchase lands and build houses, and three new churches were provided for. The peopling of the waste Spitalfields was due to the French, and in a generation nine churches had arisen there, and the workmen were so many and so busy that the silk manufacture of London was multiplied twentyfold.

South Coast

French colonists lined the south coast, where the exiles gathered around such leaders as the Marquess de Ruvigny, their aged chief who long guarded them at the French court and was now their sponsor in England; whose sons, by the way, rendered great service to England in war. These coast refugees devoted themselves chiefly to ship-

Shipping and Commerce

ping and commerce. At Exeter the tapestry weavers, however, established themselves, and in other southern towns trades were created, among them the fine linens and sail cloth. In nearly all the industrial centres the French were to be found, engaged in weaving, in printing calicoes in their unrivalled style, in making glass and paper; and everywhere setting an example of skill, thrift and cheerfulness. The paper mills extended from England into Scotland, the first being started at Glasgow. Edinburgh received a number of cambric makers, and

the burghers built them a large house on the common,
long known as little Picardya. In 1693 the city was Scotland
charged to the amount of two thousand marks for the
support of the manufactory. Others worked in silk, and
planted mulberry-gardens on the hill slopes. Helped by
the public alms at first, these Picard exiles fared prosperously, and maintained their native speech and manners, living in a house, itself of French fashion, until the
middle of the eighteenth century.

The gentry and artisans formed the bulk of the French
immigrants to England. The agricultural classes preferred Germany, Holland and Sweden, which were less
thickly peopled. It was the craftsman, carrying his
means of support in his hands or in his brain, that
enriched England and did much to make the little island
the workshop as well as the counting-house of the world.
A strong contrast these French craftsmen were to the
English workmen, who belonged in general to a rougher
and less skilled type ; who needed the greater refinement
and joyousness of the newcomers as much as the Puritans
did in New England ; and who on the whole received the
foreigners quite as hospitably as could be expected.

IV

Most heartily were the persecuted fugitives welcomed Professional
in the various countries to which they fled. At Dord- Enrichment
recht, in Holland, the burghers "received them as kins-
folk into their houses, cared for them as for their children,
and put them in the way of earning honourably their
bread," while the magistrates loaded them with privileges
and pensions. This was characteristic of the countries
generally. The French Protestant ministers and men of
letters, many of them eminent for learning, enriched
Holland by their presence. It was the artisan and agricultural class that chiefly pushed on further. Colonies
escaped through the German border to the north, and the
immigration to Hamburg embarrassed that great city by

its numbers.   Hamburg got in return, however, the linen manufacturing industry which made it famous and greatly increased its riches.

Sweden 1681

King Christian of Sweden was among the first to offer asylum to banished families, promising to grant them lands and build them churches with full religious freedom. One of the Huguenot ministers who went to Copenhagen was Phillippe Menard, afterwards French chaplain to William III.

Denmark Gains a Com- mander-in- Chief

The Refuge in Denmark included a few military officers ; one of whom was Frederic Charles de la Rochefoucault, ancestor of the Irish earls of Lifford.   This Huguenot became grand marshal and commander-in-chief of the Danish forces.   But the bulk of the French settlers were farmers, cultivating especially potatoes, the tobacco plant, which they introduced, and wheat, which they improved.

Russia Gives Free Entry

The small settlement in Russia was singular in that the Czar granted free entry and exit to any emigrants of the evangelical faith who might choose to come, and also religious liberty and chance for government service.   It is said that when Peter the Great built St. Petersburg he seemed to take pleasure in outraging the prejudice of the Orthodox Greek Church by giving all encouragement to Lutherans and Calvinists.   The imported population gave a new tone to the rising capital, different in manners and civilization from the rest of Russia.   Thus a French society grew up there, with a church built in 1723, frequented by the Swiss and English as well as by the French residents.

In Germany

In the German states the Huguenots' influence was marked.   There the French proved that gracious and civilizing power which was conspicuous subsequently in the society at Berlin.   At Celle and Hanover French was spoken as purely as in Paris, and a refinement altogether new sprang up in the German principalities.   French politeness softened Saxon brusqueness and made life much more enjoyable.

The population of Switzerland was naturally greatly enlarged by the number of refugees who there found asylum. Geneva benefited by the coming of workers in silk and wool, print manufacturers, goldsmiths and watch-makers. A greater advantage even resulted from the gathering there and at Lausanne of many families of rank, the artists and men of science, who raised the social culture. It should be noted that wherever they went the Huguenots conferred not only commercial bene-fits and carried their religion, but they elevated the culture. To their refining influence the refugees added a material benefit throughout Switzerland. They im-proved the vinegrowing and husbandry, and added the culture of orchards and kitchen gardens. This was the same thing they did in the New World; besides opening shops, starting manufactures as they were needed, and generally taking the initiative in improvements.

Germany owes not a little of its present fame as a manufacturing country to the French immigrants who were hospitably taken in when they were homeless. "Made in Germany" is stamped on many manufactures which, if the history was traced back, would show a Huguenot hand at the beginning. Jewelry, woollen goods, flannels, carpets and cloths, hats and gloves, all sorts of ornamental wares, for which Germany is known were introduced by the French artisans. There were agricultural as well as industrial settlements, and French villages dotted many a German valley. There were also many gentle families, which gradually became absorbed in the German population. The one thing that made the French unpopular was their lively, light-hearted be-haviour, which seemed frivolous to the staid German, who appreciated neither their talkativeness in church, their strange dress with short cloaks, nor their snuff-boxes.

This did not apply so much to Berlin, which got the most out of the French both in manufactures and man-ners. Hither flocked not only the best artisans, as to

Strong French
Colony

England, but especially the soldiers and nobles and gentry, until it was no wonder that Berlin was in danger of becoming more French than German, though the French element was not of the Parisian type. The trade and craft of the French colony were remarkable. The new-comers introduced numerous arts as yet unknown to the Brandenburgers when the Great Elector Frederick William welcomed the French to his dominions. Not an industry but claimed its place among the labours of the French, while most were their special or exclusive possession. As in England, paper and glass were before this only made in the commonest and coarsest kinds; now paper of the finest was made in Berlin, while the looking-glasses were said to excel those of Venice. Then there was a large mercantile element which rapidly gained supremacy, so that the Germans came to learn from them how to do business. In mining and metal founding the French opened to Germany an unworked field. The copper hitherto sent by Sweden to France was now turned into French workshops in Germany, and the iron trade helped Brandenburg on its way into the rank of kingdoms and head of an empire. She could not make her own arms.

French Gentry
in Army

The German army owed much to the French gentry, who multiplied many times their real efficiency, it was declared, by their moral sway. Two companies of Grands Mousquetaires were formed of officers only, under French Marshal Schomberg and his son. Whole regiments were formed or recruited from the body of the refugees, who thus as on the farm and in the factory richly repaid the land that gave them liberty and a home. In the social order the refugees were given the same place they had in France, and it was the aim of the German monarch to impress upon the "unpolished surface of the manner of his court something of the refinement and grace of France." There were two French churches and nine ministers in Berlin. In education the French led the way to higher medical training, and in scientific knowledge. The French College of Berlin was a notable institution. Poole goes so far as to assert that the society of Berlin was the creation of the exile, and it was the refugees who gave it that mobile course of thought, that finer culture, that tact in matters of art and that instinct of conversation which had before been the unique possession of France. They diffused their own spirit, quick, fine, lucid; the spirit of French vivacity and precision. And thus they exerted, whether in Germany or Switzerland or England, that influence peculiar to France, upon the society into the midst of which they were thrown.

Having thus seen something of the exiles in European countries, we shall be prepared to understand them and their influence in our own land, where we may be sure they would be not less influential along the same lines, social, commercial and religious. We can somewhat estimate also the loss to France of such an element; in reality its great middle class, the reliable and thoughtful and inventive class, combining the artisan, agricultural and professional, which gives to a nation its best life and its material and moral soundness and strength.

CHAPTER IV

SUFFERING FOR THE FAITH

I

A Century of
Persecution

IT is commonly thought that the history of the Huguenots in France ends with the Revocation of the Edict of Nantes, and that the record of blood and fire concludes with the great emigration of 1685. But for a hundred years thereafter the spirit of intolerance and persecution held its deadly sway. If nearly half a million Protestants left France at the Revocation, there were fully twice as many who remained in their native land, and of these only a small minority abjured their faith. Their churches had been destroyed, their pastors banished, and themselves forced to wear an outward dress of Roman Catholicism; but in their hearts they were Huguenots still, and whenever a leader was raised up for them they rallied round him and showed that the light of the Christian truth still burned within staunch French hearts.

In the Cevennes the peasants retreated into the mountain fastnesses and held the persecutor at bay for years. But numbers finally overcame them, and open resistance ceased when the last of those heroic peasants lay dripping in his own blood. Then came the "Church of the desert" with its midnight assemblies, its pastors hiding in holes and caves, its glorious martyrs.

Antoine Court

At this time the saviour of French Protestantism was Antoine Court, born 1696, two years before the illustrious Claude Brousson sealed his faith with his life at Montpelier. At seventeen Court resolved to give his life to the restoration of French Protestantism. He began to preach, gathering together a little audience of eight

74

THE HUGUENOT LOVERS, *by Millais*

or ten in some isolated barn or hole in the rocks. He
was an orator, was without fear, and was eminently
prudent withal. When he was nineteen he was made Church at
Nismes
pastor of the Reformed Church at Nismes, and a year
later, in 1716, the first synod was held, the meeting taking place in an old Roman quarry in the neighbourhood.
"The pastors were six young men, peasants of the
Cevennes, several of them younger even than Court himself. They walked all night to the place of meeting,
which meant for themselves, if taken, the gallows, and
for their audience, penal servitude for life. At dawn
the whole company knelt and invoked the presence of
the Holy Ghost, after which Antoine Court stood up.
He told them of the ruinous condition of their Church,
and counselled that discipline be restored and a form of
constitution drawn out and signed. Here are some of
their rules : 1. Assemblies to be convened once a fort-
night ; 2. Family prayer to be held three times a day ;
3. The pastors to meet twice a year in synods. Six
pastors signed the Covenant. The first was hanged in
1718, the second and third in 1728, the fourth in 1732.
One other beside Antoine Court escaped."
    In 1720 the Church at Languedoc held a midnight Treachery and
Heroism
meeting in a large cavern, Antoine Court presiding.
Treachery had been at work and two companies of soldiers burst in upon the astonished worshippers. Fifty
men, women and children were made prisoners, Court
himself having a "miraculous escape." "Some were
sent to the galleys, and nineteen were sentenced to transportation. As they entered Nismes, drenched with rain,
they sang a psalm while marching through the streets.
They started for the seaport of La Rochelle chained together and escorted by soldiers. Each night they slept
in stables and were made to lie down in dung. At La
Rochelle the whole party was stricken with malarial
fever, of which several died.
    " . . . The English ambassador induced the govern-

ment to send them to England. The English chaplain took them on board a vessel, and a large crowd heaped blessings upon them as they sailed away to exile and to freedom."

II

In 1724 Louis XV thought he would outdo his predecessor, and accordingly issued an edict, some of the provisions of which were as follows : Every minister to be put to death, and any one helping them in any way to be rewarded by penal servitude for life. Life imprisonment was to be meted out to any one attending a Protestant service. All children were to be baptized by the priests within twenty-four hours of birth. No marriage to be held legal unless performed under Roman Catholic auspices. Every one who knew when a meeting was to be held and did not betray the fact to the authorities was to lose his property and go to the gallows. Whenever a Protestant pastor was arrested every Huguenot in the district was to be fined $25,000—amounting, in nearly every instance to confiscation of entire property. The absolute fiendishness of these provisions needs no comment ; they represent the high mark of Roman Catholic craft and cruelty.

But the Reformed Church of France was not blotted out. The meetings in the forests were continued, the galleys were recruited from the ever faithful Protestant ranks, and though minister after minister was made to ascend the gallows, there were plenty of brave hearts ready and eager to take his place in the pastorate. These pastors were hunted like wolves through the country, bounties being placed on their heads whether taken dead or alive. Like criminals they were forced to resort to aliases. They travelled by night through the woods and fields. Journeying thus, Antoine Court once covered three hundred miles within the space of two months, speaking to three thousand of his people at thirty-two meetings. One pastor had a hut of stones hidden away in a ravine ;

Edict of
Louis XV

Hunted but
Persistent

this he used for his study where he prepared his sermons (surely they were sermons worth hearing). Another made his home in a hole covered over with brambles in the middle of a great plain ; here he read his Bible and slept, until one day some sheep fell into the hole and the shepherd, thus discovering the hiding-place, informed the magistrates. In 1758 Paul Rabaut, the "Apostle of the Desert," going by some lonely crossroads, would spy a placard : "Wanted, Paul Rabaut, the minister. Aged about forty; visage plain, long and thin; a little sunburned ; black hair, aquiline nose; has lost a tooth in the upper jaw," etc. The authorities rated his capture as being worth 20,000 francs—little realizing that the value of one such man as Paul Rabaut could not be expressed in terms of money.

Paul Rabaut

III

But after the middle of the century persecution grew lighter and lighter. The wishes of Romanism finally were forced to give way to the growing spirit of humanity. Toleration came at last, though with lagging footsteps. In 1762, in the city of Toulouse, the last Protestant martyr ascended the scaffold. This was Pastor Rochette, twenty-five years old. When the judge read the sentence of death, Rochette knelt and prayed in the court-room. "The recorder shed tears, so did jailers and soldiers. Rochette kindly turned to one of them : 'My friend, you would readily die for the king. Do not pity me, who am going to die for my God.'

A Better Day

Last Martyr
1762

"At 2 P. M., the last Protestant scaffold was made ready. He walked barefoot, with a placard around his neck—Minister of the Pretended Reformed Religion. Every balcony and house-top was crowded. The whole city was shocked. Pity and sympathy were on every face. Rochette stepped on the scaffold, saying, Here comes the happy day. It was coming—for the martyr first, and soon for his brethren."

The last minister to receive the death sentence was Beranger, in 1767—but only his effigy was hanged. The last pastor to be imprisoned was Broca, who was thrown into a dungeon in 1773. The last Protestant assembly to be attacked by the dragoons was the Church of Orange. Eight of those present were captured, and the officer in charge begged them to escape. This they refused, saying it was for public authority to set them at liberty. They remained in prison for two months and then a pardon from the king gave them freedom. In 1780, when the repeal of the persecuting edicts seemed imminent, the assembly of the Roman Catholic clergy sent a petition to Louis XVI asking him to recommence persecution again, but he refused. Seven years later the Edict of Toleration put in an appearance. It caused a great debate in the Parliament of Paris. One delegate declared that the Virgin had come to him in a dream and bidden him fight the heretics. Holding aloft a crucifix he demanded, "Will you crucify Jesus again?" But public opinion was for abolishing the Inquisition, and the Edict passed. It provided that Protestants could marry, bury their dead, engage in a trade, and hold private worship. In 1802 Huguenots were given the privilege of holding public services, and the Pretended Reformed Religion could at last stand on a legal equality with the Roman Catholic Church.

Edict of
Toleration

IV

The French Revolution was the ultimate result of the Roman Catholic effort to crush out Protestantism in France. In that reign of terror the Church had to meet what it had pitilessly inflicted upon the Huguenots. But the spirit of reform was to live and of religious reform. There was a great revival in France in 1827–30, which roused the French Protestants to new life. Bible, tract and missionary societies were established, Sunday-schools opened, philanthropics organized ; and in this Christian work dissenters of every shade—Wesleyans, Baptists,

Congregationalists—co-operated heartily with the Reformed Churches. In literature the French Protestants have honourable rank, and France is steadily verging towards the realization of a Protestant Republic in which religious liberty shall be secured as thoroughly as in America.

The separation of Church and State is already an accomplished fact, and the most fateful fact for France since Waterloo. Frenchmen are proud to-day to claim as ancestors those martyrs who helped with their blood in establishing the great principle of religious freedom.

The French Protestant Hospital, Victoria Park 1866.

CHAPTER V

LIFE IN THE GALLEYS

I

THOUSANDS of the Huguenots who attempted to escape from France after the Revocation were arrested and condemned to the galleys. This was a punishment far worse than torture and death. Men of gentle birth and breeding, whose only fault was their Protestant religion, were worn to death in this inhuman form of slavery, whose horrors are almost beyond description. One of the most graphic narratives of this terrible experience is given in this chapter, in order to show of what stuff the French Protestants were made, that they would undergo such merciless fate rather than abjure their faith. We can only honour and admire these heroes, while we abhor the government that permitted the galley system to exist.

The following account of life in the galleys is based upon the memoirs of a young Huguenot named Amadée, who in 1700 was convicted of the crime of trying to leave his country when he was forbidden to practice his religion in it.

Amadée was a mere stripling of eighteen when he was sentenced to the galleys for being on the frontier without a passport. His youth aroused the pity of his captors, and they made many attempts to get him to abjure his faith. One priest told him that a beautiful woman, the possessor of a large fortune, had expressed a desire to marry him in case he should renounce his faith ; and other equally attractive bribes were offered him—but all in vain, for the young man met each temptation with the answer that he was "determined to endure even the

80

galleys or death, rather than renounce the faith " in Bribery Failed which he had been educated. Finding their efforts of little avail, the priests finally declared that his soul was in the possession of the devil and therefore gave his body over to the civil authorities.

In company with a fellow prisoner, to whom he was tied and handcuffed, Amadée was led away to the prison at Tournay where he was thrown into a loathsome dungeon. Six weeks was he forced to drag out a miserable Dungeon Life existence in this human kennel—living on a scanty allowance of bread and water, sleeping on the bare pavement, and "suffering inexpressibly" from the accumulated filth of his apartment. From Tournay he was taken to Lisle, where he was thrown into a room where about thirty unfortunates were confined in total darkness —not a ray of light entering the apartment. These prisoners were of the lowest type, and their vile company was abhorrent to Amadée. He did not remain among them for long, however, for the turnkey, fancying himself insulted, removed the youth to a solitary dungeon whose floor was covered knee-deep with water. Amadée now refused to eat the portion of bread which was brought to him and resigned himself to a lingering death ; but fate, in the person of the Grand Provost of the prison, ordered otherwise. The Provost, who was himself of Protestant extraction, upon hearing that Amadée was a Huguenot, at once ordered him removed to a more comfortable quarter of the prison and saw to it that he was supplied with wholesome food and drink.

This comparatively mild detention did not last a great The Galleys while, for at the end of three months Amadée was ordered to depart for Marseilles with a party of galleyslaves. On the journey, which was one of some three hundred miles, a beautiful girl was attracted to Amadée and approached him, holding a rosary with a crucifix attached to it, which she offered him. Though he would gladly have accepted it as a token from the tender-

hearted maiden, he felt that it would be considered as a
sign of abjuration of his own faith, and heroically
declined it.   That evening she came to his prison bringing a priest, and declared her object to be his conversion.
" This," said Amadée, " was a trial that God alone
enabled me to go through.   Once I became faint from
emotions, and I was on the point of yielding.   I pressed
the soft, delicate hand, that I held, to my lips again and
again, and tried to release it, but I could not let it go.
The priest saw my yielding spirit.   ' That hand may be
yours,' he said, 'for all eternity, by renouncing your heresy
and embracing the true religion.'   Did God put those
words into his mouth to nerve me with courage?   ' No,'
I exclaimed, with new resolution ; ' it might be mine for
this life, but I should purchase it by an eternity of misery.
Let me rather die a galley-slave, at peace with my own
conscience and my God.'   Yet, when I saw her no more,
when the last glimpse of her sweet and sorrowful face was
gone, when even her white dress could no longer be dis-
cerned, I sat down and wept aloud.   At length the agony
of my soul began to yield to a still, small voice within.   I
grew calm, and thought I was dying.   ' God hears my
prayers,' said I ; ' He has sent His angels to minister to
me, to conduct me to the realms of bliss.'   Shall I confess
it?   The face of the sweet Catholic girl was ever before
me.   She seemed to emit a radiance of light through my
prison.   I know not whether my dream was a sleeping or
waking one, but methought she leaned over me, and,
raising the hand I had resigned, said in a soft, silver
voice, ' Thou hast won this for eternity.'   How often, in
successive years, when chained to the oar, have I heard
that voice and seen the beautiful vision !   God ministers
to us by His holy angels ! ''

When he arrived at his destination he was placed on
board a galley called the *Heureuse*, of which he gives the
following description : " Ours was a hundred and fifty
feet long and fifty broad, with but one deck, which cov-

*Powerful
Temptation*

*Heroic
Resistance*

A Vision

*A Galley
Described*

ered the hold. The deck rises about a foot in the middle, and slopes towards the edges to let the water run off more easily; for when a galley is loaded it seems to swim under the water; and the sea continually rushes over it. To prevent the sea from entering the hold, where the masts are placed, a long case of boards, called the coursier, is fixed in the middle, running from one end of the galley to the other. The slaves, who are the rowers, have each a board raised from the deck under which the water passes, which serves them for a footstool, otherwise their feet would be constantly in the water. A galley has fifty benches for rowers, twenty-five on each side; each bench is ten feet long, one end fixed in the coursier, that runs through the boat, the other in the band or side of the boat; the benches are half a foot thick, and placed at four feet distance from each other, and are covered with sackcloth, stuffed with flock, and a cowhide thrown over them, which, reaching to the footstool, gives them the appearance of large trunks. To these the galley-slaves are chained, six to a bench. The oars are fifty feet long, and are poised *in equilibrio* upon the apostic, or piece of timber for this purpose. They are constructed so that the thirteen feet of the oar that go into the boat are equal in weight to the thirty-seven which go into the water. It would be impossible for the slaves to grasp them, and handles are affixed for rowing.

Three Hundred Rowers

"The master, or comite, stands always at the stern, near the captain, to receive his orders. There are sous-comites, one in the middle and one near the prow, each with a whip of cords to exercise as they see fit on the slaves. The comite blows a silver whistle, which hangs from his neck; the slaves have their oars in readiness and strike all at once, and keep time so exactly, that the half a hundred oars seem to make but one movement. There is an absolute necessity for thus rowing together, for should one be lifted up or fall too soon, those before would strike the oar with the back part of their heads. Any mistake

The Master

of this kind is followed by blows given with merciless fury.   The labour of a galley-slave has become a proverb ; it is the greatest fatigue that a man can bear.   Six men are chained to each bench on both sides of the coursier wholly naked, sitting with one foot on a block of timber, the other resting on the bench before them, holding in their hands an enormous oar.   Imagine them lengthening their bodies, their arms stretched out to push the oar over the backs of those before them ; they then plunge the oar into the sea, and fall back into the hollow below, to repeat again and again the same muscular action.   The fatigue and misery of their labour seems to be without parallel.   They often faint, and are brought to life by the lash.   Sometimes a bit of bread dipped in wine is put into their mouths, when their labour cannot for a moment be spared.   Sometimes, when they faint, they are thrown into the sea, and another takes the place.''

An incident which Amadée relates shows admirably the Huguenot character with its self-sacrifice and brotherly
love.   He had been recommended to the captain of the galley for the position of steward of the provisions, and the captain had ordered him to be brought into his presence.   '' 'They tell me,' he said, ' you are the only slave that can be trusted, and you are a Huguenot.'   I answered submissively, that there were other Huguenots on board the galley that could be trusted.   'I will try you, said he, 'and give you the care of the stores ; but, remember, for the slightest infidelity you receive the bastinado.' ''   The office entitles the slave who holds it to an exemption from the oar and a dinner every day upon the captain's provisions.

''Such a situation was comparative happiness to the hard duty I was undergoing ; my heart beat rapidly.   I made no reply, for I was buried in thought.   'Dog of a Christian,' he exclaimed, 'have you no thanks ?'   At this moment a struggle, not inferior to that I had experienced once before, took possession of my mind.   'There is another Huguenot on board this galley,' said I, 'who is every way more worthy of the office than myself. He is an old man, broken down by labour, he is unable to work at the oar, and even stripes can get but little service from him. I am yet able to endure ; grant him this place, and let me still continue at the oar.' The captain seemed doubtful whether he understood me. 'I know who he means,' said the comite, 'it is old Bançillon.' 'Let him be brought,' said the commander. Bançillon was brought forward, bowed down by age and labour, his venerable head covered with white hair. The comite acknowledged that, excepting inability of strength, he had no faults, and was respected for his integrity by every one. It is unnecessary to go into the details. He was appointed to the office, and the young Amadée returned to the oar. 'How weak was my virtue!' he exclaims ; 'though it enabled me to resign the office to this venerable minister (for such he was, once), it could not restrain bitter emotions. I felt my face bedewed with scalding tears of regret, as I once more commenced my hard labour. But when, a short time after, I beheld the venerable Bançillon losing the emaciated and distressed appearance he had worn, smiling benignantly on me, and imploring for me the blessing of heaven, I no longer murmured ; I was rewarded for my sacrifice.' "

When Amadée had been a slave for seven years his galley, together with several others, engaged in a struggle with an English frigate. After describing the first part of the battle, he goes on to say : " We have seen how dexterously the frigate placed herself alongside of us, by which we were exposed to the fire of her artillery, charged with grape-shot. It happened that my seat, on which there were five Frenchmen and one Turk, lay just opposite one of the cannon, which was charged. The two vessels lay so close, that, by raising my body in the least, I could touch the cannon with my hand. A neighbourhood so terrible filled us all with silent con-

Preferring Another

Galley in Battle

sternation. My companions lay flat on the seat and in
that posture endeavoured to avoid the coming blow. I
had presence of mind enough to perceive that the gun
was pointed in such a manner that those who lay flat
would receive its contents; and I sat as upright as possible, but being chained, could not quit my station. In

Marvellous
Escape

this manner I awaited death, which I had scarce any
hope of escaping. My eyes were fixed upon the gunner,
who with his lighted match fired one piece after another.
He came nearer and nearer to the fatal one. I lifted my
heart to God in fervent prayers. Never had I felt such
assurances of divine mercy, whether life or death awaited
me. I looked steadily at the gunner as he applied the
lighted match. What followed I only knew by the
consequences. The explosion had stunned me; I was
blown as far as my chain would permit. Here I remained, I cannot say how long, lying across the body of
the lieutenant of the galley, who had been killed some
time before. At last, recovering my senses and finding
myself lying upon a dead body, I crept back to my seat.
It was night, and the darkness was such that I could see
neither the blood that was spilled, nor the carnage
around me. I imagined that their former fears still
operated upon my companions; and that they lay on
their faces to avoid the no longer threatening danger. I
felt no pain from any wound and believed myself un-
injured.

Death and
Darkness

"I remained in a tranquil state for some moments, and
even began to be amused with the motionless silence of
my fellow slaves, who, I supposed, were still lying as
they first threw themselves. Desirous to free them from
their terrors, I pushed the one next to me. 'Rise, my
boy,' said I, 'the danger is over.' I received no answer. I spoke louder; all was silence and Egyptian
darkness.

"Isouf, a Turk, had often boasted that he never knew
what fear was. He was a remarkable fellow for his truth

and honesty. 'My good fellow,' said I, in a tone of raillery, 'up, the danger is over, you may be as brave as ever. Come, I will help you.' I leaned over and took his hand. O horror! my blood still freezes at the remembrance; it came off in mine, stiff and deadly cold. The first gleam of light showed me my companions all slaughtered! Of the six on our seat I alone survived. Alas! I may well say, I was the miserable survivor; **The Sole Survivor** their toils and agonies were over. It was some time before I discovered that I was wounded, and then not by pain, but by blood which deluged me." After a long period of suffering, Amadée was considered to be sufficiently recovered to take his place again at the oar.

The winter following the above engagement, Amadée was confined to winter quarters—a short account of which he gives. During the winter months, if it chanced to be **Winter Quarters** a season of peace, the galleys were laid up for the time being. "The order is given from Court about the latter end of October. The galleys are then arranged along the quay. The galley is entirely cleared, and the slaves remain fixed to their wretched quarters for the winter. They spread their greatcoats for beds on a board, and here they sleep. When the weather is extremely cold they have a tent, made of coarse woollen cloth, raised over the galley. They never have fire or blankets. It is now a season of some rest for them, and they are permitted to earn a little money. Among the variety there are often tradesmen, tailors, shoemakers, gravers, etc. These are sometimes permitted to build wooden stalls upon the quay opposite their respective galleys. The keeper chains them in their stalls. Here they may earn a few halfpence a day, and this situation is comparative ease. There is, however, still hard labour aboard the **Comparative Ease** galley. The comites still use the lash without mercy, and often without discrimination. One of the hardest labours to Amadée, because the most tyrannical and degrading, was the exhibition to which they were constantly exposed by the officers for the entertainment of their friends. The galley was cleaned anew, and the slaves were ordered to shave, and put on their red habits and red caps, which are their uniform, when they wear any garments. This done, they are made to sit between the benches, so that nothing but heads with red caps are visible, from one end of the galley to the other. In this attitude the gentlemen and ladies, who come as spectators, are saluted by the slaves with a loud and mournful cry of 'Heu.' This seems but one voice; it is repeated three times, when a person of high distinction enters. During this salute the drums beat, and the soldiers, in their best clothes, are ranged along the sides of the boat with their guns shouldered. The masts are decorated with streamers; the chamber at the stern is also adorned with hangings of red velvet, fringed with gold. The ornaments in sculpture, at the stern, thus beautified to the water's edge; the oars lying on the seats, and appearing without the galley like wings, painted of different colours,—a galley thus adorned strikes the eye magnificently; but let the spectator reflect on the misery of three hundred slaves, scarred with stripes, emaciated and dead-eyed, chained day and night, and subject to the arbitrary will of creatures devoid of humanity, and he will no longer be enchanted by the gaudy outside. The spectators, a large proportion of whom are often ladies, pass from one end of the galley to the other, and return to the stern, where they seat themselves. The comite then blows his whistle. At the first blast every slave takes off his cap; at the second, his coat; at the third, his shirt, and they remain naked. Then comes what is called the monkey-exhibition. They are all ordered to lie along the seats, and the spectator loses sight of them; then they lift one finger, next their arms, then their head, then one leg, and so on till they appear standing upright. Then they open their mouths, cough all together, embrace, and throw themselves into ridicu-

lous attitudes, wearing, to appearance of the spectator,
an air of gayety, strangely contrasted with the sad,
hollow eyes of many of the performers, and ferocious,
hardened despair of others. To the reflecting mind
there can scarcely be anything more degrading than
this exhibition; men, subject constantly to the lash,
doomed for life to misery, perpetually called upon to
amuse their fellow beings by antic tricks.''

To conclude this melancholy history, be it said that
Amadée was released after thirteen years of this miserable
existence. Owing to the intercession of Queen Anne, of
England, a hundred and thirty-six Huguenot slaves were
given their freedom on condition that they should pay
their own expenses in leaving the country. And of these
fortunate persons the hero of this sketch made one.
After all his sufferings, it is good to know that he found
happiness and freedom.

Released After Thirteen Years

Massacre of Ribault

BOOK TWO

EARLY ATTEMPTS AT COLONIZATION

CHAPTER I

VILLEGAGNON'S FAILURE IN BRAZIL

I

THE earliest efforts to settle a body of French Protestants in the New World were inspired by Admiral Coligny, more than a century before the Pilgrims landed at Plymouth, and before the bitter religious persecutions had begun in France. Admiral Coligny was easily the greatest Frenchman of the age in far-seeing statesmanship, as he was in character the most resolute, high-minded and sagacious, and in looking at the conditions of France he saw clearly the dangers which threatened her and the people he loved. In establishing a Protestant colony he aimed at founding a refuge for the Protestants wherein they would be free from the persecutions which he realized must soon descend upon them with fury, for there was every indication that the tempest of hatred was about to burst. The bitterness and malignancy of the Romish clergy were already being aroused to feverish activity by the growth and success of the Reformed Church. Their hatred was only intensified by the fact that the virtues and sobriety of the Huguenot ministers threw into unpleasant relief their own utter lack of conscience and morals; the Christian and self-sacrificing character of their adversaries served only to heighten their rage. Their open advocacy in Parliament of introducing the Spanish Inquisition to cope with heretics gave Coligny his strongest impulse towards founding a Protestant colony, and he straightway sought the ear of Henry II. Henry's consent was gained, for to him the project appealed as an opportunity for winning to France a share of the rich domain

93

claimed as a monopoly by Spain and Portugal. The idea
of adding to the prosperity of France by increasing her
industrial resources appealed to Coligny also, but in his
case the religious motive was the dominating one.

II

Brazil was selected as the site for the first Protestant
French colony in America, and Durand de Villegagnon,
a soldier of fortune who had professed the Reformed
doctrines, was chosen as leader. In July, 1555, the
little fleet, consisting of two ships and a transport, set
sail from Havre de Grace, carrying several hundred
colonists. The character of many of these colonists was
not propitious for the success of the venture, for while
some were Protestants, including noblemen, soldiers and
mechanics, the majority were recruits from the prisons
of Paris. So many of them .deserted on the way, however, that only eighty were left to complete the voyage,
and of these but thirty were artisans. After a long and
stormy experience, the adventurers reached the wonderful Bay of Rio de Janeiro. Here they landed on an
island, constructed huts, and commenced building a fort
which they called Fort Coligny.

The condition of the colony was precarious, and unless fresh supplies of food and reinforcements of men
were received from France, the venture would prove
a failure. The island was too small to admit of
cultivation, and on the mainland the settlers were
threatened by the Portuguese, who regarded them as unlawful invaders of the soil. Many of the colonists returned to France in the ships which had brought them
over, leaving Villegagnon with a diminished band consisting mostly of the convicts he had taken from the
prisons. In addition to the dangers of famine and
destruction by the Portuguese, internal dissensions threatened the life of the colony. " Villegagnon signalized
his new-born Protestantism by an intolerable solicitude

Brazil Chosen
July, 1555

Difficult Con-
ditions

for the manners and morals of his followers. The whip
and the pillory requited the least offense. The wild
and discordant crew, starved and flogged for a season
into submission, conspired at length to rid themselves of
him ; but while they debated whether to poison him,
blow him up, or murder him and his officers in their
sleep, three Scotch soldiers, probably Calvinists, revealed
the plot, and the vigorous hand of the commandant
crushed it in the bud.''

In response to Villegagnon's letters of appeal, Coligny _Missionary Zeal_
sent out re-enforcements under Bois-Lecomte, a nephew of
Villegagnon. The better part of these fresh recruits
were Huguenots, and among them were several young
theological students from Geneva, who were full of zeal
at their opportunity to carry forward the growth of the
Reformed religion. Equally zealous were the two
ministers, Pierre Richer and Gillaume Chartier, the first
Protestant clergymen to cross the Atlantic, and who were
anxious, as the old chronicler Lescarbot says, " to cause
the light of the Gospel to shine forth among those barbarous people, godless, lawless, and without religion." This
little band of Genevans was headed by the venerable Philippe de Corguilleray, Sieur de Pont, an old neighbour of
Coligny, who had left his estates in France to enjoy the
religious privileges of Geneva. Several other noblemen
joined the expedition, which was notable for its quality.
Sailing from France on November 20, 1556, after four
months on the "great and impetuous sea," the pilgrims
landed at Fort Coligny. " The first thing we did," says
Jean de Lery, one of the Genevan students, "was to
join in thanksgiving to God."

III

From Parkman's graphic account we quote the follow- _Theological Disputes_
ing : " For a time all was ardour and hope. Men of
birth and station and the ministers themselves, laboured
with pick and shovel to finish the fort. Every day ex-

hortations, sermons, prayers, followed in close succession, and Villegagnon was always present, kneeling on a velvet cushion brought after him by a page. Soon, however, he fell into sharp controversy with the ministers upon points of faith. Among the emigrants was a student of the Sorbonne, one Cointac, between whom and the ministers arose a fierce and unintermitted war of words. Is it lawful to mix water with the wine of the Eucharist? May the sacramental bread be made of meal of Indian corn? These and similar points of dispute filled the fort with wranglings, begetting cliques, factions and feuds without number. Villegagnon took part with the student, and between them they devised a new doctrine, abhorrent alike to Geneva and to Rome. The advent of this nondescript heresy was the signal of redoubled strife. . . . Villegagnon felt himself, too, in a false position. On one side he depended on the Protestant, Coligny ; on the other, he feared the court. There were Catholics in the colony who might report him as an open heretic. On this point his doubts were set at rest ; for a ship from France brought him a letter from the Cardinal of Lorraine, couched, it is said, in terms which restored him forthwith to the bosom of the Church. Villegagnon now affirmed that he had been deceived in Calvin, and pronounced him a 'frightful heretic.' He became despotic beyond measure, and would bear no opposition. The ministers, reduced nearly to starvation, found themselves under a tyranny worse than that from which they had fled.

A False Lead

"At length he drove them from the fort, and forced them to bivouac on the mainland, at the risk of being butchered by Indians, until a vessel loading Brazil-wood in the harbour should be ready to carry them back to France. Having rid himself of the ministers, he caused three of the more zealous Calvinists to be seized, dragged to the edge of a rock, and thrown into the sea. A fourth, equally obnoxious, but who, being a tailor, could ill be spared,

Expelling the Ministers

was permitted to live on condition of recantation.   Then, mustering the colonists, he warned them to shun the heresies of Luther and Calvin ; threatened that all who openly professed those detestable doctrines should share the fate of their three comrades : and, his harangue over, feasted the whole assembly in token, says the narrator, of joy and triumph.

"Meanwhile, in their crazy vessel, the banished minis- Perils and
Privations ters drifted slowly on their way.   Storms fell upon them, their provisions failed, their water casks were empty, and, tossing in the wilderness of waves, or rocking on the long swells of subsiding gales, they sank almost to despair. In their famine they chewed the Brazil-wood with which the vessel was laden, devoured every scrap of leather, singed and ate the horn of lanterns, hunted rats through the hold, and sold them to each other at enormous prices. At length, stretched on the deck, sick, listless, attenuated, and scarcely able to move a limb, they descried across the waste of sea the faint, cloud-like line that marked the coast of Brittany.   Their perils were not past ; for, if we may believe one of them, Jean de Lery, they bore a sealed letter from Villegagnon to the magistrates of the first French port at which they might arrive.   It denounced them as heretics, worthy to be burned.   Happily, the A Disastrous
Failure magistrates leaned to the Reformed, and the malice of the commandant failed of its victims."

Soon after the return of the ministers to France, Villegagnon himself followed them, leaving the deserted colony to its fate.   The end was not long in coming, and before the close of the year 1558 a Portuguese fleet arrived in the Bay of Rio de Janeiro and overpowered the feeble resistance of the little garrison, razed the fort, and put its unhappy defenders to the sword.   Thus Coligny's first experiment in colonization failed most disastrously.

CHAPTER II

DISASTROUS ATTEMPTS IN FLORIDA

I

FOUR years after the failure of the colony at Fort Coligny, the Admiral again undertook his cherished plan of colonization. Under the leadership of Jean Ribault, who was the greatest navigator and captain of France, and a staunch Huguenot, an expedition sailed from Havre for Florida on the 18th of February, 1562. The two ships contained a goodly company of volunteers, and nearly all the soldiers and labourers, as well as the few noblemen, were Calvinists. René de Laudonnière, next to Ribault, was the leading man among them, while another of the party, Nicholas Barré, had been with Villegagnon in the expedition to Brazil.

Six weeks after setting out from France the ships made the coast of Florida, and proceeding northward reached the mouth of a large river which was named the River of May (now the St. John's) because it was the first of May when the voyagers sailed into its welcome calm. Here they landed, and immediately knelt in thanksgiving to God, and in prayer that He would bless their enterprise and bring to the knowledge of the Saviour the heathen inhabitants of this new world. Thus both these unfortunate colonies were founded in the spirit of evangelism and missions.

The friendly natives who gathered fearlessly about them watched with wonder this ceremony and the further formal proceedings whereby Ribault took possession of the country in the name of the King of France, setting up in evidence a pillar of stone, engraven with the royal arms, upon a small elevation in a grove of cypress and palm trees near the harbour.

Then the French explored the coast further, until they reached the channel of Port Royal, off the coast of what is now South Carolina. Entering the harbour, "one of the largest and fairest of the greatest havens of the world," Ribault decided here to lay the foundations of his colony. The site of a fort was chosen not far from the Beaufort of to-day, and Charlesfort was the name given in honour of the boy King who had lately come to the throne of France. When the work was under way, Ribault left a number of his men to garrison the little fort, and returned to France, to report his findings and secure larger supplies of men and means for the colony. He reached Dieppe only five months from the day of sailing. But during this brief interval France had been plunged into civil war by the unprovoked assault which the Duke of Guise had made upon a Protestant assembly in a town of Champagne, and the cold-blooded slaughter of a half a hundred inoffensive persons. In the midst of such troublous times it was impossible to get either men or money for Florida, and Ribault followed his old leader, Admiral Coligny, into the field for the Protestants. Thus the small body of men at Charlesfort was left to its fate.

Things had gone from bad to worse with them after Ribault's departure. Albert, their leader, developed into a harsh tyrant, and was finally killed on account of his cruelty. Famine stared them in the face, thoughts of home filled their hearts, and they resolved to forsake their life of dreary monotony and escape from their prison at all hazards. After infinite toil they constructed a rude ship, fitting her with sails made from their shirts and their bedding, and set forth on their long journey across the Atlantic. A long stretch of calm exhausted their supplies, and fierce gales racked their rude craft until she leaked at every seam. Many died from thirst and exhaustion, while others were barely able to sustain life by chewing upon their shoes and leather doublets. After a series of indescribable privations and sufferings

Port Royal

Charlesfort

Colony Abandoned

the survivors were driven frantic with joy at the sight of the coast of France.

II

Laudonniere's Expedition

Coligny knew nothing of the fate which had befallen his second attempt at colonization, and when the first civil war was ended by the peace of Amboise, which brought the Protestants' peace for a time, he obtained permission of the King to fit out three ships to go to the rescue of the Florida expedition. Laudonnière was placed in command, and a number of noblemen together with experienced officers and sailors joined his party. **April, 1564** This expedition sailed April 22, 1564, and safely reached the mouth of the St. John's. A graphic idea of what took place thereafter may be had from the following account, written by Laudonnière himself:

Account by Laudonniere

Afterwards, we passed between Anquilla and Anegarda, sailing towards New France, where we arrived fifteen days after, to wit: on Thursday, the 22d of June, about three of the clock in the afternoon.

. . . The next day, the 23d of this month, I gave commandment to weigh anchor, and to hoist our sails to sail towards the River of May, where we arrived two days after, and cast anchor. Afterwards, going on land with some number of gentlemen and soldiers, to know for a certainty the singularities of this place, we espied the paracoussy (chief) of the country which came towards us, **Joyous Welcome** which, having espied us, cried, very far off, Antipola! Antipola! and, being so joyful that he could not contain himself, he came to meet us, accompanied with two of his sons, as fair and mighty persons as might be found in all the world, which had nothing in their mouths but this word—*amy, amy;* that is to say, friend, friend; yea, and knowing those which were there in the first voyage, they went principally to them to use this speech unto them. There was in their train a great number of men and women, which still made very much of us, and, by evident signs, made us understand how glad they were of our arrival.

. . . I was of opinion, if it seemed good unto them, to seat ourselves about the River of May, seeing, also that, in our first voyage, we found the same only among all the rest to abound in maize and corn, besides the gold and silver that were found there : a thing that put me in hope of some happy discovery in time to come. After I had proposed these things, every one gave his opinion thereof; and, in fine, all resolved, namely, those which had been with me in the first voyage, that it was expedient to seat themselves rather on the River of May than on any other, until they might hear news of France. This point being thus agreed upon, we sailed towards the river, and used such diligence that, with the favour of the winds, we arrived the morrow after, about the break of day, which was on Thursday, 29th of June.

Having cast anchor, I embarked all my stuff, and the soldiers of my company, to sail right towards the opening of this river, wherein we entered a good way up, and found a creek, of a reasonable bigness, which invited us to refresh ourselves a little, while we reposed ourselves there. Afterwards we went on shore, to seek out a place . . . then we discovered a little hill adjoining unto a great vale, very green, and, in form, flat; wherein were the fairest meadows of the world, and grass to feed cattle. Moreover, it is environed with a great number of brooks of fresh water, and high woods, which make the vale more delectable to the eye. After I had taken the view, thereof, at mine ease, I named it, at the request of our soldiers, the Vale of Laudonnière. . . .

. . . We gathered our spirits together, and, marching with a cheerful courage, we came to the place which we had chosen to make our habitation in : whereupon, at that instant, near the river's brink, we strewed a number of boughs and leaves, to take our rest on them the night following, which we found exceeding sweet, because of the pain which before we had taken in our travel.

On the morrow, about break of day, I commanded a trumpet to be sounded, that, being assembled, we might give God thanks for our favourable and happy arrival. Then we sang a psalm of thanksgiving unto God, beseeching Him of His grace to continue His accustomed goodness towards us, His poor servants, and aid us in all enterprises that all might turn to His glory and the advancement of our King. The prayer ended, every man began to take courage.

Afterwards, having measured out a piece of ground, in the form of a triangle, we endeavoured ourselves on all sides—some to bring earth, some to cut faggots, and others to raise and make the rampart ; for there was not a man that had not either a shovel, or cutting-hook, or hatchet, as well to make the ground plain by cutting down the trees, as for the building the fort, which we did hasten, in such cheerfulness, that, within a few days, the effect of our diligence was apparent.   .   .   .

Our fort was built in the form of a triangle ; the side towards the west, which was towards the land, was inclosed with a little trench, and raised with turns made in the form of a battlement, of nine feet high ; the other side, which was towards the river, was inclosed with a palisade of planks of timber, after the manner that gabions are made.   On the south side, there was a kind of bastion, within which I caused an house for the munition to be built ; it was all builded with faggots and sand, saving about two or three feet high, with turf, whereof the battlements were made.   In the midst, I caused a great court to be made, of eighteen paces long and broad, in the midst whereof, on the one side drawing towards the south, I builded a corpse de gard, and an house on the other side, towards the north, which I caused to be raised somewhat too high, for, within a short while after, the wind beat it down ; and experiences taught me that we may not build with high stages in this country, by reason of the winds whereunto it is subject. One of the sides that enclosed my court, which I made very fair and large, reached unto the range of my munitions, and, on the other side, towards the river, was mine own lodging, round about which were galleries, all covered. One principal door of my lodging was in the midst of the great place, and the other was towards the river. A good distance from the fort, I built an oven, to avoid the danger against fire, because the houses are of palm-leaves, which will soon be burned after the fire catcheth hold of them, so that, with much ado, a man shall have leisure to quench them. Lo, here, in brief, the description of our fortress, which I named Caroline, in **Fort Caroline** honour of our prince, King Charles.

. . . In the meanwhile, I was not able, with the same store of victuals which I had, so well to proportion out the travel upon the ships which we built to return into France; but that, in the end, we were constrained to endure extreme famine, which continued among us all **Famine** the month of May; for, in this latter season, neither maize, nor beans, nor mast, was to be found in the villages, because they had employed all for to sow their fields, insomuch that we were constrained to eat roots, which the most part of our men pounded in the mortars (which I had brought with us to beat gunpowder in), and the grain which came to us from other places. Some took the wood of esquine, beat it, and made meal thereof, which they boiled with water, and eat it; others went, with their barquebuses, to seek to kill some fowl. Yea, this misery was so great, that one was found that gathered up, among the filth of my house, all the fish bones that he could find, which he dried and beat into powder, to make bread thereof.

. . . I leave it to your cogitation to think how near it went to our hearts to leave a place abounding in riches (as we were thoroughly informed thereof), in coming whereunto, and doing service unto our Prince, we left our own country, wives, children, parents, and friends, and passed the perils of the sea, and were therein arrived, as in a plentiful treasure of all our hearts' desire. As each of us were much tormented in mind with these, or such like cogitations, the 3d of August, I descried four sails in the sea as I walked upon a little hill, whereof I was exceeding well repaid. I sent, immediately, one of them which were with us, to advertise those of the fort, thereof, which were so glad of these news, that one would have thought them to be out of their wits, to see them laugh and leap for joy.

. . . Captain Vasseur and my lieutenant, which were gone to meet them, which brought me word that they were Englishmen. . . . The general (Sir Francis Drake) immediately understood the desire and urgent occasion which I had to return into France, whereupon he offered to transport me and all my company home; whereunto, notwithstanding, I would not agree, being in doubt on what occasion he made so large an offer; for I knew not how the case stood between the French and the English; and, although he promised me, on his faith to put me on land in France, before he would touch in England, yet I stood in doubt, lest he would attempt somewhat in Florida in the name of his mistress; wherefore I flatly refused his offer. . . .

As I was thus occupied in these conferences, the wind and the tide served well to set sail—which was the eighth and twentieth of August; at which instant, Captain Vasseur, which commanded in one of my vessels, and Captain Verdier, which was chief in the other—now ready to go forth, began to descry certain sails at sea, whereof they advertised me with diligence. . . .

Being, therefore, advertised that it was Captain Ribault, I went forth of the fort to meet him; and, to do him all the honour I could by any means, I caused him to be welcomed by the artillery, and a gentle volley of

Sails Espied

Sir Francis
Drake

Ribault's Ar-
rival

my shot, whereunto he answered with his. Afterwards, being come on shore, and received honourably with joy, I brought him to my lodging, rejoicing not a little, because that, in his company I knew a good number of my friends, which I entreated, in the best sort that I was able, with such victuals as I could get in the country, and that small store which I had left me, with that which I had of the English general. . . .

But, lo! how oftentimes misfortune doth search and pursue us, even when we think to be at rest! Lo! see what happened after that Captain Ribault had brought up three of his small ships into the river, which was the 4th of September. Six great Spanish ships arrived in the *Spanish Ships* road, where four of our greatest ships remained, which *Arrive* cast anchor, assuring our men of good amity. They asked how the chief captains of the enterprise did, and called them all by their names. I report me to you if it could be otherwise; but these men, before they went out of Spain, must needs be informed of the enterprise, and of those that were to execute the same. About the break of day, they began to make towards our men, but our men, which trusted them never a deal, had hoisted their sails by night, being ready to cut the strings that tied them; wherefore, perceiving that this making towards our men of the Spaniards was not to do them any pleasure, and knowing well that their furniture was too small to make head against them, because that the most part of their men were on shore, they cut their cables, left their anchors, and set sail. . . .

After he (Ribault) understood these news, he returned *A Bad Plan* to the fortress, and came to my chamber, where I was sick; and there, in the presence of several gentlemen, he propounded that it was necessary, for the King's service, to embark himself, with all his forces, and, with the three ships that were in the road, to seek the Spanish fleet; whereupon he asked our advice. . . . Then he told me that he could do no less than to continue this enterprise ; and that in the letter which he had received from my Lord Admiral, there was a postscript, which he showed me, written in these words : " Captain John Ribault, as I was enclosing of this letter, I received a certain advice, that Don Pedro Melendez departeth from Spain, to go to the coast of New France. See that you suffer him not to encroach upon you, no more than he would that you should encroach upon him."

"You see," quoth he, "the charge that I have; and I leave it unto yourself to judge if you could do any less in this case, considering the certain advertisement that we have, that they are already on land, and will invade us." . . .

The night between the 19th and 20th of September, La Cigne kept watch with his company, wherein he used all endeavour, although it rained without ceasing. When the day was, therefore, come, and that he saw that it still rained worse than it did before, he pitied the sentinels so moiled and wet, and thinking the Spaniards would not have come in such a strange time, he let them depart, and, to say the truth, he went himself unto his lodging. In the meanwhile, one which had something to do without the fort, and my trumpeter, which went up unto the rampart, perceived a troop of Spaniards which came down from a little knappe, where, incontinently, they began to cry alarm, and the trumpeter also, which, as soon as ever I understood, forthwith I issued out, with my target and sword in my hand, and got me into the midst of the court, where I began to cry upon my soldiers. . . . As I went to succour them which were defending the breach on the southwest side, I encountered, by chance, a great company of Spaniards, which had already repulsed our men, and were now entered, which drove me back unto the court of the fort . . . and, in the meanwhile, I saved myself by the breach, which was on the west side, near unto my lieutenant's lodging and gateway, into the woods, where I found certain of

Taken by
Surprise

my men, which were escaped, of which number there
were three or four which were sore hurt.   .   .   .

Being able to go no farther, by reason of my sickness
which I had, I sent two of my men, which were with me,
which could swim well, unto the ships, to advertise them
of that which had happened, and to send them word to
come and help me.   .   .   .   The 25th of September, we Escape to France
set sail to return into France. The indifferent and un-
passionate readers may easily weigh the truth of my
doings, and be upright judges of the endeavour which I
there used. For mine own part, I will not accuse, nor
excuse any ; it sufficeth me to have followed the truth
of the history, whereof many are able to bear witness,
which were there present. I will plainly say one thing—
that the long delay that Capt. John Ribault used in his
embarking, and the fifteen days that he spent in roving
along the coast of Florida before he came to our fort,
were the cause of the loss we sustained ; for he discovered
the coast on the 14th of August, and spent the time in
going from river to river, which had been sufficient for
him to have discharged his ships in, and for me to have
embarked myself to have returned into France. I note
well that all that he did was upon a good intent ; yet, in
mine opinion, he should have had more regard unto his
charge than to the devices of his own brain, which, sometimes, he printed in his head so deeply, that it was very
hard to put them out, which also turned to his utter
undoing ; for he was no sooner departed from us but a
tempest took him, which, in fine, wrecked him upon the
coast, where all his ships were cast away ; and he, with
much ado, escaped drowning, to fall into their hands,
which cruelly massacred him and all his company.

III

To this graphic story something may be added from
other sources. Once more the French proved that, while French not Colonizers
they make a most admirable element in a colony estab-

lished by others, they have not the peculiar qualifications requisite to successful colonizing when left to themselves. In this instance they invited the fate that overtook them. They had to depend upon themselves for food supplies, yet neglected to cultivate the soil, fell to quarrelling, treated the natives unwisely, and proved generally unfit for their undertaking, difficult at best. Laudonnière was weak as leader; the young nobles who had crossed the ocean to find gold could not stoop to work, and grumbled at being required to do their part in the work of fortification. The Protestants had no pastor, and complained that Laudonnière was indifferent to religion. Then came famine, owing to the failure to raise crops. The second

Bad Management

summer found scarcity at La Caroline, although the river teemed with fish. Laudonnière at last decided to return to Europe and give up his attempt. The one ship usable was put in repair and the French were making ready to depart when the English fleet appeared. The captain was friendly, relieved their necessities, and offered to transport them to France. Unhappily that was declined, but a ship was bought from the English. Soon another fleet appeared, commanded by Ribault, who had been sent to supersede Laudonnière. His fleet comprised seven ships and carried not far from a thousand men, including a number of Huguenot gentlemen. At least one minister was in the company, M. Robert. Laudonnière was able to clear himself from the charges laid against him, and was cordially treated by his old-time commander.

The Spaniards Arrive

The end drew near. Five days after Ribault's arrival a third fleet came in sight. It was the Spaniards. Ribault's larger ships had fled. Spain denied the right of France in the new world, and especially the right of French Protestants to live anywhere. The King of Spain had sent Menendez, one of his bravest and cruelest captains, to dislodge the French colony. With a fleet of

Menendez the Butcher

fifteen ships and two thousand six hundred men, Spanish

and Portuguese, Menendez attacked the body of less than half his numbers and little prepared to resist. Laudonnière's plan was to strengthen the fort, secure the help of the friendly Indians, and harass the Spanish, who had landed thirty miles south on the coast. Ribault alone insisted upon a naval engagement, and as he was in command, his will was law. Ruin resulted. A storm wrecked Ribault's ships, and left Menendez free for his work of butchery. He surprised Fort Caroline, put all to the sword save the women and children, and returned to his landing-place. Laudonnière, the minister Robert, and a few others fled, reached the coast and one of the smaller ships which Ribault had left in the river, and finally reached France. Ribault, meanwhile, with his ship-wrecked followers, made their way to La Caroline only to find the Spanish there; and a little later Ribault attempted to treat with Menendez, who would give no assurance beyond saying: "Yield yourselves to my mercy, give up your arms and your colours, and I will do as God may prompt me." Two hundred of Ribault's men refused to accept these terms and fled into the wilderness. The others, one hundred and fifty in number, **Horrible Massacre** threw themselves upon the compassion of a man who knew none for Protestants. Though Spain was at peace with France, as Ribault reminded Menendez, the answer was, "Not so in the case of heretics." Thus did this inhuman monster, sacrilegiously using the name of God, announce his action to his government. "I had their hands tied behind their backs, and themselves put to the sword. It appeared to me that by thus chastising them, God our Lord and your Majesty were served. Whereby this evil sect will in future leave us more free to plant the gospel in these parts."

Those who refused to surrender were pursued by Menendez, but after strong resistance were promised treatment as prisoners of war, and were finally sent to the galleys by the Spanish king. Thus came to its dreadful end Coligny's last hope to found a Protestant colony in America. On the spot of the La Caroline massacre Menendez placed a tablet bearing this inscription : " Hung not as Frenchmen, but as Lutheran."

A Fatal Tablet

Two years later, Dominique de Gourges, a gallant French officer, determined to avenge this slaughter of his countrymen, though he was not a Huguenot. The brutality of the Spaniards had aroused great indignation in France, yet the court remonstrances had not succeeded in obtaining any redress from the Spanish King. Hence de Gourgues took vengeance into his own hands. Selling his patrimony, with his brothers' help he fitted out three small vessels, and after a perilous voyage he reached the Florida coast, enlisted the service of the friendly Indians, and falling upon La Caroline, took prisoners the Spanish forces left to garrison it. Then he put most of them to the sword, and hung the remainder upon the trees from which Menendez had hung his French prisoners ; and upon the other side of the tablet which the Spaniard had placed near by, he inscribed these words : "I do this not as unto Spaniards, nor as unto seamen, but as unto traitors, robbers, and murderers." It was a pity that Menendez himself could not have received the punishment he so richly merited.

DeGourges' Revenge

It should be said, in closing this dreary record, that the French in their short residence had made a deep impression upon the Indians, whom they treated in a manner quite unlike that of the Spaniards and Portuguese. Their habitual gayety and good nature and kindliness attracted the natives, and the singing of the Huguenots, who were like Cromwell's men great and sonorous singers of hymns, printed itself upon the Indian memory, so that long afterwards the European cruising along the coast would be saluted, says Baird, with some snatch of a French psalm, uncouthly rendered by Indian voices, in strains caught from the Calvinist soldier on patrol. No fierce imprecation or profane expletive lingered in the

French Influence Upon the Natives

recollection of the red men, as the synonym for the French Protestant. Moreover, the Genevan students on the second expedition had succeeded in reaching a number of the Indian tribes with the truth, and obtained promises from many that they would stop their cannibalism, practiced upon their enemies.

LE MOINE'S SKETCH OF THE BUILDING OF FORT CAROLINE

CHAPTER III

THE HUGUENOT COLONY IN CANADA

I

High Aim of King Henry IV

HENRY IV entered heartily into the colonization plans of his great minister, Admiral Coligny, and after the Edict of Nantes had brought peace to France, this monarch undertook to realize his ambitious plans to build up a powerful navy, promote exploration and trade with distant parts, and carry out Coligny's scheme to establish a French colony in America. The honour belongs to this enlightened king, who strove to deal fairly with all his subjects and to protect the Protestants in their rights, of founding the first agricultural colony on our continent, and of basing it, moreover, upon the principles of religious liberty and equality.

To understand the character of this new movement of colonization and of those who engaged in it, it is necessary briefly to review the religious history of the western seacoast provinces of France. The fisher-folk and sailors of Normandy, Brittany, Saintonge, and the islands along the coast, were of the hardy sort of which explorers are **French Fishermen** made. From the year 1504 these seamen had crossed to the banks of Newfoundland and rivalled the English and Spaniards in discovery, fishing, and commercial enterprise. Many of these men were Protestant, and many of the ships engaged in these voyages were owned by Huguenot merchants, and manned by Huguenot sailors, who persisted in singing lustily Clement Marot's version of the Psalms, to the scandal of the Roman Catholics who heard them. It was as early as 1534 that Protestantism made its way into the seaboard provinces, through

112

the preaching of two of Calvin's most zealous and fiery disciples. The spread of the new doctrines was rapid, as the simpler religion appealed to the common people. A strange thing happened which aided in this quick growth of the Protestant movement. A number of monks in central France, hearing of Luther, left their monasteries and crossed into Germany to learn directly from the Reformer himself. As a result, they returned to France and began to preach against Rome in the same vein that Luther did in Germany. They were soon compelled to hide, and a number of them found refuge in Saintonge, among the seamen. The persecution that brought several of these reformed monks to the stake did not check the belief of the people in their doctrines, and again the blood of the martyrs became the seed of the church. By 1550 a large proportion of the people of this province had become Protestants, and La Rochelle, the capital town of the province, was the stronghold of Protestantism. To show how thorough the change was, it is said that when the Edict of Nantes was proclaimed in 1598 the Roman mass had not been said openly at La Rochelle for nearly forty years, while in many other Huguenot towns the Roman Catholic worship had practically disappeared, so predominantly Protestant were the people.

It was a Protestant population, therefore, that welcomed the colonization idea, not only for commercial reasons, but because experience had taught them how insecure they were in France. Even the new Edict of Henry could not guarantee continued possession of their religious liberties. The edict had inflamed the Roman Catholics, and it was plain that persecution would again break out the moment opportunity could be found. The day foreseen by the wise Coligny might dawn on any morrow, when the Protestants of France would need a place of refuge for themselves and their children.

II

Hence it was that when, November 8, 1603, Pierre de Monts, a Huguenot gentleman of Saintonge, received a royal commission authorizing him to possess and settle that part of North America embracing what is now Nova Scotia, New Brunswick and Canada, and granting him a trade monopoly for ten years, this brave Protestant leader and good man found no difficulty in securing Protestant followers. He had himself accompanied Chauvin on his first visit to the St. Lawrence, and thinking that region too severe in temperature had decided on a more southerly region for his colony. Nova Scotia was his choice. The name La Cadie had then been given to this fertile country by the French discoverer Cartier, and thus the Acadia of poetic legend came to be known. The royal grant emphasized the King's firm resolution "with the help and assistance of God, who is the author, distributor, and protector of all kingdoms and states, to seek the conversion, guidance and instruction of the races that inhabit that country, from their barbarous and godless condition, without faith or religion, to Christianity and the belief and profession of our faith and religion, and to rescue them from the ignorance and unbelief in which they now lie." Thus the purpose was declared to be spiritual as well as secular ; and the Sieur de Monts was appointed the King's lieutenant-general with powers to " subject all the peoples of this country and of the surrounding parts to our authority ; and by all lawful means to lead them to the knowledge of God and to the light of the Christian faith and religion, and to establish them therein." But there was one great difference between this missionary purpose and that of the ordinary Roman Catholic ruler. It was decreed that religious liberty should prevail in the new colony, and that all the colonists were to be maintained and protected in the exercise and profession of the Christian faith, and in peace, repose and tranquility. Calvinist

Sieur
de Monts'
Expedition

LaCadie

Missionary
Zeal and Religious
Liberty

and Romanist were to be safe to follow their own con-
sciences without molestation from the other. De Monts
was well fitted for leadership. He was a valiant soldier,
who had won the entire confidence of his sovereign, and
was a man of highest integrity and patriotism, as well as
of exemplary piety. By the testimony of his contemporaries, he was thoroughly qualified by his courage,
energy, perseverance, tact and firmness, to found New
France in America, and represented the commanding
qualities of the Huguenot gentleman.

With two ships he sailed from Havre in March, 1604, Port Royal
taking about one hundred and twenty persons. High
and low birth, Protestants and Catholics, with a Protestant
minister and a Roman Catholic priest to look after the
spiritual interests, made up the company, which was decidedly superior in character to most of those that had
previously gone forth in search of adventure. Two of
de Monts' former comrades, gentlemen of fortune and
rank—Samuel de Champlain and Baron de Poutrincourt,
accompanied him. Proceeding to the Bay of Fundy,
passing through the narrow channel into the beautiful
basin now known as Annapolis Harbour, de Monts
named the basin Port Royal, and here de Poutrincourt
decided to found a settlement and bring families from
France to develop his grant. No more favourable place
could have been found for the purpose. De Monts fixed
upon a small island at the mouth of the St. Croix for his
own colony—a site as poor as Port Royal was good ; and
after trying the hard experiences of a winter he saw his
mistake and decided to unite forces at Port Royal. Only
forty of seventy-nine of his company survived, owing to
sickness at St. Croix, and among those who died were the
priest and the minister, so that no religious teacher was
left. In this emergency, Marc Lescarbot, a Protestant
lawyer and writer, became teacher and preacher, "in
order that we might not live like the beasts," as he tells
us in his most interesting "History of New France,"

"and that we might afford the savages an example of our
way of living." It is worthy of mention that Baron de
Poutrincourt, while nominally a Roman Catholic, was
apparently in full sympathy with his Protestant associates, and was an open enemy of the Jesuits. Lescarbot
was not only teacher of his countrymen, but reached a
number of the natives, for whose conversion the Huguenots of La Rochelle daily prayed.

III

France seemed destined to defeat in the new world. If
religious troubles did not bring disaster, commercial
rivalries did. De Monts was just getting his new colony
in prosperous condition, when in 1607 his trade monopoly
was withdrawn at the instance of merchants of Brittany,
who learned with indignation that a rival threatened their
traffic along the American coast, and that exclusive rights
had been granted which shut them out from the fisheries
and fur trade. The withdrawal of his exclusive rights
crippled de Monts in his plans and led to the abandonment of Port Royal. Already a small palisaded fort had
been built, besides a mill, storehouses and dwellings, and
friendly relations had been formed with the Indians.
De Poutrincourt held his grant to the site, and took
possession of it again, but the chance for a strong colony
was lost.

De Monts now made another attempt, selecting the
interior for his new venture. For this purpose he obtained a renewal of his trade monopoly for a single year,
and taking Champlain with him, made his way up the
St. Lawrence with two vessels, one equipped for the
expedition, the other for the fur traffic which was to
bring the needed funds. In the summer of 1608, Champlain, under de Monts' authority, landed on the site of
Quebec, and established a trading-post at that strategic
point. De Monts now took in with him the rivals who
had formerly broken in upon his monopoly, and pros-

Trade Grant Withdrawn

Quebec 1608

perity attended his venture. Many merchants of La Rochelle actively engaged in the profitable trade.

Religious liberty had not as yet been interfered with, and though there were serious discussions between the Romanists and Calvinists, the friendly intercourse prevailed in the main so long as de Monts was in control. Presently, however, Champlain, who was a Roman Catholic, was appointed governor of the colony, and the religious contentions gave him much trouble. The Calvinists remained true to their faith, and on most of the "company's vessels the crews were assembled daily for prayers, after the manner of Geneva; and even good Catholics, it was complained, were required by the Huguenot captains to join in the psalmody which formed so important a part of the Protestant worship." But now came the terrible blow to the Protestants in France. Tolerant and sympathetic King Henry IV fell under the assassin's knife, and it was plain that no longer would the Huguenots enjoy their freedom of worship. De Monts gave up his hopes and plans, and surrendered his commission as viceroy of New France to the Prince of Condé, who had been a Huguenot leader, but was now engaged in politics rather than religion, using the latter as a political weapon. The proprietary rights which had belonged to de Monts passed, by the irony of fate, into the hands of the Jesuits, most inveterate and implacable of foes to the Protestant faith. One of the romances of history stranger than fiction is to be found in the passing of the title to half a continent from Protestant to Roman Catholic hands, through the missionary zeal of a French noblewoman controlled by the Jesuits on the one hand, and the financial needs of the noble de Monts, who had become governor of a Huguenot town and wanted to defend it against time of persecution, on the other. Thus began the Jesuit missions in North America under favourable auspices, and thus sounded the death-knell of a Protestant New France in North America.

Religious Troubles

DeMonts Loses Canada

Jesuits in Control

IV

France
Loses North
America as a
Result

To the Jesuits, those fomenters of wars and mischief in every country where they have been permitted to live, France owes it that North America was lost to her. The first thing the Jesuits aimed at was to get control of Acadia and Canada, and banish every heretic from the new world, then prevent any more from coming. In that simple way New France was to be kept Roman Catholic, and free from religious troubles such as had long distracted France and Germany and other nations. By the formation of a new company, the Company of New France, in which no Huguenot had place, and by the taking away of its charter from the former company, at the head of which was a Huguenot, the transformation was accomplished after a few years. Complaints of the singing of the Huguenots on shipboard brought orders prohibiting the singing of hymns, which was peculiarly distasteful to the Jesuits, of whom it was said, "They do not sing ; birds of prey never do." Champlain, as governor of Quebec, tried to enforce the orders against singing and public saying of prayers, but says : "At last it was agreed that they might meet to pray, but should not sing psalms. A bad bargain, yet it was the best we could do."

It was not long, however, before the Jesuits had grown strong enough to stop even the arrival of the singing Protestants. Under the policy of Cardinal Richelieu, who was as zealous a Roman Catholic as he was energetic and unscrupulous a minister of Louis XIII, every emigrant who went out under the Company of New France, must first profess the Roman Catholic faith. This was in the line of Richelieu's plan to crush out Protestantism in France also, and was regarded as a master stroke of policy. What it accomplished was to hand over North America to England, and to pave the way in France for the awful days of Red Revolution and a descending scale of power and influence among the world powers.

Shutting Out
Protestants

V

It was one of the reprisals of justice, one of the right-eous punishments of religious usurpation, that when the English king determined to contest the claim to North America by right of discovery, Sir William Alexander, who had a royal grant to Nova Scotia, found the best material for his expedition of conquest in the large num-bers of Huguenot seamen and soldiers who had found refuge in England from the renewed persecutions at home, and were only too glad to engage in war against the Jesuits, even though they were French. Hence we find that the admiral who had charge of Sir Alexander's squadron, fitted out for the conquest of New France, was David Kirke, while his brothers were his assistants—all natives of Dieppe in Normandy, and staunch Protestants who had fled from their country rather than deny their faith. The sailing master, Jacques Michel, was an ardent Calvinist, who had been in the employ of Guillaume de Caen when that strong Huguenot leader was at the head of the former Canadian Company organized by de Monts. Acadia was an easy prey to these bold invaders, and Kirke then turned his attention to Quebec, and on July 20, 1629, that stronghold, under Champlain, was obliged to surrender. And now the Jesuit fathers who had lately come to occupy the mission field which they proposed to hold forever shut against heretics, were prisoners in the hands of the very heretics whose destruction at home and abroad they had planned.

That Quebec again passed into French possession, be-cause peace had been signed between England and France three months before Quebec was captured, was a fortune of war; but during the three years of negotiations a Huguenot, Louis Kirk, was in command, and won the confidence and respect of all by his admirable and toler-ant conduct. His English name came from the fact that his father was a Scotchman who lived and married in France. He tried to induce the French families to re-

Sir William Alexander Claims Nova Scotia

Helped by Huguenots

Louis Kirk at Quebec

main in Quebec, and permitted them their religious liberty—an example which the Jesuit fathers, whom he permitted to say mass, never reciprocated when they were in power. It is significant, also, that it was a Huguenot, Emery de Caen, who was made the agent of France to receive back her American province. The truth seems to be that the Huguenots were men of such ability and trustworthiness that they were chosen when public service demanding highest integrity and capacity was to be rendered. We are constantly reminded of the fact that France lost her best blood when her Protestant subjects were massacred or exiled. They were the people who had convictions and courage, capacity and character such as make nations powerful and influential. And while New France was to cease to exist, the best of Old France was to enter into the making of the New World. The religious bigotry and crime and folly of the leaders of one nation, inspired by a hierarchy as pitiless as it has ever been shortsighted and grasping, were to contribute elements of inestimable value to other nations, particularly to that new one that was destined to be the wonder of them all.

1633, Canada Roman Catholic

May 23, 1633, was a decisive day for New France. On that day Champlain, again appointed governor, received the keys of the fort of Quebec from the Huguenot de Caen, and from that hour Canada was closed to the Huguenot as a colonist. None but Roman Catholic Frenchmen could acquire permanent residence. Dr. Baird is undoubtedly right when he says : "In this prohibition, religious intolerance pronounced the doom of the French colonial system in America. The exclusion of the Huguenots

France's Stupendous Blunder

from New France was one of the most stupendous blunders that history records. The repressive policy pursued by the French government for the next fifty years, culminating in the Revocation of the Edict of Nantes, tended more and more to awaken and to strengthen among the Protestants a disposition to emigrate to foreign lands. Industri-

ous and thrifty, ready for any sacrifice to enjoy the liberty
of conscience denied them at home, they would have
rejoiced to build up a French state in the New World.
No other desirable class of the population of France was
inclined for immigration. It was with great difficulty
that from time to time the feeble colony could be recruited,
at vast expense, and with inferior material. Meanwhile,
hundreds of thousands of expatriated Huguenots carried
into Protestant countries of Northern Europe, and into the
British colonies of North America, the capital, the industrial skill, the intelligence, the moral worth, that might
have enriched the French possessions, and secured to the
Gallic race a vast domain upon the North American
continent."

The John Alden House
At Duxbury

BOOK THREE

THE FRENCH PROTESTANTS IN AMERICA

PART ONE

NEW ENGLAND

CHAPTER I

THE FIRST COMERS

I

IN the list of passengers on the good ship *Mayflower* may be seen the names of a family called "Mullins," consisting of father and mother and two children: a son named Joseph and a daughter named Priscilla. But while the name William Mullins is thoroughly English, investigation proves that the man so called was not English at all. When the little ship *Speedwell* put out from Delfthaven in Holland to meet the *Mayflower* at Southampton, among the Pilgrims there was a Huguenot family, the father's name being Guillaume Molines. Already in the Old World, in that haven of Holland, the English and French refugees, sufferers alike for their religion, had clasped hands of kinship ; and in the first company that made home in the New World the Huguenots were represented, although the habit of corrupting names tended to conceal the fact. In that first awful year of starvation and suffering that followed the coming of the Pilgrims to the Massachusetts coast, Guillaume Molines, his wife, and the son perished. But Priscilla survived, and by her marriage with John Alden became the ancestress of that celebrated New England family, the Aldens. From this descent, too, was John Adams, second President of the United States. More than this, Longfellow's poem has enshrined this French girl in the affections of

The Mayflower, 1620

The Molines

Priscilla a Huguenot

125

New England as the typical Puritan maiden ; and so completely is she identified in thought and imagination with the story of the Pilgrims, that in spite of the record of history it is probable that the picture of John Alden and his fair young bride will remain the popular representation of the peculiarly English ancestors of New England.

French Traits   And yet, as a recent writer suggests, it has always been a source of wonder that an English girl could have had the ready wit to give John Alden "the tip" that released him from his ambiguous wooing and herself from the domination of the fierce little captain. "How blind we were to the Gallic coquetry with which she held on to Miles till she had secured John! She was a worthy progenitor of the Yankee girl in her ability to take care of herself. We must blot out, then, from the historic portrait the blue eyes and rosy cheeks of the English maiden whom our fancy has called up whenever we have thought of Priscilla ; and we must paint in a slender, graceful, black-haired brunette, with brown-black velvet eyes and long sweeping lashes, from under which were shot such glances as melted the hearts of all the colony ; and we must adorn the Puritan garb with some dainty ribbon." We can at once see how this different feminine element would exert its powerful influence, and how Priscilla would be a marked character.

A still greater shock will be given to tradition and family pride when it is said, further, that there are very good grounds for believing that John Alden himself had Huguenot blood in his veins. Let this case be stated by Julien, author of *Tales of Old Boston*, who made it a matter of careful research, and thought the evidence rather strongly in favour of a Huguenot origin. The Alden genealogies, he says, state vaguely that the name of Alden is not found in England, or mention a certain Mr. Alden of St. John's College, who is referred to as "one who suffered by the tyrannical Bartholomew act"—which suggests that it was a French refugee of 1572 who was

John Alden French

THE MAYFLOWER IN PLYMOUTH HARBOUR

the ancestor of this family. There is mention also of a "John Alden of the Middle Temple," to whom a coat of arms was assigned in 1607. Now the John Alden of the *Mayflower*, it will be remembered, was a cooper, whom the Pilgrims met at Southampton, just before their departure for America, and whom they induced to join their company with the understanding that he should be free to remain, or return to England as he pleased. I find in the list of persons, mostly Huguenots naturalized by royal letters patent and recorded at Westminster for the 5th of March, 1691, the name of Anne Alden, with those of her son-in-law Jean Biancard and Mary, his daughter. And there is a still more significant record of the granting of naturalization in 1575—that is, three years after the massacre of St. Bartholomew—to "Susan and Sarah Alden, daughters of John Alden of London, grocer, and Barbara, daughter of Jacques du Prier, his wife." In these records we have sufficient evidence at least to surmise that the John Alden of the *Mayflower*, as well as his wife Priscilla, was of direct Huguenot origin. Everybody is familiar with Millais' beautiful picture of the "Huguenot Lovers" of the period of the St. Bartholomew massacre. It would be a curious continuation of the story which that picture suggests if it should have a New World companion piece in the New England lovers of 1620, who on the white sand and amid the tangled sea grasses of Plymouth beach, vowed fealty to each other.

Alden Pedigree

II

The case of Priscilla Molines is more or less typical of the record of other Huguenot emigrants. Her name was distorted into the uneuphonious appellation of Mullins, and her identity was swallowed up in all its superficial aspects by the outward characteristics of her alien neighbours. It is easy to account for the changes which took place in the French names : even common English names of that period were spelled in a great variety of ways, ac-

Changes in Names

Loss of
Identity

cording to the whim or degree of learning of the user, and
so it is not to be wondered at that the strange and unfa-
miliar names of the French emigrants should have been
mangled almost out of all resemblance to the originals.
We shall find this to be the case over and over again.
And while the Huguenots did not lose the essential traits
of character which are the pride of their descendants,
they were very adaptable, and soon learned to conform to
the outward customs of the people among whom they found
themselves. They entered into the spirit of the civilization by which they were surrounded and thoroughly
identified themselves with it. For these reasons it is

Quick As-
similation of
the French

often extremely difficult to separate their history from the
history of the country at large, just as in the present instance it would be an almost impossible task to convince
the general public that Priscilla Mullins, the flower of
early Puritan civilization, was in reality a daughter of
France.

A year after the landing of the Pilgrims on Plymouth
Rock another Huguenot joined his fortunes to those of the

Phillip de la
Noye

infant state. This was Phillip de la Noye, who came over
in the ship *Fortune*. Like so many other French emigrants who came to America, la Noye was born in Holland, where his parents had taken refuge, and had there
made his acquaintance with the Puritans. Fate was
kinder to him than it had been to Guillaume Molines, and
he was enabled to gain a strong foothold in the colony.
His descendants, whose name became anglicized into
Delano, are numerous in the region where their ancestors
landed, and are to be met with in the West as well as in
New England. The late Rev. H. A. Delano, a Baptist
minister of marked gifts as a preacher, was an honoured
member of this family.

III

Touton's Peti-
tion

In the year 1662, Jean Touton, "of Rotchell in France,
Doctor Chirurgion," forwarded a petition to the "Magis-

trates of the Massachusetts Colonie'' on behalf of himself
and other persecuted citizens of that town.   The petition- A French
Surgeon
ers stated that they ''are for their religion sake, outed
and expelled from their habitations and dwellings in
Rotchell,'' and humbly crave the ''liberty to come heather,
here to inhabit and abide amongst the English in this
Jurisdiction, and to follow such honest endeavours &
ymploymts, as providence hath or shall direct them unto,
whereby they may get a livelihood, and that they might
have so much favour from the Govmt here, as in some
measure to be certayne of their residence here before they
undertake the voyage, and what privileges they may
expect here to have, that so accordingly as they find
incoridgmt for further progress herein, they may dispose
of their estates of Rotchell, where they may not have any
longer continuance.''   In October of that year the Gen- October 1662
eral Court of Massachusetts granted the petitioners the
right to take up their residence in the Colony, but how
many took advantage of the opportunity it is quite impossible to tell.   A list of the petitioners was forwarded with
the petition itself, but unfortunately it was destroyed.
Doubtless several of them found their way to Boston, for
we have evidence that Jean Touton himself arrived in
Massachusetts during the very year of the petition.   In
1687 we find him again addressing the General Court, declaring that he had ''ever since the year 1662 been an
Inhabitant in the Territory of his Majesty.''

Philip English, who was baptized Phillip L'Anglois,
came to Salem, Massachusetts, in or about the year 1670. Salem 1670
He was a high-spirited man and possessed of a great store
of energy, and he at once made a place for himself in the
affairs of that thriving seaport.   He built up a large trade
with France, Spain and the West Indies, and soon came
to be recognized as one of the most prosperous merchants
of Salem.   At one time, when at the height of his good
fortune, he was credited with owning fourteen buildings Philip English
in the town, a commodious warehouse and wharf, to say

nothing of the twenty-one vessels which brought in splendid profits under his skillful management. English had made his way to Salem from the Island of Jersey, and he was instrumental in bringing over a number of his compatriots who had taken refuge there. There is no complete record of their names, but we know that among those who came to Salem were John Touzell, John Browne (Jean Le Brun), Nicholas Chevalier, Peter Morall, Edward Feveryear, John Voudin, Rachel Dellaclose, the Valpy family, the Lefavors and the Cabots.

IV

Revocation
1685

But it was not until the Revocation of the Edict of Nantes crushed all hope of religious toleration in France and rendered the lives of Protestants unsafe, that the Huguenots began to flock to New England in any considerable numbers. In the very month of the Revocation their eyes were turned longingly towards the new world that promised them an asylum from their persecutions and an opportunity to enjoy that liberty of conscience for which they had so manfully struggled during a period of over a century and a half. On October 1, 1685, a letter was sent from La Rochelle to some unknown correspondent in Boston; it expressed the condition of the Rochellese and the faith they had in New England as a place of refuge, as the following extract will show:

Letter from
Rochelle

God grant that I and my family were with you, we should not have been exposed to the furie of our enemies, who rob us of the goods which God hath given us to the subsistence of our soule and body. I shall not assume to write all the miseries that we suffer, which cannot be comprehended in a letter, but in many books. I shall tell you briefly, that our temple is condemned, and razed, our ministers banished forever, all their goods confiscated, and moreover they are condemned to the fine of a thousand crowns. All t'other temples are also razed, excepted the temple of Ré, and two or three others. By act of Parliament we are hindered to be masters in any trade or skill. We expect every days the lord governour or Guiene, whom shall put soldiers in

our houses, and take away our children to be offered to the Idol, as
they have done in t'other countrys.

The country where you live (that is to say New England) is in great
estime ; I and a grat many others, Protestants, intend to go there.   A Haven
Tell us, if you please, what advantage we can have there, and particularly the boors who are accoustumed to plow the ground.   If somebody
of your country would hazard to come here with a ship to fetch in our
French Protestants, he would make great gain.

Five years previous, in 1680, some commissioners delegated by the Protestants of La Rochelle had visited Boston
and gained permission for a number of their countrymen
to settle in Massachusetts.   But the projected emigration
was given up, though two years later twelve persons did
find their way to Boston, coming by way of London.
They were Élie Charron, François Basset, Marie Tissau   Boston
Paré and her three daughters, and a widow named   Hospitality
Guerry, with her two sons, her son-in-law and two small
children.   This little company was very hospitably received by the good people of Boston.   They were in absolute poverty ; so great was their destitution, and so sympathetic were the people for the sufferings which they had
undergone for conscience' sake, that the governor and council recommended that on a certain day all the churches
of the neighbourhood should take up a collection to relieve
their distress, referring to them as " these Christian sufferers." At such a welcome these forlorn pilgrims must
have indeed thought that they had at last reached the
Promised Land, and it was probably the news of their
kindly reception which caused the Rochellese to look with
such yearning eyes towards Boston and Massachusetts.

V

Nor had they any cause to be disappointed when, in
1686, a company of them reached the colony.   The first   Free Citizenship arrived in July of that year, coming by way of St.   ship Granted
Christopher's.   In granting their application for admission to the colony, the council passed an order including

other French Protestants within its scope as follows : " Ordered, That upon the taking the oath of allegiance before the president, and under his hand and seal of his Majtys Territory and Dominion, they be allowed to reside and dwell in his Majtys sd dominion, and to proceed from hence and return hither as freely as any other of his Majtys subjects, and this to be an order for all such French Protestants that shall or may come into this his Majtys Territory and Dominion." By this generous action of the council, Massachusetts put herself on record as being ready and eager to furnish a home for all those who truly desired to dwell in liberty of conscience. And we can only add that she was amply repaid for her liberality by the high character and loyalty of the French refugees whom she sheltered. Bowdoin, Faneuil and Revere, are names that she could ill afford to have stricken from her annals.

Christian Charity

In August the second party of emigrants arrived. They had suffered much from the long voyage and had lost their doctor and twelve of their fellows through sickness on the way over. The survivors who landed in Boston were wasted by sickness and were almost wholly destitute of property. Their sad plight did not escape the vigilance of the ever watchful and solicitous council, which prepared a statement of the needs of the Huguenots and caused it to be read in all the churches of the colony. This paper represented them as " objects of a true Christian charity," exhorted the people to give liberally in so good a cause, and asked the ministers to " put forward the people in their charity." Captain Elisha Hutchinson and Captain Samuel Sewall, two of the leading citizens of Boston, took charge of receiving and distributing the relief fund, and everything was done to provide for the fugitives' comfort and welfare. We are told in the brief prepared by the council that this stricken company consisted of " fifteen French familyes with a religious

JOHN ALDEN AND PRISCILLA, *by Boughton*

Protestant minister, who are in all, men, women and children, more than fourscore soules."

The third party, "crowded into a small ship," reached Salem in September of that same year. The same kindness that had been shown the others was dealt out to them, and a large house (even down to the middle of the nineteenth century known as the "French House") was set apart for their use. Philip English, by this time well on the road to prosperity, was unremitting in his efforts to alleviate the misery of his countrymen, and his generosity was unbounded. Not for long, however, did these devoted emigrants stand in need of assistance. They had brought little property with them, but they were rich in thrift, perseverance, and industry, and they were soon able to take care of themselves and lend a helping hand to later arrivals.

A French House in Salem

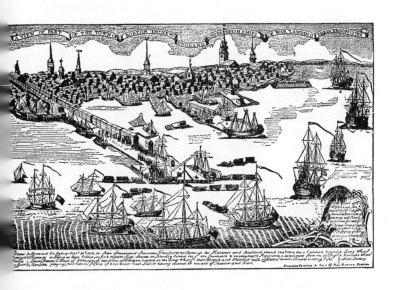

CHAPTER II

THE OXFORD SETTLEMENT

I

A WEALTHY refugee from La Rochelle, Gabriel Bernon, who reached London in 1697, was the prime mover in the French settlement of Oxford, Massachusetts. He had for some time contemplated going to America, and his design was stimulated by the offer of a grant of land on condition that he should form a settlement thereon. Bernon chose for his agent a refugee from Poitiers, one Isaac Bertrand du Tuffeau, and furnished him with the necessary funds for effecting an immediate settlement. Du Tuffeau reached Boston in the latter part of the summer of 1687, and upon presenting his credentials was given a grant of seven hundred and fifty acres of land in the Nipmuck region, on the site of the present town of Oxford.

The place selected for the little colony was far from civilization, in the heart of the forests that stretched in every direction undisturbed by the settler's axe. It could be reached only by the faint trail known as the Bay Path, which connected Boston with the valley of the Connecticut River and the settlement of Springfield; but remote and difficult of access as it was, the Oxford region had many features to recommend it. A small river flowed through the centre of a delightful valley which was walled in by a circle of rolling hills. Abundant water-power was at hand, the level plain which stretched out on either side of the river gave evidence of great fertility, while the near-by hillsides offered admirable opportunities for orchards and meadows.

To this promising locality, then, the first group of set-

Marginal note beside first paragraph: Bernon the Founder

Marginal note beside second paragraph: Nipmuck Region near Worcester

134

tlers made their way in the summer of du Tuffeau's ar- Arrival of Settlers 1687
rival in Boston.   There were not more than ten families in
the party which Daniel Bondet, an intrepid French Protestant minister who had come to Boston during the previous year, led forward into the wilderness.   Hardly had
the work of clearing the land and building the rude log
cabins been gotten under way when du Tuffeau himself
took up his residence in the colony.   Fortunately for the
colonists the winter proved to be a very mild one ; and although they had arrived too late for gathering any crops
they did not suffer for lack of food, as the woods abounded Game and Fish
in game and the numerous lakes and streams were well
stocked with fish, while from the neighbouring Indians
they were able to procure supplies of corn.   Du Tuffeau's
first care was to erect a fort on a hill which commanded
the little village and the surrounding valley.   The remains
of this fort are still extant, and show it to have been a The Fort
carefully planned and solidly built structure, consisting
of a roomy inclosure surrounded by a stockade, near the
centre of which stood a block-house about thirty feet long
by eighteen feet wide.   The fort was equipped with a well
and a powder-magazine and was adapted to resist a sudden onslaught or an extended siege ; for the settlers of
those days were forced to hold themselves in readiness
against every conceivable stroke of ill fortune.   But the
Indians were apparently peacefully disposed and the
Huguenots wasted but little thought on them.

II

The year following the establishment of the colony
Bernon himself set sail for America, bringing with him a
number of servants and several families of prospective
settlers.   This company numbered about forty persons in
all, and Bernon took upon himself the expense of fitting
out the entire enterprise.   As soon as he arrived at Bos- 1688
ton Bernon proceeded to get a confirmation of a grant of
land giving him a tract of twenty-five hundred acres

lying within the boundaries of Oxford.   A little later he
set out from Boston accompanied by Joseph Dudley, then
Chief Justice of Massachusetts and one of the principal
proprietors of the Oxford lands, who desired to show all
courtesy to the powerful and agreeable Huguenot by putting him in formal possession of his property.   Bernon's
presence gave a fresh impetus to the thriving little village.   He at once set about causing needed improvements
to be made; built a grist-mill and a saw-mill to utilize
the excellent water-power, and in many other ways provided for the comfort and welfare of the colonists.   It is
significant to note that among his earliest enterprises on
American soil was the erection of a commodious "tem-

ple" for the worship of God.   Previous to his coming,
religious exercises had been conducted in minister Bondet's "great house," which stood a little apart from the
village, but owing to the number of new arrivals it was
no longer large enough to serve as a place of gathering.

The village itself was built in the compact style to

which the refugees had been accustomed in their native
country.   All in all, the town probably contained between
seventy and eighty inhabitants during the second year of
its establishment.   Gabriel Bernon was only an occasional
resident, spending the greater part of his time in Boston.

After Bernon, du Tuffeau was probably the most important personage connected with the village.   Besides acting
as Bernon's agent he was the village magistrate, commissioned by the General Court in 1689 to "have Authority
for Tryall of small Causes not exceeding forty shillings,
and to act in all other matters as any other Assistant may
doe, as the Lawes of this Colony direct."   André Sigourney was likewise a leader in the community.   His appointment as constable of "the French Plantation," an
office which carried with it considerable respect and in-

fluence, shows how highly he was regarded by his fellow
citizens.   With Sigourney was his wife, Charlotte Pairan,
and five children, who fled with him from La Rochelle

during the winter of 1681. François Bureau came of noble blood, and fled to London with his brother Thomas from their native village of Niort, in Poitou. In 1688 François came to Oxford with his wife Anne and their two sons and two daughers. The eldest daughter, Anne, became later on the wife of Benjamin Faneuil and the mother of Peter Faneuil of Boston fame.

Besides these, there was Jean Germaine, whose name was corrupted into Germon or German, and his daughter Margaret, who came from La Tremblade, in the province of Saintonge ; Paiz Cassaneau, of Languedoc ; Daniel Johonnot, a youthful nephew of André Sigourney ; Jean Martin, his wife Anne, and their two children ; Elie Dupeux, a native of Port des Barques on the Saintonge coast ; Rene Grignon, Thomas Mousset, Guillaume Barbut, Jean Millet, Pierre Cante (Canton), Cornilly, Butt, Thibaud, Mourgues, and an Englishman named Johnson who married Susanne Sigourney. Jacques Depont was a nephew of Bernon, while Jean Baudouin was the eldest son of Pierre Baudouin, founder of the illustrious Bowdoin family in America.

III

But the little colony so prosperously begun was destined to have its full share of troubles. The practice of some unscrupulous traders in selling rum to the Indians seems to have given the settlers the first premonitions of impending disaster. In 1691 the worthy Pastor Bondet, who had an appointment from the Society for the Propagation of the Gospel to work among the Indians, wrote a letter to one of the Massachusetts authorities imploring him to use his influence in putting a stop to the traffic. After stating that the cause of his request is one which fills his heart with sorrow, he writes, "My humble request will be at least before God and before you a solemn protestation against the guilt of those incorrigible persons who dwell in our place. The rome is always sold to the

Troubles Through Traders

1691

Indians Crazed Indian without order and measure, insomuch that according to the complaint sent to me by master Dickestean with advice to present it to your honour, the 26 of the last month there was about twenty Indians so furious by drunkeness that they fought like bears and fell upon one called Remes who is appointed for preaching the Gospel amongst them. He had been so much disfigured by his wonds that there is no hope of his recovery." Bondet then goes on to beg his reader to interpose and maintain "the honour of God in a Christian habitation" and give comfort to "some honest souls which being incompatible with such abominations feel every day the burden of afliction of their honourable peregrination aggravated."

But no steps appear to have been taken to suppress the evil on the part of the authorities, for two years later André Sigourney made the following deposition :

No Help—Trouble Brewing   André Sigourney ages of about fifty years doe affirme that the 28 day of nouember last he was with all the others of the village in the mill for to take the rum in the hands of Peter Canton and when they asked him way hee doe abuse soe the Indiens in seleing them liquor to the great shame and dangers of all the company hee sd Canton answered that itt was his will and hee hath right soe to doe and asking him further if itt was noe him how make soe many Indiens drunk he did answer that hee had sell to one Indien and one squa the valew of four gills and that itt is all upon wch one of the company named Ellias Dupeux told him that hee have meet an Indien drunk wch have get a bott fooll and said that itt was to the mill how sell itt he answered that itt may bee trueth.

Canadian Priests Incite to Murder   The settlers had real cause for alarm when, in the summer of 1694, a band of Indians set on by the Canadian priests, brutally murdered the young daughter of one of the villagers named Alard, and carried off two little children. Other depredations followed, and the whole line of the outlying English colonies was threatened by the attacks of roving bands of Canadian Indians accompanied by Jesuit missionaries. The inhabitants of Oxford were continually stirred by the news of some bloody foray ;

now it would be the story of how some isolated farmhouse had been attacked in the middle of the night and its sleeping occupants butchered; or again, it would be the tale of a whole settlement put to the tomahawk. During the latter part of the summer the appearance of several bands of savages compelled the French colonists to take refuge in their fort. But though they were safe from actual danger within the confines of their strong stockade, yet they were made to suffer greatly through the destruction of their crops and a large number of their cattle, which left them in a feeble condition to meet the rigorous winter which followed. As soon as they thought it prudent to leave the protection of the fort, several of the Huguenots made their way to Boston, being under the strong impression that their isolated settlement would not be able to maintain itself in the face of the roving bands of marauders, who being perfectly at home in the woods had every advantage of their civilized opponents. Among the number who left was du Tuffeau, who had been called to account by Bernon for mismanagement of his property.

Nothing further happened to disturb the peace of Oxford until the summer of 1696. The home of the Englishman Johnson, who had married Susanne Sigourney, stood a little removed from the other houses of the town in the midst of a level stretch still known as Johnson's Plain. On August 5th, a band of Indians approached this dwelling while Johnson was some distance off, seized his three small children, André, Pierre and Marie, who were playing about the door-step, and dashed their brains out on the stones of the fireplace. The dazed and agonized mother made her escape and started out to warn her husband, but failed to find him. Johnson, unsuspecting the fate that had befallen his home, returned soon after the atrocity had taken place and was felled to the ground as he crossed the threshold. As the news of this massacre spread through the outlying districts the inhabitants were

1696 Johnson Family Attacked

one and all aroused to the danger which threatened them. A body of troops was sent out from Worcester, supported by forty friendly Indians, and for many days the neighbouring woods were scoured for traces of the murderers, but none of them were ever brought to justice.

Settlement Abandoned

The feeling of insecurity that had been gaining ground in Oxford was so heightened by the killing of the Johnson children that with one accord the refugees decided to abandon their settlement. Sigourney, Germon, Johonnot, Boutineau, Dupeul Cassaneau, Grignon, Barbut, Montier, Canton, Maillet, and Mousset retired to Boston. Depont found a new home in Milford, Connecticut. Bondet and Martin went to New Rochelle, in the province of New York; Bureau and Montel to New York. Baudouin made his way to Virginia, where his descendants may still be traced.

IV

Attempt at Revival 1699

An attempt to revive the settlement was made three years later, in the spring of 1699. The refugees who had gone back to Boston returned to Oxford and reclaimed their abandoned farms. It is probable that the energetic Bernon was the prime mover in this endeavour at resettlement, for he had expended a large sum of money in developing his Oxford property and in providing for the common welfare. The greatest loss, therefore, resulting from the abandonment of the project fell upon his shoulders. As soon, however, as the colony was revived he proceeded to invest more capital in its interests, and together with Réné Grignon and Jean Papineau established a wash-leather manufactory on the banks of the river that

New Industry

flowed through the town. This new industry gave employment to many of the villagers in hunting and trapping the game that abounded in the surrounding forests, and proved itself a decided advantage to the refugees. Loads of dressed skins were carted down to Providence and thence shipped by water to Boston and Newport, where they were made into hats and gloves by the skilled Huguenot artisans.

Jacques Laborie, a minister who had come to Boston Jesuit Intrigues from London during the previous year, accompanied the returning settlers. He brought with him his wife, Jeanne de Ressiguier, and his daughter Susanne. As he held an appointment from the corporation for promoting the Gospel in New England he at once set to work among the savages, with whom he soon came to be on the most friendly footing. It was owing to his intimacy with the Indians and his knowledge of their language that the warning of fresh intrigues on the part of the Jesuits was brought to the attention of the authorities. In spite of the treaty of Ryswick it soon became evident that the Indians Hostile priests were again endeavouring to stir up the friendly tribes to proceed against the English colonies.

In a letter to Governor Bellomont, Laborie informs him that numbers of the neighbouring Indians are preparing to leave and join the Pennacooks in New Hampshire. That they declare the "French" religion to be "plus belle que la notre" (more beautiful than ours), and that they will be furnished with silver crosses to hang about their necks, and that great promises have been made to them. Laborie is confident from the things he has heard that the priests are hard at work perfecting some scheme which they will bring forward when a propitious occasion presents itself. Rumours of such a nature kept the people of Oxford in a constant state of tension, but it was not until the summer of 1703 that 1703 actual hostilities broke out. They did their best to prepare for any sudden emergency that might arise ; a mil- Deerfield Massacre itary company was formed and the town's defenses were strengthened by building a palisade around Bernon's house to serve as a stronghold for the garrison. But after the Deerfield massacre, where over a hundred and fifty persons were slain or made prisoners, the handful of

Final
Abandonment
refugees felt that they were too tempting and easy a bait to hold their isolated position with any degree of security, and they accordingly abandoned their settlement in the spring of 1704, never to return again.

THE " BOSTON MASSACRE,   MARCH 5, 1770

CHAPTER III

GABRIEL BERNON

I

GABRIEL BERNON came of an ancient family claiming descent from the house of the Counts of Burgundy. Even without this noble lineage the Bernons had an independent patent of nobility, due to the fact that they had furnished several mayors to the independent city of La Rochelle. Gabriel, who succeeded his father André in business, was born April 6, 1664. He was a skillful man of affairs and under his guidance the house of Bernon became one of the wealthiest and most influential concerns in the flourishing seaport. The development of a considerable trade with Canada caused Bernon to take up his residence there for a number of years, and so successful was he that the governor of Canada, de Denonville, refers to him as the principal merchant in the colony. *The Bernon Family Ancient*

But Bernon was a Protestant, as his father had been before him ; indeed, the family had been one of the first in La Rochelle to adopt the Reformed religion, and it was in the Bernon mansion that many of the earliest Protestant services were held. His religion made him obnoxious to the Jesuits, who had by this time gained control of Canada and were bent on persecuting the Huguenots as heartily as did their compatriots at home, and so he was given notice to recant or quit. "It is a pity that he cannot be converted," wrote de Denonville, "as he is a Huguenot, the bishop wants me to order him home this autumn, which I have done, though he carries on a large business and *a great deal of money remains due to him here.*" *Staunch Protestants*

143

Jesuit Honour If they could not make him a Catholic they would at least make sure that his faith should cost him a fortune! Nothing daunted by this blow, Bernon returned to La Rochelle, arriving at the height of the persecution. He was at once thrown into prison where he was confined for some months, being released finally through the influence of his brothers, who had recanted. Unshaken in his faith, he made the best disposition of what property remained to him and escaped to Holland in May, 1686. From Amsterdam he made his way to London the following year and formed the project of the Oxford settlement, as we have seen.

II

In the summer of 1688 Bernon reached Boston after a voyage of ten weeks, a rapid journey for those days. His personal appearance is described, by a tradition dating from his arrival in Boston, as that of a man of commanding presence whose bearing always won the respect and consideration due to his character and ability. His figure was tall and of slender proportions; his carriage, erect and expressive of energy in every movement, yet tempered with a peculiar grace and courtly suavity. While on ordinary occasions his manner was affable and kindly, his hot temper sometimes led him to assume a tone of decided imperiousness. Thoroughly upright in all the acts of his life, thinking high thoughts, genuine in his religious feelings, thoughtful, optimistic and daring in his public and private ventures, he was naturally qualified for leadership. Misfortunes never daunted him, and left him ever the same brave, steadfast, hopeful man.

Personal Appearance 1688

Such a man would soon make his presence felt in the colony, and Bernon shortly became one of the leading citizens of Boston. After attending to the matters of the Oxford settlement and getting himself naturalized as a British subject, he devoted his attention to several industrial enterprises. Prominent among these undertakings was the manufacture of rosin and other naval stores.

A Leading Citizen

He was so successful in this that he engaged the interest of a government agent who had been sent to Massachusetts to learn what means were to be found in America for supplying the royal navy with such articles. By the advice of this agent, Bernon took a trip to London in the year 1693 to inform the admiralty of the opportunities for producing naval stores on a large scale in America, and also for the purpose of securing a patent on their manufacture. He was very favourably received by Lord Portland and other high officials, and succeeded in securing a contract from the government to supply a quantity of stores for a term of years.

Three years later he again made a visit to England on the same errand, returning to Boston with Governor Bellomont. To the governor Bernon unfolded his schemes for developing the manufactures and produce of the colony, and Lord Bellomont was greatly taken with his ideas, even recommending the royal council to appoint the refugee superintendent of naval stores in America. But it was the government's policy, at that time, to discourage colonial industries even in a case where they would manifestly benefit the public interests, and nothing ever came of Bernon's efforts in that direction.

But during these years Bernon's activities were not confined to endeavouring to overcome British insularity. His energy found vents for itself in a hundred other direc- tions. Besides retaining an active interest in the Oxford settlement he joins the Faneuils and Louis Allaire in trading with Virginia and Pennsylvania; he becomes a prosperous exporter to England and the West Indies; trades in furs with the Nova Scotians; invests considerable capital in ship-building; sets up salt-works, and undertakes the manufacture of nails. Indeed, there was hardly a department of colonial enterprise to which Bernon did not turn his attention. He did not put business first, however, but was always scrupulous to discharge his obligations as a Christian and a member of the state. He was free-handed in his dealings with his fellow refugees and aided many of them, who had been compelled to leave all their property in France, to get on their feet. When he had been a resident of Massachusetts for but two years the expedition against Port Royal was sent forward, and Bernon was not slow to contribute more than his share in furnishing arms, munition and money.

III

Removal to
Rhode Island

After a residence of nine years in Boston he removed to Rhode Island and settled first in Newport, from there going to Providence. While in Newport his career was substantially the same that it had been in Boston. He identified himself with the life of the growing town and was a leader in many of its numerous enterprises. With Daniel Ayrault for a partner he engaged largely in the West India trade, in which Rhode Island was then taking the lead. It was a hazardous business, involving great risks and great profits as well, as many wealthy Rhode Island families of to-day whose fortunes date back to the days of the "triangular trade" attest. Fortune did not favour Bernon in most of these ventures, however. He suffered losses from the French privateers which scoured the neighbouring waters, and from shipwreck, also. Greater than any loss of wealth to Gabriel Bernon was the death of his only son, who met his death in one of his father's ships that was outward bound for the Indies. Soon after leaving Newport the vessel was overtaken by a violent storm, and it is believed that she must have foundered, for none of her ship's company was ever heard from again. It was a great blow to the Huguenot, with his pride of birth and ancestry, to lose the only member of his family who could perpetuate the name of Bernon in America. Perhaps the death of his son may have influenced him to withdraw from the trade and take up his residence in Providence, for he did so not long afterwards.

Newport

But though he gradually withdrew from active partic- ipation in business affairs, he lost none of his former zeal in the cause of religion. While living in Boston he had been a devoted member of the French Reformed church, and the relations he afterwards sustained with that church were always of the most cordial nature, but on coming to Rhode Island, where there were not enough of his countrymen to support such an organization, he immediately allied himself with the Anglican communion. More fervent in his faith than the majority of the Epis- copalians in the colony, and accustomed to act rather than talk, he was largely instrumental in founding the first three Anglican churches in the province—Trinity Church in Newport, St. Paul's Church in Kingston and St. John's Church in Providence. In the year 1724, when he was eighty-one years old, he crossed over to present to the Bishop of London the needs of the church in Providence and the benefits which would accrue from sending there an able and competent minister. Surely it is not too much to say that a man who, in the declining years of his life, was willing to undertake the perils and hardships of a voyage that was at its best an uncomfort- able and hazardous proceeding—and willing to do this not for personal motives but for the well-being of others —was a man of heroic mould, and one of whom his de- scendants may well be proud.

Bernon had lost much of his property by some of his later ventures, yet enough remained to him to enable him to build a fine house in Providence "near Roger Will- iams' spring," and there he lived his last few years in quiet happiness, giving his time to writings and correspond- ence, mostly of a religious character. Up to the very last his Protestantism was pronounced and vigorous. He could never endure anything in the nature of priestly as- sumption or ecclesiastical domination, and in a letter to the vestry of Trinity Church in Newport written in his old age, denouncing a pamphlet on church order which

His Views they had sanctioned, he says: "I am a born layman of France, naturalized English, which I hold a greater honour than all the riches of France, because the English laity are not, like the laity of France, slaves of the clergy and hackneys of the Pope; wherefore rather than submit to this I abandoned my country, my fortune, and my friends, in order to become a citizen under the English government." And because of his staunch belief in the rights of the laity he found Rhode Island a more congenial place of residence than Massachusetts, with its ecclesiastical hierarchy, which smacked too much of the intolerance of Catholicism in France to meet with his entire approval.

Memorial Tablet He died in 1736, at the age of ninety-one, and was buried under St. John's Church, Providence, with every token of public respect. A tablet in the church bears the following inscription:

In Memory of Gabriel Bernon, Son of André and Suzanne Bernon, Born at La Rochelle, France, April 6, A. D. 1644. A Huguenot. After two years' imprisonment for his Religious Faith, Previous to the revocation of the Edict of Nantes, He took refuge in England, and came to America A. D. 1688. Here he continued steadfast in promoting The Honour of the Church And the Glory of God. It is recorded in the History of Rhode Island, that " To the persevering piety and untiring zeal of Gabriel Bernon the first three Episcopal Churches in Rhode Island owed their orgin," King's, now St. John's Church, Providence, Founded A. D. 1722, being one of them. He died in the Faith once delivered to the Saints, Feb. 1, A. D. 1736, A 92, And is buried beneath this Church. " Every one that hath forsaken houses, or brethren, or sisters, or father, or mother, or wife, or children, or lands, for My name's sake, shall receive an hundredfold, and shall inherit eternal life."—*St. Matt.*

IV

Bernon's Descendants Bernon's first wife was Esther Le Roy, daughter of a wealthy Huguenot merchant of La Rochelle. Sne accompanied her husband to America and died in Newport in 1710, at the age of fifty-six. The children by this

OLD HUGUENOT CHAIR AND BOSTON STATE HOUSE

marriage were Gabriel, Marie, Esther, Sarah, and Jeanne. Gabriel died unmarried. Marie married Abraham Tourtellot, a Huguenot who was at that time master of a vessel sailing from Newport. Their descendants are numerous. Esther married Adam Powell, of Newport, in 1713. She gave birth to two daughters, the elder of whom, Elizabeth, married the Reverend Samuel Seabury, of New London, Connecticut ; while the younger, Esther, married Chief-Justice Helme of the Superior Court of Rhode Island.

Sarah married the representative of a prominent New England family, Benjamin Whipple, in the year 1722. Jeanne married Colonel William Coddington, of Newport, in 1722. The issue of this union was two sons and four daughters ; John and Francis, Content, Esther, Jane and Ann.

The children of Bernon's second wife, Mary Harris, granddaughter of William Harris, who accompanied Roger Williams when he landed at Whatcheer rock in 1636, were Susanne, Mary, and Eve. There was also born to her a son, Gabriel, who died at an early age.

Susanne married Joseph Crawford in 1734. Nine children were born to them, the youngest of whom, Ann, was married to Zachariah Allen in 1778. The Honourable Zachariah Allen, son of Ann Crawford and grandson of Susanne Bernon, was born in Providence, Rhode Island, in 1795, where he died in 1882 at the age of eighty-seven. His Huguenot ancestry was always a matter of keen interest to Mr. Allen, and as president of the Rhode Island Historical Society and first president of the Huguenot Memorial Society of Oxford, Massachusetts, he was enabled to further the growing sentiment which gives to the French Protestant emigrants their rightful place among the founders of the Republic. As Baird says of Mr. Allen, "perhaps more than any other American who has lived in these times, Mr. Allen himself illustrated some of the finest traits of the Huguenot character." A

Honorable Zachariah Allen

President Rhode Island Historical Society

Brown 1813

graduate of Brown University in the class of 1813, he studied law and medicine and then engaged in business with marked success. Inheriting the versatility of his ancestor, Gabriel Bernon, his public and his private interests were of the broadest character ; he was a thorough student of the sciences, made several valuable improvements in the construction of machinery, was largely engaged in promoting philanthropic activities, and wrote several books and many papers. But above all, he was loved by all who knew him for his buoyancy, kindliness, unfailing sympathy and simple piety.

Mary Bernon married Gideon Crawford, and gave birth to seven sons and four daughters. Her younger sister, Eve, died unmarried.

THE BALLOU CHURCH 1640
(ATTENDED BY PRES. GARFIELD'S MOTHER)

CHAPTER IV

THE NARRAGANSETT SETTLEMENT

I

EVEN more unfortunate in its outcome than the A Land Scheme Oxford settlement was the attempt to establish a Huguenot community near the shores of Narragansett Bay, within the limits of the township known to-day as East Greenwich. The complete failure of this project was in no wise due, however, to the refugees themselves, but to the fact that they were inveigled by an unscrupulous land company into purchasing a tract whose title was later shown to be invalid.

In October, 1686, a body of Huguenots in London made 1686 London Contract arrangements with the "Atherton Company," which claimed the ownership of the "Narragansett Country," whereby they acquired a site for a settlement. According to the terms of the contract each family was to receive one hundred acres of upland and a share of meadow; the price for which was fixed at twenty pounds the hundred acres if paid for at once, or twenty-five pounds if settled for at the end of three years. The "Narragansett Country," comprising all that portion of Rhode Island which to-day lies south of the town of Warwick on the western side of Narragansett Bay, had long been the cause of dispute between Connecticut and Rhode Island. Connecticut claimed that her borders extended to the shores of Narragansett Bay and therefore included the disputed territory, and Rhode Island, on the other hand, as stoutly denied it. These rival claims had already been submitted to the crown for adjustment and the decision was still pending when the Huguenots made their unfortunate purchase, little dreaming that their homes would be taken from them through a judgment of the courts.

Immediately following the purchase of their town-site from the "Atherton Company," the refugees took up their residence in Rhode Island.   They numbered in all forty-eight families, ten of whom came from La Rochelle, ten from Saintonge, with perhaps as many more from Poitou ; the remainder hailing from Guyenne and Nor-

mandy.   Ézechiel Carré was the pastor and principal leader of the colony.   He had studied under Calvin at Geneva, and had already held the pastorate of two churches in France, at Mirameau in Saintonge, and La Roche Chalais in Guyenne.   Closely associated with him as a leader was Pierre Berthon de Marign (Peter Berton, or Burton), who was descended from a prominent family of Chattelerault in Poitou.   With Berton came his wife, Margaret, a native of the same town.   Pierre Ayrault, a native of Angers, province of Anjou, was the physician of the colony, and brought with him his wife, Françoise, his son Daniel, and nephew named Nicholas.   Besides these leaders the list of the colonists comprises the following names : André Arnaud, Jean Amian, Louis Allaire, Ézechiel Bouniot, Jean Beauchamps, Pierre Bretin dit Laronde, Daniel Belhair, Paul Bussereau, Guillaume Barbut, Jean Coudret, Jean Chadene, Paul Collin, Jean David, Josue David, Sr., Josue David, Jr., Pierre Deschamps, Théophile Froêtier, Jean Galay, Ézechiel Grazilier, Réné Grignon, Jean Germon, Jean Julien, Daniel Jouet, Étienne Jamain, Daniel Lambert, Pierre Le Moine, Étienne La Vigne, Moise Le Brun, Daniel Le Gendre, Jean Lafon, François Legare, Menar-deau Milard, Jacques Magni, Jean Magni, Élie Rambert, Jacob Ratier, Daniel Renaud, Étienne Rogineau, Daniel Targe, Abram Tourtellot, Pierre Traverrier, Pierre Tougére.

II

The first care of the settlers was to provide themselves

with places of shelter against the approaching winter. Homes built
According to the account left by Ayrault, some twenty
houses were built that fall, together with "some cellars
in the ground." The latter refers, undoubtedly, to the
dug-outs which many of the early settlers found it convenient to occupy until opportunity came for constructing
more comfortable and pretentious dwellings. The common type of such "cellars" was a square pit six or seven
feet deep, floored and walled with wood, and roofed with
logs covered by a layer of sod. If we may believe the
testimony of a contemporary writer and observer it was
possible for the occupants of these residences to "live
dry and warm with their families for two, three and four
years." During the winter they occupied their time in
clearing away the stones that littered their farms, felling
trees, and otherwise preparing for the planting season.
Fifty acres of land were set apart for the maintenance
of a school, provision was made for erecting a church as
soon as the weather permitted, and one hundred and fifty
acres were freely donated to Pastor Carré for his support ;
for among these worthy people, religion, education and
industry went hand in hand. And although their labours
were of necessity very severe at first they went about with
glad hearts, "for," says Ayrault, "we had a comfort ;
we could enjoy our worship to God."

In the course of a few years the appearance of "French- Frenchtown
town," as it was then called, and as the locality is known
to-day, was greatly changed. By their industry and skill
the refugees had turned a wilderness into a garden. The
"cellars" had been replaced by comfortable houses, the
forest had given way to orchards and vineyards, and
neat fences and hedges surrounded trim gardens. The
mild climate of that section of Rhode Island, resembling
Virginia, was found to be admirably adapted to the cultivation of grapes, and some persons in Boston who had
tasted the wine from them gave the judgment that they
"thought it as good as Bordeaux claret." Other plans,

too, filled the busy minds of the settlers; among them being the planting of mulberry trees upon which to breed silk-worms. In this effort to establish a profitable industry they hoped to be aided by further accessions of their countrymen, and the prospect seemed good that within a few years Rhode Island would be the home of a large number of Huguenot silk producers.

Land Claimed by the English

But though the future prospect of the settlement seemed bright, it was never realized. Within five years of its establishment only two families out of the forty-eight remained on the land they had improved and rendered fertile. For by the decision of the court it was made apparent that the refugees had been innocently occupying lands to which other parties held prior claims, and that the "Atherton Company" had deluded them with specious pretenses. In the summer of 1691 the settlement was broken up and the various families sought homes for themselves in more hospitable localities. Dr. Ayrault gives the following account of the troubles which beset the refugees:

Pitiable Plight of the Victims

The protecting of us in our liberty and property was continued not two years under said Government, before we were molested by the vulgar sort of the people, who flinging down our fences laid open our lands to ruin, so that all benefit thereby we were deprived of. Ruin looked on us in a dismal state; our wives and children living in fear of the threats of many unruly persons; and what benefit we expected from our lands for subsistence was destroyed by secretly laying open our fences by night and day; and what little we had preserved by flying from France, we had laid out under the then improvements. It looked so hard upon us, to see the cryes of our wives and children, lamenting their sad fate, flying from persecution, and coming under his Majesty's gracious Indulgence, and by the Government promised us, yet we, ruined. And when we complained to the Government, we could have no relief, although some would have helped us, we judge, if by their patience they could have borne such ill treatments as they must expect to have met with by the unruly inhabitants there settled also. Many of the English inhabitants compassionating our condition, would have helped us; but when they used any means therein, they were evilly treated. So that these things did put us then upon looking for a place of shelter, in our distressed condition ; and hearing that many of our distressed country people had been protected and well treated in Boston and Yorke, to seek out new habitations, where the Governments had compassion on them, and gave them relief and help, to their wives and children subsistance.   Only two families moving to Boston, and the rest to New York, and there bought lands, some of them, and had time given them for payment.   And so was they all forced away from their lands and houses, orchards and vineyards, taking some small matter from some English people for somewhat of their labour ; thus leaving all habitations.   Some people got not anything for their labour and improvements, but Greenwich men who had given us the disturbance, getting on the lands, so improved in any way they could, and soon pulled down and demolished our church.

It is only fair to the "Greenwich men" to state that the tract of land occupied by the French had been granted to these "unruly persons" by the legislature of Rhode Island in 1677, so that they looked upon the refugees as nothing short of interlopers. Besides doing everything in their power to dispossess the Huguenots, the people of Greenwich sent a petition to the governor in which they desired to know "by what order or Lawe or by what means those Frenchmen are settled in our town bounds," and in which they asserted that the presence of these intruders "proves great detriment to us," and prophesied that unless the French were made to vacate their illegal holdings the persons to whom the land belonged would "be utterly ruined." *Greenwich Men*

Their plan for establishing a community proving itself a failure, and having sunk the greater part of their funds in the common venture, the refugees could no longer proceed as a body but were forced to become widely scattered upon leaving the Narragansett settlement. The conditions prevailing in the province of New York seemed most favourable to the majority of the Huguenots, and of the twenty-five families who removed thither the following found homes in New York city itself: Bouniot, Coudret, the three David families, Galay, Grazilier, Jamain, Lafon, Lambert, La Vigne, LeBreton, the two *Scattered Colony*

Magni families, Rambert, Ratier, Robineau, both Targe
families, Traverrier, and Tougére.   The families of Ber-
tin, Chadene, Froêtier and Benaud joined the settlement
at New Rochelle.   The families of Allaire, Arnaud,
Beauchamps, Barbut, Deschamps, Legare and Tourtellot
went to Boston.   Germon and Grignon journeyed through
the woods to the settlement at Oxford.   South Carolina
received Amian, Jouet, Le Brun and Le Gendre, and
Milford, Connecticut, became the home of Paul Collin.
Jean Julien went only as far as Newport, while Ayrault
and Le Moine, of all the settlers, were the only ones to
remain in Greenwich.   Le Moine's descendants, under
the name of Money or Mawney, still possess the farm
which their ancestor cut out of the forest.   A few of the
emigrants, Pastor Carré among them, disappear from the
records after the year 1691, and it is impossible to trace
them to their new habitations or state what fate befell
them.

Boston Old Latin School Where French Church Met

CHAPTER V

THE FRENCH CHURCH IN BOSTON

I

THE history of the French Protestant Church in Boston forms an essential part of the story of the French who found refuge among the Puritans in this land which was destined to become one of religious liberty, although the principle of freedom of conscience had to be established through the independent stand of those who would not yield to Congregationalism in America those things from which they had fled in Europe.

The date of the organization of the French Protestants of Boston into a church is not definitely known.   Such an organization was in existence as early as 1685, with a settled minister, as is shown by the correspondence between Rev. Peter Daillé and Rev. Increase Mather, minister of the North Church in Boston and President of Harvard College.   Dr. Charles W. Baird thinks it highly probable that this congregation, like some others, may have been gathered together by the excellent Daillé, who gained the title of the " Apostle of the Huguenots in America," collecting them into churches in various sections of the country as Paul gathered the Christian converts in Asia Minor.   Daillé came to America in 1682, sent out by the Bishop of London to labour among the French emigrants in the new world.

We know that the French were treated most kindly by the ministers and the public authorities of Boston, who received the little flock of strangers as brothers fleeing from home persecution on account of their faith, and thus

Organized by 1685

Peter Daille

" Latine Schoolhouse " Granted for Meetings

157

worthy of every consideration. The Council of Boston
on November 24, 1687, granted liberty "to the French Congregation to meete in the Latine Schoolhouse at Boston as
desired." This Latin School was the beginning of the
educational system in Boston, and gave the name of
Schoolhouse Lane to what is now School Street. In the
old schoolhouse, which stood just southeast of the present
King's Chapel, the French Church continued to worship
for nearly thirty years. At least ten years earlier than
this there was an effort made to build a suitable "temple," as we learn from the Massachusetts Archives where
are preserved the Minutes of Council. Under date of
January 12, 1704 is this record :

Proposed
Temple

1704

> Upon a Representation made by Mr. Daillé Minister and the Elders
> of the French Protestant Church in Boston That his late Majesty, King
> William, had bestowed on them Eighty-three pounds to be Imploy'd
> towards building them a House for the Publick Worship of God, set-
> ting forth, That they have purchased a piece of land in Schoolhouse
> Lane in Boston for that use, Praying to be licensed to aske and receive
> the Benevolence of well-disposed persons that shall be willing to en-
> courage so pious a worke to assist them in said Building : Advised
> that License be accordingly granted and the moneys thereby collected
> to be put into the hands of Simeon Stoddard Esqr and to be applyed
> for the use afores'd and no other. And the House when built to be
> forever continued and improved for religious worship.

II

Permission
Refused

While the Council consented, the selectmen refused
their permission to build at this time, renewing however
the "offer of the free liberty to meet in the new schoolhouse," which, they said, was "sufficient for a far larger
number of persons" than that composing the congregation. Mr. Julien thinks it may fairly be surmised that
this refusal was based upon a feeling that the Huguenot
custom of observing Christmas and like festival days, together with the fact that the congregation spoke a
foreign tongue, seemed to justify to their Puritan neighbours a measure of restraint. This is not unlikely in

view of the fact that it was deemed essential to enact in
the laws of Massachusetts Bay, 1651, that "whosoever
shall be found observing any such day as Christmas, or
the like, either by forbearing labour, feasting, or any
other way upon such account as aforesaid, every such
person so offending shall pay for every such offense, five
shillings as a fine to the county."

It is known, moreover, that while Pastor Daillé was Liturgy not
admired and esteemed by the English, many of whom Liked
sometimes came to hear his eloquent sermons, yet the
stricter class of the Puritans could not be expected to
favour a liturgical worship that reminded them of what
they would fain forget, or observances which savoured to
them of popery.   Samuel Sewall, who was next door neighbour to one of the Huguenot merchants, Jacques Leblond,
enters in his famous diary a gentle protest against one of
these practices : "This day I spake with Mr. Newman
about his partaking with the French Church on the 25th
of December on account of its being Christmas day, as
they abusively call it."   Another surmise may be made,
namely, that the selectmen, who represented a government that was a combination of Church and State, did not
wish any other form of church organization to become so
firmly established as to own a house of worship, and
treated the French precisely as they did the Baptists who
desired to build meeting houses : with this difference, that
they were much more kindly and lenient in disposition
towards the French, and did not persecute them as they
did those of kindred blood who took their stand for
liberty of conscience.   There are, indeed many evidences
that the French had the cordial regard of their Puritan Regard for the
neighbours.   "'Tis my hope," said Cotton Mather, French
"that the English churches will not fail in respect to any
that have endured hard things for their faithfulness to
the Son of God."   This hope was realized.   While the
plans for a church building were delayed for a decade,
until after the death of the good minister, Daillé, who had

House in 1715 cherished the project, in 1715 a house of worship, an unpretentious brick building, was erected on the plot of
ground originally intended for it, and the French church
had a home of its own until it gave up its separate
existence.

III

The first pastor of the French church was a severe trial
Erratic Pastor both to the members and the outside friends.   Laurentius
Van den Bosch, more properly Laurent du Bois, of
French parentage, had lived some time in Holland and
adopted a Dutch patronymic.   He was erratic in the extreme.   Removing to England, he conformed to the English church, and came to America with a license from the
Bishop of London.   In Boston he speedily made himself
disliked by his disregard of rules and haughty and stubborn demeanour when reproved.   He also embroiled his
little congregation, and his conduct was so prejudicial
that Mr. Daillé wrote to Rev. Increase Mather, begging
him not to permit the annoyance occasioned by Mr.
"Vandenbosk" to diminish his favour towards the
French, since the fault of a single person ought not to be
imputed to others to their harm.

Fortunately for all concerned Vandenbosk soon left
Boston, and was followed by a man of very different
character, a most estimable minister who accompanied
Good the French Protestants from the island of St. Christopher
Bonrepos in 1686.   The coming of this company added much to
the strength of the French congregation, which was
never large in numbers, and the new pastor, David Bonrepos, was able to heal the divisions caused by his predecessor, and to enter into most pleasant relations with
his fellow ministers.   His little flock was to be pitied
that after a year of such admirable service to the cause in
Boston he was called to minister to the Huguenot colonies
in New Rochelle, Staten Island, and New Paltz, in the
province of New York.

"There are not more than twenty French families here," he wrote from Boston in the winter of 1687, "and their number is diminishing daily, as they remove into the country to buy or take up lands for cultivation with a view to permanent settlement." The way these comparatively few families held together and maintained their church is remarkable ; all the more so when it is considered that for eight years after Mr. Bonrepos left them they were pastorless, the pulpit being supplied irregularly by Ézechiel Carré, minister of the French colony in Narragansett, Daniel Bondet, of New Oxford, and occasionally by Rev. Nehemiah Walter, John Eliot's successor at the First Church in Roxbury, who was an accomplished French scholar, and was glad to render this service to the appreciative refugees.

Affairs were not promising until Mr. Daillé came to Massachusetts from New York, where he had been settled as minister of the French congregation from the time of his arrival in America. He served as pastor of the French church in Boston from 1696 until his death, nineteen years later. This was the period of greatest prosperity for the church. Mr. Daillé was received by his brother ministers with the consideration his character and talents merited. He bore a distinguished name—that of the famous minister of Charenton, Jean Daillé, one of the most learned scholars and theologians of his age. Before coming to America, moreover, Pierre had been professor in the great Protestant Academy of Saumur, the most celebrated of the four Protestant colleges of France, "for eighty years a torch that illuminated all Europe." Like other scholars of his time he wrote Latin fluently, and his letters to Rev. Increase Mather show the marks of the scholar and courteous French gentleman. He was in truth a fine type of the Huguenot, adding to his breeding and learning an earnest and unaffected piety. "He is full of fire, godliness and learning," wrote the Dutch minister Selyns of New York. "Banished on account of

Pastor Daille

A Scholar and Eloquent Preacher

his religion, he maintains the cause of Jesus Christ with untiring zeal." Such a minister and man was an influence of inestimable good to the New England colony, not simply to his own people, who revered and loved him as one who had shared the fires of persecution in the bonds of a common faith.

IV

The liturgy observed by the refugees in their public religious services, says Baird, was that which had been in use among the Reformed churches of France for nearly a century and a half. Modelled by Calvin upon primitive offices, it was of rigid simplicity, yet it was orderly and impressive. The Sunday service was preceded by the reading of several chapters of Holy Scripture. The reading was performed, not by the clergyman, but by a "lecteur," who was also the "chantra" or precentor, and who frequently united with these functions those of the parish schoolmaster during the week. In Daillé's day the "lecteur" was probably "old Mr. John Rawlins," whom the pastor remembered affectionately in his will. The reading ended with the decalogue; and then came the service conducted by the minister. It began with a sentence of invocation, followed by an invitation to prayer, and a general confession of sins. The congregation rose with the words of invocation, and remained standing during prayer, but resumed their seats when the psalm was given out for singing. This was the people's part—the service of song—in a ritual without other audible response; and all the Huguenot fervour broke out in those strains that had for generations expressed the faith and the religious joy of a persecuted race. A brief extempore prayer preceded the sermon. They closed with the Lord's Prayer and the Apostles' Creed, except when the Communion was to be administered; and after the benediction the congregation was dismissed with the word of peace, and an injunction to remember the poor, as they passed the

alms' chests at the church door. A prominent seat was
reserved in the church for the "anciens" or elders of the
congregation. These, with the pastor, constituted the
Consistoire, or Church Session. They were elected by
the people, holding office for a term of years, and had entire charge of the church government, both spiritual and
material.

V

The Earl of Bellomont, while governor of Massachu- Favourable
Opinion
setts, in an address to the General Court upon his last
visit to Boston, thus expressed his opinion of the French
refugees: "I recommend to your care the French minister of this town, who is destitute of a maintenance, because there are so few families here. Let the present
raging persecution of the French Protestants in France
stir up your zeal and compassion towards him. I wish
for your sakes the French Protestants had been encouraged among you. They are a good sort of people, very
ingenious, industrious, and would have been of great use
for peopling this country, and enriching it by trade."
Perhaps stimulated by this interest, the French Protestants in Boston presented a petition to him and to the
general court for aid in the support of the gospel ministry
among them. They "take leave to signifie that many of
their flock being already gone away who contributed
much for the subsistence of their minister, the few that
remain are not capable of furnishing the one-half that is
necessary, and they must undergo the unhappyness of
being deprived of the consolation of the holy ministry of Petition for
Aid
the word of God (whereof the unheard-of cruelty of the
persecutors of the church had deprived them in their own
country) unless they may obtain your Christian assistance." The petitioners also state that they have "borne
great charges in paying taxes for the poor of New Oxford, who by occasion of the war withdrew themselves,
and since that they have assisted many who returned to
Oxford in order to their resettlement."

This petition was referred to a committee, which reported that "for their encouragement as strangers and for the carrying on the publick worship of God amongst them there be paid unto their minister twelve punds of the publick treasury." This report was passed by both branches of the General Court, and so far as recorded was the only grant from the public funds.

The support was so slender that Mr. Daillé sometimes questioned whether he could remain ; but he lived up to his own declaration that "A minister must use every expedient before deserting his flock." Among these expedients was an appeal to the English Society for the Propagation of the Gospel in Foreign Parts ; an appeal that was seconded by Governor Dudley, who spoke of him as "an honest man and good preacher," who in the governor's belief had not more than thirty pounds per annum to live upon. The society declined, on the ground that the French church did not belong to the Anglican communion, and the pastor laboured on till his death, May 20, 1715, in his sixty-seventh year.

No minister of the early colonial days did more honour to his calling than the learned and devoted Pierre Daillé,

whose tombstone may be seen in the Old Granary Burying Ground. And however inadequate his salary, with the characteristic thrift of his people, this good man in some way managed to save up enough to be able to leave some considerable bequests in his will. His first remembrance was for the church and its ministers. He gave all

his French and Latin books—at a time when such books were of great value—to the church for the use of its ministers. He remembered their necessities, besides, by giving one hundred pounds to be let out at interest for the help and support of the minister ; and he bequeathed ten pounds towards the erection of the meeting house for which he had longed. For the rest he gave three hundred and fifty pounds in province bills or silver equivalent thereto, and his negro man-servant named

Kuffy and all his "plate, cloaths, household goods and furniture," to his "loving wife, Martha," who was his third wife ; the residue of his estate going to his brother Paul in Holland. In saving as in spirituality this French apostle set a worthy example to his brethren in the ministry. His character may be read as through an open window in a sentence in one of his private letters : "I have always determined to injure no one   His Motto by my words or otherwise, but on the contrary to serve whomsoever I might be able to serve."

<h2 style="text-align:center">VI</h2>

The French Church in Boston was to have but one more pastor, who was settled before many months. A call was given to André Le Mercier, a young man lately   Pastor graduated from the Academy of Geneva, and recom-   Le Mercier mended highly by the church authorities there, who took   from Geneva a paternal interest in the Calvinistic churches in America. A salary of one hundred pounds was offered him, the arrangement being made by Andrew Faneuil, indicating that the congregation was more prosperous than hitherto. Leaders in it were Andrew Faneuil, James Bowdoin, Daniel Johonnot, and Andrew Sigourney, each of whom at his death left a generous bequest to the pastor. This may perhaps explain in part the amount saved by Mr. Daillé, though such bequests to him are not a matter of record. Soon after the coming of the new minister the "meeting house" was built, diagonally opposite the Latin School on School Street. This pastorate continued thirty-four years. While not so brilliant a preacher as   Thirty-four Daillé, Le Mercier was pious and earnest and a diligent   Years' Pastor- worker in various fields. Two books from his pen are   ate extant : a "History of the Church and Republic of Geneva," and a "Treatise Against Detraction." He busied himself in the improvement of agriculture in Massachusetts, and was very zealous in humane endeavours to preserve the lives of seamen shipwrecked upon the

dangerous coast of Nova Scotia. In 1738 he petitioned
the governor and council of Nova Scotia for a grant of
the Sable Island, off that coast, that he might erect buildings thereon and stock the island with such domestic
animals as might be useful in preserving the lives of
escaped mariners. The grant was made, and the colonial
governments of Nova Scotia and Massachusetts issued
proclamations warning all persons against destroying or
removing the improvemènts made by the proprietor of
the island. It is said that many lives were saved by this
humane enterprise, which in a sense was the origin of the
life-saving coast service of to-day. Sable Island has continued to be the scene of frequent shipwrecks, and at
present the noble work begun by the Huguenot pastor of
Boston is carried on by government at an expense of four
thousand dollars yearly, maintaining a force of men
furnished with provisions and appliances for the relief
of shipwrecked sailors. Let it not be forgotten that the
sailors owe a debt of gratitude to André Le Mercier, the
refugee minister of Boston.

That the membership of the French Church decreased
under his ministry is not to be attributed chiefly to any
lack in him either as preacher or pastor, but rather to
the aptitude of the French for assimilation. The children became proficient in the English language, and
through their associations were led naturally to favour
the American churches. The tendency was irresistible,
and when the young people were "driven to other
churches" (a charge laid against Le Mercier with probably scant justice) it was only a question of time when
the French Church should cease to exist. This time came
in 1748, when the membership had become reduced to a
mere handful. Through intermarriage the leading French
families had formed close interests in such churches as
Trinity and King's Chapel, the Faneuils becoming prominent supporters of the latter. On the dissolution of the
French Church the meeting house passed into possession

of a new Congregational society, with the proviso that the building was to be preserved for the sole use of a Protestant sanctuary forever.   How little human provisions can control is shown by the fact that, in spite of the condition of sale, forty years later the Huguenot "temple" was sold to the Roman Catholics, and mass was said within its walls by a Romish priest November 2, 1788.   As for Le Mercier, he lived for sixteen years after the dissolution of the church, spending his last days upon an estate which he had purchased in Dorchester, Massachusetts, where he died March 31, 1764.

During Daillé's pastorate the church received a present Queen Anne of a Bible from Queen Anne for pulpit use.   This Bible Bible was highly esteemed and continued in use until the church dissolved, when it passed into possession of Rev. Mather Byles, first pastor of the Hollis Street Congregational Church, whose library was subsequently sold, the Bible going to Mr. E. Cobb, by whose widow it was presented in 1831 to the Divinity Library of Harvard University, where it is now carefully preserved.   The book is in a very good state of preservation; contains a few illustrations and maps, and the Apocrypha; and was printed in Amsterdam by the Elzeviers in 1669.

CHAPTER VI

PAUL REVERE

PAUL REVERE, born in Boston on January 8, 1735, was descended from an honourable Huguenot family—the Rivoires of Romagnieu. His father, Apollos Rivoire, came to Boston from the Island of Guernsey, when he was a lad of thirteen, and was set to learn the goldsmith's trade as apprentice to John Coney. After he had established himself in the business of a gold and silversmith, he married Deborah Hichborn; and the third child of this union was Paul Revere, craftsman, artist and patriot.

Revere received his education at the famous old "North Grammar School," which stood on North Bennett Street. After leaving school he entered his father's shop as an apprentice. He possessed a natural taste for drawing, and became very skillful in the use of the graver; executing most of the embellishments on the silverware then

manufactured in Boston. Many are the cups, spoons, mugs, pitchers, tankards, and other articles of beautiful patterns, made by him, and still owned by our New England families; some are now in every day use; all are treasured relics. If not as famous or gifted as Cellini, abundant monuments remain to prove that Revere was also an artist, as praiseworthy for the beauty and grace of his artistic creations as for their excellent handiwork. Long practice in the successful embellishment of silverware caused him to learn the art of engraving on copperplate, entirely self-taught; and numerous specimens of his handiwork in this line are still in existence, treasured memorials of a skillful and patriotic hand. Many of his pictures were political caricatures, and engravings of his-

168

PAUL REVERE, *Portrait by Gilbert Stuart*

toric scenes closely connected with the struggle for Independence.

But Revere was not wholly satisfied with leading a life of quiet prosperity. He longed for a taste of military life, and obtained his desire by joining the second expedition against Crown Point—serving through the campaign as a lieutenant of artillery. On his return to civil life he married Miss Sarah Orne and settled down to his trade. From thence on he devoted considerable of his time to engraving, and his art was immensely popular during the years preceding the Revolution. His bold attempts at copperplate engraving are rude enough to be sure; but they were considered good at the time, and were vastly better than nothing. His keen sense of humour found congenial employment in the caricatures of political events which issued from his shop and obtained a wide popularity. His art was always used in favour of the people, of the masses; he was quick at perceiving the striking features of the hour; and his ready genius to portray them made him the "offhand artist of many caricatures intended to bring ridicule upon the enemy, and the author of various sketches of interesting scenes of which he was an eye-witness."

Revere's patriotic services began in 1765, when he became one of the first members of the famous "Sons of Liberty"—an organization which soon became famous for its intimidation of the stamp-distributors and its keen opposition to any enforcement of the hated Stamp Act. He was likewise an active member of "Long Room Club" and the "North End Caucus"—the latter being the association which gave birth to "The Boston Tea-Party." Revere became the confidential messenger of the patriots and travelled thousands of miles on horseback, during troublous times, when railroads and steamboats were unknown. During all these years he had a large family to support; yet he was so constituted as to find sufficient leisure to interest himself in all the matters

Beginning of his Military Career

Popular as a Caricaturist

Sons of Liberty 1765

Boston Tea Party

Ardent Patriot

pertaining to the public good, watching closely the course of political events in the pre-revolutionary days. "With well-considered, settled opinions, his will was strong; while his general gifts rendered him competent to great emergencies, and equal to great events. The result was, that in a crisis like that of rousing the people to conflict on the eve of the first struggle for our Independence, he was the wise counsellor at home, and the daring actor in the field."

The Midnight Ride

Revere took many rides in the service of the Revolutionary party, but most famous of them all was the ride on the night of the 18th of April, 1775—"the most important single exploit in our nation's annals." Longfellow's account is known throughout the land; and therefore the insertion of the following extracts from Revere's own version of the affair is made at the risk of repeating a well-known story:

Revere's Telling of the Story

In the fall of 1774, and winter of 1775, I was one of upwards of thirty, chiefly mechanics, who formed ourselves into a committee for the purpose of watching the movements of the British soldiers, and gaining every intelligence of the movements of the Tories. We held our meetings at the Green Dragon Tavern. We were so careful that our meetings should be kept secret, that every time we met, every person swore upon the Bible that they would not discover any of our transactions but to Messrs. Hancock, Adams, and one or two more. . . .

April 18, 1775 Committee on Watch

In the winter, towards the spring, we frequently took turns, two by two, to watch the soldiers, by patrolling the streets all night. The Saturday night preceding the 19th of April, about twelve o'clock at night, the boats belonging to the transports were all launched, and carried under the sterns of the men-of-war. We likewise found that the grenadiers and light infantry were all taken off duty. From these movements we expected something serious was to be transacted.

The Lantern Signals

. . . I agreed with a Colonel Conant and some other gentlemen, that if the British went out by water, we would show two lanterns in the North Church steeple; and if by land, one as a signal; for we were apprehensive it would be difficult to cross Charles River, or get over Boston Neck. . . . I then went home, took my boots and surtout, went to the north part of the town, where I kept a boat; two friends rowed me across Charles River a little to the eastward where the

Somerset man-of-war lay. It was then young flood, the ship was winding, and the moon was rising.

They landed me on the Charlestown side. When I got into town, I met Colonel Conant and several others ; they said they had seen our signals. I told them what was acting, and went to get me a horse ; I got a horse of Deacon Larkin. While the horse was preparing, Richard Devens, Esq., who was one of the Committee of Safety, came to me, and told me that he came down the road from Lexington, after sundown, that evening ; that he met ten British officers, all well mounted and armed, going up the road.

I set off upon a very good horse ; it was then about eleven o'clock and very pleasant. After I had passed Charlestown Neck, and got nearly opposite where Mark was hung in chains, I saw two men on horseback, under a tree. When I got near them, I discovered they were British officers. One tried to get ahead of me, and the other to take me. I turned my horse very quick, and galloped towards Charlestown Neck, and then pushed for the Medford road. The one who chased me, endeavouring to cut me off, got into a clay pond, near where the new tavern is now built. I got clear of him, and went through Medford, over the bridge, and up to Menotomy. In Medford I waked the Captain of the minute men ; and after that, I alarmed almost every house till I got to Lexington.

At Lexington he gave the alarm to John Hancock and Samuel Adams, and then pressed on towards Concord "to secure the stores, etc., there." On his way, however, he met with some British officers ; "in an instant I was surrounded by four ;—they had placed themselves in a straight road, that inclined each way ; they had taken down a pair of bars on the north side of the road, and two of them were under a tree in the pasture. . . . I observed a wood at a small distance, and made for that. When I got there, out started six officers, on horseback, and ordered me dismount." And thus the "midnight ride of Paul Revere" came to an untimely end.

During the war Revere served his country in a dual capacity—as a Colonel in the Massachusetts artillery, and as a producer of gunpowder and cannon. In the capacity of Colonel, he had active command of the defenses of Boston harbour until he resigned from the service in 1779. As a manufacturer he was sent to Philadelphia by the

Council to gain a knowledge of powder making in order that the colony might make its own ammunition ; and he also was engaged to oversee the casting of cannon. He found time, meanwhile, to engrave and print the Massachusetts colony notes, and make dies for coins.

Successful Manufacturer

After the war Revere launched out into new enterprises, the most important of which was the establishment of a foundry where he undertook the casting of cannon, ironware and church bells. He perfected a process of preparing copper for use in bolts and spikes, etc., for naval purposes, and furnished the sheathing and fittings for *Old Ironsides*, and many another gallant vessel. His business prospered greatly, as his foundry was the only one in the country which could turn out sheet copper. It is interesting to note that he furnished the copper boilers for Robert Fulton's Hudson River steamboats.

Mechanics' Association 1795

A lasting monument to the ruling passion of his life is the Massachusetts Charitable Mechanics Association which, chiefly through his instrumentality, was formed in 1795. He was its first president, and continued in that office until 1799, when he declined re-election, although his interest in its affairs was undiminished and his counsel its main dependence.

Death in 1818

Revere died on May 10, 1818, at the age of eighty-three years. His body was placed in the Granary Burial Ground near that of his fellow Huguenot, Peter Faneuil, almost under the shadow of the State House whose corner-stone he helped to set and whose significance he had laboured to establish. It is pleasant to know that the last years of his useful, self-sacrificing life were passed in prosperity, and in the esteem and love of his countrymen. He was a fine type of the highly skilled artisan class which formed so large a part of the Huguenot emigration. He was equally a true representative of the Huguenots in his sturdy patriotism and devotion to the right as he saw it. He was a zealous and honoured member of the Masonic fraternity in Boston, as appears elsewhere.

CHAPTER VII

THE FANEUIL FAMILY

I

ONE of the foremost families of these early settlers from France was that of Faneuil—name indissolubly associated with Boston. In a list of the French nationality admitted into the Bay Colony by the Governor and Council, on February 1, 1691, are the names of Benjamin, John and Andrew Faneuil. As these brothers were among the refugees who were fortunate in bringing property with them to this country, it is probable that Benjamin had a financial interest in both of the Huguenot settlements—that at Oxford, Massachusetts, and at New Rochelle, New York, as his name appears in connection with them. When the Oxford enterprise was given up, after a ten years' struggle with hardship and Indians, Benjamin Faneuil chose New York for his residence, and established a home there, marrying one Anne Bureau, a French lady of that place. On a horizontal slab in Trinity churchyard, New York, is the inscription: "Here lies buried the body of Mr. Benjamin Faneuil of the city of Rochelle, France, who died the 31st of March, 1719, aged 60 years and 8 months."

Andrew Faneuil, brother of Benjamin, was one of the most prominent members of the Huguenot colony in Boston, and a leader in the organization of the French Protestant Church. He escaped from France and lived for a time in Holland, where he was married. This record is preserved: "The death of Mrs. Mary Catherine, wife of Mr. Andrew Faneuil, occurred in Boston,

[margin note: Benjamin Faneuil]

[margin note: Andrew Faneuil]

July 16, 1724, a gentlewoman of extraordinary perfections
both in mind and body.'' A portrait, representing her
as a beautiful woman, was brought to America and treasured in the family. The exact date of their coming is not
known, but Andrew's name appears on the tax list in
1691, and it is plain that he was a man of affairs in the
town at that time. Like his brother, he was doubtless
one of those fortunate Huguenots who, having an estate
in France, had been able to take a goodly portion with
him when he left his native land, and had not come
empty handed to Boston. It is evident that he made an
early investment in the city, for in a petition dated February 20, 1709, to build a wharf from the bottom of King
(now State) Street to low water mark, it is described as
"of the width of King Street, between Mr. East Ap-
thorp's and Mr. Andrew Faneiol's.'' He was soon well
established in a lucrative business, and the owner of large
real estate interests. His warehouse was on Butler Square,
out of State Street, and his mansion, one of the finest in
the city, surrounded by seven acres of admirably kept
gardens, was on Tremont Street, opposite King's Chapel
Burying Ground.

Citizen in 1691

His Fine Mansion

II

Andrew Faneuil was a positive, peculiar and interesting character. He did not remarry, though he kept up
his stately establishment, and had black and white servants in plenty. His brother Benjamin of New York had
a family of eleven children, and Andrew undertook the
care of three of them—Benjamin and Peter, the oldest
sons, and Mary Anne, their sister. He chose Benjamin,
his nephew, for his heir, on the one freakish condition
that the young man should never marry. Benjamin
agreed, and the relations went on harmoniously enough
until a certain Miss Mary Cutler, a young lady of many
personal attractions, educated, refined, and a poetess to
boot, led the nephew to choose expulsion from his home,
with his love, just as the uncle preferred exile with

Nephew Benjamin Loses a For-tune

Peter Faneuil

religious liberty to France and spiritual enslavement. Andrew was inflexible, and turned to Benjamin's brother, Peter, as his hope for a worthy heir and representative. Peter was without matrimonial inclinations and accepted the terms, becoming heir presumptive in his turn, and likewise the business partner of his uncle.   The ousted Benjamin, who had gone into business on his own account, was prospering, and all three Faneuils were happy and highly respected, and becoming rich and influential as the result of ability, integrity, and that sturdy quality of conscience that compels recognition.   Three of the New York Benjamin's daughters had meanwhile married Boston citizens—a clergyman, a lawyer, and a prosperous merchant—so that the Faneuil family was well established in the business and social life of Boston.

Nephew Peter Becomes Heir

Andrew Faneuil died in February, 1738, and the magnificence of his funeral gave evidence of the position he had attained in the city.   The newspaper report says, "Last Monday the corpse of Andrew Faneuil, Esquire, whose death we mentioned in our last, was honourable interred here, above 1,100 persons of all Ranks, beside the Mourners, following the Corpse, also a vast number of spectators were gathered together on the Occasion, at which time the half-minute guns from on board several vessels were discharged.   And 'tis supposed that as the Gentleman's fortune was the greatest of any among us, so his funeral was the most generous and expensive of any that has been known here."

A Great Funeral 1738

Peter Faneuil saw to it that every propriety was observed, and three thousand pairs of mourning gloves were distributed to the friends in attendance, while two hundred mourning rings were given to the nearer friends of the family.   The business and estate now fell to Peter. In his will, however, Andrew proved his devotion to his faith by first of all leaving his warehouse in trust for the support of the ministers and elders of the French church in Boston, which he had staunchly supported.   If the church should cease to be, as he foresaw it might through the intermarriage of the Huguenot with the Puritan element, the warehouse was to revert to his heirs.

III

How much property Andrew Faneuil left was not announced, but it was commonly understood that he was the wealthiest merchant in the province, and Peter now succeeded to that proud position. He was thirty-eight years old when he became the "topiniest merchant in the town," as Thomas Hancock put it. He was corpulent, with large, well-rounded features, had a genial disposition, and ambitions and tastes in keeping with his fortune. He was fond of display and good living, and his home was the scene of open-handed hospitality. He ordered from London a "handsome chariot with two sets of harness, with the arms as inclosed in the same in the handsomest manner that you shall judge proper, but at the same time nothing gaudy," and ordered also "two sober men, the one for a coachman, the other for a gardener; and as most servants from Europe are apt when here to be debauched with strong drink, rum, etc., being very plenty, I pray your particular care in this article." He sends for the "latest best book of the several sorts of cookery, which pray let be of the largest character for the benefit of the maid's reading." He refurnishes and restocks the mansion, and among other new articles, buys for house use "as likely a strait negro lad" as could be found, "of a tractable disposition and one that had had the smallpox."

With the waning of the French church, Peter Faneuil became a worshipper at Trinity church, of which his brother-in-law, the Rev. Addington Davenport, was rector. In one of his orders from London is this item: "Purchase for me 1 handsome, large, octavo Common Prayer Book of a good letter, and well bound, with one of the same in French for my own use." Thus the mother

Boston's Wealthiest Merchant

Peter Described

A Good Liver

Generous and Just

FANEUIL HALL AND THE OLD FEATHER STORE

tongue remained dear to him. He was one of the early
members of the Episcopal Charitable Society, and gave a
large sum to Trinity church to support the families of the
deceased clergy.   Indeed, every charity of the time had
his name on its subscription list for a generous sum.
While Peter Faneuil was liberal to all good objects, he
was scrupulous in his business transactions, and expected
to be dealt with justly, in the same spirit in which he
dealt with others.   He did not like to be wronged out of
any amount, however small, as the following extract from
his correspondence shows : ''I have been very much
surprised that ever since the death of Captain Allen, you
have not advised me of the sale of a horse belonging to
my deceased uncle, left in your hands by him, which I
am informed you sold for a very good price, and I am
now to request the favour you would send me the net
proceeds in sweetmeats and citron water, your compli-
ance with which will stop me from giving some of my
friends the trouble of calling you to an account there.   I
shall be glad to know if Captain Allen did not leave
a silver watch and some fish, belonging to a servant of
mine, with some person of your island, and with who ?
I expect your speedy answer.''

As Mr. Brown, the biographer of the family, puts it,
''While giving a pound with one hand, he was holding
the other for a penny that was justly his.'' Some branches
of his business, although endorsed by the trade and society of his time as perfectly legitimate, would be found
wanting if weighed in the balance of modern commercial
integrity—from which we may see that, after all, the
standards have been raised instead of lowered, as is often
intimated by those pessimistically inclined.   Trading with
so many ports, he received all kinds of merchandise,
wines and other liquors seeming to predominate, while
occasionally a negro slave was consigned to him.   He
lived up to his conscience, however, for he writes to one
correspondent : ''I would have you know that I am not

so fond of a commission as to go a begging for it, or to do any base thing to attain it. I bless God I have fortune enough to support myself without doing any base action." The products of the fisheries, with tobacco, tar and staves, made up the burden of his outgoing cargoes. He built sailing vessels for his own trade and for others, and in addition to his trade with foreign ports he carried on an extensive commerce with New York and Philadelphia. The whole commercial world rated Peter Faneuil as a responsible merchant, and he never wanted for business.

Slave Trade   The slave trade was then not disreputable, and Peter Faneuil, like his contemporaries, was often found engaged in it. "The merchants of Boston quoted negroes like any other merchandise demanded by their correspondents." He also did not think it wrong on occasion to evade the duties of the custom-house, though he was honest in his declaration, "I value my character more than all the money on earth." He simply shared what may be called a common commercial conscience of the times, which ever counted government as a lawful prey, and accounted smuggling as skillful rather than dishonest.

The Jolly Bachelor   Peter Faneuil became known in his circle of intimates as the "Jolly Bachelor," which name he gave to one of his ships. His sister Mary Anne looked out for the care of the household and presided with grace over his establishment. It is certain, however, that he had his love affair, and that if a certain Miss Mary Jekyll had not accepted a Mr. Richard Saltonstall instead, she might have found a husband in Mr. Peter Faneuil. After this break in his desire for a single life, he had no second, so far as is known, and his sister remained mistress of the fine mansion and generally desirable situation.

IV

With all his love of display and good living, Peter

Faneuil was a public-spirited citizen. While engrossed
in the cares of extensive business, he had vital inter-   Faneuil Hall
est in the welfare of his neighbours and friends and
in the future good of the town of Boston. From his own
experience he realized the disadvantages under which
trade was conducted without a local market. He desired
improvement in this direction, and was finally led to test
the public sentiment, which had been strangely an-
tagonistic to the establishment of a public market, by
making a proposition which is set forth in a petition,
sent to the selectmen with the signatures of three hundred
and forty prominent citizens attached. The petition declared that Peter Faneuil, Esq., "hath been generously
pleased to offer at his own cost and charge to erect and
build a noble and complete structure or edifice to be improved for a market, for the sole use, benefit and advantage of the town, provided that the town of Boston
would pass a vote for that purpose, and lay the same under such proper regulations as shall be thought necessary,
and constantly support it for the said use." So the warrant for the town meeting was posted, and the matter was
discussed pro and con, for there was a great division
of opinion. There were seven hundred and twenty-
seven ballots cast, and the yeas won by only seven votes.
Thus near did Boston come to losing Faneuil Hall and
the "cradle of liberty." But Peter Faneuil's plans in-   The Cradle of
cluded a public meeting hall in addition to a market,   Liberty 1742
and it was due to him that the people had a forum. In
August, 1742, after two years spent upon the work, the
selectmen were informed that the market was finished,
and on September 10, the keys were delivered to the city
authorities. There had been a great change in public
opinion, and now the citizens unanimously voted to "accept this most generous and noble benefaction for the use
and intention they are designed for."

The name came from no initiative of Peter Faneuil, but   Source of the
from an outside source. The records show that it was   Name

voted, on motion of Thomas Hutchinson, later royal
governor, "that in testimony of the town's gratitude to
the said Peter Faneuil, Esq., and to perpetuate his memory,
the hall over the market place be named Faneuil Hall."
In response Mr. Faneuil said, "I hope what I have done
will be for the service of the whole country." Little did
he realize how true a prophecy his words were. And in
this way this French Protestant, whose father came to
America as a refugee on account of his religious convictions, wrote his name indelibly on the pages of American
history. By vote his picture was drawn at full length at
the expense of the town, and placed in the hall; and the
Faneuil coat-of-arms, so much prized by the merchant,
was carved and gilded by Moses Deshon, bought by the
town and likewise set up in the hall. The selectmen immediately began to meet in the new and more comfortable
quarters provided for them, and selected one of their
number to purchase "two pairs of brass candlesticks with
steel snuffers, and a poker for the town's use." The
house given by Peter Faneuil was regarded as the greatest
munificence the town of Boston had received. It was
built of brick, two stories high, and in comparison with
other buildings in the vicinity of Dock Square presented
a commanding appearance. With the exception of the
old State House, all the buildings that surrounded Faneuil
Hall have been replaced. But Faneuil Hall "stands and
will remain as long as the power of patriotic citizens can
retain it. The force of sentiment is seen in its preservation; and many generations yet unborn will early learn to
cherish this New England forum." The power of the
sentiment of religion that led the Huguenots to America
is akin to the sentiment of patriotism that made them of
so much good to the new world.

History of Faneuil Hall As for the history of Faneuil Hall, it can only be said
here that it was burned in the destructive fire of January
13, 1761; was rebuilt by money secured by a lottery, the
tickets being signed by John Hancock; was enlarged and

THE FANEUIL MANSION ON TREMONT STREET, BOSTON

much altered in appearance in 1805–6 under direction of
Charles Bulfinch, who designed the State House on
Beacon Hill; and in 1898 was practically rebuilt with
steel walls, though the Bulfinch appearance was retained
outside and within. While only a small portion of the
original hall given by Peter Faneuil remains, it is still
Faneuil Hall, with all its sacred associations. In the
words of Lafayette, the great Frenchman who did so
much for America in a critical period, and whose sympathies were with the Huguenots, "May Faneuil Hall ever   Words of
stand, a monument to teach the world that resistance to   Lafayette
oppression is a duty, and will under true republican institutions become a blessing."

V

Peter Faneuil died the next year after his market and
hall had been given to Boston, March 3, 1743. The   Death 1743
market bell was tolled from one o'clock until the funeral
was over, by town order, and every honour was paid to
his memory. According to the obituary in the *News
Letter*, "he was a most generous spirit, whose hospitality
to all and secret unbounded charity to the poor, made his
life a public blessing, and his death a general loss to, and
universally regretted by, the inhabitants; the most public-
spirited man, in all regards, that ever yet appeared on the
northern continent of America." In addition to a great   Man of Public
funeral there was a public memorial service. From Will-   Spirit
iam Nadir's Almanac, under date of March 10, 1743, this
extract is taken: "Thursday 10, buried Peter Faneuil,
Esq., in the 43d year of age, a fat, corpulent, brown,
squat man, hip short, lame from childhood, a very large
funeral went around ye Town house; gave us gloves at ye
funeral, but sent ye gloves on 11 day, his Coffin covered
with black velvet, & plated with yellow plates."
John Lovell, master of the Boston Latin School, delivered the funeral oration at the memorial service held in
Faneuil Hall, and this was the beginning of such services

there.   A single quotation must suffice :   " It was to him
the highest enjoyment of riches, to relieve the wants of
the needy, from which he was himself exempted, to see
mankind rejoicing in the fruits of his bounty, and to feel
that divine satisfaction which results from communicating happiness to others.   His alms flowed like a fruitful
river, that diffuses its streams through a whole country.
He fed the hungry, and he cloathed the naked, he com-
forted the fatherless and the widows in their afliction,
and his bounties visited the prisoner.   So that Almighty
God in giving riches to this man, seems to have scattered
blessings all abroad among the people."

From this common testimony as to his charity, he must
have been entitled to large praise as a benefactor of the
needy.   He failed to make a will, and the estate which
his uncle expressly withheld from his brother Benjamin
now came into the custody of that individual, and a good
share of it into his possession.   The estate was soon scattered.   The Faneuils during the Revolutionary days were
among the Tories, and fled either to England or Nova
Scotia.   The Faneuil tomb is in the westerly corner of the
Granary Burying Ground.   After the Revolution, the
family played an unimportant part in the life of Boston ;
but Andrew and Peter Faneuil will ever be among the
noted names of the Huguenot settlers in the new world.
They represented in many respects the best traits of the
Huguenot character, and show what splendid material
France lost through her misguided policy.

CHAPTER VIII

THE BOWDOINS, DANAS, AND OTHER FAMILIES

I

JAMES BOWDOIN, elder son of Pierre Baudouin the emigrant, was born in 1676. He became a highly successful Boston merchant, was for a number of years a member of the Massachusetts council, and when he died, in 1747, was accounted to have left the largest estate ever owned by any citizen of the province. The Bowdoins 1676

His son, James, was born in Boston in 1727 and was graduated from Harvard in 1745. By the death of his father two years later he came into possession of the great estate, and for the next few years devoted himself to the care of his property and to scientific and literary studies. When he was twenty-four years old he paid a visit to Benjamin Franklin, with whom he afterwards corresponded to such good purpose that Franklin read his letters before the Royal Society of London. It is interesting to note that in one of these letters Bowdoin suggested the theory, now generally accepted, that under certain conditions the phosphorescence of the sea is due to the presence of minute animals. During his entire life he was greatly interested in natural science, and it is highly probable that he would have made still more valuable contributions to knowledge if patriotism and ill health had not cut short his studies. But although suffering from consumption for many years, he nevertheless threw himself with ardour into the turbulent political life of the day. James Bowdoin Scientist

His public career began with his election to the Massa-

183

chusetts General Court when he was twenty-six years old.

His ability soon asserted itself and three years later he was made a member of the council.   Here he distinguished himself by his firm opposition to the royal governor and to the encroachments of the crown upon the popular

liberty of the colony.   His popularity with the people became thus solidly intrenched, while the royal officers both hated and feared him.   In 1769 he was again chosen as one of the councillors and was promptly negatived by Governor Bernard.   This aroused the resentment of the Bostonians, and they showed their feeling by immediately electing him to the assembly with an overwhelming majority.   Sickness alone prevented him from attending the Continental Congress to which he was delegated in 1774, but by the end of the next year he was so far recovered as to be able to act as president of the council.

The constitutional convention which assembled in 1779 chose him for its presiding officer, and he took prominent part in shaping the action of that body.   Shortly after his election as governor of the state in 1785, he was confronted by a difficult problem in the shape of Shay's Rebellion.   His firmness and decisive action quelled the rapidly growing insurrection without resort to bloodshed, though, in taking his prompt measures he was compelled to pay the expenses of the militia largely out of his own pocket.   In the words of President Timothy Dwight, "This measure preserved the State, perhaps the Union, and deserved for the author of it a statue."   His last public service was as a member of the convention that adopted the federal constitution in 1788.

Although most of Governor Bowdoin's rapidly declining energies were devoted to politics, he yet found time to aid and further many charitable and scientific enterprises. He was one of the founders, and the first president, of the American Academy of Arts and Letters ; and willed to the society his valuable library.   He aided in establishing the Massachusetts Humane Society.   For many years he was a Trustee and Fellow of Harvard College ; and was a Fellow of the Royal Societies of London and Edinburgh. Bowdoin College has proved a splendid memorial to his generosity and interest in the public welfare.

Patron of Bowdoin College

His son, James, born in Boston in 1752, was graduated from Harvard, travelled extensively abroad, and then returned to serve in the assembly, state senate and state council. He was a delegate to the constitutional convention, and in 1804 was appointed minister to Spain. He was a man of fine tastes and scholarship and of an ardent disposition which was constantly thwarted by physical weakness. At the outbreak of the Revolution he had enlisted, and it was the keenest regret of his life that sickness had prevented him from serving. He was a generous patron of Bowdoin College, giving it six thousand acres of land, a large sum of money, and bequeathing it his library and collections of painting and scientific apparatus. He died without issue and "with him the name of Bowdoin passed away from the annals of New England."

Last of the Name

Bequests to the College

The excellent Huguenot blood of the Bowdoins persists, however, in the descendants of Governor Thomas L. Winthrop, who married Elizabeth Temple, granddaughter of Gov. James Bowdoin. The late Robert C. Winthrop, lawyer and statesman, was thus a great-grandson of James Bowdoin.

II

The sole ancestor of the Dana family in America was Richard Dana, who came to Cambridge, Mass., in 1640. The only record of the name in England is that of the Rev. Edmund Dana, a great-grandson of Richard, who went to England from America in 1761. According to the traditions of the family, Richard's father was a Huguenot who fled from France and settled in England about 1629. One of Richard's descendants, Judah Dana, is said to have had a silver cup which had once been

The Dana Family 1640

among the belongings which the refugee had carried with
him out of France. In view of the fact that the name
does not occur in England, and that no documentary
proof has come to light, the family tradition must be accepted.

Among Richard Dana's numerous descendants there
have been many men of eminence. It will be possible to
mention only a few of them here. Richard Dana, grandson of the emigrant, was born in Cambridge in 1699. He
was graduated from Harvard in 1718 and practiced law
in Boston, becoming one of the two acknowledged leaders
of the bar in that city. He was a staunch patriot and
took a prominent part in the opposition to British oppression. All the offices which lay in the people's gift were
his if he so desired, but he wished no titles. Between the
years 1763 and 1772 he called and presided over many
patriotic meetings of Bostonians. He was one of the first
members of the Sons of Liberty, and in 1765 acted as
chairman of the citizen committee which devised ways
and means to thwart the Stamp Act. His death in 1772
was felt to be a distinct loss by all the patriots of Massachusetts.

His son, Francis, born in 1743, devoted himself to the
cause of colonial rights. He was a member of the first
Provincial Congress of Massachusetts. In 1775 he went
to England with confidential letters bearing on the state
of feeling in America, in the hope of persuading Parliament to retract. A year later he was elected to the executive council of the colony, and was also sent to the
Continental Congress, where he became chairman of the
committee on the reorganization of the army. He was
one of the embassy which negotiated for peace in 1779.
In 1780 he was sent as minister to Russia, remaining there
in an endeavour to get Russia to recognize the independence of the United States—a task in which he was unsuccessful. After further service in the Continental Congress
he became a justice in the Supreme Court of Massa-

Richard Dana
Patriot

Resisting the
Stamp Act

Francis 1743

Public Spirit
and Service

chusetts, and was made chief justice in 1791, an office which he held until his death, fifteen years later.

His son, Richard Henry Dana, was for many years closely connected with American literature. He was one of the founders of the *North American Review*, and published poems, stories and essays which made him one of the most eminent writers of his day. His son, Richard Henry, Jr., will always be remembered as the author of that American classic, "Two Years Before the Mast." Richard Henry Dana Author

James Dana, born in 1735, was a famous Congregational minister. His oldest son, Samuel W., was a congressman for thirteen years and a senator for eleven. Joseph Dana, a grandson of the emigrant, was also a well-known Congregational preacher, retaining his pastorate at Ipswich for sixty-two years. His grandson, Israel T., was the leading surgeon of Maine and one of the founders of the Maine General Hospital. Judah Dana was senator from Maine in 1836, and his son, John Winchester, was governor of that State in 1847. Samuel L. Dana was prominently identified with the progress of cotton manufacturing in New England, making many improvements in the methods of printing, bleaching, etc. He also contributed to the growth and knowledge of scientific agriculture. Charles A. Dana was for many years the editor of the New York *Sun*, making a record in American journalism equalled only by Horace Greeley's. The works of James Dwight Dana, professor of mineralogy at Yale for forty-five years, are known by every geologist throughout the civilized world. Eminent Sons

This remarkable family, with its wide reaching influence in professional lines, in public life, in education and religion is a signal witness to the value of the Huguenot contribution to American life.

III

OTHER IMMIGRANTS

About the time that the companies of destitute refugees

Men of Estates were coming into Boston and Salem, other and more fortunate Huguenots made their way to New England. "Men of estates," as they were referred to in Sewall's diary, who had been able to save something from the wreck of their fortunes in France, began to seek new homes for themselves in the colonies. It has been estimated that one hundred and fifty families came to New England during the last decade of the seventeenth century. Such an estimate only approximates the real number, for the names of many families were never entered on any records that are accessible to the historian, and even of those whose names were recorded many have always been regarded as of English origin, owing to the fact that their French patronymics had become anglicized beyond all hope of recognition.

The following are the names of some of the more important refugees who were settled in and near Boston by the end of the century :

Andrew Sigourney   Andrew Sigourney, who became the ancestor of a well-known New England family, was a citizen of La Rochelle at the time of the Revocation. When the time came for a squad of dragoons to be quartered in his house Sigourney and his wife, Charlotte Pairan, decided to hold to their faith and make their escape from France. To this end they laid their plans carefully, and by making use of several ingenious devices they were able to get a portion of their property on board a friendly vessel then lying in the harbour. The day set for their attempt to escape was a holiday which they felt sure the soldiers would wish to celebrate. Accordingly they made ready a tempting Escape from France feast, and while the unsuspecting troopers were in the middle of their celebration, the family stole unobserved from the house and got aboard the ship, in which they were carried safely to England. From England they came to Boston in the summer of 1686.

Daniel Johonnot   Daniel Johonnot, nephew of Andrew Sigourney, was a member of the Oxford settlement until 1696, when he came to Boston and set up a distillery. In the year 1700 he married his cousin, Suzanne Sigourney, in the Old South Church. His business, which was a prosperous one, was carried on successively by his son Andrew and grandson of the same name.

Anthony Olivier (Oliver) was a native of Niort, in Poitou. He settled in Boston shortly after the Revocation and engaged in the chandlery trade. His daughter, Susanna, married Andrew Johonnot, and the name is still found in Boston to-day in the family of George Stuart Johonnot Oliver. *Olivier*

Peter Chardon became one of the richest merchants in the town. At the time of the Revocation he was a banker in Paris. He fled to England and was naturalized in 1687, coming to America shortly afterwards. His house, a handsome mansion for that day, stood for many years at the corner of the street which was named in his honour. His son Peter, the last of the family, died in the West Indies in 1766. Of him John Adams spoke as being one of the few young men of Boston who was on "the directest road to superiority." *Chardon*

Paix Cazneau (Casno) was one of the Oxford settlers. Returning to Boston, he went into business as a feltmaker and built up a fortune. He was active in trade and an influential citizen as late as the year 1738. He had a son Isaac and a daughter who married a refugee named Adam de Chezeau. *Cazneau*

John Chabot was probably from Bergerac, in Guienne. His name is mentioned in 1700 as among the leading members of the French Church, who are planning soon to leave Boston. From Boston he undoubtedly went to New York, for it is recorded that in 1711 a John Chabot subscribed to the building of Trinity Church steeple. *Chabot*

Peter Canton, one of the Oxford men, was in Boston as early as 1692 making rosin in partnership with Gabriel Bernon. *Canton*

Anthony LeBlond (Blond), a refugee from Normandy, *LeBlond*

was a prosperous chandler in Boston before the end of the century. His brother James must have been established in the town before the year 1690, for in that year his wife Ann joined Cotton Mather's Church. James was the father of four sons, James, Peter, Gabriel and Alexander, and three daughters, Phillippa, Ann and Marian.

Rawlings
Teacher

John Rawlings probably came to Boston as early as 1684. In 1683 he was one of the "Ruling Elders" of the French Church in Southampton, England. His name has come down to us as the honoured "French schoolmaster in Boston" for a long period of years, and he was a man of marked piety and uprightness of life. In 1696 his name was recorded as one of the elders of the French Church.

Beauchamp

Jean Beauchamp was the son of a Parisian lawyer who fled to England and died there in 1688. Jean came to Boston the year previous to his father's death. After the failure of the Narragansett settlement he became a prosperous leather dresser and owned a substantial house on Washington Street. In 1720 he removed to Hartford, Connecticut, where one of his daughters married Allan McLean, another married Thomas Elmer, a third became the wife of Jean Chenevard, while the fourth married into the Laurens (Lawrence) family.

Allaire

Louis Allaire, of La Rochelle, a nephew of Gabriel Bernon, was the founder of the firm of "Louis Allaire and Company," which carried on an extensive trade with southern ports. A descendant settled in New York and founded the Allaire Iron Works; he was philanthropic and established a model working men's village in New Jersey, the first settlement of its kind. The enterprise was not financially successful, but Allaire, the employer, was recognized as a benefactor.

Boutineau

Stephen Boutineau, a lawyer from La Rochelle, became one of the leading French citizens of Boston. He settled first in Casco, Maine (now Portland), and came to Boston in 1690. In 1708 he married Mary Baudouin, who bore to him six sons and four daughters.

A further list of the refugees includes the names of Abraham Tourtellot, who married Marie Bernon ; Peter Signac, who manufactured hats and carried on a trade in peltries from Newfoundland ; John Tartarien, of Saintonge ; David Basset, mariner and trader, one of the first refugees to make Boston his home ; Dr. Peter Basset, of Marennes ; Philip Barger, who died in 1702, leaving a son Philip ; William Barbut, of Languedoc, who was admitted into Massachusetts in 1691, and soon afterwards became an elder in the church ; Francis Legaré, of Lyons, who practiced the goldsmith's trade, bought an estate in Braintree, and founded a family of whom the Hon. Hugh Swinton Legaré was an able representative ; Thomas Moussett, who owned a tract of land in Roxbury in 1698 and was an elder in the church ; Isaac Biscon, a native of the island of Oleron ; Francis Bridon (Bredon, Breedon) who fled from the Port des Barques in 1681 ; Stephen Robineau, whose daughter Mary married Daniel Ayrault in 1703 ; Abraham Sauvage (Savage from St. Algis), in Picardy ; James Montier, from Rouen ; Jean Maillet, Joseph Roy, Bastian Gazeau, Deblois of Saintonge, René Grignon, Louis and Henri Guionneau, Louis Boucher, Jean Girote and Jean Petel.

Family
Names

CHAPTER IX

A DESCRIPTION OF EARLY BOSTON

ONE of the best descriptions of Boston and its surrounding settlements in these early days is to be found in the "Narrative of a French Protestant Refugee in Boston." Some extracts from that very valuable document will be of interest here, as they show the conditions by which the Huguenot settlers were surrounded, and give a hint as to the kind of life which went on in Boston prior to the opening of the eighteenth century. As will be gathered from the first selection, the narrative was written as a guide to refugees in London who contemplated emigrating to America. Says the author :

"First, in order to come to this country, it is necessary to embark at London, from which place a ship sails about once a month. The most favourable time to embark is the latter part of March, or the end of August and the beginning of September. These are the proper seasons ; all the more because the weather is then neither too hot nor too cold, and one does not experience the dead calms which occur frequently in summer, and on account of which vessels take four months to cross hither : besides which, the heat often produces sickness on shipboard. If one will provide himself with suitable refreshments of all kinds, he will not have to endure any discomfort. With regard to danger, one must be particular to take passage on a good vessel, well equipped with men and with cannon, and well provided with an unfailing supply of bread and water.

"There is risk only in approaching land, and on the sand banks which one finds. (After stating that ' *Cap*

192

Coot' was sighted some twenty leagues south of Boston, he continues) :   On the following day we reached Boston, after meeting a multitude of exceedingly pretty islands in front of Boston, most of them cultivated, and inhabited by peasants, and presenting a very pleasing appearance. Boston is situated within a bay three or four leagues in circumference, and shut in by these islands.   Here ships ride in safety, in all kinds of weather.   The town is built upon the slope of a little hill, and is about as large as La Rochelle.   With the surrounding land it measures not more than three miles around, for it is almost an island. It would only be necessary to cut through the sand about three hundred paces, and in less than twice twenty-four hours Boston would be made an island, with the sea beating upon it on every side.   The town consists almost entirely of houses built of wood : but since the ravages made by fires, it is no longer allowed to build of wood, and several very handsome houses of brick are at present going up.   .   .   .   There is no other religion here than the Presbyterian, Anglican, the Anabaptist, and our own. We have no Papists, at least none that are known to us.

Boston Harbour

A Wooden Town

Varieties of Religion

"One may bring with him persons bound to service, of whatever calling ; they are indispensable in order to the cultivation of the ground.   One may also hold negroes, male and female ; there is not a house in Boston, however small the means of the family, that has not one or two. Some have five or six, and all earn well their living.   The savages are employed, for the tilling of the lands, at a shilling and a half, or eighteen pence per day, with their board.   .   .   .   Negroes cost from twenty to forty pistoles, according to their skill or vigour.   There is no danger that they, or even the bond-servants will leave you, for so soon as one is missing from the town, it is only necessary to give notice of the fact to the savages, and describe the person to them, promising them some reward, and the man is soon found.   But it seldom happens that they leave you, for they would not know whither

Negro Slavery

to go, few roads having been opened, and those that have
been opened leading to English towns or villages, which,
upon your writing to them, would forthwith send back
your people to you.

High Wages   "Houses of brick and of wood can be built cheaply, as
it regards the materials, for as to manual labour that is
very dear; a man could scarcely be induced to work for
less than twenty-four pence per day and his board. . . .
The rivers abound with fish, and we have so much, both
of sea and river fish, that no account is made of it. There
are persons here of every trade, and particularly carpen-
ters for ship-building. The day after my arrival, I wit-

Ship Building nessed the launching of a vessel of three hundred tons,
and since then, two others, a little smaller, have been
launched. This town carries on an extensive trade with
the islands of America and with Spain. To the islands
they take meal, salt beef, salt pork, codfish, staves, salt
salmon, salt mackerel, onions, and oysters—a great quantity of which are caught here—preserved with salt in
barrels; and upon their return they bring sugar, cotton-
wood, molasses, indigo and other freight. As for the
trade with Spain, they carry thither nothing but dry fish,
which can be had here at eight to twelve shillings per
quintal, according to the quality. Their return cargo
consists of oils, wine, brandy and other merchandise.
. . . I came in season to see a prodigious quantity of
apples, of which they make cider that is marvellous. A
barrel costs only eight shillings, and in the taverns they
sell it for twopence per quart, and beer for twopence.

Good Opening   "If our poor refugee brethren who understand farming
should come here, they could not fail to live very comfortably and gain property; for the English are very
lazy, and are proficient only in raising their Indian corn
and cattle. . . . With regard to wild beasts, we have
here a quantity of bears and wolves in great numbers,
who commit many depredations among the sheep, when

due precautions are not taken. We have also a quantity of rattlesnakes, but they are not to be seen as yet.

"The English who inhabit these countries are, as elsewhere, good and bad; but one sees more of the latter than of the former class, and to tell it to you in a few words, there are all kinds, and consequently all kinds of life and manners. It is not that strife and quarrels occur among them, but it is that they do not lead a good life. There are some that practice no other formality of marriage than that of taking each other by the hand; and they live together peaceably; there are others, sixty years of age, who have not yet been baptized because they are not members. About a month ago, a woman forty-five years of age was baptized in our church, with five of her children. They would not baptize her among the Presbyterians because she had not become a member."

It will not do to place too much reliance upon the writer's remarks as to the moral character of the people. His associations were evidently not of the best. What he says about looseness of marriage ties does not accord with the Puritan strictness. His narrative is to be taken with the same large allowance that belongs to the tourists who spend a few weeks in America and then write volumes of description.

CHAPTER X

FRENCH SETTLEMENT IN MAINE

I

The Dresden Settlement

THE visitor to the Forest Grove Cemetery, in the village of Richmond, on the eastern bank of the Kennebec, finds a reminder of the refugee settlers in an inscription on a tombstone: "Louis Houdelette and Mary Cavalear, his Wife, French Huguenots." The Maine historians, for the most part, have failed to give credit to the French settlers, either affirming that Dresden was settled by Germans, or passing lightly over the French part of the record. But later researches have shown that the founders of Dresden were nearly all French, who had first fled to Germany after the Revocation, and had thence emigrated to the new world in company with a few German families. Dresden was settled by these people in 1752, and in many instances the families still retain the French names, with such changes as time and new environment work in nomenclature.

Stephen Houdelette

These French Protestants belonged to the Lutheran branch of the Reformed Church, and came from the eastern provinces of France. Of the forty-six French and German emigrants who left Frankfort in 1752, twenty-eight French names are known and five German, so that the colony was preponderantly French. Among the more important of these families was that of Charles Stephen Houdelette, the father of Louis. He was a lace weaver, and represented the best type of the French skilled artisan, and was equally prominent in the civil and spiritual life of the little colony. Some of his descendants still remain in Dresden, while others are scattered throughout various parts of the country. Henry

196

Clay Houdelette, direct descendant of Louis Houdelette and Mary Cavalier, was commander of a steamship plying between San Francisco and the Sandwich Islands. One of the most interesting passages in his career was the occasion on which he received knighthood at the hands of the potentate of that group of islands.

Another family was that of Jean Pochard, weaver, son of the Honourable Nicholas Pochard, mayor of Anne-sur-l'eau in France. In May, 1751, the ministers and elders of the church at Chenebie gave him a certificate for himself and family, comprising his wife and four sons, setting forth that "they and their children have lived up to the present time in a Christian manner, professing the holy religion according to the Confession of Augsburg, having committed no crime, at least that has come to our knowledge." The mental reservation at the end shows an admirable degree of caution on the part of the writers, to say the least. Jean Pochard with his family sailed from Rotterdam to Boston on the ship *Priscilla* in 1751, and reached Frankfort plantation, the first township organized for settlement on the Kennebec after the proprietors of the Kennebec Purchase came into possession, in March of 1752. Tradition says they tarried awhile at Fort Richmond, from fear of the Indians. Indeed, an Indian tragedy on Swan Island was then a very recent affair. They very soon built for themselves log houses on the banks of the Eastern River, the sites of some of which are still distinctly traceable. In 1765, John Pochard mortgaged forty acres of land situated on Dresden neck, to William Bowdoin, of Roxbury, in trust, to secure the owners of the ship *Priscilla* the sum of £27, 15s., 6d., the amount of his passage money from Rotterdam to Boston; and in 1773, James Bowdoin, administrator of the estate of William, discharged that mortgage. We can gather from this kindly action how ready were the Bowdoins to aid their fellow countrymen, and we may be sure that Bowdoin College proceeded from the same trait of char-

Marginal notes:

Jean Pochard

A "Character"

Ship Priscilla 1751

acter in the Bowdoin family.   The name Pochard became corrupted to Pushard, and one branch of the family petitioned the legislature to have their name changed to Shaw.

II

Asking for a
Missionary   These settlers were ever mindful of their religion.   In 1759, with the Houdelettes, the Gouds, the Stilphens, and others, John Pochard and three of his sons were among the petitioners who asked that Jacob Bailey be sent them as missionary.   Of John Pochard's four sons, Abraham worked at Fort Western as a hewer of timber ; tradition says George was killed by the Indians while hunting up river in the vicinity of the wilds of Augusta ; Christopher settled in Pownalboro ; and Peter, the youngest, became a shoemaker, and after marrying Daniel Malbon's daughter Betsey, settled on the lot of land where West Dresden post-office now is.   His cellar and well are still to be seen, and some apple trees planted by his hand still bear fruit. Two of his grandchildren were living in 1892, and a great-grandson preserves the old shoemaker's lapstone and other of his tools.   A copy of his will shows that he was thrifty, like his race, and died possessed of some property. He was a respected and worthy citizen.

Firm but not
Narrow   "Baptized a Lutheran in France, he attended Episcopal service until Rev. Mr. Bailey's departure for Halifax in 1779 ; and when the Congregational Church was erected in 1801, Peter became its first sexton, purchased a gallery pew for eighteen dollars, and a floor pew for forty-seven dollars.   I think these people were piously inclined without being narrow."   Writing thus, Mr. Charles E. Allen expresses a significant fact concerning their character. They would not abjure Protestantism and embrace popery, though they gave up life itself; but, on the other hand, they were not bigoted or small sectarians.   They could be brotherly in any church that upheld the great Protestant principles of liberty of conscience and a free Bible ;

and in every community they contributed to the best citizenship.

As a whole, these colonists of Dresden township were earnest and capable, though poor.   Contending against poverty, besides being menaced by Indians, snow and ice, wolves and bears, they yet managed to wrest a fair degree of prosperity from the wilderness.   By dint of hard and persevering labour they turned the forest into a farming country.   Among numerous other products, they cultivated flax with good success, and so deftly did their wives and daughters spin this into linen that many of their fabrics are in existence to-day.   Among the number of these settlers whose names have been preserved are the following :   Charles Houdelette, Louis, his son, John Pochard and his four sons, Jean Goud, Daniel Goud, James Goud, Jacques Bugnon, Daniel Malbon, Amos Paris, Philip Fought, John Stain, John Pechin, John Henry Laylor, Francis Riddle, Michael Stilphen, George Jaquin, James Frederick Jaquin.

A Good Type of Settler

III

The two letters which follow are interesting documents, and not the less so because they show a remarkably rapid progress in a new and stubborn language :

Two Characteristic Letters

FRANKFORT, September 13, 1752.

SIRS :—We have learnt from James Frederick Jaquin, lately from Halifax and settled amongst us that all those that arrived there since some short time from Urope, was by means of the letters we wrote to our friends in our country, and instead of their being transported to Boston according to our intentions, was carried to Halifax by the ill conduct of the commisary J. Crelious, which is verified by the wife and children of Malbon being there, and ye mother, brothers and sisters of Daniel Jacob likewise, and generally their own brother and brothers-in-law, or other relations, which makes us humbly entreat of the honourable company to have the goodness and regard for us, that all those the said Jaquin proposed to the gentlemen he should go and bring to our settlement from Halifax by transporting himself to Boston in the first sloop, the which persones would be very necessary amongst us, some being artist and brought up to such trades as we cant well do without, and it is our generall request to the company to have them if possible, and in particular Malbon and Daniel Jacob ; and if these cant have their families with them at Frankfort, they say of necessity though much against their inclination must go to Halifax, not being able to live with any comfort or satisfaction so near them and not be near their dear relatives ; therefore further humbly and earnestly intreat of the venerable good company to use their utmost interest to obtain said persones for their friends and for which favours shall be ever obliged.   Signed in behalf of all the French settlers at Frankfort,

CHARLES STEPHEN HOUDELETTE.

Malbon's wife's name is Margaret Humbart. If the gentleman writes to Halifax about the above mentioned persones, he desires they would let his wife know he is in good health, and that he desires nothing more in the world but to have her with him.

To Mr. Peter Chardon.

FRANKFORT, November 2, 1752.

SIR :—We ask with great humility, pardon for our importunities and trouble we give you, and we take again the freedom to write praying Almighty God for the preservation of your dear health and of all those that belongs to you.   We had great satisfaction in the grant of fourty acres of land each in this place, but at the same time the affliction to see the English quit their first lots and settle upon the French line in such a manner as to oblige some of us to take up with the other twenty acres at a great distance from the first, although we had almost finished our settlements ; and further, we are very much troubled to see said persons to our great inconvenience fit their houses in such forwardness as only to want coverings which would been likewise done if they had the tools necessary for their work.

The most honourable gentlemen of the company promised to settle all the French upon one line near one another, so as to enable them hereafter to settle a minister for Divine Service and a schoolmaster for the instruction of their children.   We desire, dear sir, you would be so good as to communicate to the honourable gentlemen of the company our former requests for sundry articles, we are in very great want of, in particular the provision our three men that went to Boston lately desired, not have half enough to carry us through the winter, and as for other necessaries every one asks for himself, besides what each desired some time ago, namely for George Gout 2 hatts, 1 a half castor, the other a felt, 3 shaves to shave wood, black pepper, smoak tobaca. For John Pochard, 2 hats, 1 shaver for wood, 1 hand saw, 2 gimlets, 1 large, 1 small ; smoak tobaca, black pepper, sewing thread for cloth, 2 chisels, small hatchet. For John Bugnont—barrel vinegar, bushel of onions, black pepper, felt hat, blanket or rugg, thread for clothes, smoak tobaca, barrel of rum for him, George Gout & Peter Gout. For Daniel Jalot, 5 yards middlin coarse cloth for clothes, hats, axe, thread, black pepper. For Peter Gout, hats, sewing thread, hand-saw, chisel, shaver, bushel of onions. For Joseph Bas, shaver, hat, bushel of onions, black pepper, tobaca to smoak, cive for flower.

Signed by

JAMES BUGNONT,
PETER GOUT,
JOHN POCHARD &
DENIS JACOB.

I have received 3 barrels, 1 of flour, 1 of Indian corn, & one of pork. I humbly intreat of you, dear sir, to ask the favour of those gentlemen to have the goodness to send me 3 barrels more of flour, 3 of Indian corn, and 2 of pork, 1 of rum, and 1 of molasses, these last two for Daniel Jacob and Joseph Bas; and for me, James Frederick Jaquin, the last comer, a small quantity of the best flax for a piece or two of linen, 19 lbs. of tobaca, 1 lb. black pepper, bushel of onions, bushel of good peas. This signed only by

JAMES FREDERICK JAQUIN.

Earliest View of New Amsterdam

CHAPTER XI

HUGUENOT INFLUENCE UPON PURITAN CHARACTER

I

W E are led constantly to wonder at the radical difference between the men and women of England and of New England. Of the same race, the same stock, they are yet so unlike as to occasion investigation into the causes of such wide divergence. No sooner were the Pilgrims and Puritans established on this side the sea than they began to differentiate from their forebears on the other side. And the peculiarities which distinguish the New Englanders are not merely in dress, accent, speech or customs, they extend to face and figure, physique and manner. Where the Englishman is phlegmatic, the New Englander is alert and wiry; where the former is burly, the latter is slight and quick by comparison. Perhaps nowhere does the difference stand out more conspicuously than in the treatment of women by the men—a treatment that has made the American husband and father a standard of excellence and genuine chivalry.

Speedy Differentiation

This wide-reaching change which came over the transplanted Puritans is of great interest to the student of race development and of the influence of mixed bloods. Whence came the greater flexibility of the Yankee intellect, the larger spirit of liberality, that great hospitality towards men and ideas? What produced the livelier and more cheerful temperament, and that darker and warmer physical colouring, so that the ruddy-cheeked, blue-eyed Saxon type became rarer among the New Eng-

Whence the Change

landers, and the brown skin and dark eyes common?
This subject is considered philosophically by Horace
Graves, of whose study, "The Huguenot in New Eng-
land," we make free use in this chapter.

So keen an author as Hawthorne, who had full chance
to observe, in his *English Note Book* sets forth in strong
colours the characteristics of the Englishmen who have
remained at home, and of those who are the product of
two or three centuries of life in America.   "We, in our
dry atmosphere," he wrote in 1863, "are getting nervous,
haggard, dyspeptic, extenuated, unsubstantial, theoretic,
and need to be made grosser.   John Bull, on the other
hand, has grown bulbous, long-bodied, short-legged,
heavy-witted, material, and, in a word, too intensely
English.   In a few centuries he will be the earthiest
creature that the earth ever saw." *Contrast Drawn by Hawthorne*

He speaks still more candidly of the British woman, as
contrasted with her American sister.   "I have heard a
good deal of the tenacity with which the English ladies
retain their personal beauty to a late period of life; but
it strikes me that an English lady of fifty is apt to become
a creature less refined and delicate, so far as her physique
goes, than anything that we western people class under
the name of woman.   She has an awful ponderosity of
frame, not pulpy, like the looser development of our few
fat women, but massive, with solid beef and streaky tal-
low; so that (though struggling manfully against the idea)
you inevitably think of her as made up of steaks and
sirloins.   When she walks, her advance is elephantine.
When she sits down, it is on a great round space of her
Maker's footstool, where she looks as if nothing could
ever move her.   Her visage is unusually grim and stern,
seldom positively forbidding, yet calmly terrible, not
merely by its breadth and weight of feature, but because
it seems to express so much well-founded self-reliance." *Ungallant but Graphic*

Hawthorne and others attributed this great difference
in the men and women of the two countries to climate, *Climate as Cause*

and this theory has been largely accepted as sufficient to account for all dissimilarities. It has been generally believed that a clearer, sunnier air has browned the race permanently, and begotten nervousness of physical and mental constitution. It is assumed that there could have been no more powerful, and indeed no other intervening cause. In support of this conclusion it is pointed out that the New England colonists were purely and exclusively English. Palfrey contends that the population "continued to multiply for a century and a half on its own soil, in remarkable seclusion from other communities." John Fiske accepts Palfrey's statement, and cites Savage as demonstrating, after painstaking labours, that ninety-eight out of every hundred of the early settlers could trace their descent directly to an English ancestry. These authorities would leave us no alternative but to conclude that climate alone must have wrought the remarkable transformation of mind, character and body, through which have been evolved and fixed the idiosyncrasies of the New Englander.

Palfrey

Fiske

II

Not a Sufficient Cause

But if climate was the potent cause, why did not the changes appear in the first century of colonial life? In 1776 the portraits of the men who won our liberties show us veritable Englishmen. Yet in 1863 the change had come about, and Hawthorne found the two peoples radically different. Climate is much slower in its effects than this. The truth is, it is impossible that the Yankee could have been so greatly differentiated from the Englishman in three or four generations merely from exposure to a climate but little unlike that of Great Britain. Having disposed of this fallacious theory, the search for an effective cause begins, and later historical researches have made it plain. This transformation came from mixture of bloods, from intermarriage between the early English colonists and some race of a slighter build, a less sombre

The True Cause

disposition, a more active mind and an intenser nature. There is no race which at once combined proximity and the other requisites except the French ; and in the French —with their clearness and quickness, their bright dispo- **The French Traits** sition—were to be found every required element. There are two classes of French ; and that which came to America to seek a home and religious liberty possessed a remarkable combination of traits—a mingling of the sanguine, light, cheerful, witty, sincere, devout, and amiable. Disposed to enjoy life, even under hardest circumstances, the Frenchman was the best of companions. As Lavater, the great physiognomist, says : " His countenance is open and at first sight speaks a thousand pleasant, amiable things. His eloquence is often deafening, but his good humour casts a veil over his failings."

This is the stock that intermingled with the Puritan and wrought the change, and it is strange that historians should not have given them larger credit for their racial influence. It is equally strange that only recently has the extent of the Huguenot immigration been recognized in any adequate degree. One reason given is that the French **A Strong Mixture** refugees came to New England from motives so much like those which brought the early settlers that these strangers did not, on arriving, exhibit the strong contrast with their English predecessors which appeared on the entry of the French exiles into other parts of our country. The Huguenots and the Puritans had both suffered bitter persecution. They had faced death from devotion to the same religious principles. Moreover they were not strangers to one another ; for when the little congregation from Scrooby sought refuge in Holland, they found Leyden full of Frenchmen who had fled from their native country. For a time both bodies of people were allowed to worship in the same edifice, and both were eagerly waiting the opportunity to put the ocean between themselves and their enemies. In one particular they differed radically, and that favoured the loss of recognition by the

Huguenots. The English were fearful lest they should lose their English name and tongue ; while the French seemed indifferent to their native speech, and were ready to translate their names into equivalent Dutch or English, according to the predominant population of the community in which they happened to be. They soon merged into New Englanders. Before the first ships reached shore, indeed, the French Molines had become plain English Mullins, as we have seen.

French at the Base

The English got away from Holland first, and those of the French Protestants who cast lots in with them speedily assimilated with their fellow voyagers. This was done so unobtrusively that only in recent days has the truth been realized that the Plymouth colony was not of unmixed English blood, but contained an element that was profoundly to affect the English stock. Thus right at the base of the first effort to settle New England is this revelation of the stealthy introduction of the Huguenot to the hearthstone and into the very hearts of the New England ancestors. It is no surprise, after this, to find that many of the eminent men of our early history were in some degree at least of Huguenot descent.

The French Contribution

What did the Huguenots contribute to the change in English character? All the lighter, happier, more refining and spiritual qualities, the joyous temperament. The thrift of the Protestant French is proverbial. It found speedy expression in New England in commerce and in devising new subjects of manufacture and exportation. We have noted how the Faneuils and Gabriel Bernon and their French fellows were of the mercantile and manufacturing class that built up Boston. As the exiled French were founders of many British industries when they settled in England, so they were most efficient in developing the resources of the new country in which they were heartily given asylum. But they were never so engrossed in trade that they allowed their passion for civil and religious liberty to expire. It was a Huguenot,

Paul Revere, who was the trusted messenger of the Boston patriots on the night before the conflict at Lexington. There is no name of traitor in all the list, though many of them, owing everything to England and regarding her as their deliverer, could not see it right to rebel against her authority, and remained on the Tory side.

III

It is all the more singular that Palfrey did not recognize the Huguenot influence upon the Puritan life, since he knew of their presence. In his "History of New England" he makes the extremely conservative statement that at least one hundred and fifty Huguenot families came to Massachusetts after the Revocation in 1685. He makes no account of those already here, nor of those who did not come directly from France, nor of those who kept coming from time to time, even down to 1776. Nor does he take account of the number who have names that seem to be English or Dutch, but which are French translated, as in the case of some of the Duboises, living in Leyden, who allowed themselves to be called Van den Bosch, and came to America under that name. Gerneau became Gano in English mouths, and at last the owners of the name let it go at that. Thus Erouard became Heroy, Bouquet is now spelled Bockee, Tissau became Tishew, and Fleurri is hid in Florence. Olivier has been confused with the English Oliver, and Burpo was originally Bonrepos. Nor was the assent to this distortion due to ignorance on the part of the Frenchmen; for Bonrepos was a learned pastor of the French church in Boston, and the refugees were generally of the higher and cultivated classes of their native land.

Loss of Identity

The merchants of the Huguenot seaports of France were already familiar with the New England seaports, and fled to Boston and Salem when the time of peril came. Many of them found shelter in neighbouring countries before coming to America, and sometimes for that reason

French-Swiss

were not recognized as French. In this way families like those of Agassiz and Audubon are known as Swiss, while there is little doubt that their origin was French. When the Cabots, the Lefavours, the Beadles, the Valpys and Philip English had established themselves in Salem, they began to bring over their fellow countrymen. English, whose real name was L'Anglois, became owner of a large number of ships and a great deal of other property. For years he imported young men to be apprenticed as sailors and young girls to be employed as domestics. They were all of Huguenot ancestry and their descendants to-day disclose their French origin in their personal appearance. Between the Connecticut River and Massachusetts Bay, young men of that line of ancestry are by no means rare, with large brown eyes, black hair and slender, graceful figures, which proclaim them Frenchmen in everything except speech ; and yet their forefathers have been inhabitants of eastern Massachusetts since the beginning of the seventeenth century. In a little seaport near Salem there are to be found to-day at least fifty family names which are distinctly French ; yet those who bear them now have never suspected that they were of other than English origin.

In this connection, it may be asked how many New Englanders would at first thought suppose or admit that Mrs. Julia Ward Howe, American of the Americans, and author of the "Battle Hymn of the Republic," had Huguenot blood in her ancestry. Yet she was the great-grandniece of General Francis Marion, which explains the strain that made a battle hymn her natural expression. Her mother had the high type of French beauty, and through all the French side of the family ran the best traits of the Huguenot blood.

How extended may have been this influence flowing into our national life may be inferred from the fact that of the twenty-five thousand or more English who were to be found in New England towards the middle or latter part

Philip English

Julia Ward
Howe

An Estimate

of the seventeenth century, the descendants are reckoned by Mr. Fiske at fifteen millions. To these few thousands of English, the Huguenots, as admitted by Palfrey, made an accession of one hundred and fifty families,—which means nearly a thousand persons, as families went then ; but after this first flood had spent its strength, nearly every ship from London, according to Baird, for many years brought additions to those who had come in the past. The exodus from France continued for full fifty years from 1666, and within that time at least a million Frenchmen were expatriated, and those the flower of the nation. It is not possible that less than four or five thousand came to dwell in New England.

The gain for New England is distinctly revealed in the development of Yankee enterprise along those very lines in which it was started by the French colonists. But these were present in the requisite number ; and when the eye is once trained and the ear attuned to detect the names which indicate Huguenot ancestry, it is astonishing how frequently they reveal themselves. If New Englanders are closely questioned concerning their ancestry, there are few who do not confess to some trace of French blood, though it be slight. This is peculiarly true of the eastern half of Massachusetts.

IV

When the Huguenots contributed their genial presence to our population, it was like the influx of a gladdening river into a thirsty land, carrying joy wherever it goes. At first, like all foreigners, they were reserved, and marriages were mostly confined to their own nationality ; but the second or third generation, under American influences which break down race barriers, found alliances that made Americans of them all. How rapidly nationalities merge in this country is seen in the case of a young man whose father was a Frenchman and whose mother was an American of English descent. His wife's mother is an

Common Ground: Love of Freedom

Irishwoman, and her father a German. Thus that marriage rolled four nationalities into one within two generations. But between the Huguenot and Puritan there was no stream to bridge over. They had in their common Calvinism and love of freedom a bond of sympathy and union that brought them into harmony as soon as their tongues had learned to speak a common language.

It is evident that the absorption of the Huguenots would occur more rapidly after the Revolution, and would manifest itself unmistakably during the first half of the nineteenth century, the time when the contrast between the New Englanders and the Old Englanders made such an impression upon Hawthorne and Emerson. The result is so noteworthy that it is marvellous that we did not long ago recognize the method of the brewing of that race of men and the material which entered into it. "There is a substance known to chemistry as diastase, which is an active element in the germination of every seed, and which, on being sprinkled, never so sparingly, over a great mass of the brewer's cloudy, pasty ' mash,' clears it instantly and leaves it a sweet, pure, transparent liquid. Such an office might the introduction of the Huguenot into New England seem to have performed, in dissipating the heaviness and dogged prejudice of our insular kinsmen." That is Mr. Graves' conclusion, and it is justified by the facts continually coming to light.

The Huguenot element, not only in New England, but equally in New York and Pennsylvania and the Carolinas, was a powerful social factor. Not numbers but character made them so effective in changing conditions. Every record we have of them in persecution and suffering and torture displays the same disposition to endure bravely and to make the best of the worst situations. Shipwreck, stormy voyages, homelessness, deprivations and perils of every kind—these circumstances only bring out the courage and cheer and uprightness and dauntless spirit of the Huguenots. And when circumstances improved,

An Illustration

A Social Factor

their genial and lovable temperament always became a wholesome quality in a life that was far too sombre and grim and gloomy when the Puritan had it to himself. Where the French were, there was the wise admixture of grave and gay, the enjoyment of life. And these much needed elements entered into the New England social A High Type development, and far exceeded climate in altering the New Englander and creating on our continent a new type, comprising the best qualities of Protestant English and Protestant French—the best type of American perhaps yet to be found. Certain it is that New England character cannot be explained without the presence of the French blood.

In an exceedingly interesting article on "The Brain of the Nation," M. Gustave Michaud says that the immigrants who peopled New England during the seventeenth century may be roughly divided into two categories: those who emigrated because they wished to improve their position through the acquisition of property, and those who wished above all to enjoy religious liberty. The latter contained among them an unusual number of men of talent. Lombroso has demonstrated the close connection which exists between exalted religious ideas and ideals and the nervous temperament characteristic of genius. In our country examples of that connection are abundant. Henry Clay, Lowell, Bancroft, Parkman, Samuel F. B. Morse, Cyrus W. Field, were sons of clergymen. Cooper, Howells and Whittier were sons of Quakers. Agassiz was the son of a Swiss pastor, himself of Huguenot descent. The Huguenots—in America still more than in England—were a hotbed of talent. And study reveals the curious influence which the blood of thousands of Huguenots who were among the very first settlers of South Carolina, now exerts upon the intellectuality of the state.

PART TWO

THE FRENCH IN NEW YORK

CHAPTER I

THE FOUNDERS OF NEW AMSTERDAM

I

French Among Early Settlers

WHILE the Dutch long had all the credit of founding New Amsterdam, which afterwards became New York, later historical researches have brought to light the fact that French Protestants had an important part in the early settlement, and were among the original company that established a colony on Manhattan Island. The Walloons were French who had fled from the province of that name, on the northern boundary of France, to escape religious persecution, and had taken up their residence in Holland, where other French Protestant refugees came at one time and another during the century that followed the massacre of St.

Jesse de Forest Bartholomew. The same Jesse de Forest that proposed to the Virginia Company to bring a French colony to America, when that offer was declined so far as material aid was concerned, repeated the proposition to the Dutch West India Company, just then forming. It was accepted, and as a result the French Protestants made up a large part of the expedition of thirty families which sailed in March, 1623, in the ship *New Netherland*, to found a Dutch colony at the mouth of the Hudson. Under the ordering of Providence, what strange results follow apparently slight causes. The English Puritans offered to establish a colony for the Dutch on the Hud-

son ; but the Dutch not being ready to move, found a
home at Plymouth instead ; while the French Protestants,
who offered to establish a colony in Virginia, since the
Virginia Company was not wise enough to accept the
offer, went to the Hudson instead of the James, and
helped found a Dutch commonwealth.

After a specially favoured voyage, early in May, fourteen years after Henry Hudson had discovered the noble
river which perpetuates his name, the ship *New Nether-*   Ship New
land sailed into the " most beautiful bay " that now shel-   Netherland
                                                               1623
ters the commerce of the world.   At that very moment a
French ship lay in the harbour, on errand to take possession of the country in the name of France, on the
ground of Verrazzano's discovery a century before ; and
thus French Roman Catholic and French Protestant met
again.   Fortunately for the newcomers, a Dutch "vessel
of several guns" chanced to lie a little further up the
river ; and between the remonstrances of the colonists and
a show of force from the *Mackerel*, the French ship sailed
away, leaving the Dutch and Walloons free to land and
make their settlement.   They found a few huts near the
southern end of the island, where a trading-post had been
maintained by Amsterdam merchants.   With this exception the country was a wilderness.

The inhabitants of the little trading-post were not all
Dutch, however, for in 1614 a child was born of Hugue-   1614
not parents.   This baby, named Jean Vigné, disputes the   First Child
right with Virginia Dare of being remembered as the   French
first white child to see the light on the continent of North
America.   The second birth to take place within the
limits of the Dutch province was that of Sarah Rapalie,   Sarah Rapalie
likewise of Huguenot blood, who was born at Orange.
The names of her parents, indeed, George Rapalie and
Catalina Trico, were the only ones definitely known hitherto of the French colonists brought over in the *New
Netherland*.   They went, with seventeen other families,
up the North River, landed and built a fort called Orange,

near what is now Albany. Of the other families, eight remained on Manhattan and took possession there for the The French Dispersed West India Company ; four newly married couples went westward and established a little post on the Delaware ; while two families pushed eastward through the wilds of Connecticut and built homes on the banks of the Hartford.

There is no list of names of these first Huguenot settlers, but by comparing the names affixed to Jesse de Forest's petition to the Virginia Company with the records of Manhattan about fifteen years after the settlement (no records being kept during the first fifteen years of the colony), the following names are gleaned : Rapalie, De la Mot, Du Four, Le Rou, Le Roy, Du Pon, Chiselin, Cornille, De Trou, De Crenne, Damont, Campion, De Carpentier, Gille, Catoir, de Croy, Maton, Lambert, Martin, and Gaspar.

II

A Happy Settlement The settlement was prosperous from the start, and the colonists happy. A ship which returned to Holland carried glowing accounts of the new country. An extract from one of the letters is as follows :

Extract from a Letter We were much gratified on arriving in this country. Here we found beautiful rivers, bubbling fountains flowing down into the valleys ; basins of running waters in the flatlands, agreeable fruits in the woods, such as strawberries, walnuts, and wild grapes. The woods abound with venison. There is considerable fish in the rivers, good tillage land ; here is, especially, free coming and going, without fear of the naked natives of the country. Had we cows, hogs, and other cattle fit for food—which we expect in the first ships—we would not wish to return to Holland.

The effect of such accounts was to bring over new colonists, among whom were many Huguenots. A Peter Minuit Huguenot Huguenot, Peter Minuit, was the second director or governor of the settlement. He reached Manhattan Fort in 1626 when the colony comprised about thirty houses closely grouped about the block-house, and tenanted by

Dutch, French, and a few English.   Minuit's family had
taken refuge in Wessel some fifty years before this date,
and there is a record in the Walloon Church of that place   1626
which shows that he acted for a time as deacon.   He was
an active, energetic man, firm in temper, friendly in disposition, just and honourable, and granted religious liberty and a fair amount of political freedom.

De Rasières, his secretary, was likewise a Huguenot   Religious
and a man of parts.   Minuit sent him to visit Governor   Granted
Bradford, of Massachusetts, regarding the relations of the
two colonies, and Bradford alludes to him as "a man of
fair and genteel behaviour."   He proved himself as a
diplomat, concealing from the English the fact of the valuable fur trade, a knowledge of which would surely have
brought the English in force against the Dutch possessions.

Among the other Huguenots who were prominent in
the first days of New Amsterdam was Johannes La Mon-   First Doctor a
tagne, the first doctor to settle on Manhattan.   He came   LaMontagne
from Leyden in 1637, from whence the family of his first
wife, Rachel De Forest, had already emigrated to New
Amsterdam.   Previous to his coming the Zieckentroosters
(comforters of the sick) were the only props which the
unfortunate sick of the colony had to lean upon.   Dr. La
Montagne was a man of varied gifts, who subsequently
occupied several stations of trust under the government.
His name appears as a member of the council, and as
official schoolmaster, and after a few years of practice he
seems to have given up the medical profession and devoted himself entirely to the civil and military service.
It is quite probable that the colonists found the fresh air   A Man of
and outdoor life of the new world too healthy to make   Affairs
the practice of medicine in New York as profitable as it
has since become.   He must have prospered in his new
work, however, for he became the owner of a "bouwery"
located at what is now the northern end of Central Park.
His daughter, Marie, married Jacob Kip in 1654.   His
farm comprised two hundred acres, for which he paid

$720 ; it was situated on Eighth Avenue between Ninety-third Street and the Harlem River. He named it "Vredendal" or "Valley of Peace." Its value to-day is high in the millions.

III

Knicker-
bockers a
Mixed Blood
The French and Dutch mingled together harmoniously, setting each other off to great advantage. How excellent was the result produced by the infusion of the facile French blood with that of the stolid Dutch may be seen in the great Knickerbocker families. Nearly every New Yorker who can trace his ancestry back to the founders of New Amsterdam will find traces of Huguenot blood in his veins, for both in the earlier and later days the inter-mixture of races was the almost constant rule. So evenly matched were the two nationalities in point of numbers by the year 1656, that all government and town procla-mations were issued in French as well as in Dutch.

Stuyvesant's
Wife a
Huguenot
Peter Stuyvesant, the famous director-general, had a Huguenot wife, Judith Bayard, daughter of a refugee minister; and during his administration he had living with him his sister, who was the widow of a Huguenot, Samuel Bayard. It was her son who founded the illustri-ous Bayard family of America. For these reasons, if for no others, he took much interest in the French exiles who sought refuge within his dominions. He not only kindly received those who came, but went further, and in 1664 offered flattering prospects to a company of Protes-tants in La Rochelle who were on the point of emigrating, carrying out his promises by presenting them with grants of land. Small bodies of French colonists kept coming, mostly from the northern provinces of France and Nor-
Bedloe's
Island Named
After Isaac
Bethlo
mandy. Among them was Isaac Bethlo, a native of Calais, who arrived in 1652, and gave his name to the island in New York harbour known as Bedloe's. It is among the strange coincidences that this island, named after a French Huguenot refugee, should become the site for that colossal statue, "Liberty Enlightening the

World," the gift of France to the United States nearly two and a half centuries later. From the outstretched arm of that figure gleams the light that illuminates the harbour, typical of the light of religious liberty which the persecuted of all lands were here to enjoy. Liberty Enlightening the World

The French did not confine themselves to the town of New Amsterdam entirely, but formed settlements on Staten Island, the upper end of Manhattan, Long Island, and in Westchester County.

Staten Island, in the bay of New York, was one of their favourite asylums. "It might properly have been called Huguenot Island." A considerable number of refugees settled there in 1657, locating their dwellings near the site of the present town of Richmond. The names of Guion, Dissosway, Bedell, Fontaine, Reseau, La Tourette, Rutan, Puillon, Mercereau, La Conte, Butten, Mancey, Perrin, Larselene, De Pue, Corssen, Martineau, Tuenire, Morgan, Le Guine, and Jouerney, have been preserved. Like the descendants of the emigrants to Ulster County, the progeny of the refugees to Staten Island still occupy, in many cases, the land held by their ancestors. The number of the island colony was constantly increased by the coming of little groups of refugees. Any completeness of record is out of the question, but it is possible to add a few names to the above list. In 1662 came Pierre Martin, Gerard Ive, and Juste Grand ; the year following, Jerome Bovie, Pierre Noue, and Pierre Parmentier had the distinction of arriving on a vessel called the *Spotted Cow*. French on Staten Island

IV

At the period just preceding the Revocation, and especially during the few years following that royal invitation to exile, the emigration to New York was greatly accelerated. From France direct, from England, from the Antilles, the refugees came in a steady stream to the growing metropolis which afforded them all a welcome. It would neither be desirable nor possible to recount the Increasing Numbers names of all who came, but in the following pages will be found a brief record of some of the refugees who established homes here, founding a posterity which has given to America many men of eminence and a multitude of those citizens who, though less noted, go to make up the bone and sinew of the nation.

The LeContes   Guillaume Le Conte, of Rouen, a descendant of the barons of Nonant on his mother's side, was one of these refugees.   By his first marriage he had a son, Guillaume, and by his second marriage, a son, Pierre.   Guillaume's descendants are to be found among the well-known Seton and Bayley families, while the honoured name of Le Conte survives through Peter's offspring.   As the Bayards, the Danas, and the Bowdoins have been publicists, so the descendants of the elder Le Conte have been men of science.   Pierre was a noted surgeon of his day.   His grandsons, Lewis and John LeConte, living together on their large plantation in Georgia, devoted themselves to the study of natural history, making contributions to our knowledge of the Georgia flora and fauna.   Of Lewis's sons, John is among the front rank of American students of physics, while Joseph is probably our foremost geologist.   John LeConte's son, John Lawrence LeConte, who died in 1883, was a brilliant naturalist, and is ranked as the "greatest entomologist this country has yet produced."

Of a different family were Pierre and Jean Le Conte, who came to New York in 1687 and acquired an estate on the western side of Staten Island.

Minvielle Mayor   Gabriel Minvielle, a native of Bordeaux, came to New York by way of Amsterdam in 1673.   He took a high station in the province at once, being elected alderman within two years after his arrival.   In 1684 he was mayor of the city, and served under four administrations.   He was married to Judith Van Beack in 1674 but had no issue ; the family name was perpetuated, however, by the children of his brother Pierre.

In 1688 Jean Barbarie and his sons Pierre and Jean settled in New York. Barbarie acquired considerable wealth, was active in politics, and distinguished himself by taking the lead in the organization of the French church. His son Pierre became one of the prominent members of Trinity Church, and served at various times as warden and vestryman. Barbarie

Jean Fouchart (Fouchard) a native of Duras, settled in New York in 1704. Denis Lambert, of Bergerac, came in 1691. Lewis Lyron came in 1696, but made his final home in Milford, Conn. At his death he gave £200 to the French Church of Boston and £100 to the church in New Rochelle. Pierre Montels, of Canet, was naturalized in England and came to New York in 1702. He had been a prosperous iron manufacturer, and before leaving home he had deeded his property to his son-in-law, Noe Cazalet, who was outwardly a "new convert." When Cazalet was examined by the priests as to his orthodoxy, he replied that he had told his children to attend the mass, but that as for himself "it must come from God." Shortly after making this declaration he, too, found it best to come to New York. Fouchard Lyron Montels

From Sedan came Jacques Tiphaine, the ancestor of the Tiffany family, distinguished merchants of New York. Henry Collier, who founded the important American family of Colliers, was a native of Paris. He reached England in 1681, but setting out on a trading voyage in 1686 he had the misfortune to be shipwrecked on the French coast and was promptly put in prison. He made good his escape a second time, however, and subsequently came to New York. Claude Requa, the ancestor of the Requa family of New York and Pennsylvania, was a child when his parents decided to come to America. The story of his emigration, which is not unlike that of thousands of others, is as follows : "They departed in the night, to save their lives, leaving the greater part of their property, which they could not convert into money. There were Tiphaine
The Tiffany
Family Collier Requa The Escape
from France eleven other families that went at the same time.   The priests used to search every house where they imagined that Bibles were concealed or meetings held.   They concealed their Bible for some time, but finally it was discovered and taken away.   They managed, however, to retain some leaves, which were concealed under the bottom of a chair.   The twelve families fled by night from Paris to La Rochelle, where they continued for some time.   But intelligence from Paris to La Rochelle soon detected their several abodes.   Their houses were to be broken into on a certain night.   They would all have been cut off, had it not been for a good man, a Catholic, who had become acquainted with them.   He gave them notice, so they fled the night before, at about one or two o'clock.   The twelve families muffled the wheels of their wagons, so as not to make any noise, but they were discovered on the way and pursued to a river, before they were overtaken.   Ten families got over the stream in safety, but two were taken. The others succeeded in getting aboard a ship which sailed for America."   During the voyage over a plague broke out on shipboard and many of the passengers died, among them being both of Claude Requa's parents.

Peril of Twelve Families

Pierre Legrand, native of Hahain, was naturalized in England in 1682.   In 1684 he was in New York, as his application for membership in the Dutch Reformed Church shows.   He seems to have lived for a year or so in Kingston, N. Y., and then returned to New York to engage in the tobacco trade.

Legrand

Among those who accepted the articles of capitulation by which New Amsterdam became New York we find the name of Jacques Cousseau, one of the French citizens, who had attained prominence.

Cousseau

The well-known Crommelin family is descended from Daniel Crommelin, son of a wealthy manufacturer of Saint Quentin.   He fled to England, from thence to Jamaica, and finally settled in New York.   His sons Charles and Isaac established the ancient country-seat of the family in

Crommelin

John Jay
First President

Henry G. Marquand
Second President

Frederick J. De Peyster
Third President

William Jay
Fourth and Present President

T. J. Oakley Rhinelander
Treasurer

Mrs. James M. Lawton
Secretary

EX-PRESIDENTS AND PRESENT OFFICERS OF THE HUGUENOT
SOCIETY OF AMERICA

Ulster County, named "Gricourt" after the old home in France.

The New York Chevaliers are descended from Jean le Chevalier, who was probably related to the other emigrants of that name who settled in Philadelphia and Charleston. He married Marie de la Plaine in the Dutch Church in 1692. From Normandy came François le Comte, who was married to Catharine Lavandier in 1693. He seems to have been one of the victims of the laws which allowed the priests to bring up Huguenot children in the Roman faith, for before his marriage he was compelled to make abjuration. Chevaliers LeComte

From Rouen came Jean Gancel, Pierre Chapron, and Abraham Dupont before the close of the century. Daniel Marchand, of Caen, came before 1692. André Foucault, descended from a family of Poitou that was noted for the sufferings it had endured in the cause of religion, was in New York by the year 1691. In 1703 the governor authorized him to open a French and English school in the city of New York. About the same time came Zacharie Angevin, likewise of Poitou. In 1701 he moved out of the city to New Rochelle, where his descendants were numerous for many years. Jacob Baillergeau, of Loudon in Touraine, was naturalized in New York in 1701, and in 1704 was licensed to practice medicine in New York and New Jersey. Thomas Bayeux, of Caen, came to New York shortly after the Revocation, and became one of the leading merchants of the city. He married Madeleine Boudinot in 1703 and left a large posterity. Foucault
Teacher

Daniel Targe, of Port des Barques, was among the Narragansett settlers, and on the breaking up of the settlement removed to New York, where his descendants survive under the transformed names of Targer and Target. François Bouquet, a ship captain from the same port, fled to England in 1681, coming to New York towards the close of the century. He was a man of property and well-known in shipping circles. The Tillou Other
Families family, of which the late Francis R. Tillou was a member, was established by Pierre Tillou, who fled from Saintonge in 1681. Jean Elizée was a fellow townsman of François Bouquet, and married his daughter Jeanne in New York in 1701.

Other immigrants with earliest known dates, were as follows : Marc Boisbelleau, 1685; André Jolin, 1686 ; Louis Carré, 1686; Gilles Gaudineau, 1686 ; John Pelletreau, 1687 ; Peter Reverdy, 1687 ; John de Neufville, 1687 ; Jacques Dubois, 1688; Jean Pinaud, died 1688 ; Aman and Gousse Bonnin, 1688 ; Daniel Merceveau, 1689; Jean Equier, 1689 ; Paul Drouhet, 1869 ; André Paillet, 1690 ; Daniel Lambert, 1691 ; Daniel Coudret, 1691 ; Jean Piervaux, 1692 ; Louis Geneuil, 1692; Elie Rembert, 1692 ; Jean Roux, 1692 ; Charles Lavigne, 1692 ; Jacques Many, 1692 ; Elie Chardavoinne, 1692 ; Jean Coulon, 1692; Jean Chadaine, 1693 ; Elie Charron, 1693 ; Estienne Archambaud, 1693 ; Isaac Quintard, 1693 ; (removed later to Stamford, Conn., where his descendants are still to be found ; Bishop Quintard, of Tennessee, is a member of this family) ; Pierre Girrard, 1694 ; Jean Doublet, 1695 ; Jean Boisseau, 1698 ; Isaac Boutineau, 1698 ; Elie Badeau, 1698 ; David Fume, 1698; Jacques Vinaux, 1699 ; Jean Faget, 1699 ; Pierre Trochon, 1700 ; André Lamoureux, 1700; Jacques Desbrosses, 1701; Pierre, Jean and Abraham Rolland, 1702; Pierre Arondeau, 1703; Pierre Durand, 1706 ; Jacques Bergeron, 1712 ; Jean Dragaud, 1729 ; Daniel Gillard, 1792 ; Pierre Rusland, 1792.

These names indicate that in the early life of New York the French played a more prominent part than in any other centre, not excepting Boston. Socially they were a most effective factor, tempering the tone of society, and in large measure creating it. That so many of the streets of the city, as Desbrosses, Lispenard, etc., were named after the French citizens, shows that they were men of note in the business and public life of the time.

The intermingling of the French and Dutch produced a strong and charming type of character, in which the best traits of both races appear. Indeed, wherever the Huguenot blood entered, it improved the type. In some the blood was mixed before coming to this country. Such cases are illustrated by Professor Johann Daniel Gros, minister of the Dutch Reformed Church in New York, and later occupant of the chair of intellectual and moral philosophy in Columbia College (now Columbia University), and author of the first text-book on moral philosophy published in America. His family was French and German from the Alsace-Lorraine section where French and German commingled. His brother, Lorenz Gros, pushed on beyond Albany up the Mohawk Valley, and built near Fonda the first gentleman's mansion west of Albany, using brick and tile imported from Holland ; a mansion still standing as strong as when built, and long a landmark in its section. He was a captain in the Continental Army, and also an officer in the War of 1812. From the fact that these families spoke German, they were indiscriminately classed among the Dutch element and their French descent was obscured. Without dates of coming are the names of Crucheron, Martiline, Gannepains, Regrenier, Casses and Cannon.

Huguenots were the first settlers in that part of Manhattan now known as Harlem (an account of their settling being given in the sketch of the De Forest family) ; and when the village of New Harlem was laid out in 1658, nearly one half of the thirty-two heads of families in the settlement were Huguenots. Other of the hardier souls among the French likewise pushed out from the original settlement ; fourteen families joined in founding Bushwick, others went to Flushing, where they introduced the fine fruit culture which distinguished that Long Island city for so many years. Later, in 1677, David Demarest gathered together a few families and formed the settlement that has since become Hackensack, New Jersey.

Huguenots First in Harlem

On Long Island

V

After the Revocation of the Edict of Nantes, the immigration to New York was so considerable that the French became an important factor in politics.   Governor Lord Bellomont wrote to the Board of Trade in 1698 :   "I must acquaint your lordships that the French here are very factious and their numbers considerable.   At the last election they ran in with the Jacobite party, and have been since so insolent as to boast they had turned the scale and could balance the interests as they pleased."   That Governor Bellomont, who was not in good favour with the people, did not despise this French influence in public affairs is proved by the fact that he tried to gain them to his side, and to this end invited Gabriel Bernon, one of the most influential Huguenots in the country, a resident of Providence, to come to his aid.   Bernon did his best in this direction, with but partial success.   The French were disposed to independence and to choose for themselves in politics as in religion.

Among the considerable social factors of the city in its day was the French Club, which was established largely through the influence of the Bayards, the family of which the long time United States Senator from Delaware was a descendant.   French became the fashionable language of the new community.   From 1648 to 1658 the French element of North America had become so important that, according to Bancroft, the public documents were issued in French as well as in Dutch and English.   It is estimated that by 1688 some two hundred Huguenot families had found a home in New York, or about one quarter of the population.   In 1661 half the inhabitants of Harlem were Huguenots.

Gabriel Bernon *(margin note)*

The French Club *(margin note)*

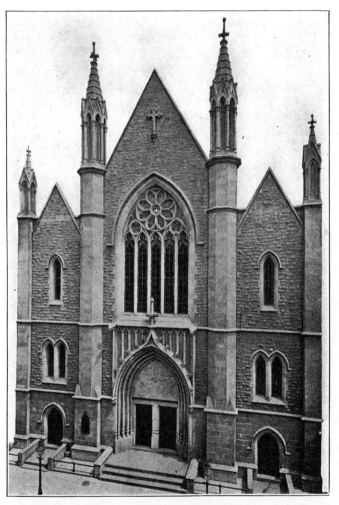

THE FRENCH CHURCH IN NEW YORK AT THE PRESENT TIME

CHAPTER II

THE FRENCH CHURCH IN NEW YORK

I

D URING the earlier years of the colony the French had no church of their own. In 1628, when the first minister, Rev. Jonas Michaelius, of the Reformed Church of Holland, came to New Amsterdam, services were conducted for both the French and the Dutch. Of the two elders who were chosen, one was a Huguenot, the "honourable director" Peter Minuit. Pastor Michaelius himself left the following account of this first organization : "We have had, at the first administration of the Lord's Supper, full fifty communicants, Walloons and Dutch : not without great joy and comfort for so many. Of these, a portion made their first Confession of Faith before us (he probably is referring to some of the unregenerate traders), and others exhibited their church certificates. Some had forgotten to bring their certificates with them, not thinking that a church would be formed and established here ; and some, who had brought them, had lost them unfortunately in a general conflagration ; but they were admitted upon the satisfactory testimony of others to whom they were known, and also upon their daily good deportment. We administer the Holy Sacrament of the Lord once in four months, provisionally, until a larger number of people shall otherwise require. The Walloons have no services on Sundays, other than that in the Dutch language, of which they understand very little. A portion of the Walloons live far away, and could not come on account of the heavy rains and storms, so that it was neither advisable, nor was it possible, to appoint any special service for so small

225

a number with so much uncertainty. Nevertheless, the Lord's Supper was administered to them in the French language, and according to the French mode, with a preceding discourse, which I had before me in writing, as I could not trust myself extemporaneously."

II

Dutch Aid

The Dutch are to be highly commended for the aid they gave the French in their religious services. In 1652 Rev. Samuel Drisius, a German, was called to be a colleague to Rev. Joannes Megapolensis, of the Dutch Reformed Church, for the reason that he was able to preach both in Dutch and French. The French were thus kindly provided for until they had a fully organized church and a **Church Founded by 1659** preacher of their own, which was not later than 1659. In 1682 there came a new era for them religiously with the arrival of Rev. Pierre Daillé. He was a rare spirit. He applied himself at once to the difficult task of preaching the gospel to his brethren scattered through the province of New York. He reorganized the French Church of New York, which prospered under his care until 1692. Even Governor Andros, who spoke and understood both Low Dutch and French, became an attendant at the French services, which were held, like the English, in the Dutch Church within the fort. Mr. Daillé next revived the church on Staten Island, then visited New Paltz and established a church there. He also founded a church near Hackensack, and repeatedly visited all the Huguenot settlements, like a modern Paul visiting the churches. He was, says Selyns, his colleague, "full of fire, godliness and learning, and maintained the cause of Jesus with untiring zeal."

First House 1688

It was in the year 1688 that the French first built a house of worship for their exclusive use. This was a very humble chapel on Marketfield Street, near the Battery, and it "was here that, every Sabbath day, the people assembled from twenty miles around, from Long

Island, Staten Island, New Rochelle, and other points, for public worship. Every street near was filled with wagons as early as Saturday evening, and in them many passed the night and ate their frugal Sunday repast, presenting a touching spectacle of purity and zeal."

This house proved too small, and they were allowed to buy land for a second and larger, a plain stone edifice nearly square, which was built in 1704, directly opposite the Custom House on Pine Street. This was the same year in which the French in Boston bought the land for their church, but were not permitted by the Congregational authorities to build. The church in New York was named "L'Eglise du St. Esprit" (The Church of the Holy Spirit), and still bears the name. The congregation worshipped in Pine Street until 1831, and then removed to what was the upper part of the city at the time, the corner of Church and Franklin Streets, where a white marble edifice, noted in its day, was erected. Meanwhile, in 1804, the church had become Episcopalian in affiliation, and as such still exists in the present Church du St. Esprit, which has its fourth home in a fine stone edifice in Twenty-seventh Street, near Madison Avenue, where the French service is maintained. Slow in its organization, the church reached its highest point of development in the sixty years from 1690 to 1750, declining in the next half century, largely because of the Revolutionary War. After 1804 there was a new lease of life.

Pine Street 1704

Church Street 1831

Twenty-Seventh Street Site

Among the names of the members are such families as Quintard, Pintard, Maynard, LeConte, Lorillard, Lamoureaux, Iselin, Guion, Girard, Galaudet, Dupuy (Depew), Anne Bureau, Basset, Bayard, Badeau and Allaire, which have figured in the professional, commercial and social life of the metropolis.

III

For over forty years Rev. Louis Rou was pastor of the French Church. In this period trouble arose over the

Pastor Rou

absorption of the French Church in New Rochelle by the Episcopalians. Gradually the influences were working in this direction, and in 1804 the Episcopal liturgy was adopted in New York as the only means of saving the church. Among the names of the pew owners at that time are Jacob Schieffelin, John R. Livingston, C. Low, John Pintard, Gulian Verplanck, all names thoroughly identified with the growth of the city, and some of them still prominent, as that of Low, the family from which came the reform Mayor of New York, Honourable Seth Lowe, formerly president of Columbia University. But the most eminent name on the roll was that of Jay, which ranks high in American history.

During Mr. Rou's pastorate also, a great excitement was occasioned by a party question. The merits of the case, according to Waldron, were as follows : Stephen De Lancey, a wealthy merchant, and among the chief patrons of the church, was dissatisfied with Mr. Rou, and procured his dismissal for his want of zeal, and some innovations which he had introduced to the church discipline. The deposed minister appealed from the decision of the congregation to Governor Burnet and his council, who sustained the appellant. Both parties published indignant memorials on a dispute which had proceeded so far that, when De Lancey was elected to the Legislative Assembly, the governor refused to administer to him the oath of office, alleging that he was not a British subject. De Lancey contended that he had left France previous to the Revocation of the Edict of Nantes, and had received denizenship, under the great seal of Great Britain, from James the Second, previous to his abdication. De Lancey was proved to be right, and the Assembly sustained his claims against the governor. Mr. Rou's assistant, the Rev. Mr. Moulinard, took part against his superior. The consistory stated that they had paid Mr. Rou in full of all demands, and could dismiss him when they pleased. Still, the council decided in Mr. Rou's favour, and directed

Question of
Citizenship

The Rappelyea Estate, foot of Thirty-fifth Street, North River

Original Bayard House, 1800, 110th Street, Harlem, near First Avenue
Home of the Bayard Family in New York

that the ministers who should officiate on the following
Sabbath in the church, must proclaim the same decision
publicly, after divine service in the forenoon. All these
efforts, however, did not produce reconciliation, as Mr.
Moulinard was much opposed to the Church of England.
A feature of the case was the proving of citizenship on
the part of the French claimant. It should be said, in
praise of Mr. De Lancey and his following that they accepted the adverse decision, and did not obstruct the
pastor in his work. Few churches in the state or country
have had a longer or more honourable history than the
French Church in New York, which has enrolled so
many influential men and women, known for uprightness
and philanthropy.

The church is at present actively engaged in philan- *The Church To-day*
thropic effort. But recently it purchased the property
adjoining its fine house of worship, on the corner of
Fourth Avenue and Twenty-seventh Street, for $150,000,
as an investment. The title will be held in the name of
some of the prominent members. The object is to procure sufficient funds from rentals to found an institution
for homeless men. If this investment results as successfully as others which the astute members of the church
have made in the past, ample provision will be made for
the proposed charity. This movement is one of the
many good movements instituted by the present pastor,
Rev. Alfred V. Wittmeyer, who has been in charge nearly
thirty years. For a long time the church has been the
real friend of homeless men. Every Sunday evening a
company of the park bench loungers attend the evening
services, the collection at which is used to provide bed
and supper for the homeless and destitute. The work
among this class has led to the founding of an institution
which will be to many a means of reformation and new
beginning. It is peculiarly fitting that such work should
be done by a church which dates back to the days of
homelessness, exile and persecution, and whose first

members knew well the meaning of a helping hand in time of need.

IV

The harmony of the French colony was much disturbed by reports, carefully circulated, that they were inviting an invasion of New York by their compatriots in Canada. In order to avoid the odium which must necessarily arise from this scandal, they called a meeting and framed the following address:

To His Excellency Lord Cornbury, Governor of New York:
We, the undersigned, pray your Excellency to inquire into the report that we were inviting our countrymen to invade this province; the report has been spread throughout the whole State, and proves pernicious to all the *French Refugees* in general, and disturbs their peace and quiet, as it obstructs that affection and familiarity which they had formerly enjoyed with the other inhabitants of this province, to their grief and resentment. We pray your Excellency to instruct your printer to publish the result, for the pleasure and vindication of our reputation in this respect. And your Petitioners, as in all duty bound, will ever pray.

The Huguenots also had some connection with Trinity parish, through one of their ministers. In 1685, the Rev. Mr. Neau, with his wife and daughter, left France for America, accompanied by other Huguenots. The Rev. Mr. Vesey, the first rector of Trinity Church, appointed Mr. Neau his catechist, which office he filled for several years, and he might be considered the founder of Trinity School—an institution distinguished among the noble charities of the city. This excellent man closed his profitable life in 1722, and was buried near the northern porch of old Trinity, where he had long worshipped and served. A granddaughter of his married the brave Captain Oliver H. Perry, who was ever ready to defend his country; and their only daughter, Elizabeth Mason Perry, married the Rev. Francis Vinton, D. D., long time rector of Trinity.

CHAPTER III

NEW ROCHELLE, THE HUGUENOT SETTLEMENT

I

IN the year 1689 the lord of Pelham Manor, Mr. John The Pell Land Bought 1689 Pell, deeded 6,000 acres of land to Jacob Leisler, a prominent Dutch merchant of New York. Leisler, who had the misfortune to be hung a couple of years after this transaction, on a charge of high treason, made the purchase on behalf of a band of refugees from La Rochelle, and the 6,000 acres of land which he took over form the present township of New Rochelle, in Westchester County.

Some of the Huguenots who joined in the settlement had lived in New York for some years previously, while others came from the West Indies, where they had hastily sought refuge ; but the greater part of the colonists came from England, as tradition has it, in one of the King's ships. They were Rochellese who left their city four years before the Revocation, fled to the neighbouring Isle of Rhé, and thence on British ships to hospitable England. The exact date of their landing in America is not known, but it must have been during the year 1689 ; local tradition points out their landing place as Bonnefoy's Point, on what is now known as Davenport's Neck. The Rochelle colonists were not the first Huguenots to settle within the limits of the Pell Grant, for in 1686 we find Maria Graton, widow of William Cothouneau, conveying a tract of land to Alexander Allaire in what is now New Rochelle, and Allaire himself sold a piece of land to Theophilus Forestier one year later.

During the year following the arrival of the refugees Early Hardships there was much suffering in the settlement, as the follow-

231

ing "humble petition of ye inhabitants of New Rochelle, humbly showeth."

That your petitioners having been forced by the late persecutions in France to forsake their country and estates, and flye to ye Protestant Princes. Their Majestyes by their proclamation of ye 25th of Aprill, 1689, did grant them an azile (asylum) in all their dominions, with their Riyall protection; wherefore they were invited to come and buy lands in the province, to the end that they might by their labour help the necessityes of their familyes, and did spend therein all their smale store, with the help of their friends, whereof, they did borrow great sums of money. They are above twenty (Ms. torn) poor and needy, not able . . . tles and clothing, much . . . they did hitherto beare above their . . . thereby reduced to a lamentable condition, as having been compelled to sell for that purpose the things which are most necessary for their use. Wherefore your petitioners humbly pray, that your Excellency may be pleased to take their case in serious consideration, and out of Charity and pity, to grant them for some years what help and priveleges your Excellency shall think convenient, and your petitioners in duty bound shall ever pray, etc.

THAUVET ELSI COTHOUNEAU.

II

Among the number of those who had lived in New York a year or so previous to the coming of the main band of settlers, and who later joined them in New Rochelle, were Theroulde, Allaire, Le Vilain, Machet, Bongrand, Thauver, Mercier, Mastier and Jouneau. The town records, which were begun in 1699, give us the names of the freeholders at several different periods. In 1708 the land was divided among the following : Daniel Lambert, Elie Badeau, Daniel Giraud, Gregoire Gougeon, Daniel Bonnet, Elie de Bonrepos, Jean Magnon, Besly, Isaac Mercier, Bartholomew Le Roux, Pierre Valleau, Jacob Scurman, Ambroise Sycart, Benjamin Faneuil, Alexander Allaire, Jean Pemeau, J. Levillain, Daniel Rayneau, Guilleaume Le Counte, François Le Counte, Zacharie Angevin, and Frederick Schorman. The next sixteen years must have seen many changes in the growing town, for the list of freeholders for 1724 has a totally different complexion. The following names were signed to a deed "granting to Anthony Lespinard a portion of land for the erection of a mill" : Besly, Oliver Besly, Simon Mabe, Francis Ganyard, Frederick Scurman, Gilleaume Clapp, John Clark, John Martin, Estienne Guerin, Benj. Petit, Josias Le Conte, Abel Devoux, Samuel Barnard, John Moras, Peter Samson, John Coutant, F. Bolt, Jr., Zaccarie Angevin, Pierre Elisse Gallaudet, Isaac Mercier, Lancinie Thauvet, Anam Guion, Andre Naudain, Alexander Allaire, Gregoire Gougeon, James Roubet, Henry Shadden, Rachel Neufille.

In 1695 letters of denization were issued to Francis Le Count, David de Bonrepos, Alexander Allaire, Henry Beignon, Esaye Valleau, Andrew Thaunet, David Bonnefoy, Louis Guion, and Louis Guion his son, Pierre Das, Pierre Palcot, Andrew Naudin, and Andrew and Louis his sons, Theophile Fourrestier, Charles Fourrestier, Ambroise Sycard, and Ambroise, and Daniel and Jacques his sons, Guilliaume Landrin, Guilliaume Cothouneau, Isaac Caillard, Marie Cothouneau, and Guilliaume Cothouneau her son, Jean Neufuille, Estensie Lavinge and Jean Coutanti, of foreign birth.

Emigrants continued to come to New Rochelle up to 1700. One of these was Daniel Bonnet, perhaps the last to come. He purchased land from Bartholomew Le Roux, and the property is still held by his descendants. The following incident is related of his flight from France : *Daniel Bonnet*

"Daniel and his wife were attempting to reach the French coast with two small children concealed in the paniers of a donkey, covered with fresh vegetables. The mother having enjoined upon the children to keep perfect silence, no matter what might occur, they had scarcely commenced their journey when they were overtaken by a gendarme who demanded to know what the paniers contained. The mother replied, 'fresh vegetables for the market.' As if doubting her words, the rough soldier *Story of Flight* rode up to the side of the donkey, and thrust his sword into the nearest panier, exclaiming as he rode away, 'Bon voyage, mes amis!' The agony of the parents may be conceived, until the soldier was well out of sight, when the panier was immediately opened, and one child was found to have been pierced through the calf of his leg.''

The
Lispenards
Another of the later arrivals was Margaret Lepperner, who came with her two children, Anthony and Susanna. Anthony became the founder of a well-known family, the Lispenards ; Lepperner being merely a malformation of the name due to the peculiar orthographic methods then in vogue. A French diary in the possession of the Lispenard family, dating back to the days before the Revocation, contains many interesting and pious entries of which the two following are fair examples :

From a
Family Diary
"September 20th, 1671.—I have been married to Abel de Forge. I beg the good Lord, that He gives us the grace to live a long time in His holy fear, and that it will please Him to give us a good paradise at the end.''

"October 2d, 1672.—My wife has been confined of a girl Margaret, at about ten o'clock of the day, on a Wednesday. Margaret died, and has given her spirit to God, between six and seven o'clock of the afternoon.''

III

A Description
of the Place
1704
From the pen of Madame Knight, who passed through New Rochelle in the year 1704, comes the following brief description of the village at that time : "On the 22d of December we set out for New Rochelle, where being come, we had good entertainment, and recruited ourselves very well. This is a very pretty place, well compact, and good, handsome houses, clean, good and passable roads, and situated on a navigable river, abundance of land, well fenced and cleared all along as we passed, which caused in me a love to the place, which I could have been content to live in it. Here we rid over a bridge made of one entire stone, of such a breadth that a cart might pass with safety, and to spare. It lay over a pas-

Berrian House

Jean Machet House

OLD HUGUENOT HOUSES AT NEW ROCHELLE

sage cut through the rock to convey water to a mill not far off. Here are three fine taverns within call of each other, and very good provision for travellers."

Very early in its history New Rochelle became a place **A Resort** of some resort, "not only for the acquirement of the French language, but on account of the hospitality and politeness of its inhabitants." And although there were no regular schools in the town for some time after its establishment, the children receiving their instruction at home, New Rochelle became rather famous for the number **Good Schools** of sons of well-to-do citizens who sent them there to be educated. The most illustrious of the boys who were thus trained in the homes of New Rochelle were John Jay, who is treated of elsewhere in this volume, General **Jay** Philip Schuyler, the Revolutionary soldier, and Wash- **Schuyler** ington Irving—three pupils whom the lay schoolmaster **Irving** of New Rochelle might well have been proud of. When we remember that, in spite of their poverty for a short period during the first trying days of settlement in the New World, these founders of New Rochelle were not mere fortune seekers, but men of birth and breeding and of good estate in France—of a far higher average of **Centre of Culture** wealth and culture than the English and Dutch of New York—we need not be surprised that the little village on the Sound soon gained a reputation for elegance and culture which far surpassed that of its neighbours.

IV

The settlers of New Rochelle were not able to build a church for themselves at once. For the first three years **Church Going** they attended communion service at the French church in New York which stood on Marketfield Street. From New Rochelle to New York was a distance of twenty-three miles by road, and the refugees admirably evinced their devotion to their faith by walking the entire distance there and back in order to take part in the Lord's Sup- **Genuine Devotion** per. Some of the women and the weaker children were

placed in the few rude carts which the emigrants possessed, and then the picturesque caravan set out on its long
journey to church, the men and the remainder of the
women walking beside the carts, many of them barefooted, yet all rejoicing, and showing by their happy
faces and the ringing hymns they sang that they took
their privations lightly.   All lesser evils were swallowed
up in the great good for which they were never tired of
giving thanks to God—the freedom to worship God openly
and without a shadow of misgiving, and the knowledge
that they were laying up for their children and their
children's children a like heritage.   But it must not be
thought that these exiles did not love their native land.
They left France with regret in their hearts, and often
turned towards their old home with pity and with long-
ing.   Of one old man it is related that every evening at
sunset he would go down to the shore of the Sound, look
off across the water in the direction of France and sing
one of Marot's hymns, while the slow tears fell upon the
sand at his feet.   Gradually others met with him, until
there gathered daily a little group of exiles to pray and
sing.

As to this attendance upon church in New York, the
fact is attested by the celebrated Huguenot, Dr. John
Pintard, the founder of the Historical Society, who says
in his *Recollections:*   "The holy sacrament was administered to the Huguenots, at New Rochelle, four times
a year, namely, Christmas, Easter, Whitsuntide, and the
middle of September.   During the intermissions that
occurred, the communicants walked to New York for that
purpose.   Prior to their departure on Sunday, they always
collected the young children, and left them in the care of
friends, while they set off early in the morning, and
walked to the city barefooted, carrying their shoes and
stockings in their hands.   They were accustomed to stop
at a rock, about twelve miles from the city, to rest and
take refreshments, where they put on their shoes and

Joy in Liberty

True to their
Faith

pursued their journey, and arrived at the French church in time for service. The earliest French church in New York was in Marketfield Street, near the Battery. It was a very humble edifice, but still, being the house of God, sufficient to attract the worshippers from States-Island and New Rochelle on the Sabbath, where they used to chant Marot's hymns—those animating strains that had so often cheered their pious fathers at the stake in the time of the bloody persecution of their fatherland. With these hymns in their heads, and the little Testaments which they brought from France concealed in their hair, they enjoyed that peace of mind which passeth knowledge, unknown to their persecutors."

The first church building was erected in 1692, and was a small edifice constructed of wood. Provision for a church had been made in the grant of land to Jacob Leisler, it being there declared that John Pell, lord of the manor, with the consent of Rachel, his wife, did (besides the six thousand acres) give and grant "to the said Jacob Leisler, the further quantity of one hundred acres of land for the use of the French church, erected, or to be erected by the inhabitants of the said tract of land." The church stood on the old Boston post road, near the location of the present Presbyterian church. About the time that the church was built Louis Bongrand donated a piece of land forty paces square to be used as a "church-yard to bury their dead." And subsequently a house and about three and a half acres of land were given "by the town to the church forever." *The First House of Worship 1692*

Church Yard

It would seem that the emigrants had a pastor two years before they had a church, as is shown by the following note to Governor Leisler : *Notes from the Pastor*

SIR: I have too much respect for your orders not to execute them punctually, so that pursuant to what you did me the honour lately to give me, I spoke to the principals of this new colony about the nomination of some persons for the vacant office of Justice of the Peace ; but as the condition you require—that is a knowledge of the English tongue—has precluded them from making the election of two or three according to your order, they cannot pitch upon any except Mr. Strang, saving your approbation which, if you will have the goodness to accord them, you will oblige them infinitely. Mr. Pinton has also delivered me, this day, an order to be communicated to the sd (said) inhabitants relative to the election and nomination of Assessors, Collectors, and Commissaries, for levying, imposing, and receiving taxes for his Majesty's service. The time is very short, since it is the twenty-seventh inst., they must be at Westchester; but they look for some forbearance and delay from your goodness in case, notwithstanding their diligence, they may not be able punctually to answer. It is not through any unwillingness to exert themselves to meet it, but you know their strength as well as I. Notwithstanding, despite their poverty and misery, they will never lack in submission to the orders on behalf of his Majesty, both for the public good and interest. This they protested to me, and I pray you to be persuaded thereof. I am with respect, and I pray God for your prosperity, sir,

The French in Citizenship

Your very humble and very obedient servant,

D. BONREPOS,
Pastor of this French Colony.

N. Rochelle, 29 *Octob.*, 1690.

The period of Dr. David Bonrepos' pastorate in New Rochelle was a short one, for in 1694 he went to the church at Staten Island. In 1695 the Rev. John Miller, describing the province of New York, says, "There is a meeting house at Richmond (Staten Island) of which Dr. Bonrepos is pastor." This charge he retained until his death in 1734.

School Master's License

His brother, Elias Bonrepos, lived in New Rochelle, and like the pastor was a man of learning and attainments. In 1705 he was licensed to keep school, as the following shows:

Edward Visco't Cornbury, Capt.-General and Governor-in-Chief of ye provinces of New York, New Jersies and Terr'es depending thereon in America and vice-admiral of ye same, &c. To Elias Bon Repose greeting you are hereby impowered and lycen'd to keep school within ye town of New Rochelle in ye county of Westchester and carefully and diligently to instruct ye children under yo' care and tuition in ye art of reading and writing during my pleasure, given under my hand

and seal at New York this 23d day of June, 1705, and in ye 4th year
of her ma'tys Reign.   CORNBURY.

The next minister at New Rochelle was the Rev. Daniel **Pastor Bondet**
Bondet. He had been a student of the seminary at Geneva,
and upon the Revocation fled into England where he was
received into orders by the Bishop of London. He accompanied the settlers to New Oxford, where he was engaged in missionary work among the Indians, and came
to New Rochelle probably during the fall of 1695. He
soon took a high place among the provincial clergy, and
in 1704 we find the clergy of New York writing of him
as follows: "Mr. Daniel Bondet has gone further and
done more in that good work (converting the heathen)
than any Protestant minister that we know; we commend
him to your pious consideration as a person industrious
in ye service of the church and his own nation, ye French,
at New Rochelle."

In 1709 the French Reformed Church of New Rochelle **Becoming**
conformed to the Church of England. The following is **Anglican 1709**
an extract from a letter of Colonel Heathcote, who was
instrumental in bringing the change to pass:

At first Mr. Bondet used the French prayers, according to the
Protestant churches of France; and subsequently on every third Sunday, as appears by the above letter, the Liturgy of the Church of England; but in 1709 his congregation, with the exception of two individuals, followed the example of their Reformed brethren in England,
by conforming to the English Church. This memorable event is thus
recorded in the charter: "That on the 12th day of June, in the year
of our Lord, one thousand seven hundred and nine, all the inhabitants
of the township of New Rochelle, who were members of the said
French Church, excepting two, unanimously agreed and consented to
conform themselves, in the religious worship of their said Church, to
the Liturgy and rites of the Church of England as established by law;
and by a solemn act or agreement did submit to, and put themselves
under the protection of the same."

Since the first wooden church had been built the num- **New Stone**
ber of communicants had greatly increased, and in 1709 **Church 1710**

a license was procured for building a new one.   The new church was begun in the summer of the following year and was completed that same autumn.   It was of stone, nearly square in shape, and perfectly plain both outside and in.   Of the building of this church a pious chronicler records that "so anxious were all to contribute something towards its completion, that even females carried stones in their hands, and mortar in their aprons, to complete the sacred work."

A Church
Secession

Shortly after the conformation to the Episcopal Church, a schism arose to rend the harmony of New Rochelle. "The seceders erected a meeting-house, styled themselves

Presbyterian
Church
Formed

'The French Protestant Congregation,' and remained violently opposed to their lawful pastors; and not only so, but in opposition to their own founders, proscribed the Church of England in her doctrine, discipline, ordinances, usages, rites and ceremonies, as popish, rotten and unscriptural."   Those were "parlous times," and if we may read between the lines, religious discussion waxed extremely warm in the otherwise peaceful village. The present Presbyterian Church is the flourishing progeny of the "seceders."

A Missionary
Pastor

Concerning Pastor Bondet the same active layman, Colonel Heathcote, writes: "He is a good man, & preaches very intelligibly in English, which language he uses every third Sabbath, when he avails himself of the Liturgy; he has done a great deal of service since his arrival in this country.   His pay is only thirty pounds ($150) per anum."   In 1714 this good man took the spiritual charge of the Mohegans, or River Indians.   In his reports he states that there were fifty communicants in his church. After labouring here twenty-seven years, he died in his sixty-ninth year, in 1722.

Pastor
Stouppe

The third minister was Rev. Pierre Stouppe, A. M.   He gives some interesting information in a letter dated Decem-

1727

ber 11, 1727, about the early settlement of New Rochelle. He writes: "The present number of inhabitants is about four hundred ; there is one dozen houses round the church, near each other, which gives the place the appearance of a town. There are several French families settled within bounds of the settlement, who worship with the congregation. Such was the commencement of the beautiful and picturesque village of New Rochelle. More than a century and a half have passed away since its founders immigrated to America, and their noble and holy principles have left good influences, evidently discernible in the refinement, morals and religion of their descendants, still bearing their patronymics. Let it not be forgotten that the Bible came with these early settlers, & was the foundation of their legislation. The Dutch and Lutheran families generally unite with the church when the service is performed in English, & they bring their children to be baptized by the French ministers." There was no school in the place, and the parents supplied the deficiency by instructing their children. There were about one hundred slaves in the settlement, who were taught to read by their masters, and were baptized and admitted to the communion. *The Bible their Basis*

In July, 1760, the revered and venerable Pierre *1760* Stouppe rested from his labours on earth, leaving behind him a reputation unsullied by a stain, after having, for the long period of thirty-seven years, faithfully discharged the duties of his mission. He was greatly respected by his people, and at the time of his death the number of his communicants amounted to eighty. As a mark of respect his remains were interred under the chancel where he had so long officiated.

His successor was Rev. Michael Houdin, the last *Pastor Houdin* French preacher in New Rochelle. This zealous missionary was born in France, in 1705. At the beginning of war between France and Great Britain he quitted Canada, where he first settled, and went to New York, where he read his recantation, being previously a member of the Church of Rome. Mr. Waldron tells us, in his *Hugue-*

nots of Westchester, that when Mr. Houdin and his wife reached New York, in June, 1744, Governor Clinton, suspicious of all Frenchmen, confined the strangers to their lodgings, and set two sentinels to guard them. His Excellency summoned them before him, when Mr. Houdin first informed him that the French intended to attack Oswego with eight hundred men, being long desirous of possessing that town. After filling the office of missionary for some years in Trenton, New Jersey, he was employed, in 1759, as a guide to General Wolfe, in his expedition against Quebec. Before he undertook this business, he preached to the Provincial troops destined for Canada, in St. Peter's Church, Westchester, from St. Matthew 10 : 28 : "Fear not them which kill the body." This church, at that time, was the only parochial place of worship in a district of many miles, including Fordham, New Rochelle, West Farms, etc. The chaplain escaped the danger of the war ; but the gallant Wolfe fell, mortally wounded, at the moment of victory, on the Heights of Abraham, September 13, 1759. After the reduction of Quebec, Mr. Houdin asked permission to return to his mission again, but General Murray would not consent, as there was no other person who could be relied on for intelligence concerning the French movements.

Returning to New York in 1761, he was appointed to New Rochelle, which village, as well as Fordham, was considered within the spiritual jurisdiction of Westchester Village, then the only parish in the county. The French church was named Trinity, and received, at this time, a charter from George the Third, dated 1762. Mr. Houdin served until his death in 1766. "He was a man of considerable learning and research, as well as of irreproachable character. He was not excelled in zeal and energy by any of his predecessors, and was followed to the grave by the regrets of his numerous parishioners. He was interred under the chancel of the old French church, in the same grave with Bondet and Stouppe. Since the

Margin notes:

Service as Interpreter and Guide

A Tribute

removal of the sacred edifice, to make way for the high-road to Boston, the mortal remains of these faithful and pious labourers, in the service of their Master, repose beneath the public way, and not a memorial stone marks the spot where they lie, or commemorates their usefulness, excellence, or piety.''

While our interest in the church as a French church ceases largely at this point, since it lost its distinctive character, it is to be noted that among the later rectors of the parish was Rev. Louis Pintard Bayard, a descendant of two of the best known Huguenot families.

New Rochelle still retains something of a French character. Here and there a house with a Huguenot history can be found, and many of the old families are represented by their descendants. The growth of New York, however, has made New Rochelle one of the favourite suburban sections, and it will soon take on a metropolitan character that will obliterate what is left of its early French atmosphere.

A Favourite
Suburb
To-day

VIEW OF THE OLD FORT, THE CHURCH, AND NEIGHBOURING HOUSES, NEW AMSTERDAM

CHAPTER IV

JOHN JAY, STATESMAN AND JURIST

I

THE most eminent of the Huguenot descendants in our early history as a nation was John Jay, who, as one of his biographers says, by reason of his character, "conscientious, upright, just and wise, like Washington, survives in the popular imagination as an abstract type of propriety." He was exceptional in character as in statesmanship.

John Jay was the eighth child and sixth son of Peter Jay and Mary, daughter of Jacobus Van Cortlandt, and thus united the French and Dutch blood and two distinguished New York families, to which a third, the Livingstons, was to be added. John was born December 12, 1745. His father was a rich merchant. His great-grandfather, Pierre Jay, was a Huguenot merchant of Rochelle, who left France on the Revocation of the Edict of Nantes, when the greater part of his property was confiscated. In the *Life of John Jay*, by his son, some account is given of the fortunes of this ancestor.

"Pursuant to an order passed in January, 1685," says this account, "the Protestant Church at Rochelle was demolished. The ensuing summer a number of troops were marched into the city and quartered on the Protestant inhabitants, and these troops were soon followed by

four companies of dragoons. The attempt made to convert or intimidate Mr. Pierre Jay proving fruitless, some of these dragoons were sent to his house to live and act at their discretion." There is no evidence that they offered personal violence to Mr. Jay or his family, but in

JOHN JAY, FIRST JUSTICE OF THE SUPREME COURT

other respects they behaved as it was intended they should. Such a situation was intolerable, and Mr. Jay lost no time in relieving his family from it. He found means to withdraw them, together with some articles of furniture, secretly from the house, and succeeded in putting them on board a vessel which he had engaged for the purpose. They fortunately set sail without being discovered, and were safely landed at Plymouth in England. He thought it advisable to remain behind, doubtless with the design to save what he could from the wreck of his fortune. It was not long before the absence of his family excited attention and produced investigation. After some time he was arrested and committed to prison. Being closely connected with some influential Roman Catholics, he was, by their interposition and good offices, set at liberty. He was fortunate enough to escape to England in one of his own vessels that arrived from Spain. As soon as his departure was known, his estate was seized, and no part of it afterwards came to the use of either himself or his family. He died in England. Augustus Jay His son Augustus, after many adventures, settled in New York in 1686, where he married Anna Maria Bayard, descendant of the Protestant professor of theology at Paris, who had left his country on account of his religion, like so many others, and made his home in Holland. Through his wife's relatives, the Bayards and Stuyvesants (Peter Stuyvesant's wife being a Huguenot), and his brother-in-law, Stephen Peloquin, a merchant of Bristol, England, Augustus Jay soon formed a profitable business connection. His son became partner in his firm ; and in 1740 his name appears as alderman, while the family became allied with the manorial families of Van Cortlandt, Phillipse, and Livingston.

II

From his father, Peter Jay, who was a typical New York merchant of the time, a gentleman of opulence, character and reputation, John inherited many marked

Peter Jay's
Piety
traits.   Peter was a very pious man.   In letters to his
son James in England he writes : "Let us endeavour to
adhere to the worship of God, observing His holy ordinances as the rule of our lives, let us disregard the
wicked insinuations of libertines, who not only deride
our most holy religion and the professors of it, but also
endeavour to gain proselytes to their detestable notions,
and so rob the Almighty of the honour and adoration
that is due to Him from His creatures."   And again,
"Don't forget to bring me Bishop Patrick's *Devout
Christian*, a book you doubtless will remember, as it contains the family prayers we always use."

Sturdy
Principle
Peter Jay was a colonist and not a Royalist, and his
son came naturally by his Whig notions.   "I have nothing to ask or fear from any man, and will not be compelled into measures."   That was the man, and that was
his son John.   Firmness of character that in excess would
have been obstinacy was a notable trait in them.   John
was brought up in Rye, in the old Jay house, a long low
building only one room deep but eighty feet long, that
grew as the family required.   He was taught by his
mother the rudiments of English and the Latin grammar.
"Johnny is of a very grave disposition and takes to
John's
Education
learning exceedingly well," wrote his father when the
lad was seven.   He was sent to grammar school at eight,
a school kept by Rev. Peter Stouppe, pastor of the
French Huguenot Church, then lately joined to the Episcopal communion at New Rochelle.   French was then
spoken generally at the school.

In 1760 he entered King's College (Columbia University of to-day), when a little over fourteen.   After graduation in 1764, he studied law, in 1768 receiving admission to the bar.   Family and ability combined to gain
Marriage 1774
him a large practice.   In 1774 he was married to Sarah
Livingston, whose father later became governor of New
Jersey.

The Revolution gave him opportunity to serve his country in most conspicuous manner, and opportunity found him ready and eager.   He took an active part in the measures that led to independence.   In the year of his marriage he was one of the committee of fifty appointed by the citizens of New York to correspond with other colonial committees concerning the Boston Port Bill.   His talents were recognized and his advancement was rapid. In September, 1774, he was elected a delegate to the Continental Congress in Philadelphia, and took a leading position in that body, although one of the youngest members.   It is sufficient proof of his position that he was charged with drawing up the Address to the People of Great Britain, and the utmost confidence was placed in his judgment. *Active Patriot*

He was a member also of the second Congress, in 1775, and wrote the addresses to the people of Canada and Ireland.   He rendered most useful service on the secret committee which corresponded with the friends of America in Europe.   His pen was able and eloquent, and none could more forcibly present the cause of the colonies. He was a member of the committee that drew up the Declaration of Independence, and doubtless had full share in that document, although he was not among its signers, owing to the fact that it was deemed essential to the cause of liberty that he take the seat in the provincial Congress of New York, to which he was elected in April, 1776.   In that body he was a leader, and it was his hand which drafted the constitution adopted by the State. *Member of Congress 1775*

Constitution Maker

III

It should not be forgotten that it was the descendant of a French Huguenot refugee who, as chairman of the committee of the New York Congress to which the Declaration of Independence had been referred, wrote and reported this resolution, which was unanimously adopted : *Resolution for Independence*

"That the reasons assigned by the Continental Congress for declaring the United Colonies free and independent States are cogent and conclusive; and that while we lament the cruel necessity which has rendered that measure unavoidable, we approve the same, and while at the risk of our lives and fortunes, join with the other colonies in supporting it."

Then the New York delegates at Philadelphia were authorized to sign the Declaration. Jay served as one of the Council of Safety in New York, and later accepted provisional appointment as Chief Justice of the State. This appointment was confirmed under the constitution, when adopted, but he was prohibited from holding any other office except that of Congressional delegate "on special occasion." Events now moved rapidly and the special occasion soon came in the secession of Vermont from New Hampshire and New York. In December, 1778, Jay was sent to Congress, and elected its president. He was the author of the letter, written in 1779 in the name of the Congress, to the people of the States on the subject of currency and finance. Then came a stress in foreign affairs, and it was necessary to send abroad the ablest men to be found. Jay was accordingly despatched as plenipotentiary to Spain, arriving there in January, 1780. He resigned his chief justiceship and the presidency of Congress to undertake a mission that proved unsatisfactory, though through no fault of his; he succeeded in gaining material help from Spain.

In 1781 he was commissioned to act with Franklin, Adams, Jefferson and Laurens in negotiating peace with Great Britain. Thus two of the five members of that most important diplomatic body were Huguenot descendants. Jay arrived in Paris from Spain in June, 1782, the provisional articles were signed November 30, 1782, and the formal treaty on September 3, 1783. During this period Jay was the one who "evinced a jealous suspicion of the disinterestedness of France and a punctilious attention to the dignity of his country"—perhaps

Marginal notes:

Chief Justice

President of Congress

Spain 1780

Negotiating Peace 1781

remembering the treatment which France had given to his forebears. When the peace treaty had been signed, Jay resigned all his commissions and came back to New York in 1784 as a private citizen, after ten years of most arduous and brilliant service for his country—a service that had contributed as much as that of any other man to the shaping of the policies and course of the young Republic.

IV

But he could not remain in private life; he was too valuable to the state. He was presented with the freedom of the city, and at once elected delegate to Congress. Before he reached America, indeed, that body had chosen him to be foreign secretary, and he held that position until the beginning of the Federal Government in 1789. He was foremost in the organization of that government, and joined Hamilton and Madison in issuing the *Federalist*. He published an address to the people of New York, in vindication of the Constitution, and worked zealously with Hamilton for its adoption by New York. From his legal acquirements and judicial temperament it was natural and fitting that under this new government he was appointed, September 26, 1789, the first Chief Justice of the Supreme Court of the United States. The two men who through their ability and influence swung New York into line for the Federal Constitution were of French blood.

Offices and Honours

First Chief Justice Supreme Court

None of the great statesmen who founded the Republic escaped detraction at some period, and Jay was in the company of Washington and others in this respect. It was necessary to make a commercial treaty with Great Britain, if war was to be averted, and Chief Justice Jay was appointed envoy to England for that purpose in 1794. He signed a treaty with Lord Grenville November 19th, after four months spent in negotiations, and landed in New York again in May, 1795. "Jay's Treaty" was fiercely attacked, particularly because of the article de-

Jay's Treaty

claring that a free ship did not make free cargo. In spite of the fact that by the treaty provisions the eastern boundary of Maine was determined, that American citizens recovered over ten millions for illegal captures by British cruisers, and that the western posts held by British garrisons were surrendered, Jay was accused of having betrayed his country, and his effigy was burned together with copies of the treaty. Washington, however, ratified the treaty, with the approval of the Senate, and its beneficial effects were subsequently recognized.

Governor of
New York

Two days before he arrived in New York from this foreign mission, Jay had been elected Governor of New York ; and in spite of the violent denunciation of his treaty was re-elected, serving six years. At the close of his second term, in 1801, he resolutely withdrew from public life, living on the ancestral estate at Bedford,

Death in 1829

Westchester County, for a quarter century. He died May 17, 1829. He declined a second appointment by President Adams as Chief Justice of the United States Supreme Court, and kept himself free from politics.

The characteristics of his ancestry now appeared prominently. He was devoted to religious and philanthropic movements, and his public utterances in his later years were chiefly as president of the American Bible Society. He was a member of the Episcopal church, in which most

Christian
Philan-
thropist

of the Huguenot churches in this country became merged, and maintained the highest character for moral purity, philanthropy, patriotism, and unyielding integrity. He was long in advance of the latter-day abolitionists. As early as 1785 he was president of a New York society for the emancipation of the slaves, and it was largely due to his efforts that slavery was abolished in New York in 1799. As a private citizen his influence was scarcely less marked than when he was in public life. In his eighty-fourth year closed a life whose purity and integrity are

Webster's
Eulogy

summed up in a sentence by Daniel Webster that forms a fitting epitaph : `` When the spotless ermine of the judi-

cial robe fell on John Jay, it touched nothing less spotless than itself." America owes a lasting debt of gratitude to this great jurist and statesman, one of the greatest
gifts France made to this country through the persecution
of her Protestant citizens.

The following " Reflection of John Jay" concerning his   Jay on his
ancestry is given in his biography :   Ancestry

After what has been said, you will observe with pleasure and gratitude how kindly and how amply Providence was pleased to provide
for the welfare of our ancestor, Augustus. Nor was his case a solitary or singular instance. The beneficent care of heaven appears to
have been evidently and remarkably extended to all those persecuted
exiles. Strange as it may seem, I have never heard of one of them
who asked or received alms ; nor have I any reason to suspect, much
less to believe, that any of them came to this country in a destitute
situation. The number of refugees who settled here was considerable.
They did not disperse and settle in different parts of the country, but
formed three societies or congregations, one in the city of New York,
another at Paltz, and a third at a town which they purchased and
called New Rochelle. At New Rochelle they built two churches, and
lived in great tranquillity. None of them became rich, but they lived
comfortably.

LIBERTY HALL, BIRTHPLACE OF MRS JAY

CHAPTER V

ALEXANDER HAMILTON, STATESMAN AND FINANCIER

I

A Huguenot
Mother

SIDE by side with John Jay among the great figures of the Revolutionary period stands Alexander Hamilton, who had in his veins Huguenot blood, on his mother's side. No more brilliant genius has our country known. Many have ranked him next to Washington. Commonly he is placed in the eminent group that includes Franklin, Jay and Adams. He was second to none in the character and importance of his services to his country. To his commanding abilities as a financier the new Republic owed its financial salvation, and for his achievements in this difficult line he received as high praise as language could bestow. It was Daniel Webster who said of him : "He touched the dead corpse of public credit, and it sprang upon its feet." And this was no hyperbole.

Birthplace
1757

His career was romantic and remarkable. He was born January 11, 1757, on the island of Nevis, in the West Indies, where his father, an English officer of Scotch blood, met and took for wife the descendant of a French refugee, one of the considerable number that found an asylum in the West Indies. The boy was destined to know little of home life. In 1772, when he was fifteen, a hurricane swept over the island. A newspaper account of the disaster was so graphic in description that its unknown author was sought for, and found to be the lad Hamilton. So impressed was the governor of Nevis with the boy's talents that he was sent to the American colonies, where he could find wider field. He was placed in a grammar

ALEXANDER HAMILTON
Nat. 1757 - Ob. 1804

From the Original Painting in the Trumbull Collection, Yale School of Art

school at Elizabethtown, New Jersey, and in less than a year was declared ready for college. Princeton would not allow him to advance as rapidly as he was able, regardless of the established four years, so he applied for this privilege at King's College in New York, and was accepted. He went through college at an amazing pace, taking such extra studies as he desired. Racing Through College

Meanwhile the storm of the Revolution was approaching. As a British subject the young man's sympathies were at first with England. But in 1774, when he was seventeen, he visited Boston, where the "tea party" and its consequences were the absorbing topic. This led him to study with the thoroughness that marked him the whole subject of the relations of the colonies to the mother country and the questions at issue. As a result he returned to New York an American. A mass meeting of patriots was held in July of that same year, and Hamilton heard the speeches. Suddenly, uninvited and unannounced, he took the platform and began to speak. At first surprise kept the people silent, as this youthful and slender student went on. Soon they forgot his age, and listened to one who knew his subject and was enlightening as well as enchaining them. That incident, which reminds us of Wendell Phillips' first anti-slavery speech, introduced Alexander Hamilton to the American public. From that day Hamilton used his voice and pen with telling effect. A recent writer says : The Tea Party Maiden Speech

During the winter of 1774–5, a coterie of Tory writers, mostly clergymen and educators, issued a series of essays presenting the British side so strongly as to threaten great harm to the popular cause, unless ably answered. These essays were soon met by anonymous replies so exhaustive and convincing as to excite the admiration of the Tories themselves. On every hand eager search was made to discover this new "Junius." The reputation of John Jay and of Governor Livingston was augmented in no small degree by the supposition that they were the authors of the patriotic answers. Great was the surprise at the discovery, after some weeks, that the real author was the Tory Essayists Answered youthful student from the island of Nevis.   Oddly enough, it turned out that one of the Tories with whom the lad had been conducting his newspaper controversy was Dr. Cooper, president of King's College.

But now the time for action came, and Hamilton, who had leaped from boyhood into manhood, devoted himself to the study of war.   So apt a scholar was he that when the New York Convention ordered the raising of an artillery company, he was made its captain.   His company was brought to a high state of discipline so rapidly that it attracted the attention of General Greene, who brought the young officer to the attention of Washington.

Nothing could hold this precocious genius back.   He was with the Continental Army on Long Island and in New Jersey.   At Princeton and Trenton he shared in the laurels.   He constructed some earthworks with such unusual skill that they were noticed by Washington, who traced them to their author.   So drawn was the great commander to the youth that he appointed him aide-de-camp to himself with rank of lieutenant-colonel, and made him secretary and confidential adviser.   This when he was twenty, in 1777.   Washington was forty-five, and members of his staff were old enough to be Hamilton's father, yet he won them all by his modesty and genuineness and ability.   For four years he served on Washington's staff, and then their official relationship came to an end through a misunderstanding.   Hamilton, however, remained with the army, preferring life on the line.   At Yorktown, commanding a corps under Lafayette, he led an assault upon a British redoubt with such gallantry, taking the redoubt at the point of the bayonet, that Lafayette was high in his praise, while Washington said, "Few cases have exhibited greater proof of intrepidity, coolness and firmness than were shown on this occasion."   By his courage Hamilton won

the name of "the Little Lion."   He had the military instinct, and would have made a great general, had his

life so developed; but he was destined for something
higher.

When the end of the war was in sight, Hamilton resigned his commission, took up the study of law at
Albany, and in four months was admitted to the bar.
In the fall of 1782 he was elected to the Continental
Congress, where he devoted his genius to the financial
and political problems that threatened the destruction
of the new Confederation. He adopted the national or
republican principle, as against the strictly democratic
idea. He believed that the best people must rule. He
felt that unless a stronger central government was formed
the people must lose what they had gained by the long
war. To create such a government became his passion.
He did more than any other man to secure the convention that wrought out the Constitution of the United
States, and in that convention he was a leading spirit
and power. Then he threw himself into the struggle to
secure the adoption of the constitution by the States.
His ends were gained, and two Huguenot descendants—
Jay and himself—had much to do with the success
achieved, which meant stability for the new Republic, if
not existence itself.

Washington as president made Hamilton the first
secretary of the treasury, and in this office his genius
blossomed. He was secretary of a treasury that had no
treasure in it. The government was not only moneyless
but in debt. Public credit had to be created. And
Hamilton created it. He caused the adoption of the
dollar first used by the United States in 1793. He induced Congress to assume the whole of the war indebtedness and pledge the resources of the United States for its
payment. In the process, to secure the necessary votes,
he made the famous bargain with Jefferson whereby the
national capital was located on the Potomac, a wise
choice. By financial measures which evoked the admiration of foreign statesmen, he bound the States into a

A National Policy

Creating the Constitution

Secretary of the Treasury

union of such cohesive force that a half century later the fibres of civil war, burning with increasing fury for four years, could not melt it.

From Public Life to Law Practice

Broad and deep he laid the foundation principles. And then, having done his duty at personal sacrifice, he left public life to practice his profession and make a living for his family. New York never had a more brilliant lawyer. Chancellor Kent said, "Hamilton rose to the loftiest heights of professional eminence. He was a very great favourite with the merchants of New York, and was employed in every important and every commercial case." He was marked by profound penetration, power of analysis, comprehensive grasp, strength of undertaking, firmness, frankness, and integrity. It was said he could win any case he undertook, right or wrong ; but he took only the case he considered right. Socially he was as popular as professionally. He was fascinating in his personality, was generous, polished, a brilliant conversationalist. In the prime of life, only forty-four, a great career seemed to lie before him, with no height that he might not reach.

The Duel and the End

Then came the tragic end. Aaron Burr, longtime a political opponent, made cause of offense, and challenged Hamilton to a duel. Burr thirsted for revenge, Hamilton felt no ill-will, tried to avoid the duel, but at length felt compelled to accept the challenge, which resulted in his death. It was nothing less than cold-blooded murder, and Burr the assassin. It is well said that not until Lincoln fell was the country again so shocked and stricken with horror. Burr, like Booth, fled, pursued by the anathemas of his countrymen. He had robbed the country of one of its greatest men, one who had rendered invaluable service at a critical time, and who deserves the honour and enduring remembrance of Americans. On his monument in Boston are carved these words, " Alexander Hamilton, Orator, Writer, Soldier, Jurist, Financier." Senator Henry Cabot Lodge says of him, " In founding a government he founded a nation. His versatility was extraordinary. He was a great orator and lawyer, and he was also the ablest political and constitutional writer of his day, a good soldier, and possessed of a wonderful capacity for organization and practical administration. He was a master in every field he entered and never failed.'' Such was the man who inherited his keen, intellectual powers from his Scotch father, and his fascinating vivacity and ardent temperament from his Huguenot mother.

The Grange, as it appeared in Hamilton's time. From an old print

CHAPTER VI

SOME PROMINENT NAMES

I

THE DE LANCEY FAMILY

ETIENNE DE LANCEY, born in Caen in October of the year 1663, came to New York in 1686, arriving on the seventh day of June. He had brought with him some of his family jewels and these he disposed of for the sum of £300. With this money (which in those days of scarce currency represented a far greater degree of value than would fifteen hundred dollars to-day) he set himself up as a merchant. He proved to be a shrewd and bold trader, and so well did his business ventures prosper that in the year 1700 he was enabled to marry the aristo-

cratic Anne van Cortland. For her he built a brick mansion on Broadway between the present Thames and Cedar Streets. It was one of the fine houses of the city, and from its windows a striking panorama of life and death could be seen; for on the one hand lay the Mall where New York's fashionable set was wont to walk of a sunny afternoon, and on the other lay Trinity churchyard where

fashionable folk rested. There was a broad veranda at the rear of the house which commanded a view of the North River, and there were stately gardens which sloped gently down to the edge of the water. Half a century later the fine old residence was turned into a tavern under the sign of the Province Arms, and for nearly fifty years it flourished as the fashionable hostelry of the town, and was the scene of many famous social and patriotic occasions. The Boreel building of to-day marks the site of Étienne De Lancey's once elegant mansion.

Before moving into their new home the De Lanceys lived for a time in the house which Étienne had first built for himself at the southeast corner of Broad and Pearl Streets. Afterwards it was used for a time as a store, and then, like the other De Lancey residence, it was converted into a tavern. Samuel Fraunces was the first innkeeper, and Fraunces' Tavern it has ever since been called. Here it was, in the long room which had once been Mrs. De Lancey's drawing-room, that George Washington said farewell to the officers of his army on the 4th of December, 1783. Many other hallowed memories cluster about the old building, as well befits the oldest landmark in the city of New York. It is pleasing to know that the De Lancey homestead has recently (1904) passed into the keeping of a patriotic society and will be preserved to future generations : nor is it without significance, as showing the important part played by Huguenot blood in the founding of the city, to note that the oldest and most historic edifice in the metropolis to-day was once the home of a French refugee. *Fraunces' Tavern*

But Étienne De Lancey did not confine his energies to laying up a fortune and building fine residences. He took a keen interest in all the affairs of the city and of the province. For several years he was a member of the board of aldermen, and for a long period, covering twenty-four years, he represented the city in the provincial assembly. It was through his generosity that the first town clock was set up in the city ; and the first fire-engine to be imported into America was brought over by De Lancey and presented to the people of New York. In these, and in a hundred other ways did he show himself a public-spirited citizen ; and as, when he came to die in 1741, none had amassed a greater fortune than he, so none had won a better title to the love and respect of his fellow-townsmen. *Alderman Public Spirited* *Death in 1741*

James, the eldest son of Étienne De Lancey, was born in New York on the 27th of November, 1703. As a boy *James DeLancey* he gave evidence of powers far above the ordinary, and everything was done for him which might foster the development of his talents. England was then the Mecca of the American educational world, and to England accordingly young De Lancey was sent by his devoted father. After graduating at the University of Cambridge he completed his training by a course of legal study at the Inner Temple, London, and returned to New York in 1725. He soon became prominent in the public life of the province, and his legal talents received an early recognition. In 1729 he was elected to the council. The following year he was appointed as the head of a commission to frame a charter for the city of New York. The "Montgomery Charter," as this instrument was known, was mainly the result of De Lancey's labours ; and for this distinguished service he was rewarded by being presented with the freedom of the city, an honour which he was the first person to receive. In 1731 he was appointed to the highest tribunal in the province as second judge of the Supreme Court, and two years later was made Chief Justice, a position which he retained with honour until the close of his life. During the next twenty years he was occupied with his judicial duties, with the care of the immense estate left to him by his father, and with many important public commissions.

City Charter

Chief Justice

During these years his influence and reputation grew among the citizens of New York and spread to England, so that in 1753 he was appointed by the Crown Lieutenant-Governor of the province. For several years, in the absence of an English governor, he was the real ruler of New York. Shortly after taking his oath of office he convened and presided over the first congress ever held in America, which met at Albany on the 19th of June, 1754. Delegates from all the colonies were present to take measures for the common defense and to devise means of conciliating the Indians. The congress is chiefly remembered, however, from the fact that Benjamin

Practically Governor

Franklin took occasion to propose a union of all the colonies by act of Parliament, a proposal which it is hardly necessary to state was not adopted. In October of the same year, Governor De Lancey granted a charter to King's College (now Columbia University). He died on the 30th of July, 1760. As a jurist he was possessed of great learning; the wise and enlightened use of his vast wealth earned for him a position of almost boundless influence and power; and he will always be remembered as one of the best and ablest provincial rulers of New York.

James, eldest son of Governor De Lancey, was born in New York in 1732. He was educated at Eton and Cambridge, and returned home at the beginning of the French War. He immediately turned soldier and went through the Niagara campaign of 1755. He was in command of the detachment which prevented the relief of Fort Niagara, and it was through his efforts that that strong position was finally taken. In the expedition against Ticonderoga in 1758 he acted as aide-de-camp to General Abercrombie. In 1760, when he succeeded to his father's estate he was the richest man in America, and for several years he devoted his time to the care of his property. But the active Huguenot blood which flowed in his veins would not permit him to live the life of a merely selfish rich man, and in the year 1768 he became a member of the assembly and engaged actively in public affairs. He soon became recognized as the leader of the conservative party in the province, bending all his energies towards a peaceful solution of the differences between the colonies and the mother country. Perhaps his most notable service was in introducing and putting through a resolution which ordered a petition sent to the king, a memorial to the lords and a remonstrance to the commons, demanding redress for the grievances of the colonists. He himself drafted the remonstrance to the commons, producing an able document which was presented to parliament by

James

Soldier

Richest Man of his Day

Edmund Burke, but which met with the contemptuous indifference of that body. With a view to impressing the needs of pacifying the colonies upon the English government, he went to London in 1775, but was unsuccessful in his efforts. While engaged in this business actual hostilities broke out in America. De Lancey remained faithful to the king and saw the confiscation of his vast estates. In our day, so far removed from the bitterness of the revolutionary struggle, we may frankly admire the loyalty of a man who preferred to lose a great fortune rather than prove a rebel to that power which had befriended so many of his persecuted Huguenot brethren. While we must disagree with his view of the situation, we must, nevertheless, give him all honour for his self-sacrifice and devotion to his principles.

William
De Lancey
Bishop

William Heathcote De Lancey, nephew of James, was born in Mamaroneck, N. Y., in 1797. He graduated from Yale in 1817, went to Philadelphia and took orders in the Episcopal Church. In 1827 he was persuaded to become provost of the University of Pennsylvania, which at that time had become greatly run down. There were twenty-one students in the institution when De Lancey accepted the provostship, but when he came to leave it in 1836 to become rector of St. Peter's Church, Philadelphia, he had raised the number to one hundred and twenty-five. After serving as rector of St. Peter's for three years, De Lancey was made bishop of Western New York on the creation of that diocese in 1839. He was an eloquent speaker and a man of excellent judgment and tact, and living at a time when the Episcopal Church in America was in a formative condition he was able to exercise a generous influence in shaping its policy. He was the first, for example, to propose the "provincial system" in the American Church, and it was Bishop De Lancey who laid out the lines along which the General Theological Seminary should work. The two most lasting monuments of his energy and devotion are Hobart

College and the training school at Geneva, N. Y. In
the grounds of the latter there is a fine chapel which was
erected in his honour shortly after his death in 1865.

Peter De Lancey, second son of Étienne, was born in Other Sons
New York in 1705. He was a man of great wealth and
influence, and from 1750 to 1768 he was a member of the
provincial assembly. His daughter Alice married Ralph
Izard, the South Carolina Senator, and his daughter
Susan married Colonel Thomas Barclay. Of his three
sons two became loyalists; the youngest, James, being a
thorn in the side of Westchester County patriots. At the
head of his troop of light horse he made frequent raids
through the countryside, and his alertness and courage
made his name one to conjure with throughout the length
and breadth of the "neutral grounds." Étienne's third
son, Oliver, was an able soldier. He gained his first experiences during the French and Indian War, taking
part in the Niagara campaign and commanding the New
York troops at the capture of Ticonderoga. During the
Revolution he raised three regiments of loyalists at his
own expense, known as "De Lancey's Battalions," and
was given command of Long Island.

Oliver's two sons both joined the British service.
Stephen served through the Revolution as a colonel in
the English army, and after the war was made governor
of Tobago, a small island of the West Indies; while
Oliver had attained the rank of general when he died in
1822.

II

THE DE FOREST FAMILY

The members of the large and well-known De Forest Jesse de Forest 1622
family of America trace their descent to the Jesse de
Forest who in 1622 propounded his scheme of colonization
to the Virginia Company. Jesse de Forest came from an
old family of Avesnes, but was forced for conscience' sake
to take refuge in Holland. His name first appears on

the records of Leyden in 1615, and three years later we
hear of him as a resident of the Hague. His fortunes
were at a low ebb at this time and the records show that
he was in the direst poverty, pledging his household
goods and the tools with which he prosecuted his trade as
dyer. He was not alone in his poverty, however, for
there were many scions of noble French houses begging
for their daily bread in the streets of Amsterdam and
other Dutch cities. Of this period of distress Mr. J. W.
De Forest writes as follows: " Perhaps there is no more
sublime spectacle in history than that of a man who
knows not where to lay his head, stepping forward to
guide and save his fellow creatures, with a perfect confidence that he can do it. The thought of our exiled ancestor, with his ten young children and his haunting debt
of fifty florins, planning and petitioning and recruiting

Planning a
Colony for a Protestant colony in America, is a remembrance
which ought to fill his descendants with pride, and to
stimulate them to courage of soul and energy of deed."

Jesse de Forest did not himself affect a settlement in
North America, but joined a band of colonists who were
bound for the coast of Guiana, the " Wild Coast," as the
Henry and
Isaac
DeForest 1636 Dutch called it. It was left to his sons Henry and Isaac
to carry the family fortunes into New Amsterdam. These
brothers sailed from Amsterdam in the tiny ship *Rennsel-
aerwick* in October, 1636, with the intention of setting up
as tobacco planters. " The upper portion of New York
island was then a mere wilderness of virgin forest and
natural clearing, inhabitated by bears, catamounts,
painted Wickasqueeks and other savage creatures, and
giving small promise of the vast civilized population
which now loads the soil of Harlem."

To the brothers de Forest belongs the distinction of
being the first white settlers in this wild region. To live
there meant exposure to many hardships and dangers,
but land was abundant and cheap and the young men
(Henry, the married brother, was thirty and Isaac was

only twenty years of age) were courageous. "From the rough, forest-clad hills," writes Mr. J. H. Innes, "seamed with deep ravines, a part of which now occupy the north end of the Central Park, these two brothers, as they explored the island of the Mannahatoes, soon after their arrival, must have seen, as they looked to the northward, towards the wide salt-water estuary which we now know as Harlem River, a level expanse of some seven or eight hundred acres in area, broken only by one or two isolated rocky eminences crowned with trees. Through the midst of this ran a small fresh-water stream, and there is little doubt that portions of the plain had been long cleared and cultivated by the Indians." Here Director van Twiller granted two hundred acres of meadow land to Henry, with the customary formalities of the times: "The said de Forest and his successors shall acknowledge their High Mightinesses, the Directors of the West India Company, as their sovereign Lords and Patroons, and at the end of ten years after the actual settlement shall render the just tenth part of the product wherewith God may bless the soil, and from this time forth shall annually deliver on account of the dwelling and house-lot, a pair of capons to the Director for the holidays." Shortly afterwards the brothers erected the first house on upper Manhattan; a solidly built dwelling forty-two feet long and eighteen feet wide, protected by a heavy palisade. It is interesting to note that the site of this house was not far from the present Harlem Lake in Central Park.

The rewards of his arduous labours, however, were not destined for Henry de Forest. Hardly had the spring plowing been completed in the year 1637 when he died of some cause unknown. The Harlem estate passed into the hands of his widow, only a small portion of the movable property going to Isaac; a half interest in a boat, half of a bull calf and the half of two kids are mentioned as belonging to him. It became necessary for Isaac, therefore, to establish a plantation for himself; and he procured a grant of one hundred acres which extended in a narrow strip from "about the present Fifth Avenue and One Hundred and Twelfth Street to the river shore in the neighbourhood of First Avenue and One Hundred and Twenty-sixth Street," including not a little of what is at present Mt. Morris Park.

The loneliness of bachelor life must have weighed heavily on Isaac, and in the records of the Dutch Reformed Church for June 9, 1641, appears the following note : "Isaac de Forest of Leyden, bachelor, was married to Sarah du Trieux of New Amsterdam, spinster." At the time of his marriage he already had a dwelling and a tobacco house on his plantation. Two years later he leased the farm on shares and moved into the village of New Amsterdam, where he opened a tobacco warehouse in the Old Church, a deserted building which stood on the Strand, now Pearl Street. From dealing in tobacco Isaac branched out into the brewing line, and by 1653 he was reckoned as a thoroughly successful brewer. In many ways did he identify himself with the life of the growing town : in 1652 he was one of the Nine Men (the advisory committee of the town); during the following year he was inspector of tobacco ; in 1656 he was appointed "Master of the Weight House" ; was made a great burgher two years later ; and served in the common council for several years.

Of the Nine Men

The Descendants

When Isaac de Forest died in 1674 he was survived by a widow and seven children ; Susannah, Johannes, Philip, Isaac, Hendricus, Maria, and David. Susannah married Peter de Riemer ; Maria married Alderman Isaac de Riemer ; Johannes died without issue. Of the remaining children, Philip, husband of Tryntie Kip, founded the Albany branch of the family ; Isaac remained in New York, where many of his descendants are living to-day ; Hendrick settled on Long Island, and left a goodly progeny ; while David removed to Stratford, Conn., where he

married Martha Blagge. From Connecticut, the little
State which has sent so many colonists out into the unsettled portions of the country, the De Forests spread until to-day they are to be found in nearly every section of
the United States.

III

GENERAL RICHARD MONTGOMERY

This noble martyr to liberty, who fell at Quebec on the
last day of 1775, was descended from the Huguenots
through that Comte de Montgomerie who mortally
wounded Henry II of France, July 10, 1559, in a tourna-
ment in honour of the marriage of his daughter. Though
the King forgave the Count, the queen mother, Catherine
de Medicis, did not, but pursued the brave Huguenot with
implacable vengeance till she brought him to the scaffold,
May 27, 1576. His family fled to Ireland and won distinction. Richard Montgomery was third son of an Irish
baronet, and was born December 2, 1738, at his father's
country seat in the north of Ireland. Liberally educated,
young Montgomery entered the British army and served
under General Wolfe in the war between England and
France for supremacy in Canada. Thus he gained his
experience for the Revolutionary days, when he espoused
the cause of the American colonies, and was elected a
brigadier-general by the Continental Congress. He was
then living on his farm at Rhinebeck, having married
into the Livingston family. The distinction conferred
upon him without his solicitation was accepted with
characteristic modesty and a patriotic sense of duty.
Writing to a friend he says: "The Congress having
done me the honour of electing me a brigadier-general in
their service, is an event which must put an end for a
while, perhaps forever, to the quiet scheme of life I had
prescribed for myself: for, though entirely unexpected
and undesired by me, the will of an oppressed people,
compelled to choose between liberty and slavery, must be

*A Revolution-
ary Leader
and Martyr*

*Leaving the
Farm for War*

obeyed." From that hour he was devoted to his adopted country. He was sent to capture Montreal, which he did after a most brilliant campaign. When the news of his signal success reached Congress, that body passed a vote of thanks and promoted him to be a major-general; but his untimely death prevented his receiving this reward of merit. Quebec was his next objective, for as he wrote to Congress: "Till Quebec is taken, Canada is unconquered." It is a romantic but tragic story, how he led his band of three hundred patriots over frozen ground and drifting snows; made juncture with Arnold, who had completed a wonderful march with a half-starved and frozen army through the wilderness of northern Maine; only to fall into a trap at last, and perish while at the head of his hapless command, leading an assault on the strongly fortified city. His last words were: "Men of New York, you will not fear to follow where your general leads! March on, brave boys! Quebec is ours!" But they marched into the jaws of swift death. Through the courtesy of General Carleton, British commander, Montgomery's body was privately interred, January 4, 1776, near where he fell. By friend and foe alike his bravery and ability were recognized and admired. His death made a profound impression, both in Europe and America, for the excellency of his character had won him affection, as his great abilities had gained public esteem. The Continental Congress caused to be executed a monument of white marble, with a classical inscription written by Franklin, which has since 1789 adorned the front of St. Paul's Church in New York. It was fitting that this monument should be executed by a Frenchman, Caffières, sculptor to Louis XVI. He was eulogized even in the British Parliament by Chatham and Burke. Forty-three years after his death his remains were removed from Quebec, by an "act of Honour" of the legislature of New York, and buried with brilliant military ceremonies near the cenotaph erected by Congress to his memory. Of

A Daring Assault on Quebec

The Chivalrous Soldier

GENERAL RICHARD MONTGOMERY AND QUEBEC

Washington's thirteen generals, elected by Congress, Montgomery was second to none. He was "the embodiment of the true gentleman and chivalrous soldier," and in his veins flowed the best of the French and English blood.

IV

PHILIP FRENEAU, POET

So expert a critic as the late Mr. Stedman asserted that the "first essential poetic spirit" in American letters is to be found in the earlier odes and lyrics of Philip Freneau. He has been fitly called the "Laureate of the Revolution," and his name will always be remembered in connection with the history of American literature as the first poet to be produced on this continent. Mr. Stedman says further of Freneau that he was "a true poet, one of nature's lyrists, who had the temperament of a Landor and was much what the Warwick classicist might have been if bred, afar from Oxford, to the life of a pioneer and revolutionist, spending his vital surplusage in action, bellicose journalism and new-world verse." *Laureate of the Revolution*

Philip Freneau was born in New York on January 2, 1752. The best Huguenot blood flowed in his veins, the Freneaus being an able and distinguished family. His grandfather, André Fresneau, emigrated to Boston in 1705; journeyed thence to Connecticut, where he was engaged for a while in mining ventures; and finally arrived in New York to take a position with the Royal West India Company. Here his son Pierre was born, who was the father of the poet. Pierre was so successful in his business affairs that the year his son Philip was born he was able to purchase a large estate in Monmouth County, New Jersey, and build thereon a handsome spacious mansion. Two years later he retired from active business and withdrew with his family to his picturesque estate. Here Philip was surrounded by everything that might tend to develop his poetic impulse. *Birth in 1752*

Princeton   After a due course of preparation in the classics he
entered Princeton College. Tradition has it that his
roommate there was James Madison. Certain it was that
Madison was among his classmates, as were Aaron Burr,
Aaron Ogden and Hugh Henry Breckenridge. While in
college he gave much of his time to writing poetry, and
the year before his graduation in 1771 he and his friend
Breckenridge published a volume of verses. The years
between his leaving college and the breaking out of the
Revolution were devoted to teaching, and various light
skirmishes with the law, with theology, and with medicine. Many of his choicest nature-lyrics were written
Martial Songs during this period. In 1775 the cause of freedom aroused
Freneau to a high pitch of activity, and he freely gave
all that he had in the way of satirical power to arousing
the spirit of the public. He did not enter the army, but
it is safe to say that his satires and his martial songs accomplished more for the cause of Independence than his
individual efforts as a soldier could have done. While
Poems of   sailing in Delaware Bay in 1780, he was taken prisoner
Patriotism   by the British man-o'-war *Iris*, and spent many weary
weeks aboard an English prison-ship. When he was at
last released, he returned to New Jersey weak from fever
and hardship, but firm in will. He now had a personal
grievance to add to the fires of his zeal against the red-
coats, and his satire and invective became more biting
and effective than at first. Many of his pieces achieved
a wide-spread popularity among the troops and the
people, and did much to foster the spirit of patriotic
ardour.

When the war was over, Freneau engaged in many
Editor   journalistic enterprises, the most notable of which was
the editing of *The National Gazette.*

Freneau espoused the cause of Jefferson, as against the
Federalists under the leadership of Alexander Hamilton,
and became involved thereby in a long train of acrimo-
nious disputes. And while Freneau was of too independ-

ent a nature to allow his paper to become a mere tool in the hands of his able friends, it was recognized, nevertheless as the semi-official organ of Jefferson and Madison. Towards the latter part of his life, Freneau forsook journalism, and in partnership with one of his brothers ventured his fortune in trade with the West Indies, the poet himself acting as commander of a brig. He seems, indeed, to have been decidedly proud of his title as "Captain Freneau." His death, which was a tragic one, occurred in December of the year 1832.

Of Freneau, Professor Bronson, one of the best of recent critics of American literature, writes: "In poems of fancy and imagination he was the most original and truly poetical poet in America before the nineteenth century. . . . The 'Wild Honeysuckle' is the high-water mark of American poetry of the eighteenth century, in delicacy of feeling and felicity of expression being at least the equal of Bryant's 'To the Fringed Gentian.' When such lines were possible in the very infancy of the national life, there was no reason to despair for the future of American literature."

V

HENRY DAVID THOREAU

In connection with Freneau we may properly speak of Thoreau, though he was a New Englander. Henry David Thoreau, born in Concord, Massachusetts, in 1817, was the great-grandson of Philippe Thoreau and his wife Marie le Gallais, French refugees who settled at St. Helier in the Island of Jersey. The events of his life are few and simple. At school and at Harvard University he did not distinguish himself as a student, but yet managed to pick up enough Latin and Greek to qualify himself as a quondam schoolmaster. The profession of teaching, however, proved to be extremely distasteful to him, and abandoning it after a short trial he devoted himself to the family occupation—pencil-making. But

A New England Character

what men call the "business of life" accorded little with
the aims and interests of Henry Thoreau. "He had
early discovered, by virtue of that keen insight which
looked through the outer husk of conventionality, that
what is called profit in the bustle of commercial life is
often far from being, in the true sense, profitable ; that
the just claims of leisure are fully as important as the
just claims of business ; and that the surest way of becoming rich is to need little ; in his own words, ' a man
is rich in proportion to the number of the things which
he can afford to let alone.' "

A Lover of
Nature

He refused to pledge himself "to some professional
treadmill, and for the sake of imaginary ' comforts' sacrifice the substantial happiness of life." He gave himself
over to a "loitering" in which idleness held no part.
Supporting himself by pencil-making, surveying, lectur-
ing and writing, as occasion demanded, he spent the bulk
of his time in the study of wild nature. "His business
was to spend at least one half of each day in the open
air ; to watch the dawns and the sunsets; to carry express what was in the wind ; to secure the latest news
from forest and hilltop, and to be ' self-appointed inspector of snow-storms and rain-storms.' "

In 1845 he built a hut near Walden Pond and retired
to a closer intimacy with nature. "His residence on the
shore of Walden Pond has often been misinterpreted,"
says Professor Bronson, in his *History of American Literature*. "It was only an episode in his life, and he never
meant to preach by it that all men should live in huts
or that civilization was a mistake. Rather it was a
demonstration, first to himself and then to others, that
man's happiness and higher life are not dependent upon
luxuries nor even upon external refinements." After
two years of life in his simple hermitage he returned to
Concord, where he supported his mother and sisters
largely through the old trade of pencil-making. He died
on May 6, 1862, at the age of forty-five.

Henry D. Thoreau

Philip Freneau

Henry Wadsworth Longfellow

John Greenleaf Whittier

Thoreau's life and writings, taken together, form a strong protest against the modern vice of over-attention to the mere externals of life. Says his biographer, Henry Salt: "He shows us that it is possible for men to-day to live as the Stoics strove to live, in accordance with Nature, with absolute serenity and self-possession ; to follow out one's own ideal in spite of every obstacle, with unfaltering devotion ; and so to simplify one's life, and clarify one's senses, as to master many of the secrets of that book of Nature which to most men remains unintelligible and unread."

It was Thoreau's distinction to be the pioneer among Americans in the nature study that is the favourite pursuit of so many to-day. He was the apostle of the simple life, and lived as he preached. He tells us of his housekeeping methods at Walden : "When my floor was dirty I rose early, and setting all my furniture out of doors on the grass, bed and bedstead making but one budget, dashed water on the floor, and sprinkled white sand from the pond on it, and then with a broom scrubbed it clean and white ; and by the time the villagers had broken their fast, the morning sun had dried my house sufficiently to allow me to move in again, and my meditations were almost uninterrupted. It was pleasant to see my whole household effects upon the grass, making a little pile like a gipsy's pack, and my three-legged table, from which I did not remove the books and pen and ink, standing amidst the pines and hickories."

If Thoreau seemed unsympathetic to certain classes of people, he loved children and animals, and was at home with them and they with him. He proved his theory "that to maintain oneself on this earth is not a hardship but a pastime, if we will live simply and wisely." Here is a characteristic description of himself by Thoreau : "Am not married. I don't know whether mine is a profession, or a trade, or what not. It is not learned, and in every instance has been practiced before being studied. The

The Life of the Soul Emphasized

A Pioneer in Nature Study

A Self-Char-
acterization

mercantile part of it was begun by myself alone.   I am a
Schoolmaster, a private Tutor, a Surveyor, a Gardener, a
Farmer, a Painter (I mean a House Painter), a Carpen-
ter, a Mason, a Day-labourer, a Pencil-maker, a Writer,
and sometimes a Poetaster. . . . My steadiest employment is to keep myself at the top of my condition,
and ready for whatever may turn up in heaven or on
earth."

Thoreau maintained sincerity to be chief of all virtues,
and may be called a Yankee stoic. He held the old
stoical maxim that all places are the same to the wise
man, and that "the best place for each is where he
stands." On the same principle, being asked at table
what dish he preferred, he is said to have answered,
"The nearest." He was a radical abolitionist, and a
patriotic American. His writings have given him high
rank among literary men, and his influence abides.
Ellery Channing, an intimate friend, thus describes his
appearance :

A Pen
Portrait

"His face, once seen, could not be forgotten. The
features were quite marked : the nose aquiline, or very
Roman, like one of the portraits of Cæsar ; large, over-
hanging brow above the deepest-set blue eyes that could
be seen, in certain lights, and in other gray—eyes expressive of all shades of feeling, but never weak or near-
sighted ; the forehead not unusually broad or high, full
of concentrated energy or purpose ; the mouth with
prominent lips, pursed up with meaning and thought
when silent, and giving out when open a stream of the
most varied and unusual and instructive sayings. His
whole figure had an active earnestness, as if he had no
moment to waste." New England and America needed
just such an influence as this scholar and genius of French
descent exerted.

Poem on the
Sea

Space forbids quotations that would show Thoreau's
pithy and witty prose style, and we can give but a single

illustration of his poetry.   These stanzas on the sea were
written at Staten Island :

> " My life is like a stroll upon the beach,
>   As near the ocean's edge as I can go ;
>   My tardy steps its waves sometimes o'erreach,
>   Sometimes I stay to let them overflow.

> " My sole employment 'tis, and scrupulous care,
>   To place my gains beyond the reach of tides,
>   Each smoother pebble, and each shell more rare,
>   Which Ocean kindly to my hand confides.

> " I have but few companions on the shore :
>   They scorn the strand who sail upon the sea ;
>   Yet oft I think the ocean they've sailed o'er
>   Is deeper known upon the strand to me."

VI

MATTHEW VASSAR

Among the men of Huguenot blood who have through
philanthropy written their names indelibly on history's
page must be placed Matthew Vassar, founder of Vassar
College, the original woman's college of the first order
established in any land.   Matthew Vassar was born in
England, but came to America when a young child with
his parents.   His father was the direct descendant of a
Huguenot exile who found a home in England.   Matthew's mother was led to brew English ale, in order to
stop the common drinking of whiskey by the farm hands.
Her brew was so popular that it largely replaced the
stronger liquor, and demands for it increased until the
son began to brew as a business.   Out of this beginning
developed the Vassar brewery, which was famous for
many years, and which made a large fortune for the
family.

Not a highly educated man himself, Matthew Vassar
appreciated education, and was of a philanthropic turn.
He wanted to do good with his money.   He established a

home for old men, and had plans for a hospital.   The
subject of woman's education interested him, and he
thought women should have as good educational advantages as men.   He was ready, therefore, to consider the
matter with Professor Raymond, who had worked out the
plans for a distinctive woman's college.   Mr. Vassar
furnished the capital, and Vassar College was started as
an experiment, with Professor Raymond as president.
Into this enterprise, which grew far beyond the original
plans, Matthew Vassar put a large part of his fortune;
and had the satisfaction of seeing the institution a great
success before he was taken away.   This was the pioneer,
but soon his example was followed—in Massachusetts by
Mr. Durant, who founded Wellesley.   To-day the women's
colleges are thriving and numerous, and hold the highest
rank, while their thousands of alumni are to be found in
all parts of the land.   Huguenot descendants may remember with just pride that the first of these institutions, and
one still in the front rank, was due to the philanthropy
and far-sightedness of one of their number.

VII

THOMAS HOPKINS GALLAUDET

The Gallaudet   One of the Huguenot emigrants from France was Peter
Ancestry
Gallaudet, who left Mauze, near La Rochelle, shortly after
the Revocation, and came to America, transferring to new
shores the traditions of a family long identified by act
and sympathy with the cause of Protestantism.   Gallaudet settled in New Rochelle, whence his descendants
have spread to various parts of the country.

One of Gallaudet's great-grandsons was Thomas Hopkins Gallaudet, who more than any other member of the
family has brought the name into prominence.   Thomas
was born in Philadelphia in 1787, and there spent his
early days.   Moving to Hartford in 1800, he entered Yale,
and was graduated in 1805.   The three following years he
spent as travelling salesman for a New York firm.   Then

for two years he tutored in Yale, and for three more attended the Andover Theological Seminary, graduating in 1814. During this educational period there were unfolded in Gallaudet the characteristics which have always marked the Huguenots—sociability, a wide range of interests and sympathies, versatility, ingenuity, and a desire to turn all faculties to account in unselfish human service.

Up to the beginning of the nineteenth century organized charity was a thing unknown in New England. Especially pitiable was the plight of the deaf mutes, of whom, it was estimated, there were four hundred in New England, all out of reach of instruction. One of these deaf mutes was Alice Coggswell, daughter of a wealthy physician of Hartford. She had been afflicted from an early age ; as she approached maturity her father was impelled to find some means of relieving her tragic situation. Several philanthropists joined with him in the effort to establish regular instruction for deaf mutes in America. The first step was to secure an American who would undertake to learn the methods of instruction abroad. Their plans reached the point of action at the very time when Gallaudet was deciding on his career. His name was at once brought forward, the more readily because he had for some time shown an interest in Alice Coggswell, and had even succeeded in teaching her a few words.

Instruction for Deaf Mutes

Gallaudet accepted the commission with a confidence which was characteristic, crossed the ocean, and after encountering many obstacles, induced the Abbé Sicard, in Paris, to teach him. Here he worked zealously for a year, varying his labour by preaching. At the end of this time he returned to America, fitted for introducing the approved French methods of instruction. From 1817 to 1830 he controlled the policy and working of the Hartford Institution for Deaf Mutes. So intense was his application during these thirteen years, in the face of a

Organizes the Hartford Institution for Deaf Mutes

steadily declining physique, that when at length ill
health compelled him to resign, he left the institution
equipped with well-trained instructors, and in shape to
continue its activities unimpaired.

Gallaudet found that the relief from continuous labour
gave him a new lease of activity. He was at once offered
several promising positions, but declined them all, and
applied himself for some years to writing books of
various kinds, principally books for children, such
as *The Child's Book of the Soul* (1830), and *Bible
Stories for the Young* (1838), for which he was admirably fitted by his pedagogic experience. In 1838 he
found congenial employment as chaplain of the Hartford
Retreat for the Insane. Here he carried on a gentle
ministry for long and profitable years, until his death in
1851. His sons have carried forward the noble work in
which he was so long engaged, and the family name is
one that will be held in high honour for splendid service
rendered in the cause of humanity. The deaf mutes of
America and the world owe a large debt of gratitude to
the Huguenot descendants who have consecrated their
lives to opening the world of thought, knowledge and
communication to a class of unfortunates.

CHAPTER VII

JOHN AND STEPHEN GANO

I

A MINISTER of prominence in New York and New Jersey during the Revolutionary period was Rev. John Gano, a Baptist. This exceptionally able man, who was to come into somewhat intimate relations with Washington, was a descendant of the French refugee family of Ganeau, which settled in Rhode Island. It was John Gano's great-grandfather Francis who came to this country to escape persecution. John was born at Hopewell, New Jersey, 1727, being thus six years older than Washington. He has left a most interesting autobiography, in which he states that he believed himself converted when about eighteen. His father was a Presbyterian, but his mother was a Baptist, and after careful consideration he thought it his duty to join a Baptist church. Thus that denomination gained a minister of great influence and usefulness. He early felt convictions of duty to enter the ministry, and decided to do so, though he shrank from the calling. He was educated at Princeton College, at "that time kept in Newark, and governed by President Burr, with whom I was a great favourite," he tells us. Before leaving college he began to preach and made a missionary journey to Virginia. He was gifted as writer and speaker, had a fine presence and great magnetism, so that his fame grew rapidly and he was repeatedly invited to pastorates before his studies were finished. Morristown became his temporary home, and subsequently he accepted the call of the church there. The church record for October, 1755, says : "Mr. Gano at the earnest request of the church concluded to settle

279

with us for the sum of forty pounds a year." He married Sarah Stites, daughter of the mayor of Elizabeth-Town, and thus became related indirectly to James Manning, the first president of Brown University, who married his wife's sister. The young minister bought a farm near Morristown, and thus managed together with his meagre salary to meet current expenses. But he was not long to remain there. Missionary in spirit he spent two years in North Carolina, among the religiously destitute people, and then returning North, organized the First Baptist Church of New York City, and for twenty-six years was its pastor and a citizen of no little repute. During this period he also served for a time as pastor of the First Baptist Church of Philadelphia, spending two Sundays of the month there ; since preachers of his rank were few and in great demand.

Chaplain in the Revolution   At the outbreak of the Revolutionary War John Gano became chaplain, and remained in the army seven years, giving a devoted and highly acceptable service. More than once he was under fire. Part of the time he served as aide to General James Clinton. He participated in the capture of the Hessians at Trenton, the overthrow of the English allies—the Pennsylvania Indians, and reached Yorktown just too late to witness the surrender of Cornwallis. When peace was at last concluded, and the happy event celebrated at Washington's headquarters, near Newburgh, April 19, 1783, Chaplain Gano was selected by General Washington to offer the prayer of **Usefulness Recognized by Washington** thanksgiving on that joyous and memorable occasion. After the war, Washington said, "Baptist chaplains were the most prominent and useful in the army." General Washington and Mr. Gano were close friends, and this compliment applied especially to him.

When peace was restored, Mr. Gano returned to his New York pastorate. In 1788 he resigned to go to Kentucky. He became at once the leading preacher of that State and for ten years rendered most efficient service

In 1798 he fell from his horse, breaking his shoulder. Soon after he was stricken with paralysis. During the Great Revival, 1800-1803, his speech was restored and he preached, as a contemporary described it, "in an astonishing manner."

Consider what an influence was exerted by this Huguenot descendant. The territory covered by his labours was larger than that of the Apostle Paul. It extended from Connecticut to Georgia and west to the Kentucky River. He was interested in all of the denominational enterprises of his time. He was one of the first home missionaries sent out by the Philadelphia Association, the first American Baptist chaplain, a loyal supporter of Hopewell Academy and Rhode Island College. He was present encouraging the movement when the South Carolina Baptists set apart the first money for the education of their young preachers. From this beginning came the Southern Baptist Theological Seminary. He gave sound Calvinistic colouring to the theology of the Virginia Baptists, and stirred all the churches to which he preached with missionary zeal. *An American Apostle*

II

Rev. Stephen Gano, son of John Gano, was a man of mark, whose chief work was done in Rhode Island, where his ancestor Francis found refuge. Like John Gano, the son possessed great personal magnetism and charm. He had the French clearness of style, vividness of imagination, warmth of temperament, and flow of language. At the same time he combined with pulpit power executive ability, and was marked by strong common sense and practical judgment. He was a leader in Providence, as John Gano was in New York and later in Kentucky. As pastor of the historic First Baptist Church of Providence—the church founded by Roger Williams, that great apostle of religious liberty—Stephen Gano exerted a wide influence. He held this pastorate from 1793 till his death in 1828, a period of thirty-five years. In every *A Worthy Son*

Pastor of First Baptist Church, Founded by Roger Williams

way this ministry was remarkable. Dr. S. L. Caldwell, one of his biographers, says : "He had what I may call a pastoral heart. Of large person, of loud, almost stentorian voice, he spoke with fluency ; often pathetic and hortatory in his application of truth, always possessed with a strong conviction of it, he had power over a large audience, which during his time filled the house."

Stephen Gano was filled with the missionary spirit that characterized the early Baptist ministry. During a journey to the West, while visiting his brother in Cincinnati, he organized the first Protestant church of any denomination in the State of Ohio. It was located in a little settlement known as Columbia, now within the city limits of Cincinnati. The church continues in existence. Interested in education, he stimulated the founding of colleges and academies, as well as of churches, and was a loyal supporter of Brown University. Two denominational leaders of their generation were thus contributed to American life by that brave Huguenot who fled from his home in France by night, and after many perils found refuge in that freest of colonies, where Roger Williams guaranteed to all the religious liberty for which he himself had twice been exiled.

SECOND FRENCH CHURCH ON PINE STREET, 1704, USED TILL 1831, NEW YORK.

CHAPTER VIII

NEW PALTZ

I

THE Huguenot settlement at New Paltz was 1677 brought about by the purchase of a tract of land from the Indian owners in the year 1677. In consideration of the rights acquired, the patentees agreed Purchase Price to pay to the Indians the following articles:

Forty kettles, ten large, thirty small; forty axes, forty adzes; forty shirts; four hundred fathoms of white network; sixty pairs of stockings, half small sizes; one hundred bars of lead; one keg of powder; one hundred knives; four kegs of wine; forty oars; forty pieces of "duffel" (heavy woolen cloth); sixty blankets; one hundred needles; one hundred awls; one measure of tobacco; two horses—one stallion, one mare.

The twelve men who thus agreed to collect the above The Twelve Patentees assortment of merchandise and put it into the possession of the Esopus Indians were all Huguenots who had come to the New World by way of the Paltz, of Palatinate. Their names, as appended to the deed with all the blissful ignorance of spelling which marked the period, were as follows: Lowies Du Booys, Christian de Yoo, Agraham Gaesbroeco, Andrie Lefeber, Jan Broeco, Piere Doyo, Anthony Crespel, Anraham Du Booys, Hugo Freer, Isaack D. Boojs, Symon Lefeber, Louis Baijvier. Previous to their coming to America, these men had taken refuge in and about Mannheim, in the Palatinate, and had there formed the ties of friendship which led to their association in the founding of New Paltz.

The first of the Mannheim party to arrive in America

was Matthew Blanshan and his wife, Maddeleen Jorisse, together with his son-in-law, Anthony Chrispel.   They sailed in the *Gilded Otter* in April, 1660, and by December of the same year were settled in the village of Wilt-

wyck, now called Hurley.   The following year Louis Du Bois and his wife Catherine Blanshan, with their two sons, Abraham and Isaac, took up their residence there also.   Simon and André Le Fevre were in Wiltwyck by April 23, 1665, on which day they united with the church.   Owing to the disturbed condition of the province at that time, no more members of the group left Mannheim until the year 1672, when Jean Hasbrouck and his wife, Anna, daughter of Christian Deyo, joined their friends.   Louis Beviere and his wife, Maria La Blan, came to New York in 1673, where they remained until the founding of New Paltz, four years later.   In 1675 Abraham Hasbrouck came to Boston, and shortly afterwards made his way to the banks of the Hudson. Hugh Frere and his wife, Mary Haye, with their three children, came over about 1676 ; as did Christian Deyo, with his son Pierre, and his daughter-in-law, Agatha Nickol, and his three unmarried daughters.   Thus slowly the little group was reunited, and when the circle was complete the project was formed whereby its members might dwell together in peace and amity.

The life of the settlement was harmonious from the first. The colonists lived on the friendliest terms with their Indian neighbours, who always considered that they had been treated with fairness in the matter of the purchase of the land ; and among themselves they acted as brothers in Arcadia.   At the commencement of the colony the patentees and their families all laboured together in clearing the land, in erecting their log dwellings, and in planting their first crops.   Afterwards, they met together and portioned out the lands among themselves by word of mouth, dispensing with the formality of deeds.

A form of town government was inaugurated that is

OLD HUGUENOT HOUSES AT NEW PALTZ

without a close parallel in our colonial history. At first the heads of the families met together and settled whatever public business there was on hand. But as the town grew in numbers, this primitive democracy gave way to a unique institution locally known as the Dusine, or Twelve Men. The Dusine was a legislative and executive body made up of twelve members who were elected annually by a popular vote. To the Dusine was given "full power and Authority to Act and Sett in Good order and unity all Common Affairs, Businessess or things comeing before them." If its powers were autocratic, its composition was certainly aristocratic; for no one but a patentee or an heir of a patentee could be elected to the Twelve. That is to say, the active government of the town was vested in the families of the twelve original settlers. This peculiar condition of government was continued until 1785, when the town was incorporated in the State government, and the previous measures of the Dusine were confirmed by a special Act of Legislature.

A Novel Town Government

The Dusine

When the first settlers of New Paltz alighted from their wagons, one of their number read a psalm of thanksgiving, and one of the earliest log buildings which was erected was devoted to uses as a church and schoolhouse. In this cabin the little community of Huguenots kept alive the traditions of the Reformation, meeting there for informal devotions led by one of their own number, reading passages from the Bible, singing the sonorous hymns which had been rendered sacred by the blood of so many martyrs, and uttering simple prayers. Five years after the establishment of the town a regular church was organized under the advice and guidance of the worthy Rev. Pierre Daillé. A translation of the first entry in the church records is as follows:

Church and School

The 22d of January, 1683, Mr. Pierre Daillé, minister of the Word of God, arrived at New Paltz, and preached twice on the following Sunday, and proposed to the heads of the families that they should choose by a majority of votes, by the fathers of families, one elder and

Missionary Daille

one deacon, to assist the minister in guiding the members of the church that meets in New Paltz ; who were subsequently confirmed in the said charge of elder and deacon.   This minute has been made to put in order the matters which pertain to the said church.

For ten years Daillé acted as pastor to his countrymen in New Paltz.   His principal field of labour was in New York, but he never failed to visit New Paltz for a time in the spring, and then again in the fall.   The difficulties and hardships of the long journeys he was thus forced to make cannot easily be overestimated ; they are a splendid testimony to the unflagging zeal and loyal devotion to duty which marked the man.   The same must be said of his successor, the Rev. David Bonrepos, who, from 1696 to 1700, journeyed from his pastorate at Staten Island to New Paltz twice a year.   After Bonrepos ceased to visit them it is probable that for the next thirty years they had no regular pastor ; for they had not, as yet, united with the Dutch Church, and those few French ministers who had come to this country were by this time dead, or

Building a Church

else settled in other pastorates.   But although there was thus every temptation to leave neglected the duties of their religion, such was neither the spirit nor intent of our refugees.   They kept up their informal worship in the log cabin until it became too small for their rapidly increasing numbers, and then they set about building a more suitable house of worship.   This edifice, which was constructed of stone, was completed in 1717, and was in use until 1773, when a larger church was built.   When the church was finally completed, the following entry was made in the record book :

Dedication 1717

Blessed be God, who has put it into our hearts to build a house where He may be adored and served, and that by His grace we have finished it in the year 1717; and God grant that His gospel may be preached here from one age to another till the day of eternity.   Amen.

Our Huguenots were no bigots or petty sectarians, for during the thirty year interval when they were without

a pastor, they took their children to the Dutch church
at Kingston, sixteen miles away, to be baptized; and
during the summer months they were in the habit of
taking the rough journey through the forest to join with   Uniting with
their Dutch brethren in receiving the communion. A   the Dutch
sixteen mile journey through the woods and unbridged
streams was no luxury; there were no spring wagons for
the women and children to ride in, and the trip had to be
made either a-foot or on horseback, for the highway of
that day was nothing more than a rude trail.

The lack of sectarianism that prevailed in the New
Paltz community was clearly shown in the choice of their
next pastor, the Rev. Johannes Van Driessen, a minister
of the Dutch faith who had been educated in Belgium.
The salary which he received was the munificent sum of
£10 a year, but it is highly probable that he devoted but
a small proportion of his time to the New Paltz congregation. The first entries which he made in the church
book were in French, and in one place he refers to the
church as "our French church." This was in 1731.
Twenty years later, however, the New Paltz church had
ceased to be distinctively French, and we find the next
pastor, the Rev. B. Vrooman, making an inquiry as to
whether the members accepted the doctrines of the Dutch
Reformed church according to the Heidelberg catechism.
Dutch was being more and more generally spoken in New
Paltz, and an interesting evidence of its rapid growth in
popular use is found in a clause of Jean Tebenin's will
wherein the old schoolmaster gives his property to the
church with the provision that if the French language
should be entirely superseded, the Bible should be sold
and the proceeds given to the poor.

Coincident with the founding of a church at New Paltz
was the founding of a school. Out of their scanty fortunes   Education
these worthy pioneers set aside a sum sufficient to employ   Appreciated
a schoolmaster. Jean Tebenin was the first to fill the
position, which he retained until 1700. Jean Cottin fol-

lowed in his footsteps. That he was treated with the greatest liberality is evidenced by the following deed of gift which the citizens bestowed upon him; this document also throws a strong light on the character of the men who made up the colony and the ideals they had in mind in regulating its growth :

A Gift to the Schoolmaster

We the undersigned gentlemen, resident proprietors of the twelve parts of the village of New Paltz, a dependency of Kingston, county of Ulster, province of New York, certify that of our good will and to give pleasure to Jean Cottin, schoolmaster at said Paltz, we to him have given gratuitously a little cottage to afford him a home, situated at said Paltz, at the end of the street on the left hand near the large clearing extending one "lizier" to the place reserved for building the church and continuing in a straight line to the edge of the clearing, thence one "lizier" to the extremity of the clearing, and we guarantee the said Cottin that he shall be placed in possession without any trouble and we allow said Cottin to cut wood convenient for his purpose for building and he is given the pasturage for two cows and their calves and a mare and colt. We the proprietors at the same time agree among ourselves, for the interest of our own homes to request said Cottin that he will not sell the above mentioned property to any one not of good life and manners, and we are not to keep said Cottin as schoolmaster longer than we think fit and proper.

Progress and Prosperity

By steady toil and exercise of thrift the descendants of the patentees raised themselves to a comfortable degree of prosperity. Within a few years after the building of the town, the original wooden houses gave way to spacious and solid structures of stone, many of which are standing to-day, still occupied by direct descendants of the builders. This is one of the marks of the town, that the families of the founders still cling to the locality. The hurry and bustle of modern American life is not felt to any great degree in New Paltz, and men may be seen tilling the fields that their great-great-grandfathers tilled before them.

For many years one of the Huguenot descendants, Mr. Ralph LeFevre, of New Paltz, has been gathering facts concerning the families which trace their origin to the

Esopus colony, and he has recently published the results
of his zealous labour in a large and handsome volume,
entitled *History of New Paltz and its Old Families*, which
goes minutely into family history. We are largely indebted to him for the facts given above, and for other
favours.

SECOND STONE CHURCH ❖ NEW PALTZ

PART THREE

PENNSYLVANIA AND THE SOUTHERN STATES

CHAPTER I

PENNSYLVANIA AND DELAWARE

I

*First White
Settlers
Huguenots*

SEVEN years before the building of Fort Nassau on a branch of the Delaware River and the granting of patents to Godyn and his colleagues, a small trading station was erected on an island (now almost entirely washed away) in the Delaware a short distance below the present town of Trenton Falls. The hardy settlers who undertook the labour of establishing this station in the wilderness, and who thus isolated themselves from all contact with civilization, were members of the band of refugees, collected by Jesse de Forest, which reached *Probably as Early as 1625* New York in the spring of 1623. Although the attempt was an abortive one and had to be abandoned a few years later, nevertheless the four young couples who made up the garrison of the trading station are entitled to recognition as the first white settlers of Pennsylvania. Unless new facts come into the light of history, we may safely say that the first homes which were built in that commonwealth which has proved such an asylum for the persecuted, were erected by the most bitterly persecuted of all European people, the Huguenots.

*Penn's Grant
1681*

Prior to the grant to William Penn in 1681, the region now known as Pennsylvania, and which then included the state of Delaware, contained many French refugees among its inhabitants. The names of most of these settlers have

290

passed into oblivion ; in some cases being irrecoverably lost, in other cases being so confused with the Dutch and Swedish colonists as to defy all attempt at separation. It is not altogether strange that the early settlers in Penn- sylvania who were of French descent lost their national identity. The majority of them did not come direct from France, but from Germany and Holland, where most of them had long resided and where many of them, indeed, had been born. During their residence in the Palatine and in Holland, they identified themselves with the in- habitants of those countries in speech and name. That faculty which the Huguenots possessed to an eminent de- gree, and which made of them such desirable immigrants, the ability to adapt themselves readily to new conditions and new environments, operated against the preservation of their identity as Frenchmen. How completely had the Gallic flavour disappeared from such a typical Ger- man name as Kieffer, or such a typical Dutch name as De Witte! Yet the Kieffers, of Pennsylvania, and the De Wittes, of New York, were once the Tonnelliers and the Le Blancs of France. And even Peter Minuit, "the discontented governor," is described as a German by our historian Bancroft. Little wonder, then, that the Hugue- not settlers in America have never received their due meed of justice at the hands of historians, and have never been given the popular recognition which they de- serve.

A majority of the French settlers in the Delaware region came over at the time of the first general influx of emi- grants from the Palatine ; roughly speaking, between the years 1654 and 1664. The names of some of the more prominent of these refugees have been preserved, and the positions which some of them held in the colony give proof of the high esteem in which the Huguenots were held among the Dutch. The first Huguenot of note to take up his residence in the Delaware colony was the ex- director of the New Netherlands, Peter Minuit, something

French
Identity Lost

Adaptability

Kieffers
De Wittes
Minuit of
French
Extraction

Influx
1654-1664

of whose history is given in another section of this book. During Minuit's residence in Delaware the colony came **Minuit founds Christiana** under the rule of Sweden, and Minuit was appointed governor. During his term of office, which was a short one, lasting only from April 28, 1638, to January 30, 1640, he founded the town of Christiana in Delaware, where he died the year following his release as governor.

After the Dutch had regained possession of the colony from the Swedes, another Huguenot was placed in a position of the highest authority. Jean Paul Jacquett, born in Nuremberg of French parents, was appointed vice-director in 1655, and was responsible to the governor of **Jacquett Vice-Director** New Netherlands for the welfare of the colony. Doubtless the fact that a refugee occupied the highest position in the colony had much to do with the coming of numbers of his brethren, for at just about this time a considerable tide of immigration set in. Later on, in 1676, Jacquett was made a justice, and was in other ways a man of great distinction in the colony. He died in 1684, at a patriarchal age. Among his descendants may be mentioned his great-grandson, Major Peter Jacquett, who was a gallant officer in the Continental Army. Two **De Haes** years after Jacquett was made justice, Captain John de Haes was elevated to the same office. Previous to this he had been commissioner to receive and take charge of quit rents, and later, collector of customs at New Castle. Another Huguenot who was prominent in the government of the colony for many years was Alexander Boyer, **Boyer** who as early as 1648 had been made deputy commissioner of Delaware.

Among the earlier settlers on the Delaware were the **Other Families** Le Fever brothers, Jacques, Hypolite and Jean. Joost de la Grange came to America in 1656 by way of Holland, and became the owner of Tinicum Island in 1662. He left a son named Arnoldus. Gerrit Rutan was a citizen of the colony before 1660, and established a family well known in Pennsylvania, of which the Hon. James

S. Rutan was a worthy representative. Other heads of families who established themselves along the banks of the Delaware were: Daniel Rouette (prior to 1683); Jean du Bois (prior to 1694); Elie Naudin in 1698, a native of La Tremblade; John Gruwell, with his sons John and Jacob; the brothers, Daniel, James and William Voshell, who were probably related to Augustine and Peter Voshell who came to New York in 1700; Dr. des Jardines (prior to 1683), who came as a naturalized Englishman; Jacob Casho; Laurens Rochia, who fled first to Ireland; and Richard Saye, of Nismes, who came in 1686. Other names appear before the end of the seventeenth century, many of them given distinction by the upright and honourable lives of their bearers, as follows: Philipe Chevalier, Henri Clerq, Albert Blocq, Math. de Ring, Mosis de Gau, Hubert Laurans, Paul Mincq, Jean Savoy, Bellevill, Cammon, Bassett, Cazier, Deto, La Pierre, La Farge, Le Compte (La Count), Larus, Sees, Setton, Janvier, Du Chesney (Dushane), Vigoure, Tunnell, Le Croix, and Hueling (Huling).

II

The Ferrèe family was descended from an old and noble family of Normandy, and at the time of the Revocation of the Edict, Daniel, one of the best representatives of the family, was a silk manufacturer of wealth and influential position. Owing to his prominence and the staunchness he had displayed in clinging to his faith, he was marked by the dragoons for the bitterest persecutions. To save his wife, Mary, and his six children from the abuse and insults of the troopers, he managed to convey them secretly to Strasbourg, where they were in comparative safety. Remaining here for some time, the Ferrèes moved to Bittingheim in the Palatinate. Here Daniel Ferrèe died. The leadership now developed upon Mary Ferrèe, and the difficulties of her position cannot be well over-estimated; an exile from her native land, living amongst a

The Ferree Family

Daniel's Flight

Mary Ferree's Heroism

strange people, and with but scant means with which to
provide for her family, the future must, indeed, have
looked black to her.   But she proved to be the stuff of
which heroines are made, and surmounting every obstacle,
managed to keep her little flock together.   As time passed
on, and her children grew to maturity, she developed the
plan of seeking out a home in the new world where her
girls and boys would have a better chance in the world

Seeks America for her Children than was offered by Germany, already overcrowded with
refugees, and far from secure from the inroads of the
Papal troops.   Her eldest daughter, Catherine, had married a young refugee by the name of Isaac le Fevre, and
he, together with the wife of Madame Ferrèe's oldest son,
Daniel, joined the little band which left the Palatinate in
1708.

Their Church Letter The church letter which Daniel received was as
follows :

Certificate for Daniel Firre and his family.

WE, the Pastors, Elders and Deacons of the Reformed Walloon
Church of Pelican, in the Lower Palatinate, having been requested
by the Honourable Daniel Firre, his wife, Anne Maria Leininger, and
their children, Andrew and John Firre, to grant them a testimonial of
their life and religion, do certify and attest that they have always
made profession of the pure Reformed religion, frequented our sacred
assemblies, and have partaken of the supper of the Lord with the other
members of the faith, in addition to which they have always conducted themselves uprightly without having given cause for scandal
that has come to our knowledge.   Being now on their departure to
settle elsewhere we commend them to the protection of God and to the
kindness of all our brethren in the Lord Christ.   In witness whereof
we have signed this present testimonial with our signature and usual
marks.   Done at Pelican, in our Consistory, the 10th of May, 1708.

    MICHAEL MESSAKOP,   J. ROMAN, Pastor,

    PETER SCHARLET,   JAMES BAILLEAUX, Deacon,

    JOHN BAPTISTE LEPLACE, Deacon.

The civil passport which Madame Ferrèe obtained is
not without interest as a historical document, and a
translation of it is as follows :

WHEREAS, Maria, Daniel Fuehre's widow, and her son, **Daniel Ferie**, with his wife and six children, in view of improving their condition and in furtherance of their prosperity, purpose to emigrate from Steinweiler, in the Mayorality of Bittingheim, High Bailiwick Germersheim, via Holland and England, to the island of Pennsylvania, to reside there. They have requested an accredited certificate that they have left the town of Steinweiler with the knowledge of the proper authorities, and have deported themselves, and without cause for censure, and are indebted to no one, and not subject to vassalage, being duly solicited it has been thought proper to grant their petition, declaring that the above named persons are not moving away clandestinely.

That during the time their father, the widow and children resided in this place they behaved themselves so piously and honestly that it would have been highly gratifying to us to see them remain among us; that they are not subject to bodily bondage, the Mayorality not being subject to vassalage. They have also paid for their permission to emigrate. Mr. Fisher, the Mayor of Steinweiler, being expressly interrogated, it has been ascertained that they are not liable for any debts. In witness whereof I have, in the absence of the Counsellor of the Palatinate, etc., signed these presents, and given the same to the persons who intend to emigrate. *[Commendations]*

J. P. DIETRICH, Court Clerk.

Dated Bittingheim, March 10, 1708.

Armed with these documents the party made its way to England to complete its arrangements for settling in America. Madame Ferrèe sought and obtained an interview with William Penn, to whom she told the story of her misfortunes and her desires for the future. Penn was deeply interested by her recital and agreed to give her a tract of land in Pennsylvania. The day following her visit he took her to see Queen Anne, and that generous sovereign also became interested in the courageous woman and promised her " substantial aid, which she in due time rendered." *[Interview with Wm. Penn] [Aid from Queen Anne]*

After a six months' residence in London the Ferrèes and Le Fevre joined a band of Huguenot and Palatine refugees who were about to set out for America under the leadership of the Rev. Joshua Kocherthal. Arriving in *[LeFevre Son-in-law]*

New York, the party continued on up the Hudson to
Esopus, where their relatives, Michail Ferrèe and Andreas
Lefevre, had already settled. Here they remained for four
1712 years, until, in 1712, it became feasible for them to remove to Pennsylvania and settle upon the lands which
had been granted to them in the valley of the Pequea.
The tract which came into their possession contained two
2,000 Acres
Tract thousand acres, in consideration for which they paid over
to Penn's commissioners the sum of one hundred and fifty
pounds.

In 1716, four years after her arrival in Pennsylvania,
Madame Ferrèe found a peaceful grave near the home
which she had established for her children. It is pleasant to know that the last years of this brave woman were
Peaceful
Death
1716 in marked contrast to the stormy years of her flight from
France and her struggles in Germany, and that she died
happy in the knowledge that her children were on the
high-road to prosperity in a land where freedom of conscience was the birthright of all her sons. Her descendants prospered and multiplied until to-day they are to be
numbered by the thousand. In every walk of life they
have earned distinction and have proved an honour to
Numerous
Descendants their Huguenot ancestry. It will be possible to mention
but a few of them in this book, for a full list would occupy pages.

In the Revolutionary struggle the family took an important part. Besides a great number of privates and
non-commissioned officers, the Ferrèes gave to the cause
such brave soldiers as Colonel John Ferrèe, of the Tenth
Pennsylvania Rifles, Colonel Joel Ferrèe, Major Michael
Ferrée and Major George Lefever. Prominent among the
members of the family who took part in the war of 1812
Soldiers and
Patriots were Colonel Joel Ferrèe (a cousin of the Revolutionary
colonel of that name) and Colonel Daniel Lefevre. In
the Civil War the most distinguished representative of
General
Reynolds the family was Major-General John F. Reynolds. His
grandmother on the paternal side was Catherine Ferrèe Le

Fevre, who was a direct descendant from Madame Ferrèe. General Reynolds' record is too well known to require repetition here; certainly no more gallant soldier was developed during the war than the commander of the First Army Corps who died so nobly at the battle of Gettysburg. His brother, William Reynolds, who died a *Rear Admiral* *Reynolds* Rear Admiral in the United States Navy, was also a distinguished member of the family and helped carry on the family traditions by his service in the Mexican and Civil Wars. The Schreiver family of Maryland is another branch of Madame Ferrèe's descendants which has made an honourable record for itself, tracing its descent from Rebecca Ferrèe. Abraham Schreiver (1771–1848) earned an enviable reputation as a judge of great legal ability and uprightness. A very distinguished descendant of *Admiral* *Schley* this branch is Admiral Winfield Scott Schley, who earned lasting glory at Santiago. Admiral Schley is descended from Mary Schreiver, daughter of David and Rebecca (Ferrèe) Schreiver, who married John Schley, the admiral's grandfather. How much of his success as a fighter Admiral Schley owes to the strain of martial Huguenot blood in his veins it is, of course, impossible to say; but when we look at the records of the Ferrèe-Lefever descendants in camp and field, we may feel sure that his debt is no inconsiderable one.

III

Three Huguenots were among the first residents of Philadelphia—Jean de La Vall, Edmund Du Castle, and *Early in* *Philadelphia* Andrew Doz. Doz, who was a refugee in London at the time of Penn's purchase, came over with Penn to investigate the advisability of planting vineyards. In 1690 he was rewarded for his services by a grant of two hundred acres of land, which included the vineyards already laid out along the banks of the Schuylkill River. Settling upon this grant, he prospered, found himself a *Doz 1690* wife and established a worthy family. His grandson, likewise named Andrew, became widely known as a thoroughly public-spirited citizen and gave away large sums of money for those days, to numerous charitable and philanthropic institutions of the city.   Other Hugue-nots who were citizens of Philadelphia at a very early date were Samuel Robinett, Gabriel Rappe, and Nicholas Reboteau, of the Isle of Rhé, and Andrew of Nismes.

In 1684 Andros Souplis and his wife came to Philadelphia.   He had been an officer in the French army, was a very brilliant young man, and soon became a great favourite with Penn.   He left behind him one son, Andrew, who changed the name to its present form of Suplee.

Isaac Roberdeau, with his wife Mary Cunyngham, a descendant of the Earl of Glencairn, fled to Philadelphia from St. Christopher at an early date.   His son, Daniel, became one of the leading merchants and first citizens of Philadelphia.   By the year 1756 he had become one of the managers of the Pennsylvania hospital, and was a leader among the early Masons, being closely associated with Benjamin Franklin, Alexander Hamilton and others.   During the years 1756-60 he was a member of the Pennsylvania assembly, and five years later he was made an elder in the Presbyterian Church.   He was an ardent patriot and gave himself unsparingly to the cause of independence.   In 1775 he served as a colonel of Pennsylvania troops.   In 1776 he presided over a public meeting in Philadelphia which wielded a large influence in favour of the Declaration of Independence.   Shortly afterwards he fitted out a couple of privateers, and when one of these vessels captured a rich prize with $22,000 in silver aboard, he promptly placed the money at the disposal of Congress.   On July 4, 1776, while he was a member of the council of safety, he was chosen as first brigadier-general of the Pennsylvania troops.   Later he was elected as delegate to the Continental Congress.   In 1778 there was a scarcity of lead in the American army,

A Leader
Among the
Masons

Daniel
Roberdeau

and General Roberdeau, securing a leave of absence from the Congress, with his private fortune established a fort in Bedford County as protection against the Indians and worked a lead mine there. At the close of the war he retired from business as well as from public life, and settled down in Alexandria, Virginia, where he was frequently in the habit of entertaining General Washington. He died in 1795. An Ardent Patriot

His son, Isaac, grandson of the emigrant of that name, early showed a love for engineering and received the best kind of technical education which the times afforded. In 1791 he acted as assistant engineer in laying out the city of Washington, and later was engaged in canal construction in Pennsylvania. In 1813 he was appointed topographical engineer in the regular army, with the rank of major. In this capacity he had charge of the survey which laid out the boundary line between Canada and the United States under the treaty of Ghent. He organized the bureau of topographical engineers in the War Department, in 1818, and remained as its chief until his death in 1829.

Among the records of Christ Episcopal Church, of Philadelphia, occur the following names of Huguenot parents (first entries alone being given): Le Tort, James, 1709; Le Boyteau, William, 1711; Voyer, Peter, 1713; Tripeo, Frederick, 1713; Chevalier, Peter, 1712; Garrigues, Francis, 1721; Durell, Moses, 1731; Fleury, Peter, 1731; Le Dru, Noel, 1732; Pinnard, Joseph, 1733; Renardet, James, 1733; Doz, Andrew; Duche, Jacob, 1734; Boyer, James, 1734; Bonnett, John, 1736; Garrigues, Peter, 1736; Doutell, Michael, 1737; Hodnett, John, 1737; Boudinot, Elias, 1738; Brund, John, 1738; Purdieu, Guilliam, 1738; La Rue, John, 1739; Le Shemile, Peter, 1741; Le Gay, Jacob, 1744; Votaw, Paul Isaac, 1747; Dupeen, Daniel, 1747; de Prefontain, Peter, 1754; Vidal, Stephen, 1754; Couche, Daniel, 1756; Paca, John, 1758; Le Dieu, Lewis, 1758; Lacallas, Christ Church Records

James, 1759; Hillegas, Michael, 1760. Among these
names are many which are held in respect to-day;
two especially being worthy of notice—Boudinot and
Hillegas.

CHAPTER II

ELIAS BOUDINOT AND STEPHEN GIRARD

I

IN 1686, Elias Boudinot, of La Tremblade, came to New York. His son, Elias, Jr., left New York some time prior to 1735 and established himself in Philadelphia. There his son Elias (third of the name) was born in 1740. The boy received a good classical education, and when the usual course of Latin and Greek was completed he set himself to study law under the guidance of the famous Richard Stockton. He was an apt scholar and soon achieved an enviable reputation at the bar. At the opening of the war, though still a young man, he was recognized as easily among the most eminent lawyers which the colonies had produced. He began his public career as commissary-general of prisoners, in 1777, and the year following was elected to the Continental Congress. Here his abilities were brought into full play and he soon became one of the most powerful leaders of that body. Four years after his first election to Congress he was chosen as its president, and in that capacity he signed the treaty of peace with England. He then wished to take up his law practice again, and succeeded for a short while. But he had proved himself too valuable a public servant for his constituents to allow him to remain in private life, and when the constitution was adopted he was elected successively to the first, second and third congresses. In 1795 Washington appointed him Director of the Mint at Philadelphia. He held this position until 1805, when he resigned and retired to Burlington, New Jersey, in order to devote his attention to study and philanthropic work. He was for many years a trustee

Elias Boudinot 1686

His Able Son Elias, Jr., 1740

Member of Congress

President

Director of the Mint

301

of Princeton College, and in 1805 presented that institution with a valuable collection of specimens in natural history. He was greatly interested in philanthropic work of a religious nature. He served on the American

Philan-
thropist

Board of Commissioners for Foreign Missions, and was generous in his contributions to that cause. He was also one of the founders of the American Bible Society, becoming its first president in 1816. Other lines of philanthropic endeavour in which he was actively engaged were the education of deaf mutes, the training of young men for the ministry, and the relief of the poor. While

Student and
Author

thus busily engaged in promoting the welfare of his fellows, he found time to undertake many arduous studies in biblical literature, and published a number of volumes on religious subjects—the most famous of these being a reply to Tom Paine. He died in 1821, full of years and good deeds. In his will he gave 13,000 acres of land to the city of Philadelphia in order that the poor might be able to buy wood at a small price ; 3,000 acres

Benefactor

to the Pennsylvania hospital, etc. Among the other bequests was the rather odd one of a fund with which to buy spectacles for the aged poor.

No short sketch of his life can do justice to Elias Boudinot. To appreciate his real significance as an actor in the drama which took place at the founding of the Republic, it is necessary to read the history of his times. As lawyer, statesman, patriot, scholar and philanthropist, he was one of the most remarkable men of the Revolutionary period.

II

Story of
Stephen
Girard

One of the most interesting characters that France has contributed to America is Stephen Girard, founder of Girard College in Philadelphia. He represented the accumulative and thrifty spirit of his race. From a penniless runaway he rose to be merchant, banker, multi-millionaire, the richest man of his day in America, and at the end a philanthropist and benefactor. He was one of the most eccentric of men ; and his homely chaise, drawn by a sleepy looking farm horse, was for years to be seen every day except Sunday at about the same hour, making its way slowly along the main business street of his adopted city. This description of him is given by a recent writer : [1] "His low, square, sturdy frame was invariably clad in a faded coat of an ancient and foreign pattern. His slouch hat half concealed a cold and melancholy face marked with deep lines of thought and care. His small, bright eye looked hard and cunning, and his firm, determined mouth and square jaw indicated the indomitable will that lay beneath the uncouth exterior."

He was born near Bordeaux, in France, May 24, 1750, of seafaring parents. His childhood was unhappy, and at fourteen he ran away from home, shipping as cabinboy on a trading vessel bound for the West Indies. During his voyages he read carefully every book he could get hold of, and gained a large fund of information. Of a keen mind, he studied thoroughly the commercial conditions and operations of the countries he visited. By and by he rose to the command of a ship, and presently became ship owner, purchasing vessel after vessel until his fleet was famous the world around. He made Philadelphia his headquarters in 1777, and became engaged in numerous enterprises. His marriage to a Philadelphia shipbuilder's daughter was unhappy, his wife becoming insane and spending twenty-five years in an asylum before death relieved her. This blasting of his domestic happiness, together with his boyhood miseries, embittered him, and led him to assume a harsh and cynical exterior foreign to his real nature.

He bent all his energies to the accumulation of wealth, and came to be regarded as a miser. The truth would seem to be, however, that all this time he had the fixed purpose of founding an institution that should through

Born 1750 in France

Self-Made

Philadelphia 1777

Miser-Philanthropist

[1] W. H. Kirkbride.

generations feed, clothe and educate the humble and homeless. Rich as he was, his tastes were of the simplest. Indeed, he lived in obscurity, in a small house on an unattractive side street, and it is said his personal expenses were not so great as those of his clerks. His breakfast and supper usually consisted of biscuits and milk, while for dinner he occasionally allowed himself a little meat.

Eccentric but Just

His eccentricities were many, and the stories told of him well illustrate this side of his character. We give two or three which are thoroughly characteristic. He was not in the habit of giving promiscuously, and seldom, if ever, gave to beggars. A very poor man once knocked at his door, begging for bread to save his wife and children from starvation. Girard drove him roughly away, but secretly followed him home, and, finding that he had spoken the truth, ordered the baker to leave four loaves a day at the house until the man procured work enough to support his family.

Respect for True Piety

He had the greatest contempt for any one who professed religion and did not practice it, but respected the man of religion who was honest and straightforward in his dealings. One of the few men that he trusted implicitly was a Mr. Inglis, an expert accountant, and a man of sincere religious opinions. Recognizing his value and his honesty, Girard offered him the position of cashier in his bank, which was refused. "You and I serve different masters, Mr. Girard, and could never agree." His views were respected and nothing further was said on the subject.

A Quaker's Method of Getting a Subscription

To get a subscription from Stephen Girard was not an easy matter. It required tact and the right introduction and many failed while a few succeeded. It is told that Samuel Coates, a genial Quaker, was one of the few men who knew how to approach the eccentric millionaire. He was a manager of the Pennsylvania Hospital, and called on Girard for the purpose of raising money for the support of that institution. "Well, how much do you want, Coates?" asked Girard in his usual brusque tones. "Just what thee pleases to give, Stephen," quietly replied the Quaker. Girard wrote out a check for $2,000, and, handing it to Mr. Coates, was surprised to see that gentleman pocket it without looking at the amount. "What! you don't look to see how much I give you?" cried Girard incredulously. "Beggars must not be choosers, Stephen," replied the Quaker.

"Give me back my check and I will change it," said Girard after a moment's pause.

"A bird in the hand is worth two in the bush, thee knows, Stephen," mildly replied the Quaker. Without another word Girard sat down and wrote him out a second check for $5,000.

His farm on the outskirts of Philadelphia was one of the best in the country, and while living in town he often drove out before breakfast to see that all was going well. He was very exacting with his hired hands, and never trusted the management of his farm to any one else, but ran it himself, as he did all his affairs. Arriving one morning a little earlier than usual he was greatly annoyed at not finding his man at work on a fence that he was building. The man's wife, noticing Girard approaching the house, hurriedly awoke her husband and sent him to his duties by way of the back door. After visiting the house Girard returned to the fence, and seeing the man at his post reprimanded him for being late. "I'd been here, sir, but went back for a spade," said the workman. "You lie! I went and put my hand in your bed and found it warm," replied Girard, and he discharged the man on the spot.

Detecting a Lie

Not only did he personally supervise the affairs of his farm, but also prided himself on performing much of the manual labour. He frequently killed as many as fifty steers with the assistance of one hired man, and in

Working with his Hands

harvest-time would spend twelve hours at a time with the pitchfork loading the hay wagon.

Financial Mainstay of the Government

This was the man who at the opening of the War of 1812 bought out the old Bank of the United States, and during the war was the financial mainstay of the government. In 1814 when the government called for a loan of $5,000,000 the subscriptions amounted to only $20,000. The credit of the country was at its lowest ebb; but Girard had faith in the nation and saved the day by coming out from behind the ramparts of his bank and advancing the entire sum. He did not stickle about the interest; he had faith, and he could wait for that, he said.

Often Misjudged

In childhood Girard had sustained an accident which blinded one of his eyes and gave a distorted twist to his features. The bitterness attendant upon this was probably the cause in part of his shyness and unsocial habits. Many of his contemporaries thought him harsh and reclusive, but this opinion undoubtedly arose from his manner rather than from any lack of kindness and humanity in Girard's heart, for the open record of his life is sufficient evidence of his altruistic nature. During the epidemic of yellow fever which swept over Philadelphia in

Yellow Fever Episode

1793, he was instrumental in organizing a hospital for the plague-stricken people and gave largely to it. And when no one could be hired to take charge of it, Girard himself, although his business interests suffered greatly from his absence, went to the hospital and for sixty days laboured with might and main to establish order and cleanliness.

Founding Girard College

During his life he gave thousands of dollars to the city of Philadelphia for public improvements and was a liberal contributor to many churches and various charities. At his death he left about nine million dollars to philanthropic enterprises, his principal bequest being the orphanage known as Girard College. This unique institution receives orphans between the ages of six and ten years, inclusive, educates them under excellent masters, trains them for mechanical, agricultural or commercial pursuits, and at the end of eight years gives them a further start in life by finding them suitable positions in their chosen trades.   Thus thousands of poor boys have been cared for and reared into useful, upright men ; and many generations of well-trained and worthy citizens have reason to rise up and call Stephen Girard blessed. The college has had a remarkable success.   Financially the estate increased in value until it is estimated at thirty-eight millions and the annual expenditures of the college are over half a million, as against forty-seven thousand dollars at the beginning.   Fifteen millions have been spent upon the maintenance and enlargement of the institution, which has an enrollment of 1,550.   A preference is given to orphan boys from Philadelphia, secondly, to those born elsewhere in Pennsylvania, thirdly, to those born in New York city, and lastly, to those born in New Orleans—these last two being the first cities he visited after reaching America.

Great Endowment

The will provided strictly that no sectarian teaching should ever be allowed in the college, but said :   " My desire is that all instructors and teachers in the college shall take pains to instill into the minds of the scholars the purest principles of morality, so that, on their entrance into active life, they may, from inclination and habit, evince benevolence towards their fellow creatures, and a love of truth, sobriety and industry, adopting at the same time such religious tenets as their matured reason may enable them to prefer."

Non-Sectarian Provision

Pure Morality

This French-American, who wished to spare other boys the sorrows of his own early life, not only has the credit of founding a distinctive institution of noble aim, but of being a pioneer in great gifts by rich men for educational and philanthropic purposes.   His was the first large benefaction of its kind in the country ; and in Girard College he reared both a monument and an example.

A Noble Monument and Example

CHAPTER III

THE BAYARDS AND OTHER FAMILIES

I

The American
Bayards

Nicholas

TRADITION traces the Bayard family back to that great French Knight who was dubbed "sans peur et sans reproche" (without fear and without reproach). The history of the American Bayards properly begins with Nicholas Bayard, a Huguenot minister who fled into Holland after the massacre of St. Bartholomew and settled in Amsterdam. His daughter, Judith, married Peter Stuyvesant, the last of the Dutch governors of New Amsterdam, and one of his sons married Stuyvesant's sister. From this alliance sprang Nicolas, Balthazar, and Peter Bayard, the founders of the American branches of the family.

Nicholas and Balthazar became prominent citizens of New York, while Peter, offending his aristocratic brethren by joining the Labadists, went to Bohemia Manor and established the Delaware branch. No American family has a more honourable record than the Delaware Bayards, who for generation after generation have been zealous for the public welfare, as the following brief sketch of some of its members will show.

Delaware
Branch

John Bayard

Colonel John Bayard, born in Bohemia Manor, Md., in 1738, was the great-grandson of Peter Bayard. When he was eighteen years old he went up to Philadelphia and there commenced his commercial career. He was very successful in business, and in the course of a few years was reckoned among the leading merchants of that flourishing city. He was a patriot through and through, and as he was a man of strong character he soon became a vital

308

force in the growing resentment against British oppression and the movement for independence. He was one of the first to join the famous organization known as the Sons of Liberty, and in spite of the injury to his business which it entailed, he was one of the first merchants to sign the non-importation agreement of October, 1765. In 1774 he was elected to the Provincial Congress ; two years later he became a member of the Council of Safety. During the campaign of 1776-7 he was in the field at the head of a Pennsylvania regiment. So brave a soldier was he that after the battle of Princeton Washington complimented him in person upon his gallantry in that action. The year following he again took up his legislative duties, serving as speaker of the Pennsylvania house of assembly. In 1781 he was appointed to the supreme executive council, and in 1785 completed his public services by representing his state in the Continental Congress. He deserved to be remembered, in the phrase of Bancroft, as "a patriot of singular purity of character." *Sons of Liberty* *Gallant Soldier*

Samuel Bayard, born in Philadelphia in 1767, was the fourth son of Colonel John Bayard. He graduated from Princeton with the class of 1784, studied law and commenced his practice in Philadelphia. In 1791 he was made clerk of the United States Supreme Court, but left that position in 1794 to become the agent of the government in prosecuting the claims before the British Court of Admiralty. On his return from London he settled in New York and commanded a large and lucrative practice. While living in New York he became instrumental in founding the New York Historical Society. In 1806 he purchased a beautiful estate in Princeton, New Jersey, becoming a country squire and philanthropist. He attended session after session of the state legislature, and for many years was the presiding judge of the Court of Common Pleas of Somerest County. Among other things, he was associated with Elias Boudinot in forming the American Bible Society, and was one of the founders and patrons *Samuel Bayard* *Founder of New York Historical Society* of the Theological Seminary at Princeton.   He died in 1840.

James
Asheton
Bayard

James Asheton Bayard, son of Dr. James Asheton Bayard, and nephew of Colonel John Bayard, was born in Philadelphia in 1767.   He graduated from Princeton in 1784 in the same class with his cousin Samuel.   Three years later he was admitted to the bar and located in Wilmington, Del.   His ability as a lawyer was soon recognized, and at the time he was elected to Congress, in 1796, he was already among the most prominent men in the profession.   A year after his election to Congress he achieved a national reputation by his management of the impeachment of William Blount.   His power as an orator and his wide knowledge of constitutional law soon brought

Federalist
Leader

him to the fore in Congress, and he rapidly developed into a leader of the Federalist party.   In 1801, when the choice lay between Burr and Jefferson, Bayard was influential, together with Hamilton, in swinging the scales in favour of Jefferson.   That same year he declined an appointment as Minister to France.   From 1804 to 1813 he represented Delaware in the United States Senate.   President Madison selected Bayard as a joint commissioner to act with Albert Gallatin, John Adams and Henry Clay in arranging terms of peace with Great Britain in 1814, and he was prominent in the negotiations which brought about the treaty of Ghent.   While in Europe he contracted a serious illness, and returned to his home in Wilmington only to die early in the following year.

Family of
Great Senators

Richard Henry Bayard, his eldest son, was born in Wilmington in 1796, graduated from Princeton in 1814, and then devoted himself to the law.   He was a brilliant lawyer, and in 1836 was made United States Senator from Delaware.

His youngest brother, James Asheton, was born in 1779.   He, too, became a lawyer, and won high distinction at the bar.   He was federal attorney for Delaware during the administration of President Van Buren, and in 1851 he became a Senator from that state, continuing until 1869. He was for a long time chairman of the committee on the judiciary, and was generally esteemed for the high sense of public honour which he evinced on numerous occasions.

His son, Thomas Francis Bayard, was born in Wilmington in 1828. He was admitted to the bar in 1851 and practised law until he was elected to succeed his father in the Senate in 1868. He served as Senator until 1885, when he became Secretary of State. In 1893 he was appointed Ambassador to Great Britain.

Last of a Noble Family

II

The Duché family is descended from Jacques Duché, a native of La Rochelle, who was naturalized in England in 1682 with his wife, Mary, and two sons, Arnold and Anthony. Anthony came to Staten Island at an early date and removed to Philadelphia a few years prior to 1700. His son Jacob, born in Philadelphia in 1708, was the father of the Reverend Jacob Duché, a noted clergyman of his day. He was born at Philadelphia in 1737, graduated from the University of Pennsylvania when he was twenty years old, and then went to Cambridge, England, to pursue his studies further. In 1759 the Bishop of London licensed him to preach in the Philadelphia churches, and that same year he returned to this country. He was a very popular preacher and by 1775 had become rector of Christ Church, the leading Episcopal congregation of Philadelphia at the time. He has come down to us in history as the minister who delivered the prayer at the opening of the first Continental Congress—a prayer so patriotic and reverent withal that the assembled patriots gave him a vote of thanks. In 1776 he was chosen chaplain of Congress. He died in 1798.

The Duche Family

Jacob Preacher and Patriot

III

The Du Pont family, long known as the great powder

The Du Pont Family

manufacturers of the country, are descended from an old Huguenot family of Rouen in France. Du Pont de Nemours was the founder of the family. His story has been written by G. Schelle, and published by Gillaumin in Paris. A writer in the *Magazine of American History*, for March, 1889, reviews the Memoir. The Du Pont works at Wilmington, Delaware, and their branches and businesses in other places, have given them a commercial reputation hardly equalled in any other calling. During the long period from the beginning of the last century to our own time many members of the Du Pont family have gained distinction by their services in the army and navy. They were represented in the War of 1812, and in the Civil War Admiral Du Pont and Colonel Henry Du Pont were both men of mark.

Du Pont de
Nemours,
Publicist

Du Pont de Nemours was born in Paris in 1739. He was precocious, noted at his twelfth year for his knowledge, and at twenty submitted to Choiseul a plan for encouraging agriculture, establishing domestic free trade, suppressing taxes, and remodelling the financial system of France. He was soon recognized as one of the most brilliant and able publicists and economists of France. He was the most chivalric champion of liberty in France, according to Madame de Stael, and successively urged the abolition of slavery, the repeal of the game laws, liberty of the press, relief from the laws controlling labour, reform in public charity, the repeal of monopolies, and other public oppressions and abuses. Benjamin Franklin especially commended his economic tables. If France had heeded him, the French Revolution would not have been necessary. He was too much of a reformer to be acceptable to a corrupt court, and during the stress of the Revolution, his life being in peril, he escaped to America, where his eldest son had established himself. Jefferson, who had known him in France, heartily welcomed him to the United States. He laboured to effect Jefferson's purpose of securing Louisiana by purchase from Napoleon, having returned to France after the Revolution. When Napoleon returned from Elba, Du Pont again took refuge in the United States, and lived with his sons near Wilmington until his death in 1817, in his seventy-seventh year.

His second son, Irénée, was the founder of the powder works. He had shared imprisonment with his father, and on reaching the United States in 1798 found the great need of a domestic supply of good gunpowder. He returned to France to study its manufacture, came back to this country, and from a small beginning built up a business which has become one of the notable industries of the country. He died in 1834.

Admiral Du Pont, one of the distinguished officers of the United States Navy, was the son of Victor, older brother of Irénée, and engaged with him in business. It was Admiral Du Pont who was the commander and hero of the Port Royal Expedition. This descendant of a Huguenot won that unexpected, absolute and decisive victory which thrilled the loyal hearts of the country with hope and thankfulness, coming as it did when only such a victory could counterbalance the alarm caused by the defeat at Bull Run. The story of this remarkable expedition is told by General Egbert L. Viele in the *Magazine of American History*, October, 1885. Admiral Du Pont had to attack with his fleet the great forts which guarded the harbour of Port Royal, in order to establish a system of blockade that would cripple the Confederacy. There were 20,000 soldiers and 5,000 sailors under the admiral's command, and his fleet consisted of seventy-seven vessels, including transports. It was a motley collection, and storms had to be overcome as well as forts ; but the brave and able commander carried out his plan, won a decisive and crushing victory, and matched Farragut's daring strategy at New Orleans.

"The planning of the bombardment, the manning of the ships, and the effective work done by the fleet," says

*Admiral
DuPont Hero
of Port Royal*

*A Brilliant
Naval Victory*

General Viele, "will pass into history as one of the most successful achievements of the kind, as it marked an era in naval warfare. It was the first time that the powerful auxiliary of steam was brought to play such a decided part in war operations. . . . Du Pont had planned the attack with the utmost precision. Every vessel had its designated place. The fleet sailed in the form of an ellipse, each ship to deliver its fire at each fort as it passed abreast. Three times this circle of death passed in its relentless course. For four hours the terrible duel was maintained, and then after a well directed broadside from the *Wabash*, all was over. . . . Such utter destruction probably never overtook a fortification."

In a private letter, dated on board the flagship *Wabash*, Port Royal, November 9, 1861, Admiral Du Pont wrote: "During the disheartening events of our passage my faith never gave way; but at some moments it seemed appalling (referring to a severe storm that scattered the fleet and wrecked a number of vessels). On the other hand, I permit no elation at our success. Yet I cannot refrain from telling you that it has been more complete and brilliant than I ever could have believed. . . . I kept under way and made three turns, though I passed five times between the forts. I could get none of my big frigates up. I believe my plan was clever. I stood against the side, and had the management the better in consequence. The confidence of the enemy was extreme that they could drive us away. They fought bravely, and their rifle guns never missed. They aimed at one bridge, where they knew they could make a hole if they were lucky. A shot in the centre let water into the after magazine; but I saved a hundred lives by keeping under way and bearing in close. I never conceived such a fire as that of this ship on her second turn, and I am told that its effect upon the spectators outside of her was intense. I learn that when they saw our flag flying on shore the troops were powerless to cheer, but wept."

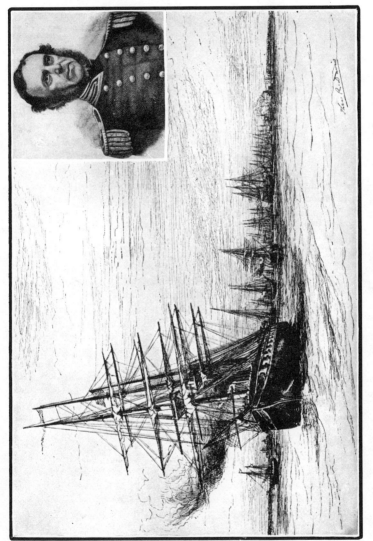

ADMIRAL S. F. DuPONT AND THE AMERICAN ARMADA AT PORT ROYAL

On the reception of the official dispatches in Washington, the general order was issued by Secretary Gideon Wells, "that to commemorate this signal victory, a national salute be fired from each navy yard, at meridian, on the day after the reception of this order."

IV

John Stephen Benezett was the founder of the family of that name. He was born in Abbeville in 1682, at the Revocation was taken to Holland, and from thence to England in 1715. He settled in Philadelphia in 1731 and became prominent in the affairs of the city, having the distinction of being the first city treasurer. He was also one of the leading members of the Society of Friends, and for some years was a pillar in the Moravian church. Of his three sons, one became a major in the Revolution, while Anthony, the youngest, grew into one of the most philanthropic citizens of Philadelphia. He advocated the emancipation of the slaves and was zealous in promoting their education, opening a night school for their benefit and showing his sincerity by teaching in it himself. He deserves to rank as the earliest abolitionist who openly dared to express his views, a pamphlet of his entitled *Considerations on the Keeping of Negroes* being the first anti-slavery work published in America. During the Revolution he was active in relieving the sufferings of prisoners and wounded, thus being in a way the forebear of the Red Cross Society.

Benezett

First City Treasurer

Anthony first Open Abolitionist

V

Michael Hillegas was the son of a refugee who fled to the Palatinate shortly after the Revocation. He was born in Philadelphia in 1728 and amassed a considerable fortune in the sugar refining business. He was an ardent patriot and at an early date placed himself and his fortunes at the service of the cause of independence. He was made the first treasurer of the United States, and his

Michael Hillegas 1728

integrity and financial ability made him a "tower of
strength" during the dreariest and most hopeless days of
the Revolution. Among the many descendants of the
Hillegas family may be named the Honourable John
Richards, who was a member of Congress in 1796, and for
many years prominent in legal and political circles in
Pennsylvania.

VI

Huguenots were among the earliest settlers of Germantown, in the vicinity of Philadelphia. Within three years
of the date of settlement we find Jean Le Brun, Jean
Dedier, Wigard and Gerhart Levering mentioned as heads
of families. The peculiarly German names Gerhart and
Wigard were due to the fact that the father of the emigrants, Doctor Rosier Levering, a refugee to Germany,
married a German lady named Elizabeth Van der Walle,
both sons being born on German soil. The Leverings
have been prominent in Pennsylvania for many years.
Wigard, a man of strong character, was the founder of
Roxborough. Among Gerhart's descendants may be
mentioned the Honourable Joshua Levering and the
Right Reverend J. Mortimer Levering.

The descendants of James De la Plaine, son of Nicholas
De la Plaine, who came to New Amsterdam via Holland
prior to 1663, are numerous in Pennsylvania and Maryland. James settled in Germantown in 1691, became a
leader in the Society of Friends, and died in 1750. Besides James, four daughters of Nicholas De la Plaine
came to Philadelphia at about the same period; Elizabeth, wife of Casper Hoodt; Judith, wife of Thomas
Griffith; Susanna, wife of Arnold Cassel; and Crejanne,
wife of Ives Belangèe,—the last three being married in
Philadelphia. John and Joseph De la Plaine, grandsons
of James, and the latter an officer in the Revolution,
removed to Maryland and established a numerous
progeny.

VII

The Garrigues family, represented in Philadelphia by William H. and Samuel E. Garrigues, traces its descent from the Garric family, of Monpellier, in Languedoc. At the Revocation, David Garric fled to England, where the name became Garrick ; while another brother took refuge in Germany, whence under the modified name of Garrigues, his descendants established themselves in Philadelphia shortly after 1700. David Garrick's Descent

Richard De Charms, one of the best known Swedenborgian preachers of the first half of the century, who held successful pastorates in Philadelphia, Baltimore and New York, was born in Philadelphia in 1796.

Abram Markos, or Marcou, was a distinguished resident of the city prior to and during the Revolution. He was born in the Danish West Indies in 1729, and was descended from Count Marcou, a native of Montbeliard, in French-Comte, who settled in the Antilles and became a prosperous planter. Abram came to Philadelphia when he was a young man and traded extensively between Philadelphia and Santa Cruz, where he was largely interested in raising sugar. He acquired a considerable holding of real estate, one of his plots being the land on which the government buildings now stand. In 1774 he organized the company of light horse now so famous as the "city troop" of Philadelphia, and became its first captain. A year later he presented the company with a silk flag, the first flag to bear the thirteen stripes symbolical of the thirteen colonies struggling for freedom. As he was a Danish subject, the neutrality proclamations of the king of Denmark prevented him from taking an active part in the Revolution. Abram Marcou

The Pennsylvania branch of the Chevalier family was founded by Pierre Chevalier, who settled in Philadelphia in 1720. His father, of a noble family of Bretagne, fled to England, where Pierre was born. Before emigrating to this country, Pierre married an English lady. He The Chevaliers

left two sons, Peter and John, whose sons became prominent merchants of the city. His daughters married well,
and among their descendants may be numbered Judge
Samuel Breese, of New Jersey, and Professor Edward E.
Salisbury, of Yale.

Other Huguenot names which occur among the emi-
grants to Philadelphia before 1750 are: Montadon, Le
Colle, Casser, Remy, Huyett, Remley, Ransier, Suffrance,
Bouton, Rena, Du Bois, Le Brant, and Piquart.

VIII

Lancaster County was a place of refuge for many
Huguenots. In the days before a permanent settlement
had been effected, there were several Huguenots in that
region who were engaged in trading with the Indians.
Among these was Captain James Letort, who with his
sons is frequently mentioned as being in the government's
employ. He afterwards settled in Philadelphia.

Samuel Boyer was one of the first of the regular settlers
to arrive, coming in 1710. The Boyer family in France
is a large and honourable one, and the American Boyers
are worthy of their heredity. Members are to be found
throughout Pennsylvania, and mention may be made of
Honourable Henry Boyer, General Philip Boyer, of the
War of 1812, Honourable Benjamin M. Boyer, member
of Congress in 1864, Colonel Zachur Boyer, of the Civil
War, and Honourable Henry K. Boyer, Treasurer of the
State and Director of the United States Mint at Philadelphia.

As news of the colony spread among the exiles in the
Palatinate, they came over in large numbers. They did
not support any separate church organization of their
own, having united with other churches while in Germany, but it is recorded that Lewis Boehm, pastor of the
First Reformed Church in Lancaster in 1771, used to deliver frequent sermons in French. The following refugees
were members of this church: Viller, De Gaston, Mel-

Lancaster County

The Boyers

Easy Assimilation

chior Boyer, Beauchamp, Fortune, Fortuney, Ferrèe, Fortunet, La Rou, Racque, Bonnett, Marquet, Rosier, De Dieu, Allemand, Huttier, Berott, Le Fever, Trébert, Le Crone, Delancey, Roller, Le Roy, Vissard, Maquinnette, Vosine, Le Brant, Raiguel, Du Fresne and Lorah. Holding membership in Trinity Lutheran Church, of Lancaster, were Hubele, Morett, Moreau, Mathiot, Santeau, De Mars, Dilliers, Cossart and Sponsilier.

Among the descendants of these emigrants are Dr. Henry Bernard Mathiot, of Pittsburg; Adam Hubele, member of the Provincial Assembly in 1775 and a colonel in the Revolution ; John Hubele, member of the Constitutional Convention of 1776, of the Committee of Safety, etc. ; General Peter Forney, an officer in the Revolution, and member of Congress in 1813 ; the Honourable David Marchand, Jr., member of Congress in 1817 ; the Honourable Joshua Mathiot, Congressman from Ohio in 1841 ; Colonel Forney, member of Congress in 1851 and an officer in the Civil War ; the Honourable Albert Marchand, member of Congress in 1839 ; Commodore John Bonnett Marchand, famous for the part he played in the naval fight in Mobile Bay ; and General John E. Roller.

Public Men

IX

Near the present town of Sheridan is still standing a massive stone mansion built by Jean Henri Cellier in 1727. The Cellier family was scattered to the four winds by the Revocation, representatives being found even in Africa, where the descendants of the branch which took refuge in Holland are among the prominent citizens of Cape Colony—one of them, General Cellier, being especially noted through his operations in the Boer War. In Pennsylvania the name has been corrupted to Zeller.

Other Parts of the State

To the Universalists the stone house erected in Oley, Berks County, by Dr. George De Bonneville in 1745, will always have peculiar interest. For this house, still well preserved, is " the undoubted birthplace of Universalism

Dr. DeBonneville

in America. In this edifice De Bonneville had a large room fitted up as a chapel where he was wont to preach the doctrine of universal redemption to his friends and neighbours who gathered to hear him." De Bonneville was descended from the Lords of Bonneville, whose ancestral seat was at Limoges. His grandfather was Francis De Bonneville, who went to England at the invitation of William III, and whose son married a member of the famous Granville family. From this marriage was born George De Bonneville in 1703. While a young man De Bonneville returned to France to preach to his Huguenot brethren, was captured and was on the point of being beheaded when a reprieve came from the king, Queen Anne of England having pleaded in his behalf. After his release he preached through Germany and Holland and finally emigrated to America in 1741. He will always be remembered as one of the prime movers in what was, perhaps, the profoundest change which took place in religious conceptions during the eighteenth century.

Birthplace of Universalism in America

A Pennsylvanian of Huguenot descent who will long be remembered by many grateful hearts is Reverend William A. Passevant, of the Lutheran Church. The greater part of his life was devoted to philanthropic enterprises. He was instrumental in founding hospitals in Pittsburg, Milwaukee, Chicago and Jacksonville. He helped establish orphanages at Rochester, Pa., and Mt. Vernon, N. Y., and was the founder of Thiel College at Greenville, Pa.

Passevant Preacher

William Chauvenent, the brilliant mathematician, was born in Milford in 1820. He was active with Maury, a Virginia Huguenot, in bringing about the establishment of the United States Naval Academy, and was the leading professor there for several years. For his patriotic efforts in establishing the academy on its present admirable basis, and for his many contributions to the scientific literature of the day, he deserves to be remembered.

Chauvenent Mathematician

General James A. Beaver is descended from a Revolu- Governor Beaver
tionary soldier, John George Beaver, who came to Pennsylvania in 1731 in the good ship *Pink*. General Beaver
served as Colonel of the One Hundred and Forty-eighth
Pennsylvania Regiment during the Civil War, and was
brevetted Brigadier for his services. He has since been
Governor of Pennsylvania, and at present is a Judge of
the Superior Court.

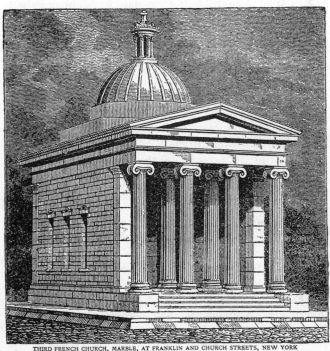

THIRD FRENCH CHURCH, MARBLE, AT FRANKLIN AND CHURCH STREETS, NEW YORK

SOUTH CAROLINA

I

MORE than a century after the disastrous failure of Admiral Coligny's plans to establish French colonies which might become asylums for Protestant refugees in America, in the very same Carolina that was the scene of devastation, demonism, despair and death, it came to pass that French settlements were established. In no section, moreover, were the French settlers more numerous and influential. The story of the state cannot be written without them. In the colonial days they ranked among the foremost citizens in public affairs, and in the War of the Revolution they stood in the front ranks of the patriots and soldiers.

One has but to mention the same of Henry Laurens, a chief among the men who resented royal tyranny and carried the Carolinas into line with Massachusetts in defense of human liberty; and in the army the name of Marion, one of the most romantic figures as well as effective fighters of the Revolution, to prove this.

Owing to the Spaniards and their hatred of the French, and particularly the Protestant French, it was left for the English, under direction of William Sayle, the first governor, to establish the first permanent settlement in

South Carolina. This was at or near Port Royal in 1670. The charter was especially inviting to emigrants. It

granted liberty of conscience to every one, and this at a time when in England conformity to the Anglican Church was pressing hard upon many good men, just as in France Roman Catholicism was driving out the Huguenots. The civil government of this new colony laid only

322

MAROT PSALM BOOK OF GABRIEL MANIGAULT

GABRIEL MANIGAULT, MERCHANT, 1704-1781
From Painting by Jeremiah Theus, Charleston, 1757

three conditions with respect to religion : 1. To believe
that there is a God ; 2. That He is to be worshipped ;
and 3. That it is lawful and the duty of every man when
called upon by those in authority, to bear witness to the
truth. Without acknowledging this no man was permitted to be a freeman, or to have any estate or habitation in Carolina. But persecution for observing different
modes and ways of worship was expressly forbidden ;
and every man was to be left full liberty of conscience,
and might worship God in that manner which he thought
most conformable to the divine will and revealed word.

Ramsay, whose history of South Carolina was written
at the beginning of the last century (published 1808), and   A Medley
who renders due credit to the French, says the early emigrants were a medley of different nations and principles.
Every year brought new adventurers. From England
there came both Cavaliers and Puritans, and many a severe
clash they had. A colony of Dutch settlers came from
New Amsterdam, after the English had taken it and made
New York of it, and these newcomers settled Johnstown,
but subsequently spread themselves over the country. It   1679
was in 1679, the year before Charleston was founded on its   French
Established
present site, that the French refugees reached Carolina to
stay. King Charles II was the direct means of their
coming. He saw the value of skilled labour to the
new colonies, and ordered two small vessels to be
provided at his own expense to transport to Carolina
a company of the foreign Protestants, who had found refuge in his realm, who proposed to raise wine, oil, silk,
and other products of the south. " Though they did not
succeed in enriching the country with these valuable
commodities," says the historian, " their descendants
form a part of the present inhabitants."

II

Then came the Revocation of the Edict of Nantes,
fifteen years after the settlement of Carolina, and this be-

came a large contributor to the growth and prosperity of South Carolina, as of other parts of the world. France's inestimable loss was the gain of nations born and as yet unborn. To South Carolina were transplanted from France the stocks from which have sprung such respectable families, some of them renowned, as Laurens, Marion, Manigault, Prioleau, Horry, Huger, Postell, Guerard, Benoist, Dubois, Dupré, St. Julien, Chevalier, Simons, and a score of others. This group of refugees settled at first on the Santee River, and from them that part of the country in old maps was called French Santee. Their religious leader was Reverend Elias Prioleau, who had brought with him a considerable part of his congregation from France. He was the grandson of Anthoine Prioli, who was chosen Doge of Venice in 1618, and was a man of unusual parts.

Honoured Names

Elias Prioleau

What these families went through for the sake of their religion is indicated in a letter written by Judith Manigault, wife of Peter Manigault, founders of a family that was long well known in the State. This lady, when about twenty, embarked in 1685 for Carolina by way of London. She subsequently wrote to her brother in France a letter, giving some account of her experiences. This is a translation of it into English :

Judith Manigault's Letter

Since you desire it, I will give you an account of our quitting France, and of our arrival in Carolina. During eight months, we had suffered from the contributions and the quartering of the soldiers, with many other inconveniences. We therefore resolved on quitting France by night, leaving the soldiers in their beds, and abandoning the house with its furniture. We contrived to hide ourselves at Romans in Dauphigny, for ten days, while a search was made after us ; but our hostess being faithful, did not betray us when questioned if she had seen us. From thence we passed to Lyons—from thence to Dijon—from which place, as well as from Langres, my eldest brother wrote to you ; but I know not if either of the letters reached you. He informed you that we were quitting France. He went to Madame de Choiseul's, which was of no avail, as she was dead, and her son-in-law had the command of everything ; moreover, he gave us to understand that he perceived our intention of quitting France, and if we asked any favours of him, he would inform against us. We therefore made the best of our way for Metz, in Lorraine, where we embarked on the river Moselle, in order to go to Treves—from thence we passed to Coblentz and Cologne, where we left the Rhine, to go by land to Wesel, where we met with an host who spoke a little French, and informed us we were only thirty leagues from Lunenburg. We knew that you were in winter quarters there. Our deceased mother and myself earnestly besought my eldest brother to go that way with us ; or, leaving us with her, to pay you a visit alone. It was in the depth of winter; but he would not hear of it, having Carolina so much in his head that he dreaded losing any opportunity of going thither. Oh, what grief the losing so fine an opportunity of seeing you at least once more, has caused me ! How have I regretted seeing a brother show so little feeling, and how often have I reproached him with it ! But he was our master, and we were constrained to do as he pleased.

We passed on to Holland, to go from thence to England. We remained in London three months, waiting for a passage to Carolina. Having embarked, we were sadly off : the spotted fever made its appearance on board our vessel, of which disease many died, and among them our aged mother. Nine months elapsed before our arrival in Carolina. We touched two ports—one a Portuguese, and the other an island called Bermuda, belonging to the English, to refit our vessel, which had been much injured in a storm. Our captain having committed some misdemeanor, was put in prison, and the vessel seized. Our money was all spent, and it was with great difficulty we procured a passage in another vessel. After our arrival in Carolina we suffered every kind of evil. In about eighteen months our elder brother, unaccustomed to the hard labour we had to undergo, died of a fever. Since leaving France we had experienced every kind of affliction— disease, pestilence, famine, poverty, hard labour. I have been for six months together without tasting bread, working the ground like a slave; and I have even passed three or four years without always having it when I wanted it. God has done great things for us, in enabling us to bear up under so many trials. I should never have done, were I to attempt to detail to you all our adventures; let it suffice that God has had compassion on me, and changed my fate to a more happy one, for which glory be unto Him.

The Spotted Fever

Hardships and Sufferings

Such was the faith that could not be overthrown by suffering and hardship. This young woman, left alone in the world, found a worthy husband in Peter Manigault.

A Noble Son

She died in 1711, seven years after she had given birth to Gabriel Manigault, who in a long and useful life accumulated a fortune so large that he was able to give a loan of £220,000—a remarkable fortune in those days—to the colonial government for carrying on its war for independence. This he did at an early period, when there was no certainty whether payment would ever be possible. Thus he repaid the debt his parents owed to the land which had given them asylum and a home.

III

Favoured Carolina

Besides these Huguenots who came direct from France, a considerable number of the refugees who came at first to New York and New England, after a short residence in those colder climates, found their way to Carolina, which became a general rendezvous, as originally contemplated by their distinguished leader Coligny shortly after the discovery of America. Another and a very considerable company of French came from Acadia, when, after Nova Scotia had been surrendered to England, the Acadians were dispersed among the English colonies, as a measure of safety. About fifteen hundred of them were sent to Charleston, and some of them rose to wealth and distinction, though the larger part of them left the country as soon as it was possible to get away.

1764 Immigration

In 1764 another colony of Huguenots came from France, in charge of Reverend Mr. Gilbert, a popular preacher, who prevailed on a number of persecuted families, after the peace of Paris, to seek a home in South Carolina, which was now highly reported of by the French residents there. On his solicitations the government of England, which appreciated the quality of the French Protestants as settlers, encouraged the project, and furnished the means of transportation. Going to England, Mr. Gilbert directed the movements of the emigrants, who found it necessary to leave France privately, at different times, and in small numbers. They rendez-

voused at Plymouth, England, and sailing from that post, reached Charleston in April, 1764. They were received with great kindness and hospitality. Vacant lands were laid out for their use, grants of land were made to them respectively by the Provincial Assembly, and means of conveyance to their settlement were provided. They named their new settlement New Bordeaux, after the capital of the province in France whence most of them came. They introduced in earnest the manufacture of silk. The historian says of them : " They have been distinguished for their industry and good morals. The climate has agreed so well with them that they have generally enjoyed good health. The manufacture of silk is still continued among them." They sent representatives to the legislature, were able in public as well as private affairs, and ranked among the first elements in the population.

Thus in her early days South Carolina proved indeed an asylum for those of different nationalities who fled from tyranny and persecution. The results to the state were most beneficial ; while as for the colonies at large, they owed much to South Carolina for the part she played during the Revolution ; and the brave sons of Carolina who engaged most notably in that memorable struggle for human rights and liberty were those very French Protestant families which had found welcome and shelter within her territory.

There was a certain period in the early days when the French refugees were a source of controversy between the proprietors and the people of English blood. The French settlers were orderly, industrious, religious, in every way exemplary citizens. Some of them had brought property with them which enabled them to buy land and settle with greater advantages than many of the poorer English emigrants. They were, moreover, of a more cultivated type, which did not make them more agreeable to their neighbours. The result was that, while the French were busy clearing and cultivating their lands, the English settlers were reviving national antipathies, and classing them as aliens and foreigners, legally entitled to none of the privileges and advantages of natural born British subjects. The proprietors, greatly to their credit, sided with the refugees, and instructed their Governor Ludwell to allow the French the same privileges and liberties with the English colonists. But the people carried their jealousy so far that the county in which the French lived was not allowed a single representative in the assembly. Wise measures served to lessen the friction, and by excluding the French from office the disturbers were satisfied. In process of time the national antipathies abated. Gradual Union The French proved their courage and fidelity, made friends by their excellent behaviour, and when they petitioned the legislature to be incorporated with the freemen of the colony, an act was passed in 1696 making all aliens then residents free, on petition to the governor and taking the oath of allegiance to King William. This same law conferred liberty of conscience on all Christians, with the exception of Papists. With these conditions the refugees, who were all Protestants, joyfully complied ; and the French and English settlers, being made equal in rights, became united in interest and affection, and lived together in peace and harmony thenceforward.

The position held by the French settlers is indicated by the fact that among the Council of Twelve nominated by the proprietors of South Carolina in 1719, two were Huguenots, Benjamin de la Consilière and Peter St. Julien.

IV

French in the Revolution It is when we come to the Revolutionary War, however, that the part played by the French comes out in strong relief. It must be realized that South Carolina had not the same present and living issues that stirred Massachusetts to rebellion. To the South the questions were more remote and of principle solely. The odious taxation was not felt by the southerners, and their relations to the home government had been tolerable. There were many reasons why the state should refrain from making common cause with other colonies, when war was the consequence. But love of liberty and devotion to principles touching human rights and liberties prevailed, and when the actual contest began at Lexington and Concord, in spite of the strong royalist following, South Carolina ranked herself beside the Puritan Commonwealth. As Ramsay says, " All statutes of allegiance were considered as repealed on the plains of Lexington, and the laws of self-preservation left to operate in full force." The Provincial Congress was immediately summoned, and great were the objects brought before it. The president **Henry Laurens Patriot** of this important body, be it remembered, was Henry Laurens, one of the French Protestants. When on the second day of the meeting it was unanimously resolved that an association was necessary, it was that same great citizen, a Huguenot, who drew up the following association and put his name as the first to it :

The actual commencement of hostilities against this continent by the **South Carolina's Bold Step** British troops, in the bloody scene on the 19th of April last, near Boston—the increase of arbitrary impositions from a wicked and despotic ministry—and the dread of insurrections in the colonies—are causes sufficient to drive an oppressed people to the use of arms. We, therefore, the subscribers, inhabitants of South Carolina, holding ourselves bound by that most sacred of all obligations—the duty of good citizens towards an injured country, and thoroughly convinced that, under our present distressed circumstances, we shall be justified before God and man in resisting force by force—do unite ourselves under every tie of religion and honour, and associate as a band in her defense against every foe—hereby solemnly engaging that, whenever our continental or provincial councils shall decree it necessary, we will go forth and be ready to sacrifice our lives and fortunes to secure her freedom and safety. This obligation to continue in full force until a reconciliation shall take place between Great Britain and America, upon constitutional principles—an event which we most ardently desire. And we will hold all persons inimical to the liberty of the colonies who shall refuse to subscribe this association.

Huguenot
Leader

In the work of this Provincial Congress, perhaps the most important which ever assembled in the state, Henry Laurens the Huguenot was easily the commanding figure and the leading influence.   His character and talents fitted him to command.   He was a gentleman, scholar, statesman and patriot, supplementing his own fine qualities by a sincere piety.   He was later to fill a larger sphere. He was among the first to see the trend of the British policy towards the colonies and to argue in behalf of the colonial rights, and it was in large measure owing to his bold and outspoken convictions that the sentiment of his state was so sound and strong.

John Huger

In the Council of Safety chosen by the Congress Henry Laurens stands first, and John Huger, another Huguenot, was a second member.   Some time later, when the Provincial Congress had voted itself to be the General Assembly of South Carolina, and had adopted an independent constitution, a legislative council and other officers were elected.   In the council were George Gabriel Powel and Le Roy Hammond ; Henry Laurens was vice-president ; John Huger was secretary.   This was an honourable Huguenot representation in the civil government.

V

When it came to military service, of which South Carolina had full share, the French were still more in evidence.   Aside from Marion, whose story will be told else-

Lieut.-Col.
John Laurens

where, Lieutenant-Colonel John Laurens, son of Honourable Henry Laurens, was a notable figure.   Highly educated, widely travelled, the correspondence between him and his father shows both the literary ability and the unusually close relationship between the two.   Possessed of a charming personality, handsome and accomplished, he had a host of friends, and promised to be perhaps the most popular citizen of his state.   He entered upon the war for independence with all the ardour of patriotism, and proved a most efficient officer and gallant leader.

He was the idol of his men, and for his known bravery and quickness of resource was chosen for difficult and dangerous service. Thus we find him detailed to dispute the difficult pass of Cossawhatchie bridge, near Charleston, with the British General Prevost and his large force ; while Laurens had only eighteen continentals and some militia under him. He persevered in the defense until he was wounded and had lost half his continentals, when the militia, in peril for the first time, retreated. In the campaigns of 1779 and 1780 Lieutenant-Colonel Laurens was actively engaged. When Sir Henry Clinton landed on the main, in his siege of Charleston, it was the intrepid Laurens who, with a corps of light infantry, briskly attacked his advance guards. While during the next year the American cause was low in South Carolina, with Charleston in the hands of the British, military operations were continued, and the value of Laurens' services was fully recognized. **Gallant and Idolized**

When the brighter days came for the colonists, he fell a martyr in the struggle for freedom. The British announced their intention to evacuate Charleston in the summer of 1782 ; but before going sent out marauding parties to seize provisions. A considerable party was sent to Combakee Ferry, and Brigadier-General Gist, with about three hundred cavalry and infantry of the Continental army, was detached to oppose them. Lieutenant-Colonel Laurens, though he had been confined by illness for several days, hearing of the expedition, rose from his bed and followed General Gist. When the British and American detachments approached within a few miles of each other, Lieutenant-Colonel Laurens, being in advance with a small party of regulars and militia, engaged with a much superior force in expectation of support from the main body in his rear. **A Martyr**

" In the midst of his gallant exertions," says Ramsay, " this all accomplished youth received a mortal wound. Nature had adorned him with a profusion of her choicest **Tribute to his Worth**

gifts, to which a well conducted education had added its
most useful as well as its elegant improvements. Though
his fortune and family entitled him to pre-eminence, yet
he was the warm friend of republican equality. Generous and liberal, his heart expended with genuine philanthropy. Zealous for the rights of humanity, he contended that personal liberty was the birthright of every
human being, however diversified by country, colour or
capacity. His insinuating address won the hearts of all
his acquaintances ; his sincerity and virtue secured their
lasting esteem. Acting from the most honourable principles—uniting the bravery and other talents of a great
officer with the knowledge of a complete scholar, and the
engaging manners of a well-bred gentleman, he was the
idol of his country—the glory of the army—and an orna-
ment of human nature. His abilities shone in the legislature and in the cabinet, as well as in the field, and were
equal to the highest stations. His admiring country,
sensible of his rising merit, stood prepared to confer
on him her most distinguished honours. Cut down in
the midst of all these prospects, he has left mankind to
deplore the calamities of war, which in the twenty-seventh
year of his life deprived society of so valuable a
citizen.''

Allowing something in this tribute to state pride and
the pathos of the event, there is no doubt that this young
man was one of the best examples of the educated Americans of his day—American by birth and principle and
affection—yet the son of a French refugee, an exile for
religion and conscience. There was no better stock than
this out of which to make the true Americanism.

VI

Major Huger   Another brave French officer who gave his life for his
country was Major Benjamin Huger, whose ancestors
came to South Carolina in 1696. Daniel Huger, born in
the province of Poitoux, France, fled to La Rochelle dur-

ing the bitter persecution of his province at Loudun, his native town, where fifteen hundred Huguenots were compelled to recant in a single night by two companies of dragoons. Stealing away from his home with his wife and child, under cover of the darkness they made their escape, and when La Rochelle could not afford shelter they came to America, being among the early settlers in South Carolina, where two children were born to them. From this family came John Huger, who was made secretary of the new state after the Provincial Congress had been dissolved ; and Benjamin Huger, who entertained the army as captain, and by merit was advanced to the rank of major. In the attack upon Charleston by the **Killed in 1779** British in 1779, by a false alarm at night the militia were led to fire upon the supposed advancing enemy. By this unfortunate mistake Major Huger, who was without the lines on duty with a party, was killed by his own countrymen. He is described as " a brave officer, an able statesman, and a highly distinguished citizen." He led his company in the defense of Fort Moultrie, which was one of the brilliant events in the state's revolutionary history.

Eminent service was rendered also by Colonel Daniel Horry, of a Huguenot family. After a long series of dis- **Colonel Horry** asters, for the greater safety of its people the State Assembly passed a severe militia law, intended to strengthen the Continental army. The extent and variety of military operations in the open country pointed out the advantages of cavalry ; and a regiment of dragoons was raised and put under command of Colonel Horry. While its work was very different from that which made the dragoons of France a terror to the innocent Huguenots, this regiment did most valiant service under its brave leader, who possessed something of the dash and daring that made Marion conspicuous. Marion himself, in his exploits, **Regiment of** received great assistance from the active exertions of the **Dragoons** French officers, Colonels Peter and Hugh Horry, Colonel

James Postell, and Major John Postell ; while in the ranks the Huguenot descendants were well represented. Certainly the French exiles had repaid the land which gave them refuge, and proved the quality of their loyalty to their adopted country.

French Exiled for Patriotism

It is significant both as to their rank as citizens and loyalty to the American cause, that among the prominent citizens of Charleston who were exiled to Florida by Lord Cornwallis were John Mouatt, John Neufville, Ernest Poyas, Samuel Prioleau, Daniel Bordeaux, Daniel Dessaussure, and Benjamin Postell. The influence of this class of patriots was so feared by the British commander that he was not content to have them paroled at home. In their attitude towards the revolution the Huguenots of South Carolina differed from the majority of those in New England and New York, who were ranked among the Tories. It is not strange that men who had been hospitably welcomed and treated by the representatives of the British government should hold loyally to it as long as its authority endured.

VII

An Early Description by an English Traveller

In 1701 Mr. John Lawson published "A Journal of a Thousand Miles travelled through several Nations of the Indians." He thus describes a visit to the first Huguenots who settled in South Carolina :

The first place we designed for was Santee River, where there is a colony of French Protestants allowed and encouraged by the lords proprietary. As we rowed up the river we found the land towards the mouth scarce anything but a swamp, affording vast cypress trees of which the French make canoes, that will carry fifty or sixty barrels. There being a strong current in Santee River caused us to make but small way with our oars. With hard rowing we got that night to Monsieur Eugee's (Huger's) house, which stands about fifteen miles up the river, being the first Christian dwelling we met with in that settlement, and were very courteously received by him and his wife. Many of the French follow a trade with the Indians, living very con-

veniently for that interest. There are about seventy families seated
on this river, who live as decently and happily as any planters in these
southward parts of America. The French being a temperate, industrious people, some of them bringing very little of effects, yet, by their
endeavours and mutual assistance among themselves, which is highly to
be commended, have outstripped our English, who brought with them
large fortunes, though, as it seems, less endeavour to manage their
talent to the best advantage. A Tribute to
Character

We lay all night at Monsieur Eugee's, and the next morning set out
further to go the remainder of our journey by land. At noon we
came up with several French Plantations, meeting with several
Creeks by the way. The French were very officious in assisting
with small dories to pass over the waters, whom we met coming
from their church, being all of them clean and decent, their houses
and plantations suitable in neatness and contrivance. They are
all of the same opinion of the church of Geneva; there being no
difference amongst them concerning the punctilios of the Christian
faith, which union hath propagated a happy and delightful concord,
and in all other matters throughout the whole neighbourhood ; living
amongst themselves as one tribe or kindred, every one making it his
business to be assistant to the wants of his countrymen ; preserving
his estate and reputation with the same exactness and concern as he
does his own; all seeming to share in the misfortunes and rejoice at
the advancement and rise of their brethren.

Towards the afternoon we came to Monsieur L. Jandron (Gendron),
where we got our dinners. There came some French ladies whilst we
were there, lately from England, and Monsieur Le Grand, a worthy
Norman, who hath been a great sufferer in his estate by the persecution in France against those of the Protestant religion. . . . We
got that night to Monsieur Gailliar's the elder (Gailliard) ; who lives
in a very curious contrived house, built of brick and stone, which is
gotten near that place. Near here comes in the road from Charlestown, and the rest of the English settlement. . . . We intended
for Monsieur Gailliar's, Jr., but were lost, none of us knowing the way
at that time, although the Indian with us was born in that country,
it having received so strange a metamorphosis. When we got to the
house we found our comrades, and several of the French inhabitants
with them who treated us very courteously. . . . After having
refreshed ourselves we parted from a very kind, loving, and affable
people, who wished us a safe and prosperous voyage.

These people were indeed kind and affable, courteous
and agreeable. They carried with them a cheerfulness Genial
Comradery

and geniality, a spirit of comradery and honour, that made them model settlers. They bore hardships with little complaint, and soon put a new face upon everything by their skill. Their plantations were sure to be the best and most attractive. Their gardening was justly **Famous Gardeners** famous, and their taste was manifest. They were not too busy wrestling with the virgin soil for livelihood to cultivate flowers and gratify their esthetic natures. In all these respects they differed materially from the Puritan type. Yet they were as devoutly and staunchly religious, as the fact of their exile proved. They generally bought lands, and some of them had means of purchasing large tracts, which they portioned out and sold at a low price to their distressed brethren. "We do not hear of any instance of oppression among them," says Allen, "either exercised towards each other or Americans."

Their Religion In South Carolina they very generally adopted the Episcopal mode of worship. The French Calvinistic church in Charleston adhered to its peculiar worship. It was built about 1693. The time of worship was regulated by the tide, for the accommodation of the members, many of whom came by the river from the settlements around. We can hardly imagine anything more picturesque than these little boats, borne on the water and filled with noble and daring beings, who had endured danger and suffering, and risked their lives, for the spiritual life of the soul. "Often the low chant was distinguished amidst the dashing of the oars, and sometimes an enthusiastic strain swelled on the ear, like those which proceeded from the lips of the martyrs when the flames curled around them."

Founded on Principle Their conduct was not marked by rash enthusiasm; theirs was a religion founded on principle. They were free from fanaticism and exaggeration. Their memorials to the government are simple and concise, and bear every evidence of truth. When they petition for their rights, it is done in a calm, conciliatory manner; and this is the more extraordinary, from the impetuous constitution of Frenchmen and the keen sense of wrongs they had endured in their own country. This spirit of forbearance, integrity and perseverance, marks them wherever they settled, North or South.

"Who does not feel," says their historian Allen, "that there is more to be reverenced in the exiled Huguenot, who has forsaken all from the highest sense of duty, who has uniformly placed his confidence in God under the severest trials, than the mighty monarch who exiled him? It is those in whom the power of virtue is formed and matured that are really great. The history of the Huguenots would be an enigma without this key to human power; but he, who feels this undying principle, cannot be trodden under foot, for he holds fast the inward consciousness of his own worth, which supports him under every oppression, and makes him strong to endure—a strength derived from genuine piety, and the deep sense of Christianity enjoined by its author." *The Strength of Piety*

In France these Huguenots were a law-loving and law-abiding people. They feared God and honoured their king. They were reared in habits of sobriety and virtue. They may be said to have inherited cultivated manners, so careful were parents to set examples to their children, and form the manner of intercourse in households and in society. Enduring the hardships of a new colony in a foreign land, they preserved the amenities of life. In their distress and in their prosperity, they never forgot that they sprung from the most polished country in the world. *A Cultured People*

The habits of both mutual and self-respect, of social intercourse and enjoyments, of activity and enterprise, created the wealth and formed the manners of South Carolina. Frank, urbane, cultivated, kind, resolute, energetic, the descendants of colonies composed of Huguenots and English and Scotch-Irish intermingled and amalgamated, hold an enviable place among the sisterhood of states.

CHAPTER V

FRANCIS MARION

I

A Revolutionary Hero

E VERY war has its conspicuous leaders, and develops heroes hitherto unknown to fame. The war of the American Revolution produced one of the most dashing and daring of these heroic and romantic personages in the South Carolina Huguenot, Francis Marion. His story reads like historical romance, however soberly and truthfully it is told. He may be called the Garibaldi of America. His name became a terror to the British. They knew that when he was about, it would be the unexpected that would happen. By the very recklessness of his attacks, by the risks he ran, by the sheer audacity of his movements, he astounded and defeated the enemy time after time, unless his name possessed something of the quality of magic. What gallant "Phil" Sheridan was in our Civil War, Marion was in the Revolution. And Francis Marion was the grandson of a French refugee from Languedoc, who found his way, with the Manigaults and Laurenses and Hugers, to South Carolina. Of thirteen children of this staunch Huguenot, the eldest was the father of Francis, who was to become an American general.

Born at Winyaw in 1733, at sixteen the boy decided on a seafaring life, but on his first voyage to the West Indies was shipwrecked, and was one of the three of the crew rescued after being six days in an open boat. This disaster and his mother's entreaties induced him to quit the sea. A life of adventure had irresistible attractions for him, and when the Indians became troublesome he found his opportunity. In 1759 he went as volunteer in his

338

brother's militia troop of horse in Littleton's expedition,
and two years later was serving as lieutenant under Capt.
William Moultrie, in Grant's expedition to the Indian
country.

When a regular army was formed in 1775 to defend *1775 Captain*
South Carolina against Great Britain, Marion was appointed a captain in the second South Carolina regiment,
and before the fall of Charleston had risen to the rank of
colonel. A fractured leg caused his absence from the
garrison at its surrender and saved him from being made
prisoner. He retreated to North Carolina, and on the *Colonel*
approach of General Gates made his way to the Santee,
where he found a number of his French countrymen ready
to put themselves under his command, to which he had
been appointed by General Gates. This corps acquired
the name of Marion's Brigade, and its exploits became
famous. Its original members were French and Irish. *Marion's Brigade*
For chief officers Marion had Lieutenant-Colonel Hugh
Horry, his bosom friend, Colonel Peter Horry, Captain
Lewis Ogier, and the Postell brothers of his own nationality ; with Major James, a gallant Irishman who had been
the means of arousing the section to resistance through
his insolent treatment by a British officer ; Major Vander-
horst, representing the Dutch blood ; and Captain John
Milton of Georgia.

II

Marion's Brigade immediately set itself to serious business. A few days after taking command, General Marion
led his men across the Peedee at Post's Ferry, to disperse a
large party of Tories. He surprised them in their camp,
killed one of their captains and several privates, and
routed them, horse and foot. This was the beginning of
a series of remarkable encounters and victories. We find *Remarkable Victories*
him, on hearing of the defeat of General Gates at Cam-
den, marching to intercept and rescue the prisoners on
their way to Charleston. One of his divisions, sixteen
men, under command of Colonel Hugh Horry, by a dash

in the dark took a British guard of thirty-two men and released 150 prisoners, with only one man wounded. When
the general cause looked hopeless, reduced in men to a
handful through desertion and discouragement, the
spirits of Marion were undaunted, and with the band of
faithful officers who were ready to follow him to the death,
he revived courage among the despondent, recruited his
forces, and by spirited attacks and steady victories of
surprising character inspired such confidence that men
flocked to his command.

Resource-
fulness

He was marvellous in resourcefulness. Once he was
attacking a far superior force of the Tories, who were ad-
vantageously posted to receive him. In the sharp conflict
that followed, suddenly Marion was heard to call out,
" Advance cavalry and charge on the left," whereupon
the dismayed Tories, thinking their flank was turned,
broke and ran for the swamp. This victory enabled
General Marion to march into Williamsburg. His successes were often due to the fact that his attacks were
surprises. In all his marches Marion and his men lay in
the open air with little covering, and with little other
food than sweet potatoes and meat mostly without salt.
The general fared worse than his men ; for his baggage
having caught fire by accident he had literally but half a
blanket to cover him from the dews of the night, and but
half a hat to shelter him from the rays of the sun. But
he established himself in impregnable positions, and be-

The Swamp
Fox

came known as the Swamp Fox, sending his scouts in all
directions, harassing the enemy at diverse points, making
unexpected assaults upon supply stores, and giving the
Tories some of their own medicine in the way of devastation.

Marion indeed so effectually thwarted the schemes of
the British against South Carolina, that a turning point
in the fortunes of the war came largely through his pernicious activity, which inspired the superior forces of the
enemy with dread, and discouraged the Tories who hoped

to win the state to the British side. To drive Marion out of the country was a favourite object of the British, and in 1781 a thoroughly organized attempt was made to destroy or disperse his now noted Brigade, which was held to be invincible. The story of the way Marion led the enemy into ambuscades and defeated them, though he was practically without ammunition, forms one of the stirring incidents of a war full of surprises and heroism. Coming later under direct command of General Greene, to the end of the war Marion continued his distinguished services. Illustrious among the patriot soldiery are the French Protestants of South Carolina, to whom it was given by the fortunes of the War for Independence to play an important part.

III

To Marion and his surroundings in the swamp we are introduced in the historical romances of William Gilmore Simms. Discounting the romance sufficiently, let us penetrate the Cypress with one of his heroes, and after hours of hard riding through thicket and morass, perhaps splashed with water and torn by the undergrowth, we shall find ourselves admitted to the famous camp of Marion. From the time of our entrance into the swamp, scouts and sentries have been safely passed at intervals along the way, the guide elected of our fancy answering sundry hootings of owls and familiar whistlings with satisfactory repetitions of the same. "Owls abroad?" has been the challenge of some coon-skin-covered head thrust out at us from the bushes, to which the responsive "Owls at home!" has been promptly given. And when, on nearer approach, the demand is made, "What owl hoots?" the due answer has been forthcoming; until at last we are permitted to dismount.

At once we become conscious of a little world out here in the woods by itself. In a hollow, the better to hide the flames, the party has built its fires, about which, in varying degrees of activity or repose, are grouped the hunted

A Hero of Romance

Picture of the Swamp

followers of the "Swamp Fox." Here a trooper is mending his bridle beneath a gigantic oak, or ash, or hickory, while a little further away another of less strenuous make-up is stretched at length, with feet to the fire, and half-closed eyes peering dreamily up through the branches into the starlit sky. Yonder a knot of younger men are busy fashioning arrows from a great pile of canes or reeds such as abound in the lowlands of this region, while a basket stands near by crowded with feathers of the eagle, crane, hawk and common turkey, to be fitted to the shafts when ready. In the hollow trunk of a tree bows and these arrows will be stored against the possible failure to capture more of King George's baggage-wagons laden with British arms and ammunition. The trees are a veritable depository for bridles, blankets, coats and cloaks, and a dozen saddles lie scattered about.

Here in his element is the typical ranger, or forester, of the period, with his scanty though picturesque costume, consisting of a mixture of Indian undress and military uniform, with his nonchalance, his drawl, and his almost uncanny cleverness in woodcraft, or the fence which is capable of deluding an enemy into the feeling that he is a friend. Even the names by which he is familiarly known among his fellows bespeak the haunts and habits to which his peculiar warfare has driven him; for, in the frank and unconventional phrase of the camp, we shall be sure to meet Hard-Riding Dick, Dusky Sam, Clip the Can, Prickly Ash, and Black Fox. Such a leader, in such surroundings, was Francis Marion, who seemed to his slower antagonists to wear a charmed life and possess wings.

And what a company it was one might have met in the Swamp on occasion. There was the powerful Rhode Islander, General Greene, in whose veins was Huguenot blood, and who was majestic alike in person and in professional dignity; as unlike Marion as one could imagine; noble Governor Rutledge, the veritable father of the peo-

ple ; the Swamp Fox himself, that famous guerrilla of
Carolina, with his modest person and demeanour, even
while he remained the sleepless master of every situation ;
the Game Cock, Sumter, with his dash and sensitive
pride ; besides William Washington, the nephew of the
commander-in-chief, and Lee, and the Huguenot Horry
and the rest.

IV

In this connection we may well give place to some **A Stirring**
verses of one of Simms' ringing martial lyrics which **Lyric**
well describes Marion and his men :

> We follow where the Swamp Fox guides,
>   His friends and merry men are we ;
> And when the troop of Tarleton rides,
>   We burrow in the cypress-tree.
> The turfy hammock is our bed,
>   Our home is in the red-deer's den,
> Our roof, the tree-top overhead,
>   For we are wild and hunted men.
>
> Free bridle bit, good gallant steed,
>   That will not ask a kind caress,
> To swim the Santee at our need,
>   When on our heels the foemen press —
> The true heart and the ready hand,
>   The spirit stubborn to be free —
> The twisted bore, the smiting brand —
>   And we are Marion's men, you see.
>
> Now light the fire, and cook the meal —
>   The last, perhaps, that we shall taste.
> I hear the Swamp Fox round us steal,
>   And that's a sign we move in haste.
> He whistles to the scouts, and hark !
>   You hear his order calm and low —
> Come, wave your torch across the dark,
>   And let us see the boys that go.

Now stir the fire, and lie at ease ;
　　The scouts are gone, and on the brush
I see the colonel bend his knees,
　　To take his slumbers too—but hush !
He's praying, comrades : 'tis not strange ;
　　The man that's fighting day by day
May well when night comes, take a change,
　　And down upon his knees to pray.

Now pile the brush and roll the log :
　　Hard pillow, but a soldier's head,
That's half the time in brake and bog,
　　Must never think of softer bed.
The owl is hooting to the night,
　　The cooter crawling o'er the bank,
And in that pond the plashing light
　　Tells where the alligator sank.

What—'tis the signal ! start so soon,
　　And through the Santee swamp so deep,
Without the aid of friendly moon,
　　And we, heaven help us, half asleep !
But courage, comrades ! Marion leads,
　　The Swamp Fox takes us out to-night;
So clear your swords and spur your steeds,
　　There's goodly chance, I think, of fight.

CHAPTER VI

THE HUGUENOTS IN VIRGINIA

I

THE earliest mention of the French in colonial Virginia occurs in the year 1610. In June of that year Captain-General and Governor Lord De la Warr arrived off the Virginia coast at the mouth of the James River. Before proceeding up the river to Jamestown, he went ashore with several of his officers to inspect the soil and vegetation of his new dominion. All were charmed with the fertility and luxuriance which they beheld on every side, and the governor, as the account runs, on discerning the richness of the soil and the mildness of the climate " determined to set a Frenchman heere awork to plant Vines which grew naturally in great plentie." Going on up the river to Jamestown, De la Warr "alloted every Man his particular Place and Business. The French prepared to plant the Vines ; the English laboured in the Woods and Grounds."

In 1619 Sir Edwin Sandys, treasurer of the Virginia Company makes mention of the vines " which by culture will be brought to excellent perfection. For the affecting whereof divers skillful Vignerons are sent. . . . Our Frenchmen assure us that no Countrie in the World is more proper for vines . . . than Virginia."

In 1621, the new governor, Sir Francis Wyatt, was instructed " to plant Mulberry trees and make silk, and take care of the Frenchmen sent about that work."

The Virginia Company expected a great future for the wine and silk trade in the New World, and in order to foster it they brought over several skillful Frenchmen. The venture did not appear to succeed, however, and not

345

Earliest Mention in 1610

French Vine Planters

1621

long after their arrival in America the French began to plant tobacco—much against the wishes of the company, who saw a greater profit slipping away from it. The numbers of the French who were brought over at the expense of the company were probably not large, and their names have utterly perished.

Petition to
Colonize

In July, 1621, Sir Dudley Carleton, British ambassador at the Hague, received the following petition :

His lordship the ambassador of the most serene king of Great Britain is humbly entreated to advise and answer us in regard to the articles which follow.

I.   Whether it would please his Majesty to permit fifty to sixty families, as well Walloons as French, all of the Reformed religion, to go and settle in Virginia, a country under his rule, and whether it would please him to undertake their protection and defense from and against all, and to maintain them in their religion.

Remarkable
Document

II.   And whereas the said families might find themselves near upon three hundred persons ; and whereas they would wish to carry with them a quantity of cattle, as well for the cultivation of the earth as for their sustenance, and for these reasons would need more than one ship ; whether his Majesty would not accommodate them with one, well equipped and furnished with cannon and other arms, on board of which, together with the one they would provide, they could accomplish their voyage ; the same returning to obtain merchandise for the regions granted by his said Majesty, as well as that of the country.

III.   Whether he would permit them, on their arrival in said country, to choose a convenient spot for their abode among the places not yet cultivated by those whom it has pleased his Majesty to send thither already.

To Build a
City

IV.   Whether, having secured the said spot, they might build a city for their protection and furnish it with the necessary fortifications, wherein they might elect a governor and magistrates for the maintenance of order as well as justice, under those fundamental laws which it has pleased his Majesty to establish in said regions.

Cannon for
Defense

V.   Whether his said Majesty would furnish them cannons and munitions for the defense of said place, and grant them right in case of necessity to make powder, fabricate balls and found cannons under the flag and arms of his said Majesty.

Husbandry

VI.   Whether he would grant them a circuit or territory of eight English miles radius, that is sixteen in diameter, wherein they might cultivate fields, meadows, vineyards, and the like, which territory they would hold, whether conjointly or severally, from his Majesty in such fealty and homage as his Majesty should find reasonable, without allowing any other to dwell there unless by taking out papers of residence within said territory, wherein they would reserve rights of inferior lordship ; and whether those of them who could live as nobles would be permitted to style themselves such.

VII. Whether they would be permitted in the said lands to hunt all game, whether furred or feathered, to fish in the sea and rivers, and to cut heavy and small timber, as well for navigation as other purposes, according to their desire ; in a word, whether they might make use of everything above and below ground according to their will and pleasure, saving the royal rights ; and trade in everything with such persons as should be thereto privileged.

Free Trading

Sir Dudley himself, who knew Jesse de Forest, the leader of the petitioners, favoured the project and referred the matter to the lords in council, who for their part turned the petition over to the Virginia Company. The answer of the directors was not unfavourable, but they refused to give the would-be colonists a ship, "being utterly exhausted and unable to afford other help than advice as to the cheapest mode of transporting themselves." The company also said in its reply, "that for the prosperity and principally securing of the plantation in his Maj's obedience, it is not expedient that the said families should be set down in one gross and entire body, but that they should rather be placed in convenient numbers in the principal cities . . . there being given them such proportions of land and all other privileges and benefits whatsoever in as ample a manner as to the natural English." It is probable that the petitioners came to the conclusion that advice was quite as cheap in England as it was in Leyden, for they engaged in no further parleying with the Virginia Company. But what was Virginia's loss was New Amsterdam's gain, for two years later the Dutch sent part of the band to the mouth of the Hudson, as we have previously related.

What Virginia Lost

II

After the fall of La Rochelle, the Baron De Sauce, a hero of the defense of that city under the Duke of Rohan, took refuge in England, and in 1629 begged permission of the government to establish a colony of Huguenots in Virginia "to cultivate vines and to make silke and salt there." The request was favourably received and he was given letters of denization for himself and son in order that he might return to France in safety to get his family and property. Careful preparations were made, and in due course of time the expedition sailed for Virginia. It landed safely on the southern side of the James River and a settlement was commenced in what is now the county of Nansemond, then known as "Southampton Hundred," a patent of 200,000 acres granted several years before.

No records of this colony have been discovered, and its fate is a matter of conjecture. Says Colonel R. L. Maury, who has carefully examined the Virginia records, "I have not been able to learn further of this colony ; manifestly it did not flourish, and must have soon dispersed, having left no enduring memorial."

The place chosen for this abortive attempt at colonization was perhaps the worst that could have been selected in all Virginia. In 1698, Col. William Byrd, in helping the government to locate the band who finally settled at Manakin Town (about twenty miles above Richmond, on the James River), wrote of "Southampton Hundred," "that part is according to its name, for the most part low swampy ground, unfit for planting and Improvement and ye air of it very moist and unhealthy so that to send French thither that came from a dry and serene Clymate were to send them to their death, and that would very ill answer his Maj'tys charitable intentions."

The settlers did not all perish, however, for Huguenot names became frequent in the records of Norfolk County.

III

" As the seventeenth century waxed so did the Hugue- Virginia Hospitable to not emigration to Virginia continuously increase." The Settlers refugees came singly, or in isolated groups and families. Among the colonial legislatures that of Virginia was foremost in encouraging applications for naturalization. In 1659, or thereabouts, it was enacted, "That all aliens and strangers who have inhabited the country for the space of four years, and have a firme resolution to make this countrey their place of residence shall be free deni- zens of this collony." In 1661 the General Assembly of 1661 Act of Admission Virginia passed an act admitting all strangers desirous of making their homes in Virginia, to the liberties, privi- leges and immunities of natural born Englishmen, upon their petition to the Assembly, and upon taking the oaths of allegiance and supremacy. New York adopted a sim- ilar measure in 1783, and South Carolina fourteen years later. The colonies were in this ahead of the home gov- ernment, which had not sanctioned such acts.

Among the Huguenots who took advantage of these Family Names laws were John Battaille, Richard Durand, De la Mun- dayes, Durant, de Hull, De Bar, D'Aubigne (Dabney), De la Nome, De Young, De Bandy, De Berry, Roger Fontaine, Stephen Fouace, Hillier, Jordan, Jourdan, La Furder, Lines, Louis, Lassall, La Mont (Lamont), Moyses, Martian, Mountery, Michael, Mellaney, Mille- chops, Moyssier, Morel, Norman, Noel, Poythers, Perin, Poleste, Paule, Perrot, Place, Pluvier, Pensax, Peron, Pere, Pettit, Pruett, Pallisder, Robins, Ravenell, Rab- nett, Rosier, Regault, Roden, Roye, Rue, Regant, Revell, Royall, Sully, Sabrell, Sorrel, Sallis, Tollifer (Tallia- ferro), Therrialt, Toton, Tranier, Vicomte, Vasler, Vaus, Vallentine, Vaulx, Vardie and Vodin.

Major Moore Faunt Le Roy, founder of a " very ancient Faunt LeRoy and numerous family of Virginia," owned a large tract of land on the banks of the Rappahannock prior to 1651. In 1683 the Huguenot Relief Committee in London " Paid

Mr. David Dashaise, Elder of the French Church in London, for fifty-five French Protestants to go to Virginia, Seventy pounds sterling." In 1687 Stephen Fouace came from London with letters from the Archbishop of Canterbury. He became rector of a church near Williamsburg, was prominent among the colonial clergy and was later made a trustee of William and Mary College. In 1689 came another Huguenot rector, the Rev. James Boisseau.

IV

In the last decade of the seventeenth century at least a thousand French Protestants came to America, receiving transportation from the Relief Committee in London. A few of these settled in Florida, a number in South Carolina, but not less than 700 of them landed in Virginia, to establish a settlement, according to the earlier idea of Jesse de Forest. In 1700 four fleets sailed from Gravesend, bringing all told more than seven hundred of the French refugees, with "the brave and devoted" Marquis de la Muce at their head, and Charles de Sailly as his associate. There were with the expedition three ministers and two physicians. Various sites had been considered for a settlement, but on arrival in Virginia the colonists were directed to a spot about twenty miles above Richmond, on the James River, where they were given ten thousand acres of land which had belonged to the extinct tribe of Manakin Indians. Thus the name of the settlement became Manakintown. Baird says no more interesting body of colonists than that conducted by Oliver de la Muce had crossed the ocean. Many of them belonged to the persecuted Waldensian race, who had taken refuge in Switzerland when driven from their Piedmontese homes by the troops of Louis XIV. Their number being too large for the Swiss Cantons to support, England responded liberally to the appeal for aid, and they were given transportation to America, together with the Huguenots. Three thousand pounds were appropriated for "the transportation of five hundred Vaudois and French refugees designed for some of his Majesty's plantations." Of individual accounts the records show the sum of £38 given " out of the collection to Mons Benjamin DeJoux, Minister, appointed to go to Virginia ; besides £24 for the providing of himself with necessities for the voyage." In August, 1700, the Bishop of London writes to the city chamberlain, "Sir : the bearer, Monsieur Castayne, is going out Surgeon to ye French now departing for Virginia. He wants £20 to make up his Chest of Drugs and instruments. It is a very small matter for such a voyage ; but if you have in your hands to supply that sum, I will answer for my Lord of Canterbury, that he shall allow of your so doing." Six pounds per head was allowed for transportation. The names of the other ministers were Claude Philippe de Richebourg and Louis Latane. They and the two surgeons had plenty of occupation in caring for the large company under their charge.

Among the list of the expenses of the journey to "Manicanton" appear the following items : "for one distiller and one Kettle, 3£ 2s ; To Mr. Stringer for fusils, coutlas, bayonetts, blunderbushes, flints, etc., 41£ 1s, for several Coates, waist coates, briches, etc., 10£ ; for blew Cloth handkerchieffs, cravats, etc., 26£ ; for a great Black Trunck to put ye goods in, 10s ; for Brandy, Sugar, figgs, raisons and sugar buiscuits for the sick, 5£ ; to ye ship's crew for brandy 15s ; for a boat to put some people ashoare, and to goe to Mr. Servant for a Certificate how he saw Capt. Hawes abuse us and our goods, and to bring ye salt, 3s ; To Capt. Hawes for Hamacks, brandy, and other extraordinarys 21£ 8s; To Cuper for his sabre broken by ye sentry upon the Shippe, 2s 6d ; for great nailes for the Pares (parish) doors, 9d ; To ye Miller to suffer our people by his fire and to dispatch them, 2s 6d ; to Corne for ye Horse, 1s."

In connection with the expenses of the journey it is

Items of Expense

Salt and Brandy

Ship Bill of
Fare

interesting to note the bill of fare which was set before the transatlantic passengers of that day. From the agreement made before commencing the voyage we take the following : "To every passenger over six years to have 7 pounds of Bread every week, and each mess, 8 passengers to a mess, to have 4 pounds Porke 5 days in a week, with pease. 2 days in a week to have 2 four pound piece of Beefe with a pudding with pease. If the kettle cannot be boyled for bad weather, every passenger to have 1 pound of cheese per day." Those who were sick fared better, according to this item among the expenditures : "for Brandy, Sugar, figgs, raisons and sugar busicuits for the sick . . . £5." While fifteen shillings were presented "To ye ships crew for brandy," and five shillings "To ye Cooke."

All the Huguenots who came over with la Muce did not settle at Manakin Town, but scattered themselves through the province along the banks of the James and Rappahannock Rivers ; some even pushing southward

Liberal Treat-
ment

into the Carolinas. Those who joined the settlement at Manakin Town were treated very liberally by the government of Virginia. By the king's orders the refugees were to be taken under the special protection of the governor, and the legislature showed every intention of making their settlement as easy and pleasant for them as lay within its power. Public subscriptions were taken for the purpose of relieving their most pressing necessities for food and shelter.

Says Beverly, in his history of Virginia : "The As-

Freed from
Taxation

sembly was very bountiful to those that remained at this town, bestowing on them large donations of money and provisions for their support. They likewise freed them from every tax for several years to come, and addressed the governor to grant them a brief, to entitle them to the charity of all well-disposed persons throughout the country, which, together with the king's benevolence, supported them very comfortably till they could sufficiently supply themselves with necessaries, which they now do indifferently well, and have stocks of cattle which are said to give abundance of milk more than any other in the country.   In the year 1702 they began an essay of wine which they make of the wild grapes gathered in the woods, the effect of which was a strong bodied claret of good flavour.   I heard a gentleman who had tasted it, give it great commendation.   I have heard that these people are upon the design of getting into the breed of buffaloes, to which end they lay in wait for their calves, that they may tame and raise a stock of them, in which, if they succeed, it will in all probability be greatly for their advantage; for these are much larger than the cattle, and have the benefit of being natural to the climate.   They now make their own clothes, and are resolved, as soon as they have improved that manufac-ture, to apply themselves to the making of wine and brandy, which they do not doubt to bring to perfection." But the endeavour to introduce the manufactures of France here at the extreme frontier of Virginia was a task too great for any set of colonists, and was doomed to failure from the first.   In planning as they did they showed the characteristic Huguenot enterprise, but the necessities of life drove them to agriculture as the only means of keeping the wolf from the door.

1702 Wine Growing

Buffalo Breeding

A letter from William Byrd thus described the settle-ment a year after its founding: "We visited about seventy of their huts, being, most of them very mean; there being upwards of fourty of y'm betwixt ye two creeks, w'ch is about 4 miles along on ye River, and have cleared all ye old Manacan ffields for near three miles together, as also some others (who came thither last ffeb'ry) have done more work than they y't went thither first.   .   .   . Indeed, they are very poor.   .   .   .   Tho' these people are very poor, yet they seem very cheerful and are (as farr as we could learn) very healthy, all they seem to de-sire is y't they might have Bread enough."

Description of the Settlement

The strict parish laws of the province were relaxed in favour of the Manakin Town settlers. In 1700 the Assembly enacted as follows :

A French
Parish
Established

Whereas a considerable number of French Protestant refugees have been lately imported into his Majesty's colony and dominions, several of which refugees have seated themselves above the falls of James River, at, or near to a place commonly called and known by the name of Manakin towne, for the encouragement of said refugee to settle and remain together, as near as may be to the said Manakin towne, and the parts adjacent, shall be accounted and taken for inhabitants of a distinct parish by themselves ; and the land which they now do and shall hereafter possess, at, or adjacent, to the said Manakin towne, shall be, and is hereby declared to be a parish of itselfe, distinct from any other parish, to be called and known by the name of King William Parish, in the county of Henrico, and not lyable to the payment of parish levies in any other parish whatsoever. And be it further enacted ; That such and so many of the said refugees, as are already settled, or shall hereafter settle themselves as inhabitants of the said parish, shall themselves and their familyes, and every of them, be free and exempted from the payment of public and county levies for the space of seven years next, ensuing from the publication of this act.

King William
Parish

V

A French
Church
Organized

Owing to such liberal treatment the colonists were enabled to have a church of their own, and at the first division of land a choice plot of the best glebe was set apart for the use of the pastor. The church which was immediately organized (as a matter of fact the colonists had come as one united church) prospered with the growth of the settlement. According to Bishop Meade, the life of this old church lasted down to about the middle of the last century, services being held in the name of the original organization until 1857. Where harmony and quiet prosperity are the rule, there is apt to be a dearth of material in the shape of records and documents. Such is the case with the church at Manakin Town. The peace was broken, however, in the year 1707, when there was an altercation between the pastor and the vestry. Abram Salle, vestryman, deposeth :

When Mr. Philipe had finished the service of the . . . the first thing he did was to demand the Register of Christenings to be delivered up to him . . . and in case he (Salle) refuse to do it he would excommunicate him; he was pleased to say this with a rage very unbecoming the place, which made me intreat him to have a little patience . . . upon this he flew out into a greater passion than before and frankly told us that he acknowledged no Vestry there was, neither would he have the people acknowledge any. Immediately upon his nameing the People, severol of his party . . . stood up . . . and took the liberty to utter many injurious things against me . . . and Michael . . . prest thro' the whole congregation to get up to where I was, and then catching me by the coat he threatened me very hardly, and by his Example sevarol of the crowd were heard to say, we must assassinate that fellow with the black beard. The said Philipe was—lowder than anybody.

VI

Rev. W. H. Foote writes of the colonists in Virginia as follows : " The colonists that remained at Manakin town, disappointed in their efforts to introduce the manufactures and productions of France, conformed their labours to the soil and climate and conditions of a frontier settlement ; and went on increasing and multiplying, and subduing the earth, according to the command of God in Eden. The ten thousand acres were soon too few for this enterprising people. They lengthened their cords and strengthened their stakes, and soon began to emigrate to portions of the unoccupied wilderness of Virginia. Goochland, and Fluvanna, and Louisa, and Albermarle, and Buckingham, and Powhatan, and Chesterfield, and Prince Edward, and Cumberland, and Charlotte, and Appomattox, and Campbell, and Pittsylvania, and Halifax, and Mecklinburg, all gave these emigrants a home. And then county after county to the west and south beckoned them on ; and they went on and grew and multiplied according to the blessing of Jacob on Joseph's children. Go over Virginia and ask for the descendants of those Huguenot families, that cast their lot, on their first landing, among the English neighbourhoods, and as

Enterprise and Growth

Assimilation and Wide Influence

speedily as possible conformed to the political usages of
the colony, and adopted the English language, and by
intermarriage were soon commingled with English society ;
and then follow the colonists of Manakin town, as they
more slowly assimilated with the English ; and number
those that by direct descent, or by intermarriage have
Huguenot blood in their veins, and the list will swell to
an immense multitude. The influence which these descendants of the French refugees have had, and still exercise, in the formation and preservation of the character
of the state and the nation, has unostentatiously and
widely extended."

Happily settled, indeed, were the French refugees in
what they made one of the garden spots of the country.
They were not far from the home of Pocahontas, the Indian princess, where, a little more than a century before,
Captain John Smith had found his brave rescuer, and put
a touch of enduring romance into the first days of the
white foreigner on American soil. The Indians were not
yet gone, and sometimes the French were made to feel a
spirit of vengeance that classed all whites as alike
enemies of the red men. To the English Cavaliers and
the French gentlemen Virginia owes its peculiar type
of cultivation, which made the plantations the scene of a
gallantry and courtliness and grace not yet extinct.
Where other nations often sent their poorest classes as
emigrants, France had driven away her best to enrich
the life of another and freer land.

One of the most distinguished of the Huguenot families
of Virginia was that of the Bufords, a corruption of the
original name of Beaufort, meaning "beautiful fort," or
castle. The name was variously spelled, as Beauford,
Bufford, and Buford, the form finally common. Some
members of this family, which was royal and allied to
Henry IV, were Huguenots, and emigrated to England
after the Revocation. From England some came to
America, and in both countries the descendants are found

to-day. The Virginia ancestor was John Beauford, of Christchurch Parish, Middlesex County. From him came a distinguished line of soldiers, who served their country well, some of them conspicuously. The Third Virginia Regiment in the Revolution had Colonel Buford at its head ; and two other military members of the family were Major-General Napoleon B. Buford, and Major-General John Buford. General James H. Wilson unhesitatingly ascribes to General John Buford the distinction of making Gettysburg possible. General Buford fired the first gun at Gettysburg, and in the address at the unveiling of his statue General Wilson said : "Strong, courageous, and generous, as they (the Bufords) were through many generations, the very flower and jewel of this family was the gentleman in whose name we gathered to-day. He selected Gettysburg for the field of battle."

General Buford was called by the soldiers "Old Steadfast." He himself said of Gettysburg : "A heavy task was before us. We were equal to it, and shall remember with pride that at Gettysburg we did our country much service." He was of the true type of French gentleman and loyal citizen.

CHAPTER VII

JOHN SEVIER AND HIS BRAVE WIFE

I

Xavier 1740

JOHN SEVIER, "The Commonwealth builder," is among the notable descendants of the Huguenot stock in Virginia. His father, Valentine Xavier, came from London in 1740 and settled in Rockingham County where Sevier was born in 1745. John received a fair education until he was sixteen years old, and the following year he married and founded the village of Newmarket, in the Shenandoah valley, thus early showing his propensity. He was a young man of exceptional dash and courage and soon became known throughout the region as an invincible Indian fighter. In 1772 he was made a captain in the Virginia line for the services he had rendered in the Indian wars, and that same year, he moved out to Watauga, a new and rude settlement on the west

Natural Leader

slope of the Alleghanies, now eastern Tennessee. Through his courage, popular address, and ability as a commander, he became the undisputed leader throughout the whole of that fertile wilderness. Space does not permit the recital of all the Indian campaigns he engaged in, or a list of the victories he won. In this manner his years were occupied until the breaking out of the Revolution, when we find him petitioning the North Carolina legislature on behalf of the settlers at Watauga, asking to be annexed to that province that "they might aid in the unhappy contest and bear their full proportion of the expenses of the war." The request was granted, and under the title of Washington District the whole of that territory which is now Tennessee was added to North Carolina as a county. Sevier was active in the local government of this vast new county and under the title of "clerk of the county" he held in reality entire control of the administration of the district.

In 1784 North Carolina ceded the territory to the Federal government in order to lighten the debts of the state. When the settlers heard of this they determined to found a government of their own and apply to the Union for admission. Sevier was elected governor of this new state, known as the State of Franklin, and for two years —as long as the commonwealth lasted,—retained his difficult position. Within sixty days after taking office, Sevier organized a court, a militia, and founded Washington College, the first school of a liberal nature which was established west of the Alleghanies. At last, however, a proclamation from Governor Caswell, of North Carolina, pronounced the new government a revolt and ordered it to be abandoned. In the face of superior forces the infant state was compelled to submit, and Sevier was captured and thrown into prison. He was rescued shortly afterwards, however, by his incensed followers, took the oath of allegiance to the United States, and was made brigadier-general of the territory. As a delegate to Congress he was the first representative to that body from the valley of the Mississippi. When Tennessee was made a state Sevier was elected its first governor, serving for three terms, and then after a short period, serving three more. In 1811 he served in Congress, and in 1815 he was again elected, but died before he could take his seat. His biographer says of him : "A rule like his was never before nor since known in this country."

The State of Franklin

Court and College

Sevier Arrested as Rebel

In Congress Governor

Unique Ruler

II

Captain Sevier's wife was a remarkable woman, a heroine of the pioneer days, whose story is a romance. Catherine Sherrill was the daughter of a North Carolinian who pushed his way into Tennessee in the Revolutionary days. Samuel Sherrill and his family were in that com-

A Colonial Heroine

pany of pioneers which halted in the Watauga Valley, where the king of the Cherokees planned to exterminate them. He brought his whole fighting strength against the fort defended by Captain Sevier. In the confusion of the battle, it is told that the French captain saw a tall, graceful girl running towards the fort pursued by a pack of savages. Exposing himself above the walls, heedless of the peril, the gallant captain shot down more than one

Gallant
Rescue

Indian who had raised his tomahawk to brain the girl, who succeeded in leaping the palisades and fell into his arms. It was in that exciting manner that the brave Frenchman first met the woman who was to be for forty years his companion in adventure, hardship and success.

Marriage
in 1780

They were married in 1780, four years after that Indian attack. From captain, "Nolichucky Jack," the idol of the pioneers, had risen to colonel by that time, and his whole regiment rode with him to the house of Mr. Sherrill, and held a "barbecue" in honour of the great event of their leader's wedding. Not long afterwards came the stress of the struggle for liberty, with its demands upon John Sevier and his wife. The few steadfast patriots of North Carolina were hard oppressed by the soldiers of Tarleton and Ferguson, and appealed to Sevier to help them. He had but a small command and no means to equip a large one ; but in this extremity the wife undertook to provide the equipment, while he immediately took the field. The result was that when Colonel Sevier rode away at the head of his famous regiment, the " ten

Sevier's
Regiment

hundred and forty," it was perhaps the best equipped regiment of the war. It was with that regiment Sevier stormed King's Mountain, and signally aided in turning the tide of the Revolution. And through all the time that he was kept in the field, his wife provided the resources. She had, besides, to manage the large estate and be financier

Woman
Manager and
Quarter-
master

and quartermaster ; and that in a region infested by hostile savages and equally hostile Tories, many of whom she met, rifle in hand, awing them by her determination.

It is said that once she rode boldly into a camp of out-
laws who had stolen her horses, told the leader that the
penalty of his crime was hanging, and promising him
speedy execution at the hands of her husband if the
property was not returned. The horses were restored to
her. Yet this woman, who knew no fear and could be
as stern as her husband, was all gentleness and kindness
to those in distress, a model housewife when peace came
and she was mistress of her happy home.

When John Sevier was induced, by his loyalty to his
Watauga people, to become governor of "the Free and
Independent State of Franklin," the result of a secession
from North Carolina, his wife supported him, though
she did not believe in the futile project. She kept an
open "Governor's House," from which no one was turned
away, and the people were as proud of the "Governor's
lady" as of him. Major Elholm, an officer of Pulaski's
Legion, writing to the governor of Georgia at this time,
said : "If Colonel Sevier is king here, his gracious lady
is certainly queen of the Franks. She is gifted with great
beauty and the art of hospitality, but above all is to be
esteemed her discreet understanding." After stirring
scenes, including the kidnapping of Colonel and Governor
Sevier and his rescue by his wife's ingenious plan, Tennessee emerged from the governmental chaos, the charge
of treason made against the French leader was dismissed,
and in recognition of his many services to his country he
was appointed general. Near Knoxville, the first and
new capital of the state, he built another home ; and a
little later his wife rode with him to witness his inaugura-
tion as the first governor of Tennessee. Six terms was
this Huguenot descendant elected governor, and his wife
was noted for her hospitality as much as for her beauty.
It is an interesting sidelight on the times that during the
first term as governor some eastern friend presented Mrs.
Sevier with a brace of silver candlesticks and an imported carpet—the first ever spread on the puncheon

*Governor's
Lady*

*Queen of the
Franks*

*First
Governor of
Tennessee*

floor west of the Alleghanies, and never used save on
state occasions. Then the candles were lighted and the
carpet was laid in the reception-room, and there Louis
Philippe and his brother, Andrew Jackson and many
other notables, had the honour to rest their feet upon it.

General Sevier died in 1815, while engaged as commissioner in establishing the boundaries between Georgia
and the Creek Nation, and all Tennessee was in mourning for the most distinguished leader in a trying period,
one of the truly great pioneers and commonwealth builders of America, where his persecuted forebears had
found refuge.   And ever associated with him in memory
is his heroic and accomplished wife.

PAUL REVERE'S BIRTHPLACE, NORTH SQUARE, BOSTON.

CHAPTER VIII

THE THRILLING EXPERIENCES OF AN EXILED FAMILY

I

THE *Memoirs of a Huguenot Family*, by Ann Maury, one of its descendants, throw an interesting sidelight upon the sufferings and triumphs of a Huguenot family in entering upon their life in the New World. When all the manuscripts in the possession of Huguenot descendants in America shall have been brought equally into the light, the history of the French blood in this country can be written from a far more intimate point of view than this present history can hope to take. The extracts we make from this most interesting but not generally accessible volume begin with the autobiographical introduction by the head of the Fontaine family, who reveals at once his deep piety. The De la Fontaines

"I, James Fontaine, have commenced writing this history, for the use of all my children, on the 26th day of March, 1722 ; being sixty-four years old. Introduction

"My dear Children—Whenever I have related my own adventures to you, or given you details of the incidents that befell your ancestors, you have evinced so deep an interest in them, that I feel I ought not to neglect making a record of the past for your use ; & I am determined to employ my leisure time in this way. I would fain hope that the pious examples of those from whom we are descended may warm your hearts and influence your lives. I hope you will resolve to dedicate yourselves wholly and unreservedly to the service of that God whom they worshipped at the risk of their lives, and that you, and those who come after you will be stedfast in the profession of that pure reformed religion for which they endured, with unshaken constancy, the most severe trials. You cannot fail to notice, in the course of their lives, the watchful hand of God's Providence, supporting and preserving them thro hardship and suffering.

"For my own part, I trust that, while recording the past mercies of God for the benefit of my descendants, I may derive personal advantage from the review. The frailties and sins of the different periods of my life, thus brought to mind, ought to cause me to humble myself before the throne of grace, and tremblingly implore pardon for the past, through the mediation of my blessed Saviour ; and the assistance of the Holy Spirit to make me watchful and circumspect for the time to come. When I look back upon the numberless, uncommon, and unmerited mercies bestowed upon me during the whole course of my life, I hope that my gratitude will be in-

Gratitude and Trust creased towards my Almighty Benefactor, and my confidence in Him so strengthened that I may be enabled for the future to cast all my care upon Him. Great as is my debt of gratitude for the things of this life, its manifold comforts and conveniences, how incalculably greater is it for the mercy to my immortal soul, in God having shed the blood of His only begotten Son to redeem it! Oh, my God! I entreat Thee to continue Thy fatherly protection to me during the few days I have yet to live, and, at last, to receive my soul into Thine everlasting arms. Amen."

Soul Window This is like looking through an opened window into the soul of the good man and seeing his beautiful character. The following synopsis of the story is given because it discloses both the Huguenot character and the sufferings for faith's sake, at the same time proving the care of God for His children.

II

De la Fontaine was the original name, as on record in

Rochelle, where Jaques de la Fontaine, grandfather of James the autobiographer, held some command in the Tower. From motives of humility the father of James cut off *De la*, the indication of the ancient nobility of the family. This commonly happened among the French refugees in the foreign parts. John de la Fontaine, great-grandfather of James, was born in 1500 in the province of Maine, near the borders of Normandy. His father procured him a commission in the household of Francis I, and he became conspicuous in the king's service. He became a convert to Protestantism on the first preaching of the Reformed religion in France, about 1535. He remained in royal service for a time because this was a safeguard from persecution on account of his religion. Besides, he was thus able to show much kindness to his Protestant brethren, whom he often shielded from oppression. He had four sons. When Charles IX issued the Edict of Pacification in 1561, the Protestants, believing this to be in good faith, generally laid down their arms, and at this time John de la Fontaine resigned his commission, thinking himself protected by the Edict in the exercise of his religion. He retired to his paternal estates, hoping to end his days peacefully in the bosom of his family, worshipping God according to the dictates of his conscience.

But the change was for the worse, instead of better, after the Edict ; now all was secrecy, and any wretched vagabond, imbued with the spirit of bigotry, could at once exercise the functions of judge and executioner. Armed miscreants broke into the houses of the Protestants at midnight, robbed and murdered their inmates with a cruelty at which humanity shudders, and were encouraged in their atrocities by priests, monks and bigots. The Protestants were again driven to recourse to arms. John de la Fontaine was hated because of his piety and zeal for the pure worship of God. In 1563 his house was attacked at night, he was surprised, dragged out of doors,

Erasing Sign of Nobility

Protestant in 1535

Persecution

Murdered
1563

and his throat cut. His wife, rushing after him in hopes to soften the hearts of their midnight assassins, was also murdered. The lives of the three younger boys were preserved—the oldest, about eighteen, perished. The second son, James, grandfather of our autobiographer, was about fourteen, Abraham about twelve, and the youngest nine. They fled from the scene of horror, with no other guide save Providence, and found their way to Rochelle, then the stronghold of Protestantism in France. These poor boys, deprived at one blow of parents and property, plunged from affluence into poverty, were taken in by the inhabitants, who gave them food and

James a Hero

shelter for little services they could render. A shoemaker, a charitable, God-fearing man, received James into his own house, treated him with affection, and taught him his trade. Before long he was earning wages which enabled him to support his younger brothers. When he reached manhood he engaged in commerce and was comparatively prosperous. He had three children who grew to maturity, two daughters and one son. The latter, father of James, was born in 1603. Henry IV called the grandfather the handsomest man in his kingdom.

A Ministerial
Family

His son James, delicate, fond of books, early evinced an inclination for the ministry, was afforded college advantages, and became a Protestant pastor over the churches of Vaux and Royan. He married an English lady named Thompson, in 1628, and they had five children, two of whom became ministers. By a second wife he had five children more, two of whom were sons and both became ministers, so that this was emphatically a ministerial family, and we do not wonder to find descendants continuing to follow in the clerical line.

A Model
Pastor

James, our author, was the youngest child of all. He says his father was a man of fine figure, pure red and white complexion, of very dignified deportment, commanding the respect of all. He was remarkably abstemious, living chiefly upon milk, fruit and vegetables.

He was never seen among his flock at feasts or entertainments, but made it an invariable rule to visit each family twice in the year. He hastened to the sick and afflicted as soon as their sorrows were made known to him. When it was known he was praying with any sick person crowds would flock to hear him. He was zealous and affectionate, of unusual attainments, having great learning, quick and ready wit, clear and sonorous voice, and always used the most chaste, elegant and appropriate language. He was invited to take charge of a church at Rochelle, with salary twice as large as that he was receiving, but refused decidedly. He had not the heart to abandon a flock who loved him so much.

III

James was born April 7, 1685. A nurse's carelessness **1685** lamed him for life. When only four he was so taken **Early Life** with hearing his father read the Scriptures and pray with the family, that he called together the servants and his sisters and made them kneel while he prayed. He was rather precocious, and early at six was placed in school. When he came of age at twenty-five, after many trying school experiences, he was possessed of the family estate, and had an apparently prosperous outlook. First came **Prosperity** the tribulations of his ministerial brother-in-law, who was thrown into prison on a false charge of proselyting, and was persecuted until finally he made his escape to England. Then his brother Peter, who had succeeded his father in the pastorate at Vaux, was seized and confined in a prison, without charge or trial, while the church was levelled to the ground. James now was surrounded by neighbours who had no church privileges, and he invited them to join him in his family devotions. They came until the number reached 150. Then they **A Benefactor** came two or three times a week, and he preached and expounded the Scriptures to them. All possible was done to escape observation which should draw persecution upon the people ; but at length a rumour got abroad that meetings were held in the parish and that he was the preacher. He was advised by friends to stop the meetings, but believed he was in the path of duty and kept on leading the services.

Arrest and Imprisonment

In 1684 at Easter the open attacks began. On deposition of a lawyer M. de la Fontaine was arrested on a charge of leading in unlawful assemblies. He advised all the Protestants to remain steadfast, and willingly went to jail to test the rights of citizens. In prison he offered prayer aloud, and established a daily prayer circle, by this means confirming in their faith the many Protestants who were brought there for no other crime than meeting together quietly to worship. The people had become so determined through this bold stand of their leader and his willingness to suffer imprisonment for the truth, that they no longer fled from the provost and his archers who were sent out to arrest them, but indeed seemed to be

Boldness and Acquittal

eager to show their courage. When M. de la Fontaine came to trial, charged with having taught in prison, given offense to the Roman Catholics who were in prison, and interrupted the priest in his celebration of divine worship, suborned evidence was produced ; but acting in his own defense, the able minister turned the tables on his persecutors, and was triumphantly acquitted in the end by Parliament, to which he appealed his case.

But the spirit of persecution became more and more bitter, and in 1685 the dragoons appeared. Then James

1685 The Dragoons

de la Fontaine left the home of his childhood, never to return to it. He had 500 francs, two good horses, on one of which his valet was mounted, and was well armed.

An Exile

From his amply furnished house he removed nothing, and within two hours after he quitted it the dragoons came and lived there till they had consumed or sold everything they could lay hands on, even to the locks and bolts of the doors. If one would abjure his religion he would be let alone, if not, death or torture was his fate. Riding rapidly forward, he visited the homes of his relatives, and found many of them had recanted, to escape the dragoons ; but as soon as possible they left France for countries where they could be free to worship according to their faith. He did all he could to stem the tide of abjuration, and failure to do so made him sick and careless of life. For three months did this heroic man travel about the country endeavouring to encourage the Protestants. He rode by night, resting by day, to avoid detection ; and would be six and seven days at a time without chance to undress. And his anxiety was increased by fear lest evil befall " that worthy and pious woman whom God gave to me afterwards for my beloved partner and helpmate, and my greatest earthly comfort —your dear mother." **Heroic Effort**

The Revocation of the Edict of Nantes (October, 1685), left no hope save in flight, and M. de la Fontaine made preparations in good earnest. His escape was most thrilling. He arranged with an English captain to take him and four or five persons to England, but as the coast was guarded to prevent emigration, which was made a crime, it was only after several days of distressing experiences that the party was able to board the ship and leave forever the shore of France. It should be realized here that this jeopardy of life and this loss of a comfortable fortune and pleasant home, together with an influential position as country nobleman, was undergone without a murmur all for the sake of religion, for the right to worship God according to conscience, when a word of recantation would have made exile and hardship unnecessary. Of such stuff were these Huguenots made. **Thrilling Escape**

Read his brave words : " A blessed and ever-memorable day for us, who then effected our escape from our cruel enemies, who were not so much to be feared because they had power to kill the body, but rather from the pains they took to destroy the souls of their victims. I bless God for the multitude of His mercies in earthly enjoyments also. He allowed me to bring to England the **Cheerful Sacrifice** dear one whom I loved better than myself, and she willingly gave up relations, friends, and wealth to be the sharer of my poverty in a strange land. I here testify that we have fully experienced the truth of the promise of our blessed Saviour, to give a hundredfold more, even in this present life, to those who leave all and follow Him. Certain it is that a man's life consisteth not in the abundance of the things that he possesseth, but in the enjoyment he has of them and it is in this sense that I would be understood, when I say that we have received the hundredfold promised in the Gospel ; for we have had infinitely more joy and satisfaction in having abandoned our property for the glory of God, than they can have had who took possession of it.''

IV

Romantic
Story

Few stories are more interesting in detail than that of this French family, as they sought to make a living in England, where ready hospitality was afforded.   When, however, through his superior commercial ability, he became a manufacturer of worsteds, jealousy was aroused that led him to give up business and leave Taunton and England.   He also discovered that while, if he would join the Church of England he could secure ready preferment, as a Presbyterian he had no hope of favour. He felt that the Episcopalians were not much different in spirit in England from the Roman Catholics in France, though the persecution was not of the same outrageous character.   And as he held to the simplicity of the Reformed worship in which he had been trained from boyhood, he preferred exile again to further persecution of

New Start in
Ireland

any sort.   He gave up once more his means of livelihood and went to Ireland, where he expected to become pastor of a church of French refugees.   He had now six children, five sons and one daughter.   In 1694 he became pastor in Cork, and started another manufactory, making broadcloth.   Here he was happy and prosperous, and the church increased daily. But his cup of happiness was dashed to the earth through the coming to the church of one Isaac de la Croix, who had already caused dissensions in two other churches, and now did the same thing at Cork. As a result the pastor resigned, to the great grief of his people. "Thus you see," says he, "how much injury may be done by one quarrelsome, malicious individual in a church. The poor minister is under the necessity of sacrificing his own comfort for the peace of the church. I was certain that if I did not resign a schism would be created, and did my best to prevent it."

After this M. Fontaine was ready to leave Cork, and made a venture in the fishery line, which led him to become famous as a defender of an exposed point on the Irish coast against French privateers. For his services, which were of a most romantic character, recalling the most exciting pirate stories, he received recognition and a pension from the British government. He finally settled in Dublin, establishing a school there, and maintaining relations with many notable people. Philanthropic Service

In 1714 his sons visited Virginia and became owners of a plantation, and gradually the children settled on this continent. The daughter married a Frenchman named Maury, and the editor of this *Memoir* is a great-granddaughter of that branch of the family; while the Fontaines are among the honoured names of the South. Sons go to Virginia

V

John Fontaine, son of James, who wrote the *Memoir*, desired to be a soldier and saw service in Spain. Planning for the good of his brothers and sisters he took ship at Cork for Virginia, sailing December 3, 1714. These notes are taken from his *Journal:* John Fontaine's Journal 1714

Struck by a tempest, for days there seemed little hope, the vessel tossing at the mercy of wind and overwhelming waves. In these conditions this prayer, recorded in the journal, must be regarded as remarkable, indicating the strength of character and faith that marked this family :

Prayer at Sea in Storm

We are almost wasted by the violent motion of the ship, being without masts; but we still trust in Thee, O God, and wait patiently for our deliverance by Thy almighty hand. Stretch forth Thine arm to us, O Lord, and bear us up in this our distress, lest we sink and fall under the weight of our sins. Suffer us not to repine against Thee in our trouble, but let us confess that we merit to be afflicted. Thou hast, O Lord, given for us Thy only Son, our Lord Jesus Christ : to His merits we fly, and through Him we hope for salvation. Do Thou pardon us, O Lord, and accept of these our imperfect prayers, and if Thou seest fit to take us to Thyself, do Thou also cleanse us, that we may be worthy of appearing before Thee. All these thoughts came now before us, because we see death as if it were playing before our eyes, waiting for the sentence of Almighty God to destroy us. Nothing makes this sight so terrible as our sins, and it is our weakness and ignorance that makes us think more of death now than when we are at our homes, and in our accounted places of security. If we rightly considered, we should think ourselves safer here than if we were in prosperity at home, for it is the devil's greatest cunning to put in our hearts that we are in a safe place, that we have long to live, and that a final repentance will be sufficient for our salvation. O God, give us grace that while we live, we may live unto Thee. and have death always before our eyes, which most certainly will not cheat us, but come at last and take us out of this troublesome life, and if we are prepared for it, then shall we have our recompense for past watchfulness ; therefore, let us cast off this world, so far as it may be prejudicial to our everlasting inheritance, and seek after Thy laws, expecting mercy through the merits of our blessed Saviour and Redeemer. Amen.

Reaching Virginia 1715

For six weeks the ship was tossed about in almost continuous storms, before she could again make the English coast, the idea of crossing the Atlantic having been abandoned on account of the loss of sails and masts. In another month the vessel was repaired and sailed again, The First Sunday and this time the voyage was made in three months.

At nine of the morning on May 26, 1715, they saw land, and that night entered the mouth of the Potomac River. Here is the record of his first Sunday on shore of the new world :

29th, Sunday.—About 8 of the clock we came ashore, and went to church, which is about four miles from the place where we landed. The day was very hot, and the roads very dusty. We got to church a little late, but had part of the sermon. The people seemed to me pale and yellow. After the minister had made an end, every one of the men pulled out his pipe, and smoked a pipe of tobacco. I informed myself more about my own business, and found that Williamsburg was the only place for my design.

This design was to establish a plantation for the family. He made a horseback journey to Williamsburg, became *To Establish a Plantation* acquainted with Governor Spotswood, and later formed a solid friendship with that functionary, going in his company on a number of long journeys of inspection through the unsettled country. His journal of their experiences is exceedingly interesting, and as historical material valuable. He proves how carefully the Lord's day was observed by the statement that on Sunday they saw a number of deer and two bears, but did not shoot them because it was the Sabbath. While out in the forest on *Sabbath Observance* their travels, they never omitted at least having prayers read on Sunday. He decided to take up 3,000 acres of land, and thus Virginia became the home of the Fontaine and Maury families—Miss Fontaine, the only daughter, having married M. Maury.

VI

Before returning to England, John Fontaine sailed from Hampton for New York, landing on Staten Island, *Journey to New York* of which he says : "There are some good improvements here ; the inhabitants are mostly Dutch ; the houses are all built with stone and lime ; there are some hedges as in England." From Staten Island they went by the ferry to Long Island, and then had an eight mile horseback ride to reach Brooklyn and the ferry to New York. "As soon as we landed we went and agreed for our lodgings with a Dutch woman named Schuyler, and then I went to see Mr. Andrew Freneau at his house, and he received me very well, after which I went to the tavern, and about

ten at night to my lodgings and to bed.'' Next day he
waited upon Governor Hunter, who invited him to dine;
thence to see the mayor, who kindly received him.
Next day he rode about seven miles out of town to
Colonel Morris's, ''Who lives in the country, and is
judge or chief justice of this province, a very sensible
and good man.'' Next day he saw the town. ''There
are three churches, the English, the French, and the
Dutch Church; there is also a place for the Assembly to
sit, which is not very fine, and where they judge all
matters. The town is compact, the houses for the most
part built after the Dutch manner, with the gable ends
towards the street.'' ''The French have all the privileges that can be, and are the most in number here, they
are of the Council and of the Parliament, and are in all
other employments.'' He was dined and wined with
true hospitality by the Irish Club, the French Club, and
various friends he made, including Mr. Hamilton, the
postmaster-general.

From New York he went to Philadelphia, going to
church in Amboy, New Jersey, on the way. Philadelphia
he found built very regularly upon rising ground on the
Delaware River. ''The inhabitants are most part Quakers, and they have several good meetings, and there are
also some English churches.'' He had a letter to Mr.
Samuel Perez, but says ''He had no service for me.''
Then they continued the overland journey to Virginia,
much of the way through wild territory, in which they
had some exciting experiences with robbers.

Then Peter his brother arrived from England, and the
work of establishing the plantation in King William
County proceeded. Peter was a preacher, and was soon
presented to Roanoke parish. Another brother, James,
with his family, arrived in the autumn of the same year,
1717, and the next year his brother-in-law, Mr. Matthew
Maury, with his family, completed the party. All had
to go through chills and fever in the process of acclima-

Seeing the
Town

Philadelphia

The Family
Plantation
Established

tization, and Peter suffered greatly from this cause. He returned to England in 1719 for a visit.

VII

After the Fontaines emigrated to Virginia, they were in the habit of meeting annually, to hold a solemn re- **Annual Family Reunion** ligious thanksgiving, in commemoration of their remarkable preservation when attacked by French privateers in the south of Ireland. A sermon preached by Rev. Peter' Fontaine, on one of these occasions, is preserved, bearing date of 1st June, 1723, text, Rom. 15 : 5, 6. His three points are : Firstly, The duty here enjoined, that is, to glorify God. Secondly, The manner of performing it, that is, with one mind and one mouth. And Thirdly, Put you in mind of your high obligations to comply with this duty, not only because of the signal deliverance which we are met to celebrate, but by reason of that infinite number which God hath vouchsafed to favour us with at other times, no less worthy of our remembrance and thanks.

A distinguished son of this famous family was Matthew Fontaine Maury, "The Pathfinder of the Seas." He **Matthew Fontaine Maury** was born in Spottsylvania County in 1806. He became a midshipman in the navy at nineteen, but his career as an active officer was cut short by an accident which lamed him for life. After that he devoted himself to study, and his contributions to useful knowledge have been excelled by those of no man of his time. He was the founder of the modern science of hydrography. His great work, "The Physical Geography of the Sea," published in **Founder of Hydrography** 1856, made him at once world famous ; it was the pioneer venture in a new field, and though new facts have been and will be added to our store of knowledge of ocean winds and currents, it will always be remembered that Maury "blazed the trail." He was the first to plot out the path of the Gulf Stream ; he originated the system of **Deep Sea Sounding** deep sca sounding ; he was the first to suggest the laying

Ocean Cables of oceanic cables ; he organized the system of crop observation which has proved of such countless value ; and in
a hundred other ways that are not sensational did he
labour to benefit mankind.   If sheer usefulness were the
universal test applied to greatness, Matthew Fontaine
Maury, next to George Washington, would be the greatest Virginian.

PART FOUR

THE FRENCH IN VARIOUS RELATIONS

CHAPTER I

AMERICA'S DEBT TO FRANCE DURING THE REVOLUTION

I

WHILE in one sense not strictly germane to our subject, it is certainly fitting to recognize here A Most Valuable Ally the immeasurable debt of gratitude which America owes to France for the aid given to the young Republic in its War for Independence. This aid it was that undoubtedly enabled us to gain the victory that put a new nation on the world's map ; a nation that was to be the first to set the example of true democracy, and to start that great idea of political equality which during the nineteenth century brought the people of nearly every nation in Europe to a consciousness of their power, and largely to their rightful place in government. It is the judgment of most historians that France turned the scale in favour of the colonies in their unequal struggle. It was when the American cause was seemingly hopeless, when there was no national credit, that France gave recognition and espousal to our cause. It matters not what were the controlling motives which led the French government to take the American side. The result was in the interest of humanity and of right.

Not only did the French government give recognition Lafayette the Lover of Liberty and financial aid at a time when these were invaluable, but some of the best blood of France came over to render

377

personal assistance in the field. As for the motives that impelled the foremost among them, the young and gallant Marquis de Lafayette, to leave courtly luxury and ease for camp life in a strange land, no one questions their purity and unselfishness. He is taken at his own words when he tells us his "heart was enlisted" when he "heard of American independence." We shall not forget what a comfort this young French nobleman was to Washington, who needed just such inspiration and companionship as Lafayette could give. Washington, who was not given to overpraise, said of him, "This noble soldier combines all the military fire of youth with an unusual maturity of judgment." The American commander-in-chief relied upon this French officer as upon few men, and the friendship between them was one of the fine outgrowths of the war. On Lafayette's side there was the deference and courtesy not only born of his exquisite breeding, but of an intense admiration for a character whose greatness he appreciated from the first ; while Washington also found much to admire in the brilliant young soldier and true gentleman who was as devoted as himself to the cause of human freedom. More than once the American commander had reason to be out of humour with some of the French officers, who assumed too much by reason of their rank at home ; but Lafayette was his comfort and dependence, always to be counted upon in an emergency.

Lafayette in the French Revolution   After the war Lafayette continued to render all the aid in his power to the Republic he had helped establish. A man of influence in his own country, he co-operated with the American diplomats, and was a steadfast friend until France came to her Revolution, and his hopes for such liberty there as the American Republic knew seemed forever blasted. A recent writer[1] gives an account of the later years of Lafayette's life, and of the honours paid to

[1] Augustus E. Ingram, deputy consul of the United States in Paris.

his memory by Americans. "When we visit the grave of Lafayette in the remote and obscure little burying ground of the *Dames Blanches*, in the eastern fringe of Paris," he says, "we are reminded of the sad, dark years that came later in his life, and the unpretentious tomb of his wife, close beside her husband's, tells of her heroic share in his sufferings."

II

Soon after Lafayette's return to France, the Revolution broke forth, and he took an active part in it. But he was too republican to suit the aristocrats and too moderate to suit the revolutionists. Denounced by the Jacobins, he was obliged to flee from France, but was captured by the Austrians, and confined in the damp, dark dungeons of Olmutz. Meanwhile in Paris the Reign of Terror was running its course. Among its victims was Madame de Lafayette, who was thrown into prison, partly because she was the daughter of the Duke d'Ayen, partly because she refused to disown her husband. Still more terrible was the fate of her mother and sister, who perished under the guillotine. The scene of their execution is not far from the spot where Lafayette lies buried.

Heroism of Madame de Lafayette

After the downfall and death of Robespierre, Madame de Lafayette was released and soon succeeded in finding her husband's Austrian prison. Refused permission to see him unless she shared his captivity, she accepted heroically these harsh terms. The damp, unwholesome dungeon soon seriously affected her health, but as she could only escape at the cost of separation from her husband, she declined to leave, preferring to sacrifice her life. When the devoted pair had endured five years of imprisonment, Napoleon secured their release, but Madame de Lafayette was liberated only in time to die a free woman. In 1815 Louis XVIII granted to the families of the victims of the Revolution the right to be buried near their martyred relatives. Thus the little cemetery of the *Dames Blanches* came into existence, since it was near the old quarry where thirteen hundred victims were buried, and there Madame de Lafayette's body was placed. Later her noble husband was laid by her side, and their son, George Washington Lafayette, is buried near by.

America does not forget Lafayette. His name lives in our history closely associated with that of the great American chief whom he venerated. As Decoration Day rolls around each year, Americans in Paris make a pilgrimage to the little cemetery and place flowers upon the tomb of the hero, and words of appreciation are spoken. In our own country there are statues of him in the public squares of many of our large cities. Nor are there wanting tokens of American appreciation in the French capital itself. In the quiet, picturesque little *Place des États-Unis* (Place or Square of the United States), under the shady chestnut trees, stands a beautiful bronze group by Bartholdi, the same French sculptor who designed the colossal statue of "Liberty Enlightening the World," which graces New York harbour, representing Washington and Lafayette, hand in hand, with the flags of the two republics entwined, and an inscription reading :

" *Hommage à la France, en reconnaissance de son généreux concours dans la lutte du peuple des États-Unis pour l' Indépendance et la Liberté.*"

(Homage to France, in recognition of her generous aid in the struggle of the people of the United States for independence and liberty.)

III

Some years ago some five million school children of America contributed their pennies for the erection of another statue of Lafayette in Paris. The French government gave a site in the gardens of the Louvre, and during the summer of the exposition of 1900 the unveiling of a

LAFAYETTE AT MOUNT VERNON WITH WASHINGTON

staff model of the proposed statue was made the occasion of great rejoicing and the manifestation of friendship between the sister republics.   Paul Wayland Bartlett, an American sculptor, was commissioned to design the statue, and most effectively he has executed his work.

While Lafayette was by no means the only Frenchman who served in the Rebellion, his is the conspicuous name, as his was the most consecrated spirit, and it is not necessary to particularize concerning others.   They were all brave and competent men, who were astonished at the quality of manhood they found in the little-trained and half-equipped colonials, every one of whom had imbibed the spirit of independence, and was able to fight on his own initiative when necessary, instead of being military puppets like the ordinary European soldier.

It is one of the strange providences of history that the nation which thrust forth its Protestant citizens and thus weakened itself immeasurably among the world powers, should have been the means of materially assisting in the establishment of the greatest Protestant nation and one of the foremost world powers.   Roman Catholicism could drive out of France her best people, but it could not plant successful and permanent colonies in America, nor long keep advantages momentarily gained.   Nor is the day far distant, if the signs of the times count for anything, when France will read the lessons of her own history, and secure her own future by becoming a land where religious liberty shall be as dearly prized as in our own.   That will mean a Protestant nation as the only progressive one.

While the noble Lafayette, who rendered such inestimable service to the cause of American liberty, was not of Huguenot blood or creed, he was nevertheless in sympathy with the cause of religious liberty, and became its advocate at a critical period.   When he had returned to France, crowned with the laurels he had won in the American struggle for independence, and imbued with

Lafayette a Champion of the Protestants

the spirit of the American people, he was stirred at the condition of affairs in the homeland, and at once became a zealous pleader for the oppressed Huguenots. He argued with all his eloquence the right of the Protestants at least to be permitted to marry and to die according to their faith. His efforts were not successful at that time, but, true to his high character, he cared nothing for the obloquy which his stand brought upon him from the ecclesiastics. It is probable that he would have gained the amount of liberty he sought for the Protestants had not the clergy exhorted the king in opposition. Not daunted at this failure, Lafayette again in the Assembly of Notables pleaded for the heretics, and was now more favourably listened to. He was even seconded in his just and fair propositions by the Bishop de Langres, and a petition was presented to the king. As a result an edict was registered which secured the Protestants in their civil relations, after nearly two centuries of bloodshed. The bigots of course denounced the bishop as anti-Christ, and spared no abuse or defamation of Lafayette for using his dominant influence to secure this act of simple justice. After the Revolution, which was the inevitable outcome of conditions that had made such continued persecution of the Huguenots possible in France, Napoleon granted religious toleration, although Roman Catholicism remained as the State Church. After another century, in which the church has been as of old the enemy of political and religious liberty, the French government has broken with Rome, and the Republic will probably see to it that religious liberty shall henceforth be actual, and every form of religious persecution cease.

Civil Rights
Secured

CHAPTER II

THE LOUISIANA PURCHASE

A Rich and Needed Territory

NEXT to the debt America owes France for her aid in the Revolution is the gratitude due her Emperor Napoleon for the sale of the Louisiana territory to the United States. While the first aid helped us put a new nation on the map, it was the second that enabled us to own territory that was indispensable to the United States if she was to be the predominant power on the American continent. Until that purchase our government was hemmed in on all sides. England had Canada on the north, and was likely very soon to take from France the Louisiana territory just as she had taken from France her Canadian possessions. With England in possession of this great section on our western boundary, with Spain still on the south and in the far west, it would have been easy for England to gain the ascendancy on the continent after all, and the United States would have covered but a small portion of the North American continent.

We must realize this in order to estimate what vast service Napoleon rendered us when for his own selfish purposes he consummated the Louisiana Purchase for a sum amazingly small in comparison with the value of the territory. He needed money, it is true, and twenty-two millions were something. The amount indeed loomed large to the American commissioners, who were not authorized to enter into any such financial engagement. But it was not the money that chiefly influenced Napoleon. He had good reason to believe that England would soon drive out the French and seize the territory, and he desired to have the United States rather than England enter into possession of it. It is an interesting fact that he was doubtless influenced in his decision by Marbois, one of the two commissioners whom he appointed to treat with the American representatives. Marbois had an American wife, and he radically favoured the sale; while Talleyrand as vigorously opposed it.

The Greatest Land Sale in History

By this purchase, the most stupendous land transfer in history, the United States was placed in position subsequently to acquire the Spanish region, and thus to gain its present territorial proportions. There are now fourteen populous and prosperous states of the Union comprised within this section, which includes a large part of the world's granary. Jefferson did buy a wilderness, but it has been made to blossom as the rose. Prosperous and populous cities and towns exist where in 1803 nature and the savage held sway, and the "wilderness" contains nearly one-fifth of the 80,000,000 of our people. There are three times as many people in the Louisiana Purchase now as there were in the whole United States when the sale was completed, and the centre of population as of political and industrial power is fast moving towards the Mississippi. The state of Missouri alone has more people than the thirteen colonies had when they won their independence. St. Louis, a single city, has more inhabitants to-day than New York, Philadelphia, Boston, and all other cities of the country put together in 1800. Then think of such centres of wealth, industry and culture as Denver, Omaha, St. Paul and Minneapolis, Sioux City, Kansas City, with the host of smaller but not less progressive cities and towns.

The Field

Such has been the field opened up to commerce and industry. Under the homestead laws a vast number of immigrants swept into this region, in addition to the thousands attracted from the eastern section. When we realize that other nations have furnished us with 22,000,-000 of their people since 1820, and 16,000,000 of these since 1862, the year in which President Lincoln signed the significant homestead act, we shall see what a complex population has to be dealt with in the Louisiana Purchase, as well as in the great cities of our land. But fortunately, the assimilation of foreign elements is far easier and quicker on the prairies than in the cities. While it is true that in the Louisiana Purchase there is the greatest number of languages heard anywhere, and that a large percentage of the population in the various states had its nativity in other countries, it is also true that nowhere else could be found such rapid Americanization of all these diverse elements.

And here once more we note the overrulings of Providence. This Louisiana Purchase was opened up to civilization by the Jesuit missionaries who made their way down the Mississippi, bent on converting the Indians and establishing a new France, Roman Catholic and free from any Protestant taint, in America. Many of these pioneers were brave and self-sacrificing men, who gave their lives for the cause. But every attempt to keep out the Protestants failed : and it was with the opening of the region to the same religious light and liberty enjoyed in the older states that progress came and a new civilization. As with Roman Catholic France, so with Roman Catholic Spain. Neither nation found it possible to keep the advantage gained by priority of possession ; both were gradually conquered and compelled to withdraw before the Anglo-Saxon, who represented in religion the very antipodes of the spirit of the Latin and Roman Catholic peoples. In this he who will may see the hand of God, working out human destiny along the lines of true religious and political liberty. Since Protestantism is democratic in its essential principles, it must prevail in a democracy. Autocracy in America is no more possible in religion than in government.

Protestantism Dominant

CHAPTER III

THE FRENCH IN FREEMASONRY

I

Patriots in Freemasonry

IT was perhaps natural that the French Protestants who came to America should be favourable to Freemasonry, this being an institution that had been put under the ban by the same Roman Catholic Church which had so bitterly oppressed them and driven them into exile. Aside from this, there was everything in the spirit of the ancient fraternity that would appeal to them. Hence there are many names of distinguished Huguenot families in the Masonic rolls of the period of the Revolution, as in the rolls of later days.

Freemasonry in this country early took high rank from the character of the leaders who wore the lambskin apron. It was enough to establish its worth in the estimation of multitudes that George Washington was a Freemason and was proud of the fact. He was not alone in this regard among the leaders during the Revolutionary period. Albert Gallatin, Paul Revere, the Boston patriot, General Joseph Warren, who fell at Bunker Hill, Francis Marion, the intrepid South Carolina cavalryman, DeSaussure, and many others of equal patriotism and loyalty, were members of the order. The French officers, who came to aid in our struggle for Independence, under the lead of the noble Lafayette, in most instances became Freemasons while here. General Lafayette, with his son, George Washington Lafayette, and his companion, Colonel La Vasseur, all Freemasons, visited Fredericksburg, Virginia, November 27, 1824. This visit was made the occasion of a grand reception. The general was escorted into the town by hundreds of mounted militia, with martial music, amid the greatest display and wildest enthusiasm on the part of the people. On the following day, Lafayette was made an honourary member of the Fredericksburg Lodge, which was organized in 1752. This lodge has the honour of being General George Washington's "Parent Lodge," and the records state that on the fourth day of November, A. L., 5752, the "light of Freemasonry" first burst upon his sight. Visitors to the library of the Grand Lodge of Massachusetts, A. F. & A. M., in the Masonic Temple, Boston, look with deep interest upon the Masonic relics treasured there. Among them is a Masonic apron worn by the Marquis de Lafayette at the laying of the corner-stone of the Bunker Hill Monument, June 17, 1825. Thus, among the other attachments which bound the gallant Frenchman so closely to Washington were the ties of Masonic brotherhood. Another apron to be seen in the Temple, is one that was worn by General Oliver, of Boston, at a lodge meeting when General Washington was present.

It is an interesting fact that the French Lodge, *L'Amenité*, in Philadelphia, was the first to hold a lodge of sorrow in this country, and did so upon the death of Washington in December, 1799. This French Lodge was chartered by the Grand Lodge of Pennsylvania, and included in its membership a large number of Huguenot descendants, one of whom, Simon Chaudron, delivered before the lodge a funeral oration on George Washington, on January 1, 1800. He said in part : — Lodge L'Amenite, Philadelphia

A new spectacle bursts on the eye of philosophy. The whole universe perhaps, for the first time, will unite in offering a tribute of gratitude to the memory of a mortal . . . the modest Hero, whom impartial truth this day proclaims the defender of the human race. . . . He took up arms only for the defense of the soil that gave him birth, and only to prevent its devastation. It was without doubt that, then fighting against Frenchmen, he learnt what powerful aid might be derived from that brave and generous nation for the establishment of liberty in the new world. . . . To us Frenchmen, Oration on Washington who have been so kindly received on these peaceful shores, it belongs to pay distinguished respect to the wisdom of the Hero whom we deplore; we, whom cruel fate has torn from our homes, without suffering us to carry away anything but tears and our innocence, to interest the pity of mankind, should ever hold him in grateful remembrance.

II

Modern Freemasonry owes more than is commonly known to the Huguenot blood. The records show that the four "Immemorial Lodges," which established the Grand Lodge of England, June 24, 1717, had for their leading spirits James Anderson, a Scotch Presbyterian minister of London, and John Theophilus Desaguliers, LL. D., of Christ Church, Oxford, a French Huguenot, and the son of a clergyman. He was a Fellow of the Royal Society, and engaged so earnestly in the "revival" and promotion of Freemasonry that he deserves the title of "The father of modern speculative Freemasonry." The present Grand Lodge of England, which was instituted in London in 1717, is largely indebted to him for its existence. In 1719 Desaguliers was elevated to the throne of the Grand Lodge. He did much to make Freemasonry a living institution for the good of humanity, and his learning and social position gave a prominence to the order which brought to its support noblemen and other men of influence. With others he instituted the "Plan of Charity," which was subsequently developed into what is now known in the Grand Lodge of England as the "Fund of Benevolence." It was from the union of these four lodges that the Fraternity spread into Scotland and Ireland and then to the Continent—France, Germany and Italy. In Germany, Frederick the Great became Grand Master and constituted lodges. In Italy, the affiliation with Freemasonry of the great leaders, Garibaldi, Cavour, Mazzini and Victor Emmanuel, who were active in the abolition of the temporal power of the papacy and the establishment of the kingdom of Italy, was one of the

Grand Lodge
of England
1717

facts which caused a renewal of the attacks of the Roman Catholic Church upon Freemasonry.

III

America was frontiered and bulwarked with the spirit of Freemasonry. A recent writer says: "Out from its living heart sprung those principles and sentiments of true liberty and impartial laws which led to the formulation of the Declaration of Independence. Our Revolutionary fathers held Freemasonry as their Egeria. Its fires purified their patriotic hearts. Franklin shed the luster of his glowing name upon it. It actuated the spirit of Paul Revere on his midnight ride, and its impassioned voice swelled from Bunker Hill to Mount Vernon in links of fraternal patriotism. Very many of the generals of the American Revolution were Brothers of the Mystic Tie. Many of those distinguished men who signed the Declaration of Independence and the Constitution of the United States were members of the Fraternity. The important part Freemasonry played in the struggle for liberty, and the debt of gratitude our glorious Republic owes to the Fraternity, are to-day little known outside the Craft, and but vaguely comprehended by the rank and file within it. Its principles were woven into the warp and woof of our Constitution. The name of Washington stands out in bold relief on the Masonic roster of the United States. He was a type of the order which numbers among its members the best and noblest in the world."

One of the fundamental principles of Freemasonry is that of religious liberty. Out of this principle grows the absolute separation of Church and State which is a fundamental principle of our government. It is this principle which has called down upon Freemasonry the papal decrees, which forbid any Roman Catholic to join this Fraternity on penalty of excommunication. The spirit of Freemasonry is exactly that of the French Protestants and

The Order in America

Freemasons in 1776

Freemasonry Tolerant

the English Puritans and Pilgrims—the spirit that founded our free Republic, in which freedom of conscience is recognized.   Here there is not merely toleration for the varying religious views, but in matters of opinion all are free and equal.   Hence there has been a close union between Protestantism and Freemasonry—both standing for civil and religious liberty and the rights of man.

One of the strong defenses of Freemasonry was called forth by the Encyclical Letter of Pope Leo XIII against "Freemasonry and the Spirit of the Age," dated April 20, 1884.   The unwarranted charges made in this official letter against Freemasonry were answered by "A Reply of Freemasonry in behalf of Humanity," from the Supreme Council, thirty-third degree, of the Ancient Accepted Scottish Rite of Freemasonry, for the Southern Jurisdiction of the United States of America, through Albert Pike, Grand Commander.   We quote from his Allocution these forcible words :

In Defense of Liberty

If the Encyclical Letter of Leo XIII, entitled, from its opening words, *Humanus Genus*, had been nothing more than a denunciation of Freemasonry, I should not have thought it worth replying to.   But under the guise of a condemnation of Freemasonry, and a recital of the enormities and immoralities of the order, in some respects so absurdly false as to be ludicrous, notwithstanding its malignity, it proved to be a declaration of war, and the signal for a crusade, against the rights of men individually and of communities of men as organisms ; against the separation of Church and State, and the confinement of the church within the limits of its legitimate functions ; against education free from sectarian influences ; against the great doctrine upon which, as upon a rock not to be shaken, the foundations of our Republic rest, that "men are superior to institutions and not institutions to men " ; against the right of the people to depose oppressive, cruel and worthless rulers ; against the exercise of the rights of free thought and free speech, and against, not only republican, but all constitutional government.

In the eye of the Papacy it is a crime to belong to an Order thus constituted requiring only belief in God and immortality, and allowing full liberty of conscience in religious belief ; and this the letter of Pope Leo preaches to Roman Catholics living in a Republic, the very

Liberty of Conscience a Crime

corner-stone of which is religious toleration, and which was peopled in large measure, at first, by Puritans, Quakers, Church of England men, and Huguenots.

The gist of the Pope's charge, and the reason for chief dread of its spread among Roman Catholics, may be found in the statement of the Encyclical, that Freemasonry exerts itself for this purpose, that the rule of the Church should be of no weight, that its authority should be as nothing in the State; and for this reason they everywhere assert and insist that sacred and civil ought to be wholly distinct. By this they exclude the most wholesome virtue of the Roman Catholic religion from the laws and administration of a country; and the consequence is that they think whole States ought to be constituted outside of the institutes and precepts of the church.

In other words, the Roman Church protests against that fundamental principle of constitutional government, dear above almost all else to the people of the United States, that Church and State should act each within its proper sphere, and that with the civil government and political administration of affairs the Church should have nothing to do. The people of the United States do not propose to argue that with the Church of Rome.

IV

The first permanent foothold of Freemasonry in North America was made in the town of Boston, Mass., in the year 1733. It was then that under a dispensation issued by the Grand Master of the Grand Lodge of England to Henry Price, Esq., of Boston, the First Lodge of Boston and the Saint John's Grand Lodge were instituted.

First Lodge in Boston 1733

The records of the First Lodge—now called St. John's Lodge—and of the other early lodges in Boston, disclose a large number of Huguenot names. The following names of brethren, evidently of Huguenot blood, are drawn from the lists of members of St. John's lodge, with the year of taking membership affixed.

Philip Audibert,	1741.	Nicholas Faucon,	1805.
Belthazar Bayard,	1748.	Thomas J. Gruchy,	1742.
Francis Beteilhe,	1734.	Francis Johonot,	1742.
Nathaniel Bethune,	1736.	William Joy,	1742.
John Boutin,	1743.	Gabriel Johonot,	1780.
Samuel Cazeneau,	1800.	John Joy,	1762.

Lewis DeBlois,	1753.	Louis A. Lauriat,	1819.
Stephen DeBlois,	1737.	James Montier,	1739.
Alexander Delavoux,	1739.	John Nappier,	1739.
Lewis Dolobartz,	1744.	John Odin,	1750.
Philip Dumaresque,	1764.	Andrew Oliver,	1740.
Thomas Durfey,	1740.	Francis J. Oliver,	1800.
Peter Fabre,	1780.	Peter Oliver,	1749.
Nicholas Farritoe,	1748.	Thomas Vavasour,	1748.

Luke Vardy, 1734.

Francis J. Oliver, 1800, was a Harvard graduate, an eminent merchant and banker, a member of the Legislature, and president of the American Insurance Company and of the City Bank. He was M. W. Grand Master of Masons in Massachusetts during three years, 1817-1819.

Lodge of
St. Andrew
Boston 1756

The Lodge of St. Andrew, in Boston, was chartered by the Grand Lodge of Scotland in 1756. The lists of members of this Lodge present the names of many members of Huguenot blood, among whom are the following :

Isaiah Audibert,	1777.	Peter Nogues, Jr.,	1766.
John Boit,	1780.	Israel Obear,	1761.
Gibbons Bouvé,	1773.	James Oliver,	1782.
Edward Cailleteau,	1763.	Thomas Oliver.	1776.
Isaac DeCosta,	1756.	William Palfrey,	1761.
John DeCosta,	1768.	St. DeMertino Pry,	1779.
William Darracott,	1766.	Col. Henry Purkitt	
Moses Deshon,	1761.	(Purruquet),	1799.
George DeFrance,	1782.	Paul Revere,	1761.
Philip Lewis,	1757.	Rev. James Sabine,	1823.
Philip Marett,	1762.	Andrew Sigourney,	1766.
Benjamin Mayhew,	1769.	Andrew Sigourney,	1794.
Robert Molineux,	1793.	Elisha Sigourney,	1789.

In this Lodge's records appears the name of Fosdick, 1768, which links the author's family with the Huguenot exiles, and in some measure explains his personal interest in the subject of which this volume treats.

Andrew
Sigourney

It is a noteworthy fact that Andrew Sigourney, 1794, was the founder of the first benevolent fund of its kind

established by Freemasons.   When he was Grand Treasurer of the Grand Lodge of Massachusetts, 1810–19, he
gave his last year's salary, amounting to one hundred
and seventy dollars, to found a Charity Fund for the
Fraternity, to be used for the benefit of its members, or
of widows and orphans, in case of need.

V

The name of Paul Revere is as familiar to the **Paul Revere**
present generation as household words. His Masonic
career began in the Lodge of St. Andrew in 1761. In
1782 he was a charter member of a new Lodge which
took the name of " Rising States." He was Grand Master of Masons in Massachusetts for three years, 1795-1797,
during which time he signed the charters of twenty-
three new Lodges, all of which are now in existence except two.

Of Paul Revere as a Freemason, this is said by Charles
Ferris Gettemy, in *The True Story of Paul Revere*, just
issued : " In none of the civic activities of the time was
he more prominent than in the affairs of the Masonic fraternity.   One of the most eminent and widely known
Masons of the Revolutionary era, he, in the language of a Masonic eulogist (G. Ellis Reed, W. M. of
Revere Lodge), 'served his country and his beloved Fraternity with a spirit that should inspire every Brother ;
a spirit composed of the three great essentials, freedom,
fervency, and zeal.'   ' In the Green Dragon Tavern,' says
E. Bentley Young in his oration at the Centennial celebration of Columbian Lodge in 1895, 'where he first saw
Masonic light, he met his patriotic Brethren in secrecy to
devise means for impeding the operations of the British,
then in possession of the city.   Masonry and patriotism
were identified in his person and in those of his compatriots who met him in retirement.'

" Entering Masonry through St. Andrew's Lodge, September 4, 1760, he maintained a zealous interest in the

affairs of the fraternity for the remainder of his life, filling the high office of Grand Master of the Massachusetts Grand Lodge in 1795, 1796, and 1797.   One of the most picturesque ceremonials of his career, and indeed of the early years of the constitutional history of Massachusetts, occurred during the first term of his grand mastership : the laying of the corner-stone of the new State House— the 'Bullfinch front' as it was called in later years—on Beacon Hill.   The authorities having requested the Masonic Order to participate in the dedication exercises, the various lodges assembled in the Representatives' Hall of the Old State House on State Street, and, with the state officials, marched to the Old South Meeting House, where an oration appropriate to the occasion was delivered by George Blake.   These exercises over, the procession re-formed and marched to Beacon Hill.   Arriving at the site of the new capitol, the stone, being duly squared, levelled, and plumbed, Governor Samuel Adams made a brief address, to which Grand Master Revere for the Masons responded :

" 'Worshipfull Brethren.   I congratulate you on this auspicious day; —when the Arts and Sciences are establishing themselves in our happy country, a Country distinguished from the rest of the World, by being a Government of Laws, where Liberty has found a safe and secure abode, and where her sons are determined to support and protect her. Brethren, we are called this day by our honourable & patriotic Governor, his Excellency Samuel Adams, to assist in laying the corner-stone of a building to be erected for the use of the Legislative and Executive branches of Government of this Commonwealth.   May we, my Brethren, so square our actions thro life as to show to the World of Mankind, that we mean to live within the compass of Good Citizens, that we wish to stand upon a level with them, that when we part we may be admitted into the Temple where Reigns Silence and Peace.' "

" It is utterly impossible," commented the unenterprising *Columbian Centinel*, " to do justice to the scene which presented itself on this brilliant occasion."

When Washington retired to private life the Grand

Lodge of Massachusetts sent him a fraternal greeting signed by Grand Master Revere, and upon his death the Massachusetts Masons arranged a mock funeral parade, Revere being one of the pall-bearers. A memorial urn carried in the procession was cared for many years by Revere at his home. Revere, with John Warren and Josiah Bartlett, sent a letter on behalf of the Grand Lodge dated January 11, 1800, to the widow of Washington, requesting a lock of the dead statesman's hair, to be kept as an "invaluable relique of the Hero and Patriot." The request was granted, and the memento has remained to this day one of the cherished possessions of the Grand Lodge, preserved in a golden urn made by Paul Revere.

Friendship Lodge, instituted in Boston in 1793, contained a considerable French element. One of the Masters of the Lodge was Le Barbier Du Plessis, whose name revives memories of that great Huguenot Prime Minister who would have saved France from shame and loss had the King but followed his advice instead of that given by the ecclesiastics. Other members of Friendship Lodge were Le Charles Descard, Preslin Janeau, George de France, M. D., Sy. Prea, John Beteau, and Messrs. Truene, D'Amour and Jeaureau. *Friendship Lodge Boston 1793*

John Jutau became the Master of Perfect Union Lodge, instituted in 1781, which was distinctively a French Lodge. In 1785, Mr. Jutau was Senior Grand Warden of the Grand Lodge of Massachusetts, in which were enrolled also the names of William Truan, Andrew Demarest, Dr. St. Medard, Peter La Mercier, and others. *Perfect Union Lodge Boston 1781*

There was still another Lodge, the Harmonic, instituted December 8, 1792, but it was not exclusively French. The first Master was George Gideon.

Lewis Frederick Delesdernier was a member of Warren Lodge in Machias, Maine. The Lodge was instituted September 10, 1778. His parents were Huguenots. He was visited by Albert Gallatin in 1780.

The Huguenots who settled in Boston, as earlier chapters

have made clear, became citizens of influence and much respectability. Some of them were leaders in the mercantile, social and religious circles. Here they entered into an atmosphere of liberty and opportunity which they wisely used. They established themselves so firmly and well in this community that their descendants—men of integrity and influence—remain to this day. In the town of Boston, and later in the city, as well as in the Masonic Lodges, to which so many of them belonged, they were active and useful, being ever outspoken and zealous on the side of toleration, liberty and equality.

L'AMENITÉ LODGE, No. 73, PHILADELPHIA

February 22, 1800, was a day set apart by Congress as a "Washington Day" throughout the United States. It was observed in Philadelphia by the Freemasons. Nine lodges participated in the exercises at Philadelphia. L'Amenité Lodge, No. 73, held a special open lodge of its own and Brother Simon Chaudron was the orator. The lodge was appropriately draped, and a catafalque in the centre of the lodge room was surrounded by 300 lights.

L'Amenité Lodge was organized by French refugees, and chartered May 20, 1797. Its first officers were: W. M.—Tanguy de la Beissiere; S. W.—Gabriel Decombaz; J. W.—Armand Caignet. Among the members were Abbé La Grange, Belin Gardette, and Simon Chaudron, the orator of February 22, 1800. Chaudron delivered his address in the presence of the Grand Lodge of Pennsylvania, and it was the first Masonic eulogy, in the French language, that was ever spoken upon Washington. The address was printed in the French and English languages. In view of the strained relations at the time between France and the United States, Chaudron's address had much political significance. L'Amenité went out of existence in 1823.

CHAPTER IV

THE ORDER OF THE CINCINNATI

I T was at a critical juncture in affairs that the Order
of the Cincinnati was formed for a specific and patri- Order of the
Cincinnati
otic purpose. Washington himself was a leader in
the movement. When the Revolutionary War was finally
over and the army was about to be disbanded, Washington had his headquarters at Newburgh, in the building Organization
and Obje
which is now preserved and occupied as a museum.
General Knox, one of his favourite officers, was in command of West Point, a few miles below on the Hudson.
At Newburgh Washington made his farewell address to
the army. When it came to disbanding, however, there
was trouble, because Congress had left the officers and
men without pay, and the spirit of mutiny was rife. In-
flammatory speeches were made at Newburgh, and the
mutineers threatened to band themselves together and go
about the country overawing the people, as a means of
gaining their dues. This situation, which was serious,
led Washington, Knox and others to conceive the Order
of the Cincinnati as a means of checking this mutinous
movement. A meeting was held at the headquarters of
General Steuben, at the VerPlanck homestead, Mount
Gulian—a homestead founded, by the way, by the Huguenot Romboud, of whom we shall speak elsewhere. At May 13, 1783
this meeting the new society was born, May 13, 1783.

From an interesting history of the Order, written by
William E. VerPlanck, a descendant of an ancient family,
we derive the facts which follow. Preliminary meetings
were held near New Windsor, a suburb of Newburgh, by
the American officers who were in sympathy with the
principles of the Order. Knox was perhaps chiefly in-

Washington
and Knox

strumental in the organization.   The original articles are
still preserved.   The object of the society was "to commemorate the success of the war against Great Britain
and the reciprocal advantages which would ensue to the
colonies, thereby establishing themselves as sovereign and
independent states, to perpetuate sentiments of patriotism, benevolence and brotherly love and the memory of
the hardships of the war experienced in common."   The

Original
Articles

articles also declare that "the officers of the American
Army do hereby in the most solemn manner associate
themselves into one Society of Friends to endure as long
as they shall endure, or any of their oldest male posterity,
and in failure thereof the collateral branches who may be
judged worthy of becoming its supporters and members."

The Name

"The officers of the American army having been taken
from the citizens of America possess high veneration for
the character of that illustrious Roman, Lucius Quintus
Cincinnatus, and being resolved to follow his example by
returning to their citizenship, they think they may with
propriety denominate themselves the Society of the Cincinnati."

Then follows a statement of their principles which are
of an exalted and patriotic character.   Provision was
made for the establishment of state societies, and also of
district or local societies.   In order that relief might be
immediately extended, it was provided that "each officer
shall deliver to the treasurer of the State Society one
month's pay, which shall remain forever to the use of the

Benevolent
Aim

State Society, the interest only of which, if necessary, to
be appropriated to the relief of the unfortunate."   It was
also provided that "all officers of the American army—
as well as those who have resigned with honour after
three years' service in the capacity of officers, have the
right" to membership.   Provision was made also for an
Order "by which its members shall be known and distinguished, which shall be a medal of gold of a proper
size to receive the emblems and suspended by a deep

blue ribbon two inches wide edged with white descriptive of the Union of America and France ; the principal figure: Cincinnatus—three senators presenting him with a sword."

The French connection came from the fact that honour- French Honourary ary membership in the new Order was conferred on Lafayette and the other French officers both of the army and navy who had so nobly aided in the struggle for Independence. This number included "His Excellency, The Chevalier de la Luzerne, Minister Plenipotentiary," the Counts D'Estaing, De Grasse, De Barras, and "His Excellency, the Count De Rochambeau."

The first to sign the articles was Washington, the second General Heath, the third General Lincoln, and the fourth General Greene, with Generals Knox, Putnam, and thirty other officers following. Thus began an Order that has survived, and been not only a benevolent organization, but one deeply interested in public affairs. Washington was the first president-general of the Society, and held the office until his death, when he was succeeded by Hamilton. Thus the second president was of Huguenot blood. Naturally the Society was a warm supporter of Washington in his terms as president, and in consequence became identified politically with the Federal party. It was six years after the organization of the Cincinnati that the Society of Tammany, or the Columbian Order, was formed in New York, this being at first a benevolent society, but soon becoming political, and antagonizing the Order of the Cincinnati.

In May, 1883, the Society of the Cincinnati celebrated Centennial Celebration 1883 its centennial at the old Gulian mansion where it was born a hundred years before. The mansion had been enlarged, but the original part remains, and the room in which the Order was organized has been carefully preserved and is known as the Cincinnati room. Newburgh and West Point were also visited by the celebrating party. Five or six of the original state societies survive, though the work of the Order was long since accomplished.

CHAPTER V

FRENCH LEADERS IN REFORM AND IN INVENTION

I

Governor LaFollette

HOW the Huguenot blood has diffused itself through the country is illustrated in the case of Robert Marion LaFollette of Wisconsin, one of the political reformers, who conceived it to be his mission to break up a great political machine, and as a result met and defeated an imposing array of hostile forces in his party. It is not our purpose here to enter into his campaigns or decide as to merit in disputed cases. But it is in point that we find in this champion of the people against monopoly a descendant of the same refugee stock that in almost every instance was on the side of liberty and right.

Wisconsin Boy of Kentucky Huguenot Stock

Governor LaFollette was born on a farm in Dane County, Wisconsin, June 14, 1855. His father was a Kentucky bred French Huguenot; his mother Scotch-Irish. Again and again we have met that strong combination, the same that shone out in Alexander Hamilton. The family moved to the West, where the son was to find his opportunity and make his mark in public life. The death of the father occurred when Robert was less than a year old, but the resolute mother kept her little family of four children together, and at fourteen "Little Bob," as his followers call him, became the working head. He remained on the farm till he was nineteen, then sold it and moved to Madison, where the State University attracted him. The French blood in him "stirred to sentiment and the boy thrilled for glory." He had a decided gift of oratory, and won the college contests and

debates with ease.   After graduation he went to work in
a law office, and in five months was admitted to the bar,
which indicates his remarkable mental facility and grasp.
In 1880 he began to practice, but very soon was running   In Public Life
for office.   Public life seemed to possess for him irresistible attraction.   He won the office—that of district attorney—and a wife, a college classmate, one result of
co-education and a not uncommon one.   He made an
excellent record in his first office, but already the machine politicians did not like him, because his methods
differed from theirs, and he had broken into politics
without asking the consent of the party powers.   He developed a remarkable talent for getting at and getting a
hold on the people, so that they would vote for him
whether he had the machine endorsement or not.   By
and by LaFollette clashed decidedly with the State party
"boss," and then he determined to stand or fall for himself, and to stand.   That was the Scotch pertinacity, and
with the French frankness and geniality it gained the
day for him.   The story of his successes has much of romance and strenuousness in it, but always LaFollette
won, and in office was what he promised the people he
would be, their friend, honest and true.   He went to
Congress, because he made up his Scotch mind and set
his French wit to work to do it ; and then he determined
to be governor of Wisconsin, and governor he became,
although the machine said he never could be elected.
From that high place he passed to the United States
Senate.   Whatever his future may be, this western descendant of the Huguenots has made his name known
far and wide, and honourably known as a public man
engaged in doing his duty in every office to which the
people, who believe in him, called him.   Certainly the
quality of reform runs in the Huguenot blood to the latest
generation.

II

While less noted publicly than the statesmen and soldiers of French blood who rendered such signal service to America, none of them all deserve to rank higher in the scale of usefulness and benefaction than Thomas Blanchard. His ancestors were among the exiles, known as Gabriel Bernon's colony, who undertook to found Oxford, in what is now Worcester County. This county is distinguished, as the late Senator Hoar wrote, as the very home and centre of invention. "I do not think any other place in the world, of the same size, can boast of so many great inventions as the region covered by a circle within a radius of twelve miles, of which the centre is the city of Worcester." To name but three of many, in that circle were born Eli Whitney, inventor of the cotton gin that doubled the value of every acre of cotton producing land at once, and revolutionized one of the leading industries of the world; Elias Howe, inventor of the sewing machine, one of the greatest boons ever known to woman, which made a new household economy possible; and Thomas Blanchard, subject of this sketch, inventor of the machine for the turning of irregular forms. Senator Hoar regarded this as the most important and difficult of all the inventions named, notwithstanding the vast value of the other two.

The story of Thomas Blanchard, Huguenot descendant, has recently been told by Hon. Alfred S. Roe, author of many historical monographs. We make free use of it in this connection, glad that a man of such inventive ability as Thomas Blanchard can find the wider recognition he deserves. He should have place among the first inventors because he is credited with the discovery of a new principle in motion, that of the eccentric. There is scarcely a machine shop in the world to-day that does not in some shape have instances of this French-American's genius.

After the disastrous ending of the colonizing attempt at Oxford, a branch of the Blanchard family settled finally in Sutton, where on a farm Thomas was born,

June 24, 1788. But he had no liking for farming. He
was a born mechanic, and the despair of his industrious,
plodding father. Owing to an unfortunate impediment
of speech, which in later years he overcame, the lad was
thrown much upon his own resources as a child. His
ingenuity was early shown, as when he secured charcoal
from the home fireplace for his experiments, and at thir- Apple-Paring
teen made an apple-paring machine which revolutionized Machine
the drying of that much-valued fruit. At eighteen, a
brother having established a tack factory in Millbury,
Thomas was transferred from the farm to help in the extremely monotonous occupation of heading each object
by the blow of a hammer. It did not take his ingenious
mind long to elaborate a machine which made tacks
more rapidly than the ticking of a watch, and also made
them better than those made by hand—a machine in
which no essential improvements were made in more
than twenty years. Experts declared it almost perfect Tack Machine
from the start. This was pretty good for a stuttering
schoolboy, so long the butt of his Sutton associates.
This tack machine was sold for $5,000, only a fraction of
its real value ; and from the proceeds Thomas established
a shop in which he was able to continue his inventive
work unhindered.

Up to this time, during scores of years there had been
no advance in the polishing of gun barrels. The rounded
part could be readily reached, but the flattened portions,
those at the breech where the stock was added, had to be
worked by hand, and it cost a dollar apiece properly to
finish them. There was an armory in Millbury, and the
proprietor learning of the genius in the confines of that
very town, sent for him and let him know the needs of
the occasion. Glancing along the lathe and beginning a
monotonous whistle, as was his wont when in a study, he Gun-Barrel
soon evolved a simple improvement in the shape of a Cam
cam motion, and the making of gun-barrels was simpli-
fied forever.

"Well done," says Mr. Waters. "I shouldn't wonder if you yet invented a machine for turning gun-stocks."

"W-w-ell, I'll t-try," was the laconic reply.

A train of thought had been set in motion which in time brought out the machine for turning irregular forms. His success in the Millbury armory soon secured a call for him to the government establishment in Springfield, where he set the lathes in order, all the time apparently dwelling on the words of Colonel Waters. When his work in Springfield was done and he was driving back to his Worcester County home, he much surprised certain people by exclaiming, as he drove along, "I've got it! I've got it! I've got it!" They at once pronounced him crazy, as no doubt those Syracusans did who saw the naked philosopher coursing through their streets, shouting "Eureka!"

For two years the world saw little of the young mechanic, for he shut himself in his shop and there pursued his experiments until he was able to tell Colonel Waters that what the latter in pleasantry had hinted at, had become an actuality. To be sure, it was only a miniature machine, but it was so evidently practical that other workmen were called in and a complete lathe was erected, thus giving to his native county and to the town of Millbury the credit of the first machine for the turning of irregular forms. Meanwhile, Washington had heard of his success, and he was requested to set his lathe up in the Springfield Arsenal, a request with which he complied, and it remained there long enough to have another similar one made, when the original was returned to Millbury, where it continued in constant use for more than twenty years.

International Fame of His Invention

England heard of the invention, and sent over representatives to examine and report. They were astonished at what they saw, and reported accordingly, but John Bull could not be convinced so easily, and a second messenger was sent with tough pieces of oak, thinking them too hard for any mere machine. Much to the astonishment of the Englishman, the specimens of hard wood were transformed at once into the most perfect of stocks. The report was accepted, and $40,000 worth of the lathes were forthwith ordered. As is usual with all great inventions, there was little disposition to allow Blanchard to enjoy any great results from his labours, and he himself stated in Washington, before a Congressional committee, when he applied for the second renewal of his patent, that thus far he had received little more than his board and clothes for what he had done, while litigation had cost him more than $100,000. Fortunately for the inventor, Rufus Choate was then in Congress, and his wit and wisdom coming to the rescue of the genius, he secured a renewal of the patent. To show the possibilities of his machine to turn irregular forms, he actually set up in the national capitol one of the lathes, and there in the presence of all who cared to look, using plaster figures as models, he turned in marble the heads of Webster, Clay, and others, far more exactly than the hand of an artist could fashion them. The witty Choate said Blanchard had "turned the heads of congressmen," and so he had, and they were sufficiently appreciative to grant him what he asked.

Convincing Congress

The foregoing invention alone would have given Blanchard immortality, but he did not stop here. He made steamboats of such light draught that they could run over rapids and shoals, and he invented methods of bending wood so as not to impair in the least its native strength. He could bend a shingle at right angles and leave it as strong as before. His invention was particularly valuable in the bending of timber for the knees of vessels. Beginning to realize on the many inventions he had made, he took a house in Boston, and there, in comfort and dignity, spent the remaining years of his life. Middle-aged people can remember when the old-fashioned right-angled slate frames gave way to a continuous frame with rounded

corners. Many such people may now learn for the first
time that each and every frame thus employed had paid
a small royalty to Thomas Blanchard, a royalty, however, in the aggregate amounting to many thousands of
dollars. It is said that the manufacturer for whom the
invention was made refused to pay Blanchard two thousand dollars outright for the invention, preferring to pay
him a royalty of five per cent. His feelings may be
imagined when he paid over to the genius more than two
thousand dollars the first year.

A World
Benefactor

He improved the manner of making the handles of
shovels, saving material and making a stronger handle.
The principle of his inventions was applied in so many
ways that to-day the world is full of what Blanchard did.
Millions of boot and shoe lasts are made every year, and
every one is a tribute to the Sutton boy. To drop out for
a single day, from the factories and machine shops of the
world, the inventions and applications of Thomas Blanchard, would throw the mechanical world into inextricable
confusion. When the nation gets tired of erecting statues
to soldiers, perhaps it will remember the men who helped
to make life worth living.

Blanchard lived till April 16, 1864, when he ceased
from earth, and his mortal remains were borne to Mount
Auburn, where hero-worshippers may find his grave on
Spruce Avenue ; his monument being surmounted by a
bust of the great inventor, while upon the base is a medal-
lion or relief of the lathe which gave him his world-wide
reputation.

CHAPTER VI

HUGUENOT HOME LIFE IN AMERICA

I

THIS subject is treated in a very interesting manner by Helen Evertson Smith in a volume entitled *Colonial Days and Ways*. We make such use of her work as will give our readers a picture of the home life, customs, and amusements of the French in New Rochelle and at other points. This will also show the influence which the French had upon their neighbours. The art of living happily seems to be a native possession of the French, while it is not so with the Anglo-Saxon. His disposition is to take himself and life too seriously. That was the fault and defect of the Puritan; though it must be said that this is a fault far less grave in its consequences than the modern one of not taking life seriously enough. The Huguenots hit a happy mean for the most part, and infused joy into their environment.

The Art of Living Happily

Whether they had been rich or poor in France, there were few of the Huguenot refugees who were not poor when they reached America. Notable exceptions have been cited, like those of Gabriel Bernon, but they were the exceptions. Whatever their fortunes, however, the refugees were gentle, trained in many arts, and possessed of the keen perceptions, the courtesy, and the easy adaptability of their race. Home life among them was different from that of any of the other colonists, because they came from a land more advanced in some things than either Holland or England.

Gentle and Courteous

The Puritan was keen-witted, with rigid notions of morality, and a harsh spirit towards those who disagreed with him, particularly in religion. The conditions of his

Three Races Contrasted

407

life were hard, but full of mental, moral and physical health. He despised no handicraft, neglected no means of cultivation, shirked no duty (nor did he permit any one else to do so, if he could help it), and fought his way upward, unhasting, unresting, honestly, persistently. The Dutchman was milder than the Puritan, but as stiff-necked, and an inborn republican as well as an educated Calvinist. Slower, narrower, more prejudiced, he was less agressive. To his commercial and industrial instincts our country owes much of its prosperity.

The Huguenot—to complete the comparison between these three races which came together in the formation of the colonial life and character—was devout, less ambitious, affectionate of heart, artistic, cultivated, adaptable and also highly endowed with the commercial instincts **Characteristic Cheerfulness** and skilled capacities. He brought to America the arts, accomplishments and graces of the highest civilization then known, together with a sweet cheerfulness all his own. Not a colony or a class but was ameliorated by his influence, and consciously or unconsciously, we all love him. His was, indeed, essentially a lovable nature. No character could be truer or nobler or at bottom probably more affectionate than the Puritan, but the manifestation of qualities was very different. The French did not think it a shame or crime to show freely the love they felt. They were natural where others were restrained.

It is certain, from the nature of things, that the home lives of all these different bands of colonists must have **Differences in the Home Life** differed widely. None had luxuries and few had comforts, as we now understand these terms, but each had some possessions, some ways, some deficiencies, and some attainments which belonged to none of the others. Improved conditions came rapidly, and in improvements one would be sure to find the French in the lead.

II

As we have intimated, although most of the refugee

Huguenots had been prosperous in France, and not a few had been wealthy and influential noblemen and citizens, not many had been able to take much money away with them—the circumstances of their flight precluded that; but they had all brought energy, industry, thrift, and power of endurance, as well as that truly delightful birthright of their nation, an invincible lightness of heart, while many of them also possessed skill in some hitherto peculiarly French handicraft, or in mechanical methods of unusual scope; and others had equally high talent in the professions, in trade, and in civil affairs.

Like the Plymouth Pilgrims, the Huguenots came without any backing of national trade or class interest; but while the first came to preserve civil and religious rights, the latter were exiles who had lost their rights and fled for life, and were of all social grades, embracing a few noblemen, a larger number of the class of gentlemen, or the lesser nobility, and professional men, merchants, bankers, manufacturers and artisans. In spite of previous social conditions, the oneness of the French was a wonder to the English and Dutch, who kindly welcomed them. The persecuted were bound together by a common blood, language, peril and faith. In their little settlement at New Rochelle there was for many years as near an approach to apostolic ways of living as has been seen, probably, since apostolic days. They had all things in common, cared for their own poor, and formed a brotherhood such as Christianity was intended to produce the world over. Every household became a little industrial colony. Those who had never before laboured now learned to do so, and hardships were cheerfully borne.

Daily life in the Huguenot household was probably less toilsome than was common among other colonists. In- telligent, industrial and resourceful, there was a kind of co-operation among the French. Equality of living and enjoyment prevailed. The conditions were naturally trying for many years to those who had been gently born and nurtured in France, but the best was made of existing circumstances, and the people of New Rochelle soon were distinguished by the amount of comforts and even luxuries they gathered about them.   Their homes, to judge by the specimens which remain in New Rochelle, were neither large nor fine, but they were substantial and as comfortable as was then possible.   Tradition says that the first to utilize the remnants of worn-out garments by cutting them into strips and weaving them into carpets were the French.   The rag carpet was in its day an advance agent of comfort and culture ; and one may recall the Connecticut deacon who asked Mrs. Lyman Beecher, who was the first to introduce a carpet into Litchfield, if she thought she could " have all thet an' heaven too ? " Among the earliest importations of the French settlers were the spinning wheels and looms of better quality than were previously known here.   Immigrants from fruit-growing and wine-making districts of France brought grafts and roots, and naturalized most of the hardier va-

Taste in Decorations rieties.   A few were able to import hangings, mirrors, china and furniture of rare beauty ; but in general they possessed only those articles of furniture which could be made here.   However humble these might be in themselves, they would surely be made decorative by little touches which only the French hand could give, just as the same delicate touches would be seen in the toilets of the women.

Where the English and Dutch dyed linen yarn of heavy quality and wove it into ugly stripes and checks for bed and window curtains, the French used either white linen or that with but one colour, dainty shades of light blue or dusky green or a subdued gold colour made by dyes of which they had brought the secret with them being preferred.   These linens, made into hangings bordered by an embroidered vine or arabesque design in white upon the gold, or of varied colours upon the all

E. Hamilton

Sa. Jay

Jno Bayard

Saml Provoost

white, were delicately beautiful, and became heirlooms in many a family.

"The bedroom of my mother's grandmother L'Estrange," says the author, "has often been described to me. The floor was painted as nearly as possible to match the subdued gold of the linen hangings. The ceilings and side walls were whitewashed with lime. The windows and dressing-tables were hung with tastefully arranged draperies, bordered with a grapevine pattern embroidered in white, and further trimmed at the edge with a knitted fringe of white linen yarn. The tall four-posted bedstead of carved mahogany was provided with a tester, with long draw-curtains. Over the high and downy bed lay a fringed and embroidered coverlet of the same linen. An immense stuffed chair, running easily upon wooden globes the size of billiard balls, which were the precursors of the modern caster, had a very high back and side wings, against which the head might rest. The linen yarn for the draperies of this room was all said to have been spun by the first Mme. L'Estrange and her daughters, and it was afterwards woven under their direction and embroidered by themselves."

A French Colonial Bedroom

The cultivated taste and the dainty arts brought from France made the homes of the Huguenots much more attractive in appearance than those of the other colonists, even though the latter might have far more wealth. The same difference was manifest in dress. The Frenchwoman's fine eye for colour, and her delicate skill with brush, needle and bobbin, united to produce more attractive results. Similar touches of taste and skill appeared everywhere, and gave distinction to the Huguenot homes, whatever the owner's social standing in France. As neat as their Dutch neighbours, they devised labour-saving methods to maintain perfect cleanliness without being slaves to it. As liberal as the English, they were far more economical, and by their skill in cooking they rendered palatable and digestible the coarsest fare. They

Home Attractions

could not equal the Dutch women in rich dishes, sweet cakes and preserves, nor the English in roasts and pastries, but in wholesome dishes for daily consumption they far excelled both, and particularly in bread making. They were the first to introduce yeast, where leaven was the common resort.   We owe to them delicately flavoured soups, the light omelettes, and the delicious entrées, besides the rolls and buns.

III

A Hard Lot for Loyal Souls

In spite of temperamental light-heartedness, the Huguenot had a peculiarly hard lot.   He was not a voluntary colonist, but a refugee.   Now there is no more patriotic people than the French.   They love their country and homes and customs.   The Huguenot was ready to sacrifice everything but his religion in order to remain in his own land.   An exile, his feeling towards the government and Church which had made him an outcast was bitter. It was due to this that the Huguenot refugee ceased to speak his own language as speedily as possible, and sought to forget France and the past.   To the land of their adoption the Huguenots transferred to the full all the inborn loyalty of their characters.   During Great Britain's long wars with France the Huguenot descendants, in England or the colonies, bore their part in the arm service.   Many of the best families in New Rochelle sent representatives to fight the French and Indians. The Huguenots made loyal and noble American citizens.

Change of Names

The abandonment of connection with France is shown clearly in the change of names, to which reference has elsewhere been made.   The spelling was apt to follow the pronunciation of the new friends and neighbours.   Thus Bonne Passe (Good Thrust, a name of honour when good swordsmen were valued) became shortened to Bon Pas, then changed to Bunpas, followed by Bumpus, and finally contracted to Bump.   L'Estrange was known as Streing, Strange, Strang, and sometimes Strong.

Doctrinally the Huguenots and Puritans were the same, but in practice they differed not a little. The Puritan was a very strict keeper of the Sabbath, beginning at sunset of Saturday a twenty-four hours' abstinence from any avoidable work, as well as from any pleasure save that which his devoutness found in religious services. The Huguenot Sunday began and ended as now. Like Calvin himself, the refugees did not think it necessary to avoid all pleasant things on Sunday more than on other days, and all who had friends living near the wayside stopped in to visit them as they returned from church ; for the Sunday time that was not devoted to church services and to an hour of catechizing at home was not considered as ill spent in cheerful social intercourse. In Calvinistic Switzerland, as in Roman Catholic France, it had been customary to indulge, after church hours, in any form of innocent amusement. The Huguenots seem to have drawn the line just short of this. But on week days their national joyousness and light-heartedness was bound to display itself in as many ways as circumstances would permit. Tableaux and little comedies were frequent, while dancing was the expected amusement in most households at every evening gathering, and these took place as often as possible. This made the pleasure of the home life in marked contrast to much of the severer life around them, and drew upon the Huguenots many reproaches. Children were instructed with a degree of gentleness and consideration quite in contrast with the sterner ways of the English or Dutch. Cheerfulness and even gaiety was the rule. A gloomy Huguenot was an anomaly to be pitied and apologized for. Such happy dispositions as were common among the French produced a very great impression, and their customs did much to break down an unnatural restraint that could not exist permanently without defeating the high ends aimed at by zealous and godly people.

The French boarding and day schools for young ladies

The French
Schools

which were established in New Rochelle were eagerly pat-
ronized by the English and Dutch, whose daughters
hitherto had possessed few educational advantages.
These schools were the originals of the young ladies'
seminaries and fitting schools, or finishing schools,
which held the field until the day of women's colleges,
which was ushered in by a Huguenot descendant—Matthew Vassar, founder of Vassar College. From the first
the French language was taught, and all the "ladylike
accomplishments" of the time were imparted. English
teachers were employed to teach the grammatical use of
their own tongue, written and spoken ; but it may be
imagined that this was not considered as of nearly as high
importance as the more showy accomplishments, which
could be acquired at these schools only. These accomplishments included enough of music to enable a young
woman to play a little for dancing, or to warble a few
songs in her fresh sweet tones to the accompaniment of
the spinet ; enough of French to read it easily, write it
fairly well, and hold a not too monosyllabic conversation.
Then much was made of instruction in the arts of painting and embroidery, and more of that truly high art,
gentle manners—the manners not only of persons of gentle

Graceful
Accomplish-
ments

birth, but of those so early taught by precept and example
that their graces seem to have been born with them, a part
of their very selves. The pupils were taught how to avoid
all awkwardness of movement or carriage ; how to bear
themselves gracefully erect ; how to enter and leave a
room, to greet properly all ages and conditions, to ar-
range and preside at a dinner table with elegance, to
dress with taste and effect, and to dance gracefully. In-
cidentally with all these things, a great deal of valuable
instruction was given in the finer graces of courtesy and
courteous speech, and all that gentle consideration for
others which is at once the flower and root of good breeding. Who shall say that this education was not fitting,
and that the colleges of to-day, with their mannishness,

do not lack some of the feminine elements which tend to produce rounded womanhood and to make woman a home queen.

The Huguenots endeavoured to transmit to their children the traditions of politeness they had brought from France. Even in their games and amusements good manners were taught, and certainly the delightful traits of courtesy and thoughtful kindness and fine breeding have persisted in the French Protestant blood, and are notable in the fine families which perpetuate the stock in our land.

Manners Transmitted

*Fraunce's Tavern Broad and Pearl Streets
Originally the DeLancey Homestead*

CHAPTER VII

AN EARLY FRENCH ESTIMATE OF AMERICAN CHARACTER

What is an American ?

THE American character is a composite, representing many nationalities. In the early blend there were four distinct types—English, Scotch, French and Dutch. What we commonly call the Americans, with reference to the early colonists and their descendants—using the term thus in a restricted sense—came from the intermixture of these stocks or from the unmixed blood. It will be interesting to read the estimate which a French-American colonist gives of America and the Americans in the last decade of the eighteenth century. The following extract is taken from the *Letters from an American Farmer*, published in London in 1782, the author being J. Hector St. John de Crévecœur :

Answer by a French-American Farmer

"I wish I could be acquainted with the feelings and thoughts which must agitate the heart and present themselves to the mind of an enlightened Englishman, when he first lands on this continent (America). . . . Here he sees the industry of his native country displayed in a new manner. . . . Here he beholds fair cities, substantial villages, extensive fields, an immense country filled with decent houses, good roads, orchards, meadows, and bridges, where an hundred years ago all was wild, woody and uncultivated ! . . . He is arrived on a new continent ; a modern society offers itself to his contemplation, different from what he had hitherto seen. It is not composed, as in Europe, of great lords who possess everything, and of a herd of people who have nothing. Here are no aristocratical families, no courts, no kings, no bishops, no ecclesiastical dominion, no invisible

416

power giving to a few a very visible one; no great manufacturers employing thousands, no great refinements of
luxury. The rich and the poor are not so far removed
from each other as they are in Europe. Some few towns
excepted, we are all tillers of the earth, from Nova
Scotia to West Florida. We are a people of cultivators, **An Industrious Free
People**
scattered over an immense territory, communicating with
each other by means of good roads and navigable rivers,
united by the silken bands of mild government, all re-
specting the laws, without dreading their power, because
they are equitable. We are all animated with the spirit
of an industry which is unfettered and unrestrained, because each person works for himself. . . . A pleasing uniformity of decent competence appears throughout
our habitations. The meanest of our log-houses is a dry
and comfortable habitation. Lawyer or merchant are
the fairest titles our towns afford; that of a farmer, is the
only appellation of the rural inhabitants of our country.
. . . Here man is free as he ought to be; nor is this
pleased equality so transitory as many others are. Many
ages will not see the shores of our great lakes replenished
with inland nations, nor the unknown bounds of North
America entirely peopled. Who can tell how far it ex-
tends? Who can tell the millions of men whom it will
feed and contain? for no European foot has as yet trav-
ersed half the extent of this mighty continent!

"The next wish of this traveller will be to know
whence came all these people? They are a mixture of **A Blood
Mixture**
English, Scotch, Irish, French, Dutch, Germans, and
Swedes. From this promiscuous breed, that race now
called Americans has arisen. . . .

"By what invisible power has this surprising meta- **Metamorphosis of Law
and Liberty**
morphosis been performed? By that of the laws and that
of their industry. The laws, the indulgent laws, protect
them as they arrive, stamping on them the symbol of
adoption; they receive ample rewards for their labours;
these accumulated rewards procure them land; those

lands confer on them the title of freemen, and to that
title every benefit is affixed which man can possibly require. This is the great operation daily performed by
our laws. From whence proceed these laws? From our
government. Whence that government? It is derived
from the original genius and strong desire of the people
ratified and confirmed by the crown. This is the great
chain which links us all, this is the picture which every
province exhibits. . . .

"He is an American, who leaving behind him all his
ancient prejudices and manners, receives new ones from
the new mode of life he has embraced, the new government he obeys and the new rank he holds. He becomes
an American by being received in the broad lap of our
great Alma Mater. Here individuals of all nations are
melted into a new race of men, whose labours and posterity will one day cause great changes in the world. Americans are the western pilgrims, who are carrying along
with them that great mass of arts, sciences, vigour, and
industry which began long since in the east; they will
finish the great circle. The Americans were once scattered all over Europe; here they are incorporated into
one of the finest systems of population which has ever
appeared, and which will hereafter become distinct by
the power of the different climates they inhabit. The
American ought therefore to love this country much better than that wherein either he or his forefathers were
born. Here the rewards of his industry follow with
equal steps the progress of his labour ; his labour is
founded on the basis of nature, self-interest ; can it want
a stronger allurement? Wives and children, who before
in vain demanded of him a morsel of bread, now, fat and
frolicsome, gladly help their father to clear those fields
whence exuberant crops are to arise to feed and to clothe
them all ; without any part being claimed, either by a
despotic prince, a rich abbot, or a mighty lord. Here
religion demands but little of him ; a small voluntary

Melted Into a
New Race

New Man of
New Ideas

Rev. Alfred V. Wittmeyer, Ph.D.
Founder Huguenot Society of America

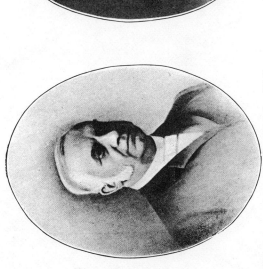

Professor Henry M. Baird, D.D., l.L.D.
Historian of the Huguenots

salary to the minister, and gratitude to God ; can he refuse these ? The American is a new man, who acts upon new principles ; he must therefore entertain new ideas, and form new opinions. From involuntary idleness, servile dependence, penury, and useless labour, he has passed to toils of a very different nature, rewarded by ample subsistence. This is an American.''

CELEBRATION OF THE ADOPTION OF THE CONSTITUTION IN 1788.

[*The most imposing part of the gorgeous pageant was the Federal ship on wheels, with Hamilton's name emblazoned upon each side of it, its crew going through every nautical preparation and movement for storms, calms, and squalls, as it moved slowly through the streets of New York City. When opposite the Bowling Green a salute of thirteen guns was fired*]

CHAPTER VIII

THE FRENCH AS A FACTOR IN AMERICAN CIVILIZATION

I

Huguenot
Influence

IN attempting to estimate the influence of the Huguenots in America, three facts must be taken into account : first, that they were Frenchmen ; second, that they were Frenchmen of marked ability ; and third, that they had been fitted by long and severe persecution for exceptional influence.

The French
Protestant
Type

The characteristic Frenchman is a marked man in any zone. In physique he is slender and supple ; in intellect imaginative, ingenious, artistic. As a man he is remarkably light-hearted, inclined to hopefulness, loving mental and moral sunshine ; and has, withal, a passionate devotion to his native land and its institutions. In addition, he possesses fine moral fibre, together with an intensely religious nature. The Huguenots who came to America were French through and through. The national blood flowed strongly in their veins ; they loved France, and because they loved her deeply they soon became intensely loyal to their adopted country. In suffering, in peril, in the face of death, in the darkest hours, they sang songs and ever turned their faces towards the brighter side of things. Yet they did not lack seriousness, but were thoroughly religious and were ready to die, if need be, for their religious convictions.

Men of
Marked
Ability

The Huguenots were Frenchmen of marked ability. They were drawn from all classes and from all occupations, but were the best of their various ranks and callings. It is the uniform testimony of unprejudiced history that the Protestants of France were her strength in

420

agriculture, in manufacturing, and in commerce, and that the insane policy of the crown in lending itself to the papal determination to exterminate them bespoiled France of much of her material wealth and glory and sank her into the depths of moral degeneration. And of this Protestant body, the brain and heart of a whole race, it was the exceptionally strong, vigorous and purposeful soul who succeeded in eluding the clutch of the emissaries of Rome and in reaching America. Those lacking in physical strength, or financial resources, or unusual tenacity of purpose, became the victims of their relentless persecutors. An elect race, men of remarkable ability, of exceptional mental and moral worth, of deathless allegiance to their faith and to the rights of man, were the French Protestants who shared with their English brethren the perils and joys of founding the American Republic.

Further than this, the long years of harrowing and terrible persecution had given to the Huguenots a character of peculiar fibre and force. The close surveillance which their persecutors held over them was so exacting and minute that they were forced into the most careful scrutiny of their every act and of the whole manner of their lives. Thus did their tormentors instil into them foresight and prudence and a deep wisdom in the conduct of life. In addition, persecution drove them to the Word of God and they became the "direct offspring of the Bible." Its study was their consolation, and came to be their strength—proving in this case, as it has proved in countless other cases, to be an inspirer of vigorous minds and sturdy moral natures. In the early days of the persecution, Clement Marot had translated the Psalms of David into French rhythm, and the singing of these psalms became a Huguenot characteristic. They chanted them at their services, in their homes, at their work, at social gatherings, on the streets, in dungeons, on board the galleys, at the stake or the scaffold : and the influence

Strong in Character

Marot's Hymns

of these hymns in giving the Huguenots comfort and courage and strength was remarkable. Engrafted upon their natures as Frenchmen was a biblical breadth and depth, and a manly gentleness of character.

II

A High Type of Race

It was, then, a high and peculiar type of French blood that was infused into the English colonial life; and marked results followed. First of all, it quickened material prosperity. By the addition of these skilled artisans, agriculture and commerce and the mechanical arts received a new impulse. They brought to perfection the cultivation of rice and tobacco, improved the native vines, introduced new fruits such as the quince and pear, and added greatly to the variety and quality of American garden products. In commercial enterprise they were

Skilled Thrifty Prosperous

unequalled, and such merchants as the Faneuils, the Lispenards, the Allaires, the Marquands, the De Lanceys, the Manigaults, were names to conjure with. The share of the colonial wealth held by the Huguenots was out of all proportion to their numbers, for of all the peoples who enjoyed the bounties of the New World they were the most prosperous. The same enterprise which caused the settlers of the Narragansett colony to set out mulberry trees, for the purpose of silk culture, at the same time they planted the crops which were to serve their immediate needs, found an outlet in the improvement of settled manufactures and in the introduction of new ones. In the weaving and dyeing of cloth, in the manufacture of felt, gunpowder, sugar, etc., they were pioneers, as they were likewise in the development of American mineral resources.

Moral and Religious Life

The infusion of the Huguenot blood had a second marked result—it produced a higher type of moral and religious life. It modified and softened the harsher and more austere views of the Puritans in New England and thus helped to produce a higher and more efficient type

President James A. Garfield

Hannibal Hamlin

General John C. Fremont

General Robert Anderson

Admiral Dewey

U. S. Senator Robert La Follette

EMINENT AMERICANS OF HUGUENOT DESCENT

of religious manhood. In the province of New Netherland the Huguenot influence was felt in lending a greater
spirituality to the solid worthfulness of the Dutch, and
in Pennsylvania the result was the same. While the
fervour of the Southerner, outside of its climatic causes,
is directly traceable to the intermingling of the Huguenot
and Cavalier.

The facility and adaptability which characterized the
Huguenot emigrants was a factor of great strength in giving the new race its peculiar ability to work out the
whole scheme of American government. The basis and
body of the colonial life was predominantly English—a
life of remarkable vigour, strength and genius. But the
Englishman after several years on American soil was no
longer an Englishman, but an Englishman Americanized.
He had been changed into a radically different and superior man. In producing this change climate and environment had their effects ; the colonial life wrought
out its disciplinary and modifying results. But the
change in character, efficiency, genius and power were
too deep and radical to be explained in this way. It can
be understood only by remembering that a continuous
stream of French life was poured into the larger English
current, sweetening and purifying its waters and making
them more healthy and life-giving. This commingling
of two powerful nations produced a race of men that
neither France nor England could possibly have produced had either been the sole possessor of American
soil. It needed both Huguenot and Englishman to
make the American. This new race, the offspring of two
great nations, faced tremendous responsibilities and assumed a herculean task. It undertook to transmute into
practical and enduring shape the dream of statesmen of
all ages. It undertook to build a nation unlike any nation of the past in all its deeper features ; to erect a
structure that should not only endure but become stronger
with the passing of the years. Civil and religious liberty

Americaniza-
tion

A Strong
Blend

was to be the foundation stone. The essential thing in its accomplishment was the race of men who were to undertake the mighty task. The foundation was laid and steadily the building went up. It took on form and beauty and realized the dream of sage and prophet. Time has tested its foundations; unlooked for strains have come to its walls, but foundations and superstructure endure, so wise and successful was the work of the builders. All honour, then, to the persecuted refugees who lent their influence and their lives to the building of the Republic.

III

America's debt to France is not likely to be fully recognized, so deep below the surface does it reach. Pointing out how Providence deduces the greatest events from the least considered causes, Bancroft instances how "a Genoese adventurer, discovering America, changed the commerce of the world; an obscure German, inventing the printing press, rendered possible the universal diffusion of increased intelligence; an Augustine monk, denouncing indulgences, introduced a schism in religion, and changed the foundations of European politics; a young French refugee, skilled alike in theology and civil law, in the duties of magistrate and the dialectics of religious controversy, entering the republic of Geneva, and conforming its ecclesiastical discipline to the principles of republican simplicity, established a party, of which Englishmen became members, and New England the asylum." There is the chain. Not only the Huguenots, but also the Pilgrims and Puritans, with their incalculable influence upon the life of the nation, are under deepest obligations to that Frenchman, John Calvin.

It is to Calvin, indeed, far more than to Luther, that America owes the Protestantism that is the foundation of its liberties and life. The Dutch brought in the Lutheran element, but their influence religiously was much less in the development of the national character than

America's Debt to France

Links in the Chain

Debt to Calvin

that of the New England Puritans, who were the spiritual offspring of Calvinism. It must be remembered that Henry VIII did not free England from the Roman Catholic church by substituting a reformed religion or a radical reform in morals. He only set himself up as a spiritual head instead of the Pope at Rome. He simply "became pope in his own dominions, and heresy was still accounted the foulest of crimes. Almost all the Roman Catholic doctrines were asserted, except the supremacy of the bishop of Rome. The Pope could praise Henry VIII for orthodoxy while he excommunicated him for disobedience. It was Henry's pride to defy the authority of the Roman bishop, and yet to enforce the doctrines of the Roman church." Thus Luther would very likely have perished by fire had he been an Englishman instead of German. Henry limited the privilege of reading the Bible to merchants and nobles. It was under Edward VI, England's only Puritan king, that the way was opened to changes within the church in England; and these changes were wrought through Calvinism. In the regency the reforming party had the majority, and Calvin, burning with zeal to include England with the Reformers of the continent, urged a uniform confession of Christian doctrine. "As for me," wrote Calvin to Cranmer, "if I can be made use of, I will sail through ten seas to bring this about." The forty-two articles promulgated as the creed of the English church were Calvinistic, and the Book of Common Prayer, revised by Cranmer, did away with most of the Romish superstitions. Calvin said of it: "The Anglican liturgy wants the purity which was to have been wished for, yet its fooleries can be borne with." So much had been gained that he could put up with the unwillingness of the English Puritans to separate themselves altogether from the Roman usages. Many of the English people, however, demanded a more complete reform, and this culminated in the Puritan revolt which led to exile and colonization in America, where religious

What Henry VIII Did for Reform

Edward VI the Puritan

The Forty-two Articles

liberty was to be a foundation stone. It was the simplicity of worship in the Reformed churches of France
and Switzerland that set the type for the Puritans of
England.

Luther and Calvin Differentiated

The difference between the Lutheran and Calvinistic
types of reform is finely brought out by Bancroft, [1] in one
of his most discriminating passages :

"The reform had made great advances among the
French and the Swiss. Both Luther and Calvin brought
the individual into immediate relation with God ; but
Calvin, under a more stern and militant form of doctrine,
lifted the individual above pope and prelate, and priest
and presbyter, above Catholic Church and national
church and general synod, above indulgences, remissions,
and absolutions from fellow-mortals, and brought him
into the immediate dependence upon God, whose eternal,
irreversible choice is made by himself alone, not arbi-
trarily, but according to his own highest wisdom and
justice. Luther spared the altar, and hesitated to deny
the real presence ; Calvin with superior dialectics, accepted as a commemoration and a seal the rite which the
Catholics revered as a sacrifice. Luther favoured magnificence in public worship, as an aid to devotion ; Calvin, the guide of republics, avoided in their churches all
appeals to the senses, as a peril to pure religion. Luther
condemned the Roman Church for its immorality ; Calvin for its idolatry. Luther exposed the folly of superstition, ridiculed the hair shirt and the scourge, the purchased indulgence, and dearly-bought, worthless masses
for the dead ; Calvin shrunk from their criminality with
impatient horror. Luther permitted the cross and the
taper, pictures and images, as things of indifference ;
Calvin demanded a spiritual worship in its utmost
purity. Luther left the organization of the church to
princes and governments ; Calvin reformed doctrine,

Calvinism Republican

---

[1] History of the United States, Vol. I, p. 312ff.

GREAT-GRANDFATHER OF JOHANNIS De PEYSTER
The First of This Family in New York

SOME OF THE De PEYSTER FAMILY PLATE

ritual and practice ; and, by establishing ruling elders in each church and an elective synod, he secured to his polity a representative character, which combined authority with popular rights. Both Luther and Calvin insisted that, for each one, there is and can be no other priest than himself; and, as a consequence, both agreed in the parity of the clergy. Both were of one mind that, should pious laymen choose one of their number to be their minister, 'the man so chosen would be as truly a priest as if all the bishops in the world had consecrated him.' "

Religion of a Free State

This clearly shows how the Protestantism that had become distinctive in America was the direct result of the teaching and polity of the French reformer, theologian and statesman who has been one of the foremost and most potent agencies in human civilization. It was because Richelieu, the keen statesman of France, saw that the Huguenot faith was in its very nature opposed to royal absolutism, and that the divine right of kings could not exist if the people came to hold the divine sovereignty taught by Calvin, that he was willing to go to all lengths to crush it out of France. Thus directly and indirectly the French have contributed to America the principles of religious and civil liberty upon which all our institutions are founded. Of far deeper influence than that which came through immigration has been the influence of that reform in religion which began in France before the day of Luther, and which had its supreme leader in John Calvin, who found opportunity to do through the Swiss Republic what he could not do in Rome-bound France, his native land.

Popular Sovereignty

APPENDIX

I

FRENCH AID IN THE REVOLUTION

A volume published in Paris in 1903, entitled *Les Combattants Français de la Guerre Americaine* gives a full list of French officers, sailors and vessels engaged in the War of the Revolution, together with a list of the officers and men who aided the Army. There were sixty-two vessels armed, manned and equipped by France in aid of the American colonies, and there were thirteen regiments of soldiers. Both vessels and troops were officered by Frenchmen.

THE ARTIST DURAND

The Durand family of New Jersey, which numbered several members who took rank among the remarkably skillful American mechanicians and artists, was descended from Huguenots who came to this country early in the eighteenth century. The two members best known were Cyrus Durand, who became a silversmith, and later engaged in the construction of machinery during the period prior to the War of 1812; and Asher Brown Durand, who began as engraver, and became a painter of distinction. He was called "one of the fathers of American landscape," having for nearly fifty years devoted himself to landscape painting. He produced the best known engraving in the United States, that of John Trumbull's famous painting of "The Declaration of Independence." His portraits of Andrew Jackson, John Quincy Adams, James Madison, Edward Everett, and Bryant were also notable. He lived to be ninety. He died in South Orange in 1886.

JUDGE TOURGEE

A Huguenot descendant who won more than ordinary distinction as an author and patriot was Judge Albion W. Tourgee, whose book of the reconstruction period, *A Fool's Errand*, had a sale of more than 200,000 copies, unprecedented in that day. As bearing on the race problem, the KuKlux Klan, and the difficulties of sectionalism, it produced a profound effect. Judge Tourgee served in the army, was severely wounded, and never wholly recovered from the effects of campaign life. He was appointed United States Consul at Halifax, and later at Bordeaux, France, the land of his ancestors, where he died in 1905.

SOME SENTENCES FROM THOREAU'S DIARY

We must be at the helm at least once a day; we must feel the tiller rope in our hands, and know that if we sail, we steer.

How vain it is to sit down to write when you have not stood up to live.

Silence is of various depths and fertility, like soil.

Praise should be spoken as naturally and simply as a flower emits its fragrance.

All fear of the world or consequences is swallowed up in a manly anxiety to do Truth justice.

We are all pilots of the most intricate Bahama channels. Beauty may be the sky overhead, but Duty is the water underneath.

The man of principle never gets a holiday. Our true character silently underlies all our words and actions, as the granite underlies the other strata.

Paul Revere

The Paul Revere Memorial Association has been formed in Boston, with purpose to purchase and preserve the old home of Paul Revere. This is believed to be the oldest building now in Boston. It was erected between 1679 and 1681. A fund of $30,000 will be raised, and the building will be devoted to educational and historical usefulness.

Paul Revere engraved the plates, made the press, and printed the first promissory notes of the State of Massachusetts Bay, when the exigencies of the struggle for independence made paper currency necessary. He had a shop on what is now Cornhill, and this was the ample sign over the door:

Paul Revere and Son, at their bell and cannon Foundry in the North part of Boston, Cast Bells of all sizes ; every kind of brass Ordinance, and every kind of composition work for ships, etc., at the briefest notice. Manufacture copper into Sheets, Bolts, Nails, Spikes, rivets, etc., from Maleable Copper.

They always keep by them every kind of copper Sheathing for ships. They now have on hand a number of Church and Ship Bells of different sizes, a large quantity of Sheathing Copper from 16 up to 30 oz. ; Bolts, Spikes, Nails, etc., of all sizes, which they warrant to be equal to English manufacture.

Cash and the highest price given for old Copper and Brass.

A French Engineer

It is interesting to remember that America owes the noble plan of the national capital to a French engineer, Major Charles Pierre L'Enfant, in whose honour it is proposed to erect a suitable memorial in one of the parks which he laid out.

The Society of Soul Winners

Rev. Edward O. Guerrant, D. D., a descendant of the Virginia Huguenots, originated a most interesting work among the mountain people of Kentucky, Tennessee and North Carolina. The religious destitution appealed to him, and in 1897 he started the America Inland Mission, with one missionary and faith for capital. The work grew, support came from unexpected sources, until the receipts for 1902 were above $7,000, and seventy faithful men and women were employed in the most destitute places, preaching, distributing Bibles and tracts, teaching Sunday-schools and day schools, caring for the sick beyond the reach of physicians, clothing the poor, building churches, and in every way,blessing the thousands to whom they ministered. More than five hundred were received into the church that year, showing the results of the Soul Winners' faithfulness. This is the obligation assumed by the members of the Soul Winners' Society:

"By the help of God, and for His glory, I will try to win at least one soul for Christ, my Lord, every year I live, and give what I am able to send the gospel to my perishing countrymen."

PROTESTANT PIONEER PREACHERS

The Calvinist ministers who came to Acadia from Geneva in 1557 were the first Protestant ministers in the Western Hemisphere. Robert was the first Protestant minister to set foot on the continent of North America. The Huguenots were thus in the lead of all others.

THE AMERICAN HEROINE

Deborah Sampson, named the "American Heroine," who served as a Revolutionary soldier for nearly three years, her sex never being suspected, was a descendant of Bathsheba LeBroche. She enlisted under the name of Robert Shurtleff, and served under Captain George Webb in the Fourth Massachusetts Regiment. She was wounded at Tarrytown, and fought in the battles of White Plains and Yorktown. She exhibited unusual heroism, was esteemed a gallant as well as faithful soldier, received an honourable discharge, and was granted a pension by the government. She was as modest as she was fearless, and was impelled to her course by patriotism. She was born in Plympton, Massachusetts. The story of her career has been written by Mrs. Deborah Sampson Gannett.

THE HUGUENOT CHAPEL

One of the chapels to be erected as a part of the Protestant Episcopal Cathedral of St. John the Divine in New York is to be called the Huguenot Chapel. This will be the second chapel in a series of seven. Mrs. Edward King, of New York, gave $100,000 for the building of this memorial to the Huguenots who have had from the beginning such honourable part in the making of the Metropolis of the New World.

MANY DISTINGUISHED MEN

From a study of the names contained in Appleton's *Encyclopedia of American Biography*, Hon. Henry Cabot Lodge finds that among the men in America prior to 1789 who were of sufficient distinction to be named in the *Encyclopedia*, there were 589 Huguenots, they holding fourth place in the list. This is sufficient testimony as to the character and ability of these Protestant French.

PRESIDENT JOHN ADAMS

In his History of Independence Hall (published by James Challon &

Son, Philadelphia, 1859), D. W. Belisle says: "The maternal ancestor of John Adams was John Alden, a passenger in the *Mayflower*, and thus he inherited from his parentage the title of a Son of Liberty. The last words he ever uttered were, 'Independence forever!'" Thus it appears that the Huguenot "Priscilla" was the ancestress of one of our Presidents.

EARLY SOCIETY IN NEW YORK

In the society which marked the early days of the Republic, in New York, then the seat of the Continental Congress, Mrs. John Jay, wife of a Huguenot descendant, was the acknowledged leader. Her talented husband was secretary for foreign affairs. Her "Dinner and Supper list" for 1787-8 contains the names of the men and women prominent in that day. General Washington was among the honoured guests in that hospitable mansion. Mrs. Jay was a Livingston. Early in the list are the names of Colonel John Bayard, distinguished member of a Huguenot family, and his wife. Other names are Alexander Hamilton, "the vivacity of whose French blood would make him a welcome guest at every social gathering"; Dr. John Rodgers, Presbyterian minister, and his wife, who was of the Delaware branch of the Huguenot Bayard family; and Dr. Provoost, bishop of New York, a chaplain of Congress, of combined Dutch and Huguenot descent. Two other names of note among the Huguenots were Elias Boudinot and Daniel Huger, the latter of the South Carolina family so honourably represented in the Revolution. The DeLancey family was represented, as were the Izards of South Carolina. Both in Congress and society the Huguenot families were at the front.

WASHINGTON AND A HUGUENOT MAIDEN

The great Washington, in his early life, was smitten, according to well established tradition, by the charms of a maiden of French blood, the fair Mary Philipse, who later became Mrs. Morris. Her father's mansion, still standing on Harlem Heights and known as the Jumel Mansion, was subsequently Washington's headquarters.

TRACING SOME OBSCURE LINES

IT is not assumed in the case of the names here given that a French ancestry is certain; simply that there is fair reason for believing it. No harm will be done if the genealogical case is not made out.

Backus. Isaac Backus, Baptist author and minister, born Jan. 9, 1724, at Norwich, Conn., died in 1806 at Titicut, Conn. Descendant in fifth generation of William or Stephen Backus, who came to Norwich, Conn., from Norwich, England, in 1637. Backus doubtless from Beccues, a Walloon. DeSue Beccues was witness to a Walloon baptism in Norwich, England, as the records of the Huguenot Society show.

Deland, DeLand, Delane, Delaune. Philip Delane or Deland, probably a Huguenot, came to Newbury, Mass., in 1694. Rowland Deland, the probable ancestor, is given as a member of the Walloon Church at Norwich, England.

Belmont, Bellomont, Beaumont. Beaumonts abound in Huguenot literature. LeSieur de Beaumont was a refugee in Acadia in 1604. Richard Coot, Earl of Bellomont, governor of New York and Massachusetts in 1696, was of Flemish origin. Coot is a Huguenot name in Canterbury Church records. While the Belmonts come from the Palatinate, Rhenish Prussia, the family is French in origin.

Garrison. William Lloyd Garrison's grandfather Joseph was an English settler on the St. John's River in 1767. His origin is obscure. Garrison was a common Walloon name in England after the Huguenot refugees had gone thither. Isaac Garrison, a Huguenot from Montaubon, France, became a citizen of New York in 1765. It is not at all improbable that the great Abolitionist had Huguenot blood in his veins.

Eustis. William Eustis, governor of Massachusetts in 1825, was a descendant of William Eustis of England. The family is of Norman blood, Eustace the Count of Boulogne being the English progenitor.

Hale. Nathan Hale, of Connecticut, who was executed as a spy in the War of the Revolution, was descended from the Hales of Kent, England, of whom Sir Nicholas de Hales was the Norman ancestor.

Fauntleroy. Moore Fauntleroy, founder of the Virginia Fauntleroys, was of Huguenot origin, his father being John Fauntleroy of Southampton, England. Moore, the immigrant, was a man of property, member of the Virginia House of Burgesses.

Moultrie. General William Moultrie, who defended Sullivan's Island from British attack in 1776, was of the Huguenot blood, as the South Carolina records show. His brother John was governor of East Florida in 1775. The family is one of the first in South Carolina.

Lyon. General Nathaniel Lyon, of Connecticut, a brave commander in the Civil War who died at Wilson's Creek, August 9, 1861, was a descendant of William Lyons, who came to Roxbury from England in 1635 in the ship *Hopewell.* The English ancestor was Sir Roger de Leonne, a native of France.

Legare. Hugh Swinton Legaré, born in Charleston, S. C., Jan. 2, 1789, died in Boston June 20, 1843, was attorney-general in President Tyler's cabinet, and was attending the dedication of Bunker Hill Monument when stricken with fatal illness. He was a direct descendant of Solomon Legare, a Huguenot refugee from Bristol, England, to Charleston, S. C., in 1686. Solomon Legaré was one of the founders of the Congregational Church—Circular Church—in Charleston.

Ross. Mrs. Betsey Ross, who made the first United States flag, very likely had French blood in her veins, although proof positive is wanting. She came from the Griscom family, and the name is in the Huguenot records frequently. The name of Ross, also, is common among the Huguenots as Ros. The flag was made upon an order from a committee consisting of General Washington and Colonel George Ross, her husband's uncle. Her ancestor, Samuel Griscom, built the first brick house in Philadelphia in 1682.

Russell. This family is of Norman origin, and Huguenot. The family of Le Rozel, from the place of that name in Lower Normandy, reaches back into the eleventh century. In England the Russells have been among the prominent families since the middle of the twelfth century. The name, given as Rushell, Rozel, Rosel, Rousselle, frequently occurs in the Walloon records at Canterbury. Russell and Rousell, Rouselle and Roussel were in the list of " Foreigners resident in England in 1618–1688." The Russells were also on the original passenger lists to America in the seventeenth century, at least a dozen entries of them bound for New England. In the New World as in the Old, the family has won distinction. The late Governor Russell of Massachusetts belonged to the best type of American citizenship.

Vasse. Colonel Joseph Vasse, or Vose, who commanded the First Massachusetts Bay Regiment in the Revolutionary War, was a direct descendant of Robert Vose, or Vasse, who came from England to America in 1654 and bought 174 acres of land in Milton, including a portion of the famous Brush Hill. In England the name was spelled Vaux, retaining the Norman origin. It is not unlikely that the name Foss comes from the same source.

St. Clair. General Arthur St. Clair had Norman blood in his veins. He was born in Scotland in 1736, died in Pennsylvania in 1818. He was a general in the Revolutionary War. He married in Boston Phœbe Bayard, daughter of a Boston Huguenot, Balthazar Bayard. His wife's mother was a half-sister of Governor James Bowdoin. The St. Clairs or Sinclairs of Scotland were of Norman descent from Walderne, Count de Santo Claro, whose wife was daughter of the Duke of Normandy.

Warren. General Joseph Warren, whose name will live as long as Bunker Hill is remembered, was born in Roxbury, Mass., June 11, 1741. The origin of his Boston ancestor, Peter Warren, is obscure. He married Sarah Tucker, and Tucker is a Huguenot name, corrupted from Tuttiett or Touchet. The father of General Warren married in 1710 Mary Stevens, daughter of Doctor Samuel Stevens, who first produced the russet apple. The name of Stevens is found as Stiffens, Steffens, Stephens, in Huguenot annals. So also the name Warren, Warene and Werene, is common in Walloon records. Very probably Peter Warren, ancestor of General Warren, was Pierre Warrene, a Huguenot. He was first known in Boston in 1659.

Reverdy. Peter Reverdy and his son Benoni came to New York from London with Pastor Peiret on the ship *Robert* in 1687. Peter was the reputed author of certain Memoirs of Sir Edmund Andros. He was chosen coroner of Newcastle, Delaware, in 1693. Reverdy was a Poitou family, Huguenot.

Johnson. Reverdy Johnson, of Maryland, the son of John Johnson and ——— Ghiselin, daughter of Reverdy Ghiselin, of Maryland, was a Huguenot, his mother being a descendant of Jan Ghiselin, a Huguenot refugee to England in 1566.

Some English Surnames of French Derivation

THE following names of families, of French descent and derivation, have been selected from Barber's *British Family Names*. Many of our American families can trace through this source French blood, in very many cases known to be Huguenot. Names given in the various chapters are not repeated here. The list will be of interest, whether the American connection can be traced or not. The abbreviations used are these: "H.," for Huguenot; "Prot. Ref.," Protestant Refugee; "L.," London.

AGNEW (from Aigneau).
Alexander (originally Alexandre).
Allard; Huguenot.
Alloth (H., near Vermeil, 1688).
Ames or Eames (Prot. Ref., L., 1618).
Angler (H., Anger).
Annes, or Annis (Prot. Ref., L., 1618).
Arch (H., L., 1618).
Arnold (H., L., 1618).
Arnott (H., Arnaud, L., 1657).
Arundell (H., L., 1618).
Astor (Norman, 1180).
Avery (H., Norwich, 1622).

BAILEY (H., Belley, L., 1688).
Bain (H., Norwich, 1622).
Baird or Beard (H., L., 1618).
Baker (Becke, Prot. Ref., Norwich, 1622).
Ballinger (Bellanger, Prot. Ref., L., 1688).
Barr (De la Barr, H., L., 1618).
Barrell (H., Barill, Canterbury, 1622).
Barrett (Norman, Barette).
Bassett (H., Sandwich, 1622).
Batchelder, or Batchelor (H., Batchelier, L., 1682).
Bean (Prot. Ref., Bienne, Norwich, 1622).
Beaumont (Norman).
Bellew, or Bellows (Norman, Bellot).
Bellin (H., Belin, Belyn, L., 1618).
Bence (Benson, H., Sandwich, 1662).
Bendon, or Benton (H., L., 1618).
Benn, Bennett, Benny (H., Benedict, L., 1688).
Bevis (from Beauvais, France).
Bezant (H., Beaussaint).
Billyard (H., Dover, 1622).
Bissett (H., Bissot, L., 1618).
Blewitt (Norman, LaBlouette).
Boffin (H., Bovin, L., 1685).
Bogert (H., Boygard, L., 1681).
Bone (H., Bohon, L., 1621).
Bonehill (H., Bonnel, L., 1618).
Bonner (H., Bonnard, L., 1618).
Boosey (H., Bussey, L., 1618).
Bowcher, Boucher, Bowker (H., L., 1618).
Boyd (H., Boyard, L., 1687).
Brade (H., Breda, L., 1688).
Brain, or Brine (H., Breon, L., 1688).
Brand (Prot. Ref., L., 1618).
Brasier, Brazier (H., Bressuire, Norwich, 1622).
Breeden (H., Briden, L., 1681).
Brett (French, LeBret).
Brewer, (Brueria in Normandy).
Briggs (H. Bruges, L., 1618).

Brill (Prot. Ref., Brille, Sandwich, 1622).
Brothers (Brodder, Prot. Ref., Sandwich, 1622).
Brown (Norman-French, LeBrun).
Bruce (Brousse, from Breux, Normandy).
Brunyee (Brune, Prot. Ref., L., 1618).
Bryan (Brionne, Normandy).
Bryant (from Breaunt, Normandy).
Bubier (Norman).
Buck (LeBuc, Prot. Ref., L., 1618).
Buckett (Bouquet, Prot. Ref., L., 1685).
Bull (Bole, Prot. Ref., L., 1618).
Buller (Bolen, Prot. Ref., L., 1618).
Burden (Fr., Burdon).
Burdett (Bourdet, H., L., 1685). Probable ancestry of Robert J. Burdett, the humourist.
Burgoyne (Norman-French).
Burr (Bure, Belgian, Prot. Ref., L., 1687).
Burt (Norman-French).
Bush (Bosch, Flemish, Prot. Ref., L., 1618)
Bushell (H., L., 1618).
Busick (Boussoe, H., L., 1685).
Butcher (H., L., 1685).
Buttle (Butel, H., L., 1685).
Byles (H., from Bueil, France).
Byron (Norman-French, Biron).

CADE (H., Cadet).
Camp (H., L., 1618).
Campbell, and Gamble (Norman-French).
Campion (Prot. Ref., Norwich, 1622).
Cantrell (H., L., 1618).
Capel (LaChapelle, H., L, 1618).
Card (H., Cardes, L., 1681).
Caron (H.. L., 1687).
Carry, or Carr (H., L., 1685).
Carter (Cartier, H., L., 1618).
Cartwright (Cauterets, Norman).
Case (H., De la Cuse).
Chaffe (H., LeChauve, L., 1682).
Chamberlain (Chambellan, H., L., 1618).
Chambers (H., Chambray, L., 1618).
Chaplin (Norman-French, Capelen).
Chattin (H., Chattaine, L., 1618).
Cheney (Fr., Chesnais).
Choffin (H., Chauvin, L., 1684).
Churchill (Nor. Fr., DeCourcelle).
Clark (H., Norwich, 1622).
Clements (Flem., Clement, Prot. Ref., L., 1618).
Cloake (H., Clocke, L., 1618).
Close (Prot. Ref., L., 1618).
Closson (Prot. Ref., L., 1618).

Cocker (H., Norwich, 1622).
Cockerell (Fr., Coqueril).
Cockle (Cokele, Prot. Ref., Norwich, 1622).
Codd (H., L., 1618).
Cogger (Coege, Flem. Ref., L., 1618).
Cole (Flem. Ref., L., 1618).
Colley (H., Colleye, 1618).
Collier, Colwer (Fr., Collioure).
Coppinger (Flem. Ref., L., 1618).
Corbett (Fr., raven).
Corbin (Norman-French).
Corke (H., Corque, L., 1618).
Courage (H., Correges).
Courteney, or Courtinay, or Courtney (H., name).
Coward (H., Chouard, 1688).
Cozens (Cousin, H., 1688).
Creamer (Prot. Ref., L., 1618).
Cross (Prot. Ref., St. Croix, 1618).
Crowley (Fr., Crulai).
Crudge (Prot. Ref., L., 1688).
Cruso (Creusot, Prot. Ref., Norwich, 1622).
Culley (Flemish Couillet).
Curtis (H., Courtois, Norwich, 1622).
Cushing (Nor. Fr., LeCuchon).

Dagg (Dague, H., Canterbury, 1622).
Dagget (Dackett, Flem. Ref., Norwich, 1622).
Dams (D'Ames, Prot. Ref., Norwich, 1622).
Dangerfield (Dangerville).
Daniel (H., L., 1618).
Danvers (from Anvers, France).
Dennis (St. Denis, H., L., 1682).
Derlyn, Darling (H., Norwich, 1622).
Derrick (H., L., 1622).
Devine (Desvignes, H. Norwich, 1622).
Dewey (Belgian, Prot. Ref., Dhuy, L., 1618).
Dewfall (Duval, Prot. Ref., L., 1687).
Doubleday (Doublet, H., L., 1685).
Doughty (Daude, H., L., 1687).
Doy (H., L, 1618).
Drake (Nor. Fr., Fitz-Drac, Prot. Ref., L., 1618).
Draper (Drapier, H., Dover, 1622).
Drew (Dreux, H, Norwich, 1622).
Drewry, or Drury (DeRouvray, Nor. Fr.).
Driver (DeRivers, Nor. Fr.).
Drought (H., Droart, L., 1618).
Durrant, or Durant (Durand, Fr.).
Durrell (Durell, H., L., 1687).

Emery (H., L., 1685).
Eve (Prot. Ref., L., 1618).
Everson (Prot. Ref., Flemish, L., 1618).
Ewing, or Ewen (Prot. Ref., L., 1618).

Fabb (H., Fabri. L., 1678).
Fairy (Verry or Ferry H., L., 1618).
Fanning (Norman).
Farjon (Fargeon, H., L., 1685).
Faulkner (Fauconnier, H., L., 1681).
Fawcett, Fassett (Fr. Fossord).
Fear (H., L., 1618).
Fellows, Fellowes (H., L., 1687).
Fenn (Fene, H., Norwich, 1622).
Ferrett (H., Dover, 1622).
Filbert (Fr., St. Philbert).
Finch (Fl., DeVinck, Prot. Ref., L., 1622).
Flowers (H., L., 1618).
Fleury (H., L, 1687).

Foggs, Fogg (H , Foucat, L., 1685).
Foljambe (Nor. Fr., Fulgent).
Forman, Furch (Forment, H., L., 1618).
Fox (Flemish, H., L., 1618).
Foy, Faith (H., L., 1618).
Freeman (Fl., Freyman, Prot. Ref., Norwich, 1622).
Fremont (Fr., Frimont).
Fromant (Fromeau, H., L., 1618).
Frusher (H., Fruchat, L., 1687).
Fuller (Fr., Fouleur).
Furber (H., Foubert, L , 1618).

Gabbett (H., Gabet, L., 1688).
Gaches (H., Gauchez, L., 1688).
Galley (H., Gallais, L., 1687).
Gallyon (H., Gaillen, L., 1618).
Galpin (H., Galopin, L., 1684).
Garrard (H., L., 1618).
Garret (Fr., Garet).
Garrick (Fr., Garrigues).
Gaskin (Fr., DeGascoigge, from Gascony).
German (H., Germon, L., 1618).
Giddings, or Giddens (H., Guidon, L., 1687).
Gifford (Giffard, full cheeked).
Gillot (diminutive of Gill, H., L., 1618).
Gilyard (Gilliard, H., L., 1687).
Gimlett (Gimlette, H., L., 1618).
Glass (H., Glace, L., 1618).
Goacher, Goucher (Fr., Goucher, H., L., 1618).
Goddard (H., Godart, L., 1618).
Godfrey (Fr., Godefroy, H., L., 1681).
Goding (Fl., Godding, Prot. Ref., L, 1685).
Goodenough, Moodenow (Fr., Godineau).
Goodfellow (Fr., Bonenfant).
Goodhew, or Gooehue (Fr., Godeheu).
Goss, or Goose (H., Norwich, 1622).
Gosling (Gosselin, Prot. Ref., L., 1622).
Gower, Gowers (Fl., Prot. Ref., Govaerts, L., 1618).
Grant (Fr., Grands).
Grave, or Graves (Nor. Fr., De la Greve).
Gray (H., L., 1618).
Gruel (H., Gruelle, L., 1628).
Gubbins (H., DeGobion, L., 1618).
Guerin (H., Gueron, L., 1628).
Gurner, or Gurney (H., L., 1618).
Gye (H., Gay, L., 1684).

Hague (H., LeHague, Prot. Ref., L., 1621). From this family came the eloquent preacher, Rev. William Hague, D. D., Baptist historian and minister.
Hall (Fl., Prot. Ref., L., 1699).
Hamblett (H., Hamlett, L., 1622).
Hanchett (Prot. Ref., Hansett, L., 1618).
Hardy (Nor. Fr., bold, strong ; H., L., 1684).
Harry (Harrye, H., L., 1681).
Harvey (H., Herve, L., 1681).
Hassatt (Prot. Ref., Sandwich, 1622).
Hay (De la Haye, H., Dover, 1622).
Hayes (Hees, H., L., 1618).
Hebbert (Hebart, Prot. Ref., L., 1685).
Herbert (Herbart, Prot. Ref., Canterbury, 1622).
Hewett (H , Huet, 1621).
Hood (H.,Ude, L., 1618).

Hook (H., Huc, L., 1618).
Hooppell (H., Dover, 1622).
Howell (H., L., 1618).
Howes (Fl., Housse, Prot. Ref., Canterbury 1622).
Howitt (H., Canterbury, 1622).
Hubbard, Hubert (H., Houbart, L., 1618).
Hidden, or Iddon (Nor., Hidden, Prot. Ref., L., 1618).

JACKMAN (H., Jacquement, Canterbury, 1622).
Jacobs (Fl., Prot., Ref., L., 1618).
James (St. James, Prot. Ref., L., 1621).
Jarvis (H., Gerveis, L., 1688).
Jasper (Fl., Jaspard, H., L., 1621).
Jay (Jeyen, H., L., 1621).
Jolly (H., L., 1681).
Joyce (Nor., Joyeuse).
Joy (H., L., 1685).
Julian (Fr., Julien).
Juliet (H., L., 1618).

KING (Fl. Ref., L., 1618).

LACY, or Lacey (Nor., Lessay, DeLacey)
Lambert (Fr., St. Lambert, Fl. Ref., L., 1618 ; General Lambert, Governor of York).
Landers (from Landre in Burgundy).
Lane (Fr., Laigne).
Larter (LaTour, H., L., 1618).
Lawrence, Laurence (Fr., Laurentin, H., L., 1618).
Laws (Prot. Ref., Norwich, 1622).
Lawson (Nor. Fr., Loison).
Laycock (H., Lecocq, Dover, 1622).
L'Amoreaux, Lamoreau (H., L., 1687).
Lepper (H., Lepere, L., 1618).
Lessey (H., Lesee, L., 1621).
Lewis (DeLuis, H., Norwich, 1622).
Littlejohn (Fr., Petitjean).
Living (Fl., H., Livain, Norwich, 1622).
Loe, or Low (H., DeLoe, L., 1618).
Lofting (Prot. Ref., L., 1688).
Long (DeLonga, Prot. Ref., L., 1621).
Longfellow (H., Longueville, L., 1685).
Luce, Loose (Prot. Ref., L., 1618).
Lovebond (H., Lovingsbone, L., 1621).
Lovell (H., Louvel, L., 1618).
Lower (Fl. Ref., L., 1618).
Lucy (Loulset, Prot. Ref., L., 1634).
Lumbard, Lombard (H., Lombuart, L., 1687).
Lyon (Prot. Ref., Norwich, 1662).

MACE (H., Mes, L., 1618).
Mackley (Fl., Prot. Ref., L, 1618).
Maitland (H., Mattalent, Nantes).
Major (H., L., 1688).
Male (DeMaisle, H., Dover, 1622).
Marcon (Marquent, Prot. Ref., Canterbury, 1622).
Marlow (Fr., Marlieux).
Marr (H., Marre, L., 1618).
Marshall (H., Marechal, L., 1618).
Martin (H., St. Martin, L., 1688).
Martineau (Fr., Martigne). Family of famous James Martineau, philosopher.
Massey (H., Macey, L., 1684).
Mason (H., Macon, L., 1618).
Mate (H., Mette, L., 1618).
Maule, or Moll (H., L., 1618).
Mayhew, or Mayo (H., Mahieu, Mayeux, Norwich, 1622).

Mayne (H., Mayenne, L., 1687).
Maynard (H., Menard, Dover, 1622).
Means (Prot. Ref., Minnens, L., 1687).
Mear (H., L., 1618).
Meen (H., Migne, L., 1618).
Merritt, Merry (Marit and Meret).
Mercier (H., L., 1618).
Meyrick (DeMeric, Prot. Ref., L., 1621).
Michell, Mitchell (H., L., 1618).
Miles (Norman French). General Miles is of this blood.
Mills (Fl., Miles, Prot. Ref., Norwich, 1622).
Minett (Minet, Prot. Ref., L., 1688).
Minter (Minder, Prot. Ref., L., 1618).
Molineux (Moliner, Prot. Ref., L., 1618).
Money (H., Monnaye, L., 1618).
Munsey, or Monsey (H. L., 1618).
Montague (Montaigu).
Moon, Moen (Fl., Moine, H., Sandwich, 1622).
Moore (Fl., Mor ; H., More, L., 1618).
Morrell (H., Morel, L., 1618).
Morriss, Morris (Meurisse, H., Canterbury, 1622).
Moss (Norman-French).
Mott (De la Motte, H., L., 1621).
Mountain (H., Montaigne, L., 1618).
Mouse (H., Mousse, Moze, L., 1687).
Munn (Prot. Ref., L., 1618).
Myhill, Mayall (H., L., 1618).

NEALE (DeNeel, H., L., 1688).
Nollett (Fr., Nolleau, H., L., 1687).

OLIVER, Olivier (H., L., 1682).
Onions (Angiens, Norman).
Overy (H., Ouvry, L., 1618).
Osborne (Osbern), Osler (l'Oiselor), Norman.

PAGE (H., LePage, L., 1688).
Paine (Fr., Pain, H., L., 1618).
Paley, Pallett (H., Paillette, L., 1688).
Palmer (lePaumier, Fl. Ref., L., 1618).
Parry (H., Parre, L., 1687).
Paskell (H., Paschal, L., 1687).
Pate (Patte, H., Canterbury, 1622).
Paton, Patton, Peyton (H., Canterbury, 1622).
Pattison (Fl. Ref., L., 1618).
Paul (H., St. Paul, L., 1618).
Paulett (Poulet, H., L., 1687).
Peacock (Fl. Ref., L., 1618).
Pear (A., Pierre, L., 1687).
Pears, Pearse (Fl., Piers, Peres, H., L., 1688).
Pearson (Pierresene, Prot. Ref., L., 1688).
Peberdy, Peabody (Nor. Fr, Pabode).
Penny (Peigne, Peno, Prot. Ref., Norwich, 1622).
Perkins, Peterkin (little Peter, Fl.).
Perowne (H., Peronnez, L., 1618).
Peters (Peeters, Prot. Ref., L., 1518).
Pettit (H., Petit, 1618).
Phantam, Vendome, Vandam (Prot. Ref., L., 1618).
Phillips (Fitz-Philip, Prot. Ref., L., 1618).
Picard (H., Picard, L., 1621).
Picken, Pickens (Fr., Picon).
Pickett, Pigott (H., Pegot or Pigot, L., 1685).
Pillow (H., Pilot, 1622).
Pinchen, Pynchon (H., Pincon or Pinchon, 1622).

Pinner (Pineur, Prot. Ref., Norwich 1622).
Plummer (H., le Plumer, L., 1682).
Plunkett, or Plunkitt (Nor. Fr., de Plugenet).
Pollard (H., L., 1618).
Pond (Fl., Pont, Prot. Ref., L., 1618).
Poole (Poule, Prot. Ref., L., 1621).
Porter (H., Portier, Norwich, 1622).
Pott (Fl., Pot, Prot. Ref., L., 1618).
Potter (Fr., Potier).
Poulter (H., Poultier, Canterbury, 1688).
Powell (H., Puel, L., 1618).
Pratt (H., DuPrat, L., 1687).
Prevost (H., Rye, 1621).
Prim, Prime (H., L., 1618).
Prince (H. Prins, L., 1618).
Prue (H., Preux L., 1687).
Pullen, Pullein (H., Poullain, L., 1622).

QUINCEY (from Quince in Maine; DeQuincey).

RANNEY (H., Rene, Renie, Fl., Renaix, L., 1688).
Reason (DeReasne, Prot. Ref., L., 1618).
Reay, Ray (DeRea, Ray, H., L., 1688).
Rebbeck (H., Rebache, L., 1688).
Revill, Revell (H., Revel, Reville, L., 1618).
Ricket (Ricquart, H., Canterbury, 1622).
Robin (H., Robain, L., 1687).
Robinson (Robyns, Prot Ref., L., 1618).
Roche, Roach (H., de la Roche, L., 1687).
    Possibly the family from which John Roach, or Roche, the American ship-builder, was descended.
Rogers (Fr., Rogier).
Rose (Nor., Ros, Rose, H , L., 1684).
Roswell, Russell (Rousselle, H , Canterbury, 1622).
Rouse (H., LeRoux, L., 1618).
Rowan, Rowen (H., Rouen, L , 1618).
Rowell (H., Rouelles, L., 1687).
Rowland (H., Dover, 1622).
Rowley (from Norman Reuilly).

SACH (Sac, Prot. Ref., L., 1618).
Sartoris (H., Sartorius, L., 1684).
Savage (Fr., Sauvage).
Seymour, Saymer, Simore (H., 1618).
Seeley (H., Sill, L., 1688).
Seguin (H., L., 1688).
Sherrard (Sheraret, F., Prot., L., 1618).
South (H., L., 1618).
Spear, Speer (Fl., Spiers, Prot. Ref., L., 1622).
Stephens (H., L., 1618).
Sturgeon (H , Lestourgeon, L., 1683).
Summers (H., Somers, L., 1618).
Summerville (from Sommervieux, Nor.).
Symonds, Simonds (H., Simon, L., 1618).

TABER (Taborer, Prot. Ref., L., 1678).
Tardy (H., L., 1688).
Taverner (H., Tavernier, L., 1622).
Terry (H., Terriss, L., 1618).
Thompson (H., L., 1618).
Tibbles (H., L., 1618).
Tiffen (H., L., 1618).
Tolver (H., Tolleve, Norwich, 1622).
Torrey (Thouret, Prot. Ref., L., 1618).
Tree (Tre, Prot. Ref., L., 1618).
Tyron (H., Trion, L., 1618).
Tulley (H., Tulye, L., 1618).
Turnbull (Nor., Tournebu).
Tyrrell, Tirrell (Fr., Tirel).

VALENTINE (H., 1618).
Valiant (H., Vaillant, 1681).
Vawdrey (H., DeValdarrie, Norwich, 1622).
Vernon (H., L., 1618).
Viall (H., Viel, L., 1684).
Vincent (H., St. Vincent, L , 1618).
Vye (H., De la Fuye, L., 1683).

WALTERS (Wauters, Prot., Ref., L. 1621).

Some Eminent Huguenot Names

Henry Wadsworth Longfellow's mother was a lineal descendant of John Alden and Priscilla Molines, and the strain of Huguenot blood accounts for some of the finest qualities in the character of New England's most loved poet.

The good Quaker poet of New England, John Greenleaf Whittier, was proud of the Huguenot blood he inherited from Thomas Whittier, the ancestor who settled in Salisbury in the days of the early colonists. Through the peaceful training of the Quaker the Gallic blood pulsed swiftly when wrong was to be righted, and liberty of conscience as well as of person was inwrought into his religious creed.

Mrs. Martha J. Lamb, the historian, author of *The History of New York*, and for many years editor of the *Magazine of American History*, which became of much value under her control, was of Huguenot descent through her mother's family, the Vintons. She was deeply interested in the Huguenots and many articles in the magazine were devoted to them. She was a leader in establishing the Huguenot Library now in possession of the Huguenot Society of America, and served on the Library Committee until her death in 1893. She was secretary of the first Sanitary Fair in 1863: noted for philanthropic and public spirit.

General Frederick Dent Grant traces his Huguenot descent through the family of DeLille and of De la Noye (Delano), who was a member of the Narragansett Settlement.

Of the Presidents of the United States, there is a strain of Huguenot blood in John Adams, Garfield, and Roosevelt—the latter representing the best type of the mingling of the Dutch and French races.

Hon. Richard Olney, Secretary of State under President Cleveland, and one of the foremost lawyers of New England, traces direct descent to Andrew Sigourney, who was one of the settlers in Oxford. With the late Senator Bayard, this makes two Secretaries of State of recent date who were of Huguenot blood.

A Historic Huguenot Chair

In the rooms of the Bostonian Society there is a very old Huguenot chair, which was brought to Boston from Lyons, France, in 1685, by a Mr. Waldo, whose family was said to belong to the Waldenses, and who left France to escape religious persecution. His son, Nathan, born in Boston, emigrated to Connecticut, taking the chair with him. Later it became successively the property of Nathan's son Edward; of Edward's daughter Johanna, wife of Josiah Cleveland, and of her daughter Thankful, wife of Thaddeus Palmer; and of Thankful's daughter Lucy, who gave it to Rev. John Cleveland, D. D., of Providence, R. I. More recently it belonged to the late Mrs. Jane G. Alden, Novelist, and is now loaned to the Bostonian Society by her daughter, Mrs. Albert DeSilva, of Roxbury, by whose permission a picture has been obtained, which may be seen elsewhere in this volume.

The Huguenot Society of America

This Society was organized in 1883. Rev. Alfred V. Wittmeyer, Ph. D., pastor of the French Church in New York, was the founder. Honourable John Jay was the first president, and Dr. Wittmeyer, secretary. Henry G. Marquand was the second president, and Frederick J. de Peyster the third. The Society has done much to bring the Huguenot descendants into acquaintance and fellowship, has fostered family pride and stimulated research, and has created a racial consciousness. Its publications have afforded a medium of historical value. Through its exercises in commemoration of the Bi-Centenary of the Revocation of the Edict of Nantes (held in New York in 1885), and of the Ter-Centenary of the Promulgation of the Edict (held in New York in 1898), attention was widely drawn to the subject of the Huguenots in America. The membership is national, and about four hundred names are on the rolls, including many families prominent in various sections of the United States.

The present officers are: President, Colonel William Jay; Vice-Presidents, George S. Bowdoin, Theodore M. Banta, Hon. H. W. Bookstaver; Henry M. Lester, Esq., New Paltz; Hon. A. T. Clearwater, Kingston; Nathaniel Thayer, Boston; Hon. Richard Olney, Boston; William Ely, Providence; Prof. Allen Marquand, Princeton; Col. H. A. Dupont, Delaware; Herbert Dupuy, Pittsburg; Col. Richard L. Maury, Richmond, Va.; Rev. Robert Wilson, Charleston, S. C.; Treasurer, T. J. Oakley Rhinelander; Secretary, Mrs. James M. Lawton, New York; Chaplain, Rt. Rev. Bishop James H. Darlington.

The honourary members are: Rev. A. V. Wittmeyer, founder; Prof. Henry M. Baird, the historian; A. Giraud Browning, president Huguenot Society of London; Meschinet de Richemond, LaRochelle, France; LeBaron De Schickler, Paris; LeDocteur Beringuier, Berlin, president German Huguenot Society; LePasteur N. Weiss, Paris; Rev. Charles S. Vedder, pastor Huguenot Church of Charleston, S. C.; James S. Van Courtland. The list of deceased members includes Dr. Thomas Gallaudet, Hon. Elisha Dyer, Prof. Joseph LeConte, Hon. Sir Henry Austen Layard, Mrs. Martha J. Lamb, Rev. William Hague, Hon. Abraham S. Hewitt, Col. Johnston L. DePeyster, Prof. D. D. Demarest, Hon. Thomas F. Bayard, Dr. Edward Bayard, Dr. Charles W. Baird, the historian, H. LeGrand Cannon, Henry G. Marquand, Bishop Quintard, and Hon. Robert C. Winthrop, of Boston, a lineal descendant of Pierre Baudoin (Bowdoin). The late Mrs. Robert Anderson, wife of General Anderson, was a long time member.

THE BI-CENTENARY COMMEMORATION IN NEW YORK

The names of the General Committee of Arrangements indicate the character of the Huguenot representatives of the present time, and show also how fully the original Huguenot settlements were represented. For these reasons the list will be of interest:

Members representing the Huguenot Society of America—Joseph H.

Gautier, M. D.; Ashbel G. Vermilye, D. D.; Frederic J. de Peyster; Benjamin F. de Costa, D. D.; Pierre Lorillard; LeGrand B. Cannon; Lawrence Turnure; Louis Mesier; Prof. David D. Demarest, D. D.; Rt. Rev. Charles T. Quintard, LL. D.; Prof. Charles A. Briggs, D. D.; Henry G. DeForest; Peter W. Gallaudet; Rt. Rev. Edmund de Schweinitz, D. D.; Walter S. Gurnee; Henry G. Marquand; Morey Hale Bartow; Rev. Alfred V. Wittmeyer, Ph. D.

Members representing the original Huguenot Settlements in America— New York: Hon. John Jay, Edward F. deLancey. Staten Island: Hon. Chauncey M. Depew, R. H. Disosway. Long Island: Augustus Rapelve, Henry E. Pierrepont. New Rochelle: Henry M. LeCount, Henry M. Lester. New Paltz: Abram duBois, M. D., Ralph LeFevre. Boston: Hon. Robert C. Winthrop, George S. Bowdoin. New Oxford: Hon. Richard Olney, John G. Whittier. Narragansett: William Ely, Thomas M. Potter, D. D. Maine: Hon. Hannibal Hamlin, Gov. Joshua Chamberlain. Delaware: Hon. Thomas F. Bayard. Pennsylvania: Charles M. duPuy, William R. Valleau. Virginia: Charles M. Maury. Charleston, S. C.: Robert N. Gourdin, Daniel Ravenel. Purysburg, S. C.: Cornelius J. Huguenin, Wilmot de Saussure. New Bordeaux, S. C.: J. A. Gibert, M. D., Rev. Benjamin Allston.

PRESENT MEMBERS OF THE HUGUENOT SOCIETY OF AMERICA

ADAMS, MRS. GEORGE F. (Demarest).
Adams, Washington I. L. (Flandreau).
Alden, Mrs. Charles H. (Cazneau, Germon).
Allen, Dr. Paul (Byssel).
Anderson, Miss Maria L. (Bayard, Poingdextre).
Ashbridge, Miss Mary P. (Pechin).
Atterbury, Mrs. Anson P. (Bayard).
Atterbury, John T., Lewis B., Rev. W. W. (Boudinot, Carre).
Aymar, Benjamin, Miss Elizabeth, Miss Harriet, Jose (Aymar, Magny).

BACOT, WM. SINCLAIR (Bacot, De Saussure).
Bailey, Pearce, M. D. (Jerauld, Dutee).
Balch, Thos. Willing (de Frouville).
Bangs, Mrs. Fletcher (Gaineau).
Banta, Theodore M. (Demarest, Sohier).
Barbour, Wm. Delamater (de la Maitre, du Bois).
Barbour, Mrs. William (Mercereau).
Barrell, Harry Ferdinand (Rapalle, Trico).
Bascome, Mrs. Western (De Lancey).
Bent, Mrs. Richard M. (Dombois).
Berrien, William Mitchell (Berrien).
Bishop, Mrs. Wm. D., Jr. (Gratiot).
Bissell, Mrs. Sanford (Byssel).
Blackwell, Miss R. R. (Bayard).
Blackwell, Wm. Bayard (Bayard).
Blodgett, Mrs. F. J. (Aymar, Belon).
Blood, John Balch (Molines).
Bogert, Theodore P. (Benezet, Testard, Crommelin).
Bolmer, Mrs. Gertrude (Laborie, Durand, Gilet).
Bontecou, Fred. T. (Bontecon, Collinot).
Bookstaver, Hon. Henry W. (Bodine, Felter).

Boucher, Miss S. (Quentin, Quereau).
Boughton, C. V. (Bouton).
Boughton, Wm. Hart (Bouton).
Bowdoin, George S. (Baudoin).
Bowdoin, Miss Isabel G. (Baudoin).
Bowdoin, Temple (Baudoin).
Boyd, Herbert Hart (Chevalier).
Brewster, Saml. Dwight (Pinneo).
Brokaw, Howard C. (Broucard, Le Febre).
Brokaw, Irving (Broucard, Le Febre).
Brokaw, Isaac Vail (Broucard, Le Febre).
Brokaw, William Vail (Broucard, Le Febre).
Brown, Dr. P. Richard, U. S. A. (Richard, De Bruyn).
Bull, Dr. Charles S. (Seguin, Mercereau).
Burruss, Mrs. Nathaniel (Perrin, Thorel).

CAMERON, MRS. M. P. B. B. (Papillon).
Campbell, Mrs. H. Godwin (Mercereau).
Cannon, Col. Le Grand B. (Le Grand, Cannon, Bouton).
Casey, Mrs. Joseph J. (Venable).
Cattus, Miss Emma E., Mrs. John C. (Aymar, Vincent).
Clarkson, Banyer (Jay, Bayard).
Clarkson, Mrs. E. L. de P. (De Peyster).
Clarkson, Matthew (Jay, Bayard).
Clearwater, Hon. A. T. (Baudoin, Bridon).
Clinch, Rev. N. Bayard (Bayard, De Peyster, Chevalier).
Cockroft, Miss E. (De Vaux, Tourneur, Colyer).
Coles, Henry R. R. (De Peyster, De Rapalye).
Cooper, Miss Marian N. B. (Jay, Bayard, De Kay).

Coutant, Dr. Richard B. (Coutant, Bonnefoy).
Coxford, Mrs. William (Perrin, Thorel).
Cutting, Robert Fulton (Bayard, Pintard).
Cutting, William Bayard (Bayard, Pintard).

DANFORTH, MRS. ELLIOT (Mercereau, La Tourette).
Darlington, Charles F. (Reyneau).
Darlington, Rev. James H. (Reyneau).
Dashiell, Nicholas L. (De Lecheilles).
Daw, George W. (Das).
De.Benneville, James S. (De Benneville).
de Forest, Robert W. (de Forest, Bertholet).
De Lamater, Ezra Doane (Le Maistre).
De Luze, Philip Schuyler (de Luze).
Demarest, Rev. Wm. H. S. (Des Marets).
Demonet, Eugene A. (Faure).
De Peyster, Frederic J. and family (de Peyster).
De Peyster, Gen. John Watts (de Peyster, de Lancey).
De Peyster, Miss M. Justine (De Peyster, de Lancey).
Depew, Hon. Chauncey M.
Devotion, Misses Elizabeth, Harriet and Sarah (Devotion).
Deyo, Robert Emmet (Doyau, du Bois).
De Zouche, John J. (de Souche).
Dickinson, Charles D. (Laurier).
Dodge, Francis Edward (d'Espard).
Dominick, Bayard (Dominique, Blanchard).
Dominick, Henry B. (Dominique, Blanchard).
Du Bois, Wm. A. (Du Bois).
Du Bois, Wm. Maison (Du Bois, Le Fevre, Blanshan).
Dumont, John B. (Dumont).
Du Pont, Col. Henry A. (Du Pont).
Du Puy, Miss Eleanor G. (Du Puy, Chardavoyne, Valleau).
Du Puy, Herbert (same as above).
Duyvee, Rev. Joseph (Durie).
Duval, H. Rieman (Duval).

ECKARD, REV. L. W. (Bayard).
Ellis, John Gillett (Gilet, Byssell).
Ellis, Mrs. Wm. R. (Gilet, Byssell).
Elting, Peter J. (Du Bois, Le Fevre).
Ely, William (Bernon).
Ely, William D. (Bernon).
Embury, Aymar (Aymar, Belon, Magny).
English, William E. (Du Bois, Blanshan).

FABER, REGINALD STANLEY (De Dibon).
Falconer, Wm. H. (Fauconnier).
Farlow, Mrs. W. G. (L'Hommedieu).
Farnham, Elijah S. (Molines).
Farnham, Mrs. George A. (Vermeille).
Faulkner, Dr. Richard B. (Du Puy, de Vaux).
Ferree, Miss Annie D. (Ferree, Blancon).
Ferree, Barr.
Ferree, Samuel Patterson.
Flagg, Rev. Edward O. (Villeponteux).
Flandreau, Felix E. (Flandreau).
Floyd-Jones, Mrs. E. (L'Escuyer).
Fontaine, William M. (de la Fontaine, Boursiquot, Chaillon).

Foote, Mrs. N. A. M. (Gilet).
Foster, Rev. Daniel Requa (Requa).
Fowler, Mrs. A. H. (Gratiot).
Freeman, Alden (Molines, Vassall, Bonne).
Freeman, Joel Francis (Bonne).
Frizzell, William H. (De Courcy, Frizzell).
Fuller, Linus E. (Molines).

GALLAUDET, PROF. E. M. (Gallaudet, Prioleau).
Garden, Hugh R. (De Saussure).
Garretson, Mrs. J. B. (Delaplaine, Cresson).
Gautier, Dudley G. (Gautier).
Gillett, Mrs. C. M. (Gilet Byssel).
Goddard, Mrs. F. W. (Cortelyou).
Goldthwaite, Mrs. C. C. (Flandreau).
Graham, Walter (Chardavoyne, Dupuy, Valleau).
Grant, Gen. Fred. D. (De la Noye, de Lille).
Green, Elmer Erving (Du Bois, Het, Sauzeau).
Grinnell, Wm. Milne (Molines).
Gross, Samuel Eberly (Du Bois, Blanshan).
Guion, Rev. Wm. B. (Guion).
Gurnee, Augustus C. (Garnier).

HALL, GEORGE P. (de Rapalie, Trico).
Harris, Mrs. Thos. Cadwalader (Jaudon).
Hartley, Mrs. Marcellus (de Boncourt, Byssel).
Haslock, William F. (Dombois).
Haughey, Mrs. E. McLean (Coutant, de Pre).
Hegeman, Miss A. M. (Hegeman, de Champ, Perot).
Heins, George L. (Fauconnier, Valleau).
Helffenstein, Dr. A. E. (Fauconnier, Valleau, Chardon).
Heroy, William W. (Erouard, Coutant).
Hillman, William (Guion).
Hodges, Alfred (Provoost).
Hoffman, Mrs. E. A. (Mercereau, Chadaine).
Holbrook, Mrs. L. (Perrin, Thorel).
Holland, Rev. William J. (Benezet).
Hopkins, Mrs. E. A. J. (De Vaux, Tourneur).
Hook, Mrs. E. Warren (Le Maistre, Du Bois, Le Comte).
Hubbard, P. Mascarene (Mascarene).
Huidekoper, Mrs. F. W. (de Mandeville, des Marets).
Hunter, Mrs. F. K. (Waldo).
Hunter, Jas. W. (Thelaball).
Huntington, Rev. Wm. R. (Baret).

IRELAND, OSCAR B. (Guion).

JACKSON, MISS MARGARET A. (Robert, de la Borde, La Tour).
Jackson, Samuel Macauley.
James, Edward W. (Dauge, Thelaball).
James, Mrs. J. W. Harry (Molines).
Jay, Col. William (Jay, Francois, Bayard).
Johnson, James L. (Le Baron, Bayeux, Boudinot, Papin).
Joline, Mrs. Adrian H. (Coutant).
Jones, Mrs. F. Cazenove (De Cazenove, de la Mar).
Jouet, Cavalier H. (Jouet, Coursier).

Julien, Gustavus D. (Cantine, Blanchan).
Julien, Rev. Matthew C. (Cantine, Blanchan).
Juillard, A. D. (Juillard).
Juillard, Mrs. A. D. (Cossit).

KENDALL, MRS. S. L. DU BOIS (Du Bois, Bentyn).
Kingsland, Mrs. J. Bayard (Bayard).
Kress, Mrs. Idabelle S. (Des Marest, Baton, Bonnefoy).

LA BACH, JAS. O., Paul M. (Des Marest, Sohier).
Ladew, Mrs. H. S. (Du Bois, Blanshan).
Lanier, Charles (Lanier).
Lathrop, Miss Emma G. (de Forest, du Trieux).
Lathrop, Kirke (Gilet, Byssell).
Lawton, Mrs. G. Perkins (De Forest, Du Cloux).
Lawton, Mrs. James M. (Bayard, de Peyster, Masse, Poingdextre).
Lawton, Mrs. Thomas A. (Molines).
Lea, Mrs. Henry (Jaudon).
Le Boutillier, Clement, John, Mrs. Margaret, Thomas, Dr. Wm. G. (Le Boutillier, Guitton, Le Maistre, Pellier).
Le Conte, Dr. Robt. G. (Le Conte).
Lee, Julian Henry (Mallet).
Lester, Henry M.
Loomis, Mrs. H. P. (Boudinot, Carre).
Luquer, Mrs. L. McI. (Jay, Bayard).
Luquer, Nicholas (L'Esquyer, de Rapalie, Trico).
Luquer, Thatcher T. P. (L'Esquyer, de Rapalie, Trico).

MACDONALD, MRS. MALCOLM (Ferree, Le Fevre).
Maddox, Mrs. Virginia K. (D'Aubigne).
Maltby, Miss Dorothy L. (Rapalje, Trico).
Mann, Mrs. C. Addison (Cazneau, Germon, Molines).
Marschalk, Edwin A. (Fauconnier, Valleau, Chardon).
Marquand, Prof. Allan (Marquand).
Maury, Charles W. (Maury, de la Fontaine).
Maury, Col. Richard L. (Maury, de la Fontaine).
McAllister, Miss Julia G. (De Lancey, Manigault, Marion).
McMurtry, Mrs. Clara L. (Molines).
Merritt, Mrs. Schuyler (Du Bois, Blanshan).
Mesier, Louis (Mesier).
Miller, Kingsbury (Rapelie, Trico).
Mitchell, Cornelius B., Hon. Edward (Berrien).
Mitchell, Hon. J. Murray (Berrien).
Mitchell, William (Berrien).
Moffat, Mrs. R. Burnham (Jay, Bayard).
Moore, Mrs. John W (De Maree, Sohier).
Morris, John E. (Bontecou, Collinot).
Morris, Robert Oliver (Bontecou, Collinot).
Morrison, Mrs. G. Austin (De Camp, de Mandeville).
Moseley, Mrs. William H. (Molines, Gaillard).
Mottet, Frederick (Mottet).
Mount, Misses C. A., Susan (De Gray).
Murray, Charles H. (Bascom).

NICOLA, MRS. CHARLES A. (Pinneo).
Norwood, Miss Catherine (Stelle, Legereau).

OGDEN, WM. B. (Bernon).
Oliver, General Paul A. (Ambrose, Prioleau, Gallaudet).
Olney, Peter B. (Sigourney).
Olney, Mrs. Peter B. (Sigourney).
Olney, Hon. Richard (Sigourney).
Orr, Mrs. A. E. (L'Esquyer, de Rapalie, Trico).

PAYNE, MRS. HENRY C. (L'Estrange, Le Mestre).
Peabody, Mrs. Ellen R. (de Rapalie, Trico).
Pechin, Mrs. Edmund C. (Gaillard or Gaylord).
Pechin, Miss Lila S. (Pechin).
Peets, Mrs. Cyrus B. (Harger).
Pelletreau, Vennette F. (Pelletreau, Gouin).
Perkins, Mrs. Charles P. (Gaineau).
Perot, Joseph S. (Perot).
Pierce, Mrs. Dean (Mascarene).
Pinney, Mrs. Maria W. (Gaillard or Gaylord).
Plummer, D. Bowdoin (Beaudoin).
Porter, Mrs. Henry K. (De Camp, Perrot).
Potter, James B. M., Jr. (Le Moine).
Potter, William H. (Le Moine).
Prall, Rev. William (Mercereau).
Putnam, Mrs. Erastus G. (Boudinot, Bayeux, Papin).

QUINTARD, GEORGE W., (Quintard Fume).

RALPH, MRS. C. M. B. (Chevalier, Renaudet).
Randolph, Mrs. Edmund D. (Molines).
Rapelje, Jacob G. (de Rapelye, Trico).
Rapelye, Henry S. (de Rapalje, Trico).
Rawson, Mrs. Warren (Petit).
Rees, Prof. John K. (Du Bois, Blanshan).
Reilly, Mrs. Thomas A. (Molines).
Remsen, Mrs. Margaret S. (De Peyster).
Reynolds, Mrs. Benj. (Gaillard or Gaylord).
Rhinelander, Philip, T. J. Oakley (Rhinelander, Robert. La Tour, de la Borde, Renaud, Mercier).
Rice, Mrs. Charles E. (Gaillard or Gaylord).
Richards, Charles S., Mrs. Susan A. (Rapelye, Trico).
Rieman, Mrs. Annie L. (de Rapalie, Trico).
Rivers, Capt. W. C., U. S. A. (Flournoy).
Robert, Miss Mary E. (Robert, La Tour, de la Borde).
Roe, Mrs. Charles F. (Des Marest, Le Sueur).
Roosevelt, Mrs. James (de la Noye, de Lille).
Rumsey, Mrs. William (de Kay).
Rundall, Clarence A. (Doyou, Du Bois, Blanshan, Ver Nooy).
Russell, Mrs. Henry G. (Bernon).

SAHLER, MISS FLORENCE L. (Du Bois, Blanshan).
Sanger, Hon. Wm. Cary (Requa).

Sargent, Mrs. Charles S. (Bernon).
Schauffler, W. G. (Byssel).
Schieffelin, W. Jay (Jay, Bayard).
Schuyler, Mrs. Montgomery (Prevot, Vincent, Felle).
Seacord, Morgan H. (Sicard, Arneau, Bonnet, Coutant).
Sell, Dr. Edward H. M. (Seul).
Sellew, Dr. Frederick S. (Selleu).
Shannon, Mrs. P. M. (Molines).
Shelton, E. De Forest (De Forest, Du Trieux, du Cloux).
Shelton, Miss J. De Forest (same as above).
Shepard, Benjamin (Molines).
Sherman, Mrs. Byron (Molines).
Shonnard, F. V. (Mizerol, Praa).
Simons, C. Dewar, J. Dewar (Bacot, Mercier, de Saussure, Peronneau).
Smith, Miss Amanda M. (Rapalie, Trico).
Smith, A. Augustus (Pengry).
Smith, Miss L. Cotheal (de Cotele).
Smith, Mrs. Rosa W. (Molines).
Smith, Miss Sarah P. (Rapalie, Trico).
Snitzler, Mrs. John H. (Laborie, de Resseguier).
Snow, Mrs. James Pardon (Le Conte).
Spencer, Mrs. L. V. B. (Benin).
Stanton, F. McM., Mrs. John, John R. (De Maree, Sohier).
Stelle, Frederick W. (Stelle, Legereau).
Stelle, Morton B., Jr. (Stelle, Legereau).
Stelle, Wm. Watts (Stelle, Legereau).
Stevenson, Richard W. (Le Fevre, Duryee).
Stimson, Frederic J., Mrs. H. C. (Boudinot, Carre).
Strong, Mrs. Allen H. (de Rapalje, Trico).
Swan, Mrs. H. Tilden (Molines).
Swift, Mrs. Edward Y. (Le Baron)
Swords, H. Cotheal (de Cotele).
Swords, Miss P. Caroline (de Cotele).

TAYLOR, MRS. VAN CAMPEN (Rapelie, Trico, Cortelyou).
Thayer, Geo. W. (Molines).
Thayer, Nathaniel (Bayard).
Thayer, Samuel R. (Molines).
Thayer, Mrs. Stephen Van R. (Bernon).
Thomas, W. Grassett (Grassett).
Thompson, Mrs. Ellen S. (Laborie, Durand, Gilet).

Townsend, Mrs. Howard (Bayard).
Trevor, Henry Graff (L'Espenard).
Troxell, Miss Clementine R. (Michelet, Mangeot).
Turner, Rev. C. H. B. (Tourneur, Poinsett, Fouchereau).
Turnure, Lawrence (Tourneur).

UTLEY, MISS ELIZABETH M. (Pardieu).

VAN BUREN, MRS. ROBERT A. (Aymar, Belon, Magny).
Vanderpoel, Miss M. V. B. (Le Baron).
Van Deventer, Mrs. L. F. (Flournoy).
Van Kleeck, Henry (de Rapelle, Trico, Du Bois, Bruyn).
Van Rensselaer, C. S. (Bayard).
Vaughan, Miss Matilda R. (Fauconnier, Pasquereau, Valleau).
Velazquez, Miss Mariana (de Peyster).
Vermilye, Rev. A. G. (Vermilye).
Voute, J. Oscar (de la Voute).

WAGNER, HENRY (Godde, Teulon).
Wallis, Miss Miriam K (Garnier).
Ward, Mrs. Charles Dod (Lequie).
Ward, Henry Chauncey (Gaillard or Gaylord).
Wardwell, Mrs. Helen E. (Aymar, Belon, Magny).
Warner, George C. (De Forest).
Weisse, Dr. Faneuil D. (Faueuil).
Wells, Miss J. Chester (Baret).
White, Mrs. Eliza M. C. (de la Noye, De Lille, Molines).
Wilcox, Mrs. Wm. W. (Seleu).
Williams, Miss Anne S. (De Votion).
Williams, Mrs. Catherine P. (De Votion).
Wilson, Rev. Robert (Mazyck, Ravenel, Le Serrurier, de St. Julien).
Woolsey, Prof Theodore S. (Chevalier).
Wright, Mrs. William J. (Rapalie, Trico, Cortelyou).

YOUNG, MISS ELIZABETH F. (Du Bois, Ferree, Deyo, Blanshan).
Young, Mrs. Emilia F. (Du Bois, Ferree, Deyo, Blanshan).
Young, Mrs. Wm. Hopkins (Hasbroucq, Doyau, Le Blanc, Du Bois).

INDEX

ACADIA, Huguenot settlement, 114
Adams, John, 431
Alden, John, pedigree of, 126
Allaire, Alexander, 231
Allaire, Louis, 190
Allen, Zechariah, 149
Amadee, sufferings of in the galleys, 80–89
America, French attempts to colonize, 93–112
American Bible Society, founded by a Huguenot, 19
American character, French estimate of, 416–419
American civilization, French as a factor in, 420–427
American Protestantism, debt of to Calvin, 427

BANCROFT, GEORGE, 424
Baird, Charles W., 11
Baird, Henry M., 11
Ballou, Hosea, 20
Bayard family: Judith, 216; Mrs. Samuel, 216, 308-311
Bayard, Thomas F., 311
Beaver, James A., general and governor, 321
Bedloe's Island, 216
Bellomont, Governor, 224
Bethlo, Isaac, refugee, 1652, 216
Benezett, John Stephen, earliest open abolitionist a Huguenot, 315
Bernon, Gabriel: Founder of Oxford settlement, 134; sketch of his life, 143-148; residence in Newport, 146; death in Providence, 147; tablet to, 148
Bible, The, cause of reformation in France, 43; clergy's ignorance of, 40; Queen Anne's, 167; Huguenot reverence for, 421
Blanchard, Thomas, inventor, 402-406
Bondet, Daniel, Reverend, 239
Bonrepos, David, Reverend, 238, 286
Bonne Passe (Bumpus), 412
Boyer family of Pennsylvania, 318
Boston: Hospitality to Huguenots, 131, 132; French Church in, 157; a Huguenot's description of, 192
Boudinot, Elias, 19, 304
Bowdoin, James (Baudouin), 183
Bowdoin, James, governor, 183
Bowdoin College, 185
Brazil, attempted French colonization in, 94-97
Briconnet, Guillaume, Bishop, 42
Bulfinch, Charles, 181

CALVIN, JOHN, America's debt to, 424; contrasted with Luther, 426
Canada: Huguenot settlement of, 116
Carre, Ezechiel, 161
Champlain, governor of Canada, 120
Character, Huguenot type of, 206, 413, 420, 421; moral and religious, 422

Chardon, Peter, 189
Chartier, Gillaume, first Protestant clergyman to cross Atlantic, 95
Cheerfulness, a Huguenot characteristic, 408
Chevaliers, The, of Pennsylvania, 317
Choate, Rufus, 405
Civilization, American, French as a factor in, 420
Clemens, Samuel L., 35
Coligny, Admiral, 49; murder of, 57
Colonization plans, 93, 98
Colonial Congress, 19
Colonial Days and Ways, 407
Colonization: French schemes of, 93; Villegagnon's failure in Brazil, 93; disastrous attempts in Florida, 98; in Canada, 112
Columbia College, 223
Constitutional Convention of 1779, 184
Court, Antoine, 74

DANA family: Francis, 186; Richard Henry, 187; James, 187; Samuel W., 187; Charles A., 187
Daille, Peter (Pierre) Reverend, 161, 226, 285
De Bellamy, Governor, opinion of Protestants, 48
De Bonneville, George, 319
Decatur, Stephen, 20
De Forest family, the, 212, 264
De Gourges, Dominique, 110
De la Noye, Phillip, 128
Delano, H. A., 128
DeLancey family: Etienne, 258; family mansion in New York, 258
Delaware: Minuit's residence in, 292
Demarest, David, founder of Hackensack, 223
De Monts, Pierre, expedition of, 114-117
De Rasieres, Huguenot, 215
De Quincey, 34
Dewey, Admiral George, 20
Dragooning, 55
Dresden settlement, Maine, 196-201
Duche family, 311
DuPont family, 311-313
Dupont, Admiral, 20, 313
Reformed Church in New York, a Huguenot pastor of, 223

EDICT of January, 49
Edict of Nantes, 54; revocation of, 54
Edict of Toleration, 78
Encyclical of Pope Leo XIII, answered, 390
English, Philip (L'Anglois), 129
Etienne, Robert, 40

FANEUIL, BENJAMIN, John, Andrew, 173; Andrew, 173, 174; Benjamin, 174; Peter, 175-182; his character, 177; gift of market to Boston, 179; tribute to, 182
Faneuil Hall, 19, 180, 181
Farel, Guillaume, 42

445

Ferree family, 293
Fiske, John, 15
Florida, French colonization scheme, 97
France: Loss of western world, 18; Huguenot persecutions in, 43-61
Freemasonry, The, French in, 386-396
Fremont, General John C., 20
French Church in Boston, 157
French Church in New York, 225; aided by Dutch, 226; first house, 1688, 226; later church edifices, 227; members, 227, 228; adoption of Episcopal liturgy, 228; present philanthropic work of, 229
Freneau, Philip, poet, 269-271

Gallaudet family, the, 276-278
Galleys, Life in the, 80-92
Gano, John and Stephen, 279-282
Germany, influence of Huguenots in, 70
Germantown, Pennsylvania, early French settlers of, 316
Girard, Stephen, 302-307
Girard College, 307
Great Britain, Huguenots in, 67
Green, Richard Henry, 34
Gros, Johann Daniel, 223
Grose, Howard B., 13
Guerrant, Edward O., 430

Hamilton, Alexander, 20, 252-257
Harlem, settled by French, 223
Hawthorne, Nathaniel, 203
Henry of Navarre, Henry IV, 54
Hillegas, Michael, 315
Holland, debt of to Huguenots, 65
Home life, Huguenot in America, 407-415
Houdelette, Henry Clay, 197
Howe, Julia Ward, 208
Hubele, Adams and John, 319
Huguenots: Estimate of, 15; in England, 16; origin of the name, 38; persecutions of in France, 43 ff.; flight of, 56; invincible spirit of, 61; in Europe, 64-73; superiority of in arts and trades, 64; later persecutions of, 74 ff.; influence of upon Puritan character, 202-211; as a factor in American life, 420-427; home life of, 407; traits of character, 413

Indians, hostile at Oxford settlement, 141

Jay, John, 19, 244-251
Jesuits, intrigues of, 141
Joan of Arc, 25; before the Dauphin, 28; trial, 30; sentence, 32; martyrdom, 34; estimates, 34 ff.
Johonnot, Daniel, 188

Kirk, David and Lewis, 119

Laborie, Jacques, 141
Lafayette, Marquis de, 377; Decoration Day observance in Paris, 380
La Follette, Robert, 400, 401
La Montague, Johannes, 215
Latin School, Boston, 182
Laudonniere, story of expedition, 100
Laurens, Henry, 327
Leclerc, John, martyr, 44
LeContes, The, Gillaume, 218; Pierre, 218; John and Joseph, 218; John Lawrence, 218

LeFevre, Jacques, 42
LeFevre, Ralph, 288
LeMercier, Andre, 165
Lescarbot, Marc, 115
Levering family, the, 316
Lodge, Henry Cabot, estimate of Huguenots, 19
Louis XV, Edict of against Huguenots, 76
Louisiana Purchase, 383
Lovell, John, oration of, 181
Luther, Martin, 426

Maine, French colony in, at Dresden 196
Manakintown, Va., 348
Manigault, Gabriel, 19, 326; Judith, letter of, 324
Marchands, The, of Pennsylvania, 319
Margaret of Angouleme, 43
Markos, Abram, organizer of "City Troop" of Philadelphia, 317
Marion, Francis, 19, 338-344
Marot, Clement, hymns of, 62, 421
Maury, Ann, 373
Mayflower, Huguenot passengers on, 125
Meaux, Reformation at, 43
Memoirs of a Huguenot Family, 363
Menendez, Don Pedro, 108
Minuit, Peter, 214, 292
Molines, Priscilla (Mullins), the Puritan maiden, 125
Montgomery, Richard, Revolutionary martyr, 267

Names, changes in, 291, 412
Narragansett settlement, the, 151; list of colonists, 152; troubles of, 154; dispersion, 155, 156
New Amsterdam, French settlers of, 212; first child born in, French; 213; names of first settlers, 214; second governor a Huguenot, 214; first doctor a Huguenot, 215; fusion of Dutch and French in, 215
New Bordeaux, French settlement in South Carolina, 327
New Paltz, Huguenot settlement, history of, 283-289
New Rochelle, Huguenot settlement, 231; land bought in 1689, 231; names of families, 232, 233; description of, 234; centre of culture, 235; French Church of, 237-241; French life of, 409; schools of, 414
New York: French among settlers of, 212; French families of, 218-222; type of character, 223; French club in, 224; French Church in, 225; social leadership in, 432

Oliver, Anthony, 189
Orange, French colony of, 214
Oxford settlement, 134-142; families of, 137

Palissy, Bernard, 58 ff.
Passevant, William A., minister and philanthropist, founder of hospitals, 320
Pennsylvania: Huguenots first white settlers of, 290; Huguenot families, 293, 298, 299
Protestantism, English, 16
Puritan, Dutch and Huguenot contrasted, 408
Port Royal, naval victory of, 313, 314

RABAUT, PAUL, pastor, 77
Rapalie, Sarah, 213
Rag carpet, introduced by French, 410
Ramsay, South Carolina historian, 323
Revere, Paul, 19, 168-172; Freemason, 386, 432
Reynolds, General John F., 20, 296, 297
Reynolds, Admiral William, 297
Ribault, Jean, expedition of, 98-111
Richelieu, Cardinal, 17
Roberdeau, Daniel, 298
Rochelle, La, 39
Rochette, Pastor, last Protestant martyr, 77
Roman Catholic Church: corruption of in France, 39; persecution of Protestant reformers, 43
Rou, Louis, Reverend, 227
Russia, French colony in, 70

SALEM, Huguenot refugees in, 129, 130
Sampson, Deborah, 431
Santee River (French Santee), Huguenot colony, 324
Schley, Admiral W. S., a Huguenot, 20, 297
Schomberg, Huguenot, 17
Sevier, John, 358
Sigourney, Andrew, 188
Simms, William Gilmore, 341
Smith, Helen Evertson, author, 407
South Carolina, Huguenots in, 322; hospitable treatment of, 327; prominent French names, 324; French Church, Charleston, 336; John Lawson's Journal of a Visit to, 334
Staten Island, French settlement on, 217; names of settlers, 217

St. Bartholomew's Day, 50 ff.
Stouppe, Peter, Reverend, 240
Stuyvesant, Peter, wife a Huguenot, 216
Sunday, Huguenot observance of, 413
Superstitions fostered in France, 41

TIFFANY family (Jacques Tiphaine ancestor), 219
Touton, Jean, 128
Thoreau, David, 271-275
Trinity School, New York, 280

UNIVERSALISM, founded in America by a Huguenot, DeBonneville, 320

VAN DEN BOSCH, LAURENTIUS, 160
Vassar College, founded by a Huguenot descendant, 276
Vassar, Matthew, 20, 275
Vassy, massacre of, 49
Vaudois, persecution of the, 45
Vigne, Jean, claimed to be first white child born in North America, 213
Villegagnon, failure in Brazil, 93
Virginia: Huguenots in, 345; petition to establish colony in, 346; Manakintown colony, 348; Huguenot families, 343; French Church in, 354; the Beauford or Buford Family, 357

WALLOONS, French Protestants, 212
Washington, George, Masonic eulogy of, 387
Wittmeyer, Alfred V., Reverend, 229

NAMES OF HUGUENOTS IN AMERICA MENTIONED IN THIS VOLUME, BUT NOT GIVEN ELSEWHERE IN THIS INDEX

AMIAN, JEAN, 152
Andre, Arnaud, 152
Angevin, Zacharie, 221
Ayrault, Daniel, 146

BADEAU, ELIE, 232
Baillergeau, Jacob, 221
Barbarie, Jean, 219
Barbut, Gillaume, 152, 191
Barger, Philip, 191
Basset, David and Peter, 191
Bayeux, Thomas, 221
Beauchamps, Jean, 152
Beaver, John George, 321
Belhair, Daniel, 152
Bergeron, Jacques, 222
Besly, Oliver, 233
Beviere, Louis, 284
Biscon, Isaac, 191
Blanshau, Matthew, 284
Blocq, Albert, 293
Bonnin, Aman, 222
Boucher, Louis, 191
Bouniot, Ezechiel, 152
Boutineau, Stephen, 190
Bovie, Jerome, 217
Boyer, James, 299
Boyer, Samuel, 318
Brund, John, 299
Bussereau, Paul, 152

CANTON, PETER, 189
Carre, Louis, 222
Cellier, Jean Henri, 319
Chabot, John, 189

Chadaine, Jean, 222
Chadene, Jean, 152
Chapron, Pierre, 221
Chardavoinne, Elie, 222
Chardon, Peter, 189
Charron, Elie, 131
Chauvenant, William, 320
Chevalier, Peter, 299
Chevalier, Phillip, 293
Clapp, Gillaume, 233
Collin, Paul, 152
Cothouneau, William, 233
Coudret, Daniel, 222
Coudret, Jean, 152
Couche, Daniel, 299
Coulon, Jean, 222
Cousseau, Jacques, 220
Crommelin, Daniel, 220

DAVID, JEAN, 152
David, Josue, 152
DeCharms, Richard, 317
De la Plaine, Nicholas, 316
De Neufville, 222
Deyo, Christian, 284
Desbrosses, Jacques, 222
Deschamps, Pierre, 152
Dissosway, 217
Doutell, Michael, 299
Doz, Andrew, 297
Drouhet, Paul, 222
DuCastle, Edmond, 297
Duche, Jacob, 299
Dubois, Jacques, 222
Dubois, Louis, 283

Dupeen, Daniel, 299
Durand, Pierre, 222
Durell, Moses, 299

EQUIER, JEAN, 222

FLEURY, PETER, 299
Forney, Peter, 319
Foucault, Andre, 221
Fouchart, Jean, 219
Freer, Hugo, 283
Frere, Hugh, 284
Fume, David, 222

GANCEL, JEAN, 221
Garrigues, Francis, 299
Gaudineau, Gilles, 222
Geneuil, Louis, 222
Germon, Jean, 152
Gillard, Daniel, 222
Giraud, Daniel, 232
Girrard, Pierre, 222
Goud, Jean and Daniel, 199
Grande, Juste, 217
Gros, Lorenz, 223
Guerin, Estienne, 233
Guion, 217

HASBROUCK, JEAN, 284
Hodnett, John, 299
Houdelette, Charles Stephen, 197
Hubele, Adam, 319

IVE, GIRARD, 217

JAQUIN, GEORGE and James F., 199
Jardines, Dr., 293
Jolin, Andre, 222
Julien, Jean, 152

LAMBERT, DANIEL, 152
Lambert, Denis, 219
Lamoreaux, 227
Laurans, Hubert, 293
Lavigne, Charles, 222
Lavigne, Estensie, 233
Laylor, John Henry, 199
LeBoyteau, William, 299
LeBlond, Anthony, 190
LeBrun, Jean, 316
LeBrun, Moise, 152
LeDieu, Lewis, 299
Lefever, Jacques, 292
Lefevre, Simon, 283
Legare, Francois, 152
Legare, Hugh Swinton, 191
LeGendre, Daniel, 152
Legrand, Pierre, 220
Lepperner, Margaret, 234
LeRoux, Bartholomew, 232
LeTort, James, 299, 318
Levering, Joshua, 316
Lorillard, Pierre, 227
Low, C., Seth, 228
Lyron, Lewis, 219

MABE, SIMON, 233

Magnon, Jean, 232
Malbon, Daniel, 199
Many, Jacques, 222
Marchand, Daniel, 221
Martin, John, 233
Martin, Pierre, 217
Mathiot, Henry Bernard, 319
Maynard, 227
Merceveau, Daniel, 222
Mercier, Isaac, 232
Minvielle, Gabriel, 218
Montels, Pierre, 219
Moussett, Thomas, 191

NAUDIN, ELIE, 293

PACA, JOHN, 299
Paillet, Andre, 222
Paris, Amos, 199
Parmentier, Pierre, 217
Passevant, William A., 320
Pelletreau, John, 222
Perry, Oliver H., 230
Piervaux, Jean, 222
Pinaud, Jeau, 222
Pinnard, Joseph, 299
Pochard, Nicholas, Jean, 179

QUINTARD, ISAAC, 222

RAMBERT, ELIE, 152
Rappe, Gabriel, 298
Reboteau, Nicholas, 298
Rembert, Elie, 222
Renardet, James, 299
Renaud, Daniel, 152
Requa, Claude, 219
Reverdy, Peter, 222
Riddle, Francis, 199
Robinett, Samuel, 298
Rochia, Laurens, 293
Rolland, Pierre, Jean, Abraham, 222
Roller, John E., 319
Rouette, Daniel, 293
Roux, Jean, 222
Rusland, Pierre, 222
Rutan, Gerrit, 292

SAUVAGE, ABRAHAM, 191
Saye, Richard, 293
Scurman, Jacob, 232
Signac, Peter, 191
Stain, John, 199
Stilphen, Michael, 199

TARGE, DANIEL, 152, 221
Tillou, Francis R., 222
Tissau, Marie, 131
Tourtellot, Abram, 152, 191
Tripeo, Frederick, 299
Trochon, Pierre, 222

VIDAL, STEPHEN, 299
Vinaux, Jacques, 222
Votaw, Paul, 299
Voyer, Peter, 299